T0344522

Transformational Concepts and Tools for Entrepreneurial Leadership

Saeed Siyal
School of Public Affairs, Zhejiang University, China & Business School, NingboTech University, Ningbo, China & College of Business and Economics, United Arab Emirates University, UAE

Vice President of Editorial	Melissa Wagner
Managing Editor of Acquisitions	Mikaela Felty
Managing Editor of Book Development	Jocelynn Hessler
Production Manager	Mike Brehm
Cover Design	Phillip Shickler

Published in the United States of America by
    IGI Global Scientific Publishing
    701 East Chocolate Avenue
    Hershey, PA, 17033, USA
    Tel: 717-533-8845
    Fax: 717-533-8661
    E-mail: cust@igi-global.com
    Website: https://www.igi-global.com

Library of Congress Cataloging-in-Publication Data

Names: Siyal, Saeed, 1989- editor.
Title: Transformational concepts and tools for entrepreneurial leadership /
  edited by Saeed Siyal.
Description: Hershey, PA : Business Science Reference, [2025] | Includes
  bibliographical references and index. | Summary: "There are few books
  that specifically address the topic of entrepreneurial leadership from a
  cross-cultural perspective"-- Provided by publisher.
Identifiers: LCCN 2023047333 (print) | LCCN 2023047334 (ebook) | ISBN
  9798369300787 (hardcover) | ISBN 9798369300794 (ebook)
Subjects: LCSH: Entrepreneurship--Cross-cultural studies. |
  Leadership--Cross-cultural studies.
Classification: LCC HB615 .T7353 2024 (print) | LCC HB615 (ebook) | DDC
  338.93--dc23/eng/20231120
LC record available at https://lccn.loc.gov/2023047333
LC ebook record available at https://lccn.loc.gov/2023047334

British Cataloguing in Publication Data
A Cataloguing in Publication record for this book is available from the British Library.

To my Loving Mother and Father

Your unwavering love, support, and sacrifices have been the foundation of all my achievements. Though you are no longer here to share in this moment, your spirit and guidance have been with me every step of the way. This success is a testament to your belief in me and the values you instilled.

I dedicate this achievement to your memory, with endless gratitude and love.

Table of Contents

Detailed Table of Contents

Chapter 1
An Assessment of How to Build a Diverse Entrepreneurial Leadership Team 1
Daniel Kwalipo Mbangula, University of Namibia, Namibia

In highlighting the significance of cultivating an inclusive culture for increased creativity, innovation, and adaptability, this chapter explores the crucial elements of building a diverse entrepreneurial leadership team. In-depth analysis and insights into the essential elements and tactics of assembling a diverse entrepreneurial leadership team are the goals of the chapter. Another goal of this chapter is to provide organizations that want to embrace diversity and inclusion among their leadership ranks with useful advice and doable suggestions. Concerns about a lack of knowledge about the advantages of diversity in entrepreneurial leadership teams may be covered in this chapter. It will underline how crucial it is to recognize and appreciate the contributions that different points of view make. Concerns about organizational culture's resistance to change will be discussed in this chapter.

Chapter 2
Building a Diverse Entrepreneurial Leadership Team 23
Kiran Thakur, University Canada West, Canada
Badr-un-Nisa Chand, University Canada West, Canada
Saeed Siyal, Zhejiang University, China

Entrepreneur leaders are visionaries who can transform the organization with their open mindset, flexible approach and learning attitude. Leaders are responsible for identifying the right talent, communicating the vision, empowering the teams, and embracing diversity to outshine. Entrepreneurial teams can significantly impact the organization's performance by bringing collective knowledge together to innovate sophisticated solutions and reduce the risk of uncertainties. This chapter encompasses the concept of diverse entrepreneurial teams, entrepreneurial leadership and its evolution, driving forces responsible for transitioning from traditional to entrepreneurial leadership, tips for building high-performance entrepreneurial teams, entrepreneurial leadership and implications for contemporary organizations.

Chapter 3

Surjit Singha, Kristu Jayanti College, India
Sateesh Kumar T. K., Kristu Jayanti College, India
M. Biju, Kristu Jayanti College, India

Entrepreneurship can foster innovation, creativity, and economic growth in diverse teams and organizations. Building an entrepreneurial culture in diverse teams and organizations requires understanding diversity, strategies for overcoming obstacles, developing entrepreneurial skills, and utilizing technology. This chapter examines the significance of entrepreneurship in diverse teams and organizations, the benefits of diversity in entrepreneurship, strategies for building an entrepreneurial culture, developing entrepreneurial skills, overcoming obstacles, and the role of technology in encouraging entrepreneurship.

Chapter 4

Shivani Dhand, Lovely Professional University, India
Kiran Thakur, University Canada West, Canada
Priyanka Chhibber, Lovely Professional University, India

Effective leadership in fast-changing environment necessitates a wide range of skills and competencies. The theory of Multiple Intelligences (MI) challenges the traditional conception of intelligence as a single, fixed characteristic. People have distinct forms of intelligence that may be nourished and developed through time. MI can assist leaders in adapting to change, building diverse and inclusive teams, and driving innovation. The leadership of the twentieth century witnessed a shift from one type of intelligence to another due to changing societal needs. Much previous research has attempted to draw out the relationship between MI and leadership performance. This chapter reviews the definitions and models in the field of MI and the connection between MI and leadership. The chapter highlights the leadership shift over time and examples of successful MNCs and SMEs resulting from entrepreneurial leadership in the context of multiple intelligence.

Chapter 5

Theresa Obuobisa-Darko, Ghana Communication Technology
University, Ghana

Using the social exchange theory, the paper explains why Entrepreneurial leadership influences employee engagement and employee's innovative behaviour towards organisation success. Findings indicate that entrepreneurial leaders influence employee engagement and employee innovative behaviour because of their People, Learning and Purpose oriented mindset. These enable the leader to influence employees positively and the employees reciprocate by being engaged, thus strive to achieve goals, work with vigour, dedication and absorbed and exhibit innovative behaviour by generating new ideas, promote and implement them for organisation success. The chapter makes a novel theoretical contribution by utilizing social exchange theory to explain the relationship between entrepreneurial leadership, employee engagement and employee's innovative behaviour. A model is developed to guide future empirical studies.

Grounded in the context of evolving markets and technological advancements, the research seeks to unravel the intricate interplay of entrepreneurial leadership styles and their impact on innovative disruption. Through in-depth interviews with a diverse group of entrepreneurs, executives, and industry experts, the study aims to capture nuanced insights into the strategies, challenges, and outcomes associated with entrepreneurial endeavors in disruptive environments. Employing qualitative research methods, including thematic analysis and participant observation, the research strives to uncover patterns, identify key drivers, and explore the contextual nuances that influence the success or failure of entrepreneurial initiatives amid disruptive forces. The findings of this study are expected to contribute to the theoretical understanding of entrepreneurial leadership and innovation disruption while providing practical implications for business leaders, policymakers, and scholars navigating the ever-changing landscape of modern business ecosystems.

This study analyzes the implications of institutional environment and sustainability on entrepreneurship ecosystems. It is assumed in a complex, uncertain and turbulent institutional environmental sustainability affects the development of national, regional, and local entrepreneurship ecosystems. The method employed is the meta-analysis and reflective based on the theoretical, conceptual, and empirical review of the literature. It is concluded that the institutional environmental sustainability influences the national, regional, and local entrepreneurship ecosystems.

Chapter 8

Entrepreneurial leadership is shaped by cultural influences, presenting diverse interpretations across different societies. This chapter examines the multifaceted nature of entrepreneurial leadership through a cultural lens and explores its implications for cross-cultural leadership development. Drawing on established cultural dimensions proposed by scholars like Hofstede and Trompenaars. Through case studies from various countries, the chapter illustrates the cultural nuances in entrepreneurial leadership practices.

Chapter 9

The development of business products and practices that have the potential to generate profits while also improving the environment is an urgent task that must be completed as soon as possible. The objective of the study is to investigate the possibilities for the continued growth of environmentally responsible business ventures. The word cloud method was utilized in the current study to analyze the keywords from the earlier studies. In addition, a tree map, a word count table, and a correlation between entrepreneurship and other variables could be observed. This conceptual research paper makes use of various secondary sources of published literature. This study highlighted a number of different facets that had been investigated in earlier studies. It has been discovered that the word "entrepreneurship" is now frequently used in conjunction with "green" and "sustainability." It will be useful for future investigations because it is possible to understand previously observed trends in greater detail.

Chapter 10
The Dragon's Approach: Entrepreneurial Leadership in the Chinese Cultural
Context 217
   Mohamad Zreik, Sun Yat-sen University, China

This chapter examines entrepreneurial leadership in the context of China's distinct sociocultural environment, taking into account the country's rapid economic development and robust entrepreneurial spirit. At first, it provides an overview of China's history, government, and economy. Then, it delves into how "guanxi" and "mianzi"—two concepts central to Chinese culture—influence the way business leaders in China operate. Key aspects of Chinese entrepreneurial leadership are presented, and the chapter discusses how these elements match up with or differ from globalized notions. As an added bonus, it provides techniques of measuring these factors in a Chinese setting. Insights from Chinese business success stories are provided as the chapter finishes. Leaders in today's increasingly globalized world can benefit from gaining a deeper appreciation for the cultural nuances of China's entrepreneurial leadership setting.

Foreword

Entrepreneurial leadership is more essential, driving not only economic growth but also the creative innovations and societal transformations needed to address global challenges. In Transformational Concepts and Tools for Entrepreneurial Leadership, Dr. Saeed brings a wealth of knowledge and strategic insight to this complex field, offering a comprehensive guide for navigating the demands of Entrepreneurial Leadership with agility, resilience, and vision.

Saeed's work stands out for its unique blend of foundational principles and practical tools that can serve both emerging and seasoned leaders. Through detailed exploration and case examples, this book introduces transformational strategies designed to inspire entrepreneurial leaders to think beyond traditional frameworks and embrace innovative solutions. By shedding light on the connections between leadership, entrepreneurship, technological advancement, and sustainability, this book is not merely a manual but a call to action - encouraging leaders to rethink their roles and responsibilities in a world where impactful change is more than a goal; it's a necessity.

The insights in this book stems from rigorous research and a clear commitment to advancing leadership that is ethical, adaptable, and inclusive. Saeed's emphasis on actionable strategies will help leaders cultivate critical skills - such as adaptability, strategic foresight, and collaborative problem-solving - that are key in today's fast-evolving landscape. This book presents a toolkit for leaders looking to foster entrepreneurial thinking within their teams and organizations, equipping them to turn challenges into opportunities and to cultivate a mindset that values continuous learning and innovation.

It is with great pleasure and admiration that I introduce Transformational Concepts and Tools for Entrepreneurial Leadership. As you read Saeed's work, may you find inspiration and guidance that not only enhances your leadership journey but also empowers you to contribute meaningfully to the world around you.

Miao Qing
Zhejiang University, China

Preface

In the dynamic and fast-evolving world of entrepreneurship, leadership is a critical determinant of success. As organizations increasingly operate in a global landscape, navigating the complexities of cultural diversity has become essential for leaders. Entrepreneurial leadership, in particular, plays a pivotal role in driving innovation, fostering resilience, and ensuring sustainable growth. However, the interpretation and practice of entrepreneurial leadership can vary widely across different cultures. As global interconnectivity intensifies, so does the need for a cross-cultural understanding of entrepreneurial leadership—a concept that is far from universal.

Transformational Concepts and Tools for Entrepreneurial Leadership aims to bridge this gap by examining the multifaceted nature of entrepreneurial leadership through a cross-cultural lens. This book delves into both theoretical frameworks and practical applications, offering readers a comprehensive understanding of how entrepreneurial leadership is perceived and enacted in different cultural contexts. By exploring the nuances of this construct, we provide insights that can guide leaders in adapting their approach to suit diverse teams and global environments.

What sets this book apart is its unique focus on developing and measuring a cross-cultural construct of entrepreneurial leadership. Few books offer a perspective that blends both theoretical rigor with practical relevance on this specific subject. Through a combination of detailed theoretical discussions, practical guidance, and illustrative case studies, this book serves as a valuable resource for entrepreneurs, business leaders, HR managers, academics, and students alike. It is designed not only to offer insights into entrepreneurial leadership but also to provide actionable tools and strategies for those aiming to succeed in a multicultural and globalized world.

We hope that the concepts and tools presented in this book will inspire readers to adopt a more nuanced and culturally aware approach to leadership. By understanding and embracing the diversity of entrepreneurial leadership, individuals and organizations will be better equipped to thrive in today's interconnected business landscape.

ORGANIZATION OF THE BOOK

Chapter 1: An Assessment of How to Build a Diverse Entrepreneurial Leadership Team

This chapter underscores the importance of fostering an inclusive culture to enhance creativity, innovation, and adaptability within entrepreneurial leadership teams. It delves into the core strategies necessary to cultivate diversity at the leadership level, offering organizations practical guidance on how to effectively embrace diverse perspectives. The chapter also addresses the challenges organizations face in understanding the benefits of diversity, particularly in leadership roles, and provides actionable solutions for overcoming resistance within organizational cultures. By emphasizing the value of different viewpoints, this chapter equips leaders with the tools needed to build strong, innovative teams in today's competitive landscape.

Chapter 2: Building a Diverse Entrepreneurial Leadership Team

Entrepreneurial leadership is characterized by visionary thinking, adaptability, and the ability to foster innovation through diverse teams. This chapter explores the transition from traditional leadership models to more entrepreneurial ones, highlighting the essential role of diversity in leadership. By assembling high-performance entrepreneurial teams, leaders can draw on a wealth of collective knowledge, driving innovation and minimizing uncertainties. The chapter also offers practical tips for identifying talent, communicating vision, and empowering teams. The discussion extends to the implications of entrepreneurial leadership for contemporary organizations, providing a robust framework for leaders aiming to thrive in a globalized economy.

Chapter 3: Creating a Culture of Entrepreneurship in Diverse Teams and Organizations

In this chapter, the focus shifts to the development of an entrepreneurial culture within diverse teams and organizations. By fostering entrepreneurship, organizations can drive innovation, creativity, and economic growth. The chapter outlines strategies for overcoming obstacles related to diversity and offers techniques for developing entrepreneurial skills within teams. It further highlights the critical role that technology plays in encouraging entrepreneurship. Through practical insights, this chapter equips organizations with the tools needed to build an entrepreneurial culture that leverages diversity as a competitive advantage.

Chapter 4: Embracing Multiple Intelligences: The Future of Leadership in a Changing World

This chapter explores the evolving demands of leadership in a rapidly changing global environment, emphasizing the importance of Multiple Intelligences (MI). MI theory, which challenges traditional notions of a singular intelligence, is positioned as a key factor in successful leadership. By fostering different forms of intelligence, leaders can adapt to change, build inclusive teams, and drive innovation. The chapter reviews MI's role in leadership evolution and provides case studies from successful multinational corporations (MNCs) and small to medium-sized enterprises (SMEs). It highlights how entrepreneurial leadership, informed by MI, can lead to transformative outcomes in diverse business environments.

Chapter 5: Entrepreneurial Leadership: The Best Promoter of Employee Engagement and Innovative Behavior for Organizational Success

This chapter employs social exchange theory to explore the influence of entrepreneurial leadership on employee engagement and innovative behavior. It argues that entrepreneurial leaders, with their focus on people, learning, and purpose, foster an environment where employees are motivated to engage and contribute creatively. The chapter presents a novel theoretical model to explain the reciprocal relationship between entrepreneurial leadership and employee behavior, offering a framework for future empirical studies. Practical insights are provided on how entrepreneurial leadership can drive employee dedication, innovation, and overall organizational success.

Chapter 6: Exploring the Nexus of Entrepreneurial Leadership and Innovative Disruption: A Qualitative Study

This chapter investigates the relationship between entrepreneurial leadership styles and their role in driving innovative disruption in rapidly changing markets. Through qualitative research, including in-depth interviews with entrepreneurs and industry experts, the chapter uncovers strategies, challenges, and outcomes associated with entrepreneurial efforts in disruptive environments. Key drivers of success, as well as the nuanced factors that contribute to the failure or success of such initiatives, are explored. The chapter offers practical insights for business leaders and policymakers, enriching the theoretical understanding of entrepreneurial leadership in the context of innovation disruption.

Chapter 7: Institutional Environment and Sustainability in Entrepreneurship Ecosystems

This chapter examines the influence of institutional environments on the sustainability of entrepreneurship ecosystems at national, regional, and local levels. Utilizing a meta-analysis and reflective review of the literature, the chapter explores how complex, uncertain, and turbulent institutional environments shape entrepreneurial ecosystems. It concludes that sustainability is a critical factor in the development of these ecosystems, providing valuable insights for policymakers and entrepreneurs aiming to navigate and thrive within challenging institutional settings.

Chapter 8: Interpretations of Entrepreneurial Leadership Across Cultures: Implications for Cross-Cultural Leadership Development

This chapter delves into how entrepreneurial leadership is interpreted differently across various cultures, drawing on the work of cultural scholars like Hofstede and Trompenaars. It explores the implications of these cultural differences for cross-cultural leadership development, offering case studies from around the world to illustrate the diverse approaches to entrepreneurial leadership. By understanding these cultural nuances, leaders can develop more effective strategies for fostering entrepreneurship in global contexts.

Chapter 9: Prospects of Green Entrepreneurship Development: A Review of Literature Using R-software

Green entrepreneurship, which seeks to balance profit with environmental sustainability, is the focus of this chapter. Using R-software for literature analysis, the chapter reviews trends in green entrepreneurship and its relationship with other business variables. Visual representations, such as word clouds and correlation tables, highlight key themes in the literature. The chapter emphasizes the growing convergence of entrepreneurship with concepts like "green" and "sustainability," offering valuable insights for future research and practical applications in environmentally responsible business ventures.

Chapter 10: The Dragon's Approach: Entrepreneurial Leadership in the Chinese Cultural Context

This chapter examines the unique characteristics of entrepreneurial leadership in China, shaped by its sociocultural values and rapid economic growth. Concepts such as "guanxi" (relationships) and "mianzi" (reputation) are explored, showing how these cultural elements influence Chinese business practices. The chapter provides a comparative analysis of Chinese entrepreneurial leadership and global leadership frameworks, offering techniques for measuring leadership effectiveness in China. Through success stories and cultural insights, the chapter equips global leaders with a deeper understanding of how to navigate entrepreneurial endeavors in the Chinese context.

IN CONCLUSION

In conclusion, this edited reference book brings together a comprehensive collection of research and insights on entrepreneurial leadership, emphasizing the profound impact of diversity, culture, and innovation in shaping the future of organizations. Each chapter offers a unique lens through which entrepreneurial leadership can be understood, whether it is through the cultivation of diverse teams, the integration of multiple intelligences, or the exploration of leadership within specific cultural contexts. The collective contributions presented here highlight not only the evolving role of entrepreneurial leadership in driving organizational success but also its power to foster innovation, engagement, and sustainability in a rapidly changing world.

As editors, we believe that the insights provided by the authors in this volume will serve as a valuable resource for scholars, practitioners, and leaders navigating the complex terrain of modern business ecosystems. The diversity of topics covered—from green entrepreneurship and leadership across cultures to the nexus between innovation and disruption—offers a holistic understanding of how entrepreneurial leadership can adapt to and thrive in the face of global challenges. By bridging theory and practice, this book encourages readers to rethink traditional leadership paradigms and embrace new approaches that prioritize inclusivity, creativity, and long-term impact.

Ultimately, this volume stands as a testament to the dynamic and multifaceted nature of entrepreneurial leadership, offering both theoretical depth and practical guidance for those striving to lead with vision, resilience, and a commitment to innovation. We hope that the ideas explored in this book will inspire and equip leaders to drive meaningful change within their organizations and beyond.

Saeed Siyal

School of Public Affairs, Zhejiang University, China & Business School, NingboTech University, Ningbo, China & College of Business and Economics, United Arab Emirates University, UAE

Acknowledgement

I would like to express my heartfelt gratitude to all those who have supported and encouraged me throughout the process of Editing this book. I am truly thankful for the prayers of my Late Parents, unwavering support of my family, friends, and colleagues. Their belief in me has been a constant source of inspiration. I would also like to extend my appreciation to the experts and professionals who have generously shared their knowledge and expertise, helping me to shape this book into its final form. Lastly, I am grateful to the readers who will soon embark on this journey with me. Thank you for your interest and support.

I would like to express the presence of my little son, Qalb E Momin, whose boundless energy and innocent curiosity have brought joy and inspiration to my life.

Chapter 1
An Assessment of How to Build a Diverse Entrepreneurial Leadership Team

Daniel Kwalipo Mbangula
https://orcid.org/0000-0003-0670-3295
University of Namibia, Namibia

ABSTRACT

In highlighting the significance of cultivating an inclusive culture for increased creativity, innovation, and adaptability, this chapter explores the crucial elements of building a diverse entrepreneurial leadership team. In-depth analysis and insights into the essential elements and tactics of assembling a diverse entrepreneurial leadership team are the goals of the chapter. Another goal of this chapter is to provide organizations that want to embrace diversity and inclusion among their leadership ranks with useful advice and doable suggestions. Concerns about a lack of knowledge about the advantages of diversity in entrepreneurial leadership teams may be covered in this chapter. It will underline how crucial it is to recognize and appreciate the contributions that different points of view make. Concerns about organizational culture's resistance to change will be discussed in this chapter.

INTRODUCTION

Guiding a new venture team requires leadership, which is inspiring a group of followers toward a particular objective in an organization with relevant knowledge (Hogan & Kaiser, 2005). Speaking of new ventures, the majority of successful

DOI: 10.4018/979-8-3693-0078-7.ch001

entrepreneurship is the result of a venture team working together as opposed to lone individuals. Chen (2007) drew attention to the idea of the lead entrepreneur in the literature on entrepreneurship, defining it as the person who guides the other members of the team toward the team's objective. Team members' performance will be impacted by the lead entrepreneur's leadership style because of their influence when they work to accomplish entrepreneurial objectives while overcoming unidentified obstacles (Renko, El Tarabishy, Carsrud & Brännback, 2015). This chapter will delve into how to build a diverse entrepreneurial leadership team. First the chapter will provide a comprehensive understanding of the importance of diversity in entrepreneurial leadership teams. Furthermore, the chapter will highlight the best practices in inclusive hiring, mentorship, and training programs that contribute to the formation of a diverse leadership team then it will address the concerns and challenges related to building a diverse leadership team, offering solutions to overcome barriers and resistance. Finally, the chapter will emphasize the role of leadership in promoting and sustaining diversity, encouraging the development of leaders who champion inclusive practices.

Background

The concepts of Diversity, Equity, and Inclusion (DEI) have become essential for organizational success and sustainability in the fast-paced, international workplace of today (Kalev et al., 2006). DEI is a comprehensive strategy that goes beyond token representation and instead highlights the value of recognizing, appreciating, and utilizing employees' varied experiences, backgrounds, and viewpoints in the workplace (Cox & Blake, 1991). It aims to establish an inclusive atmosphere in which all people are treated equally, respected, and given equal opportunity for personal growth and development, regardless of their colour, ethnicity, gender, age, sexual orientation, disability, or any other attribute (Thomas, 2004). The critical role that DEI plays in today's workplace has been highlighted by extensive research and international advocacy (Herring, 2009). Businesses across the world have realized that, in addition to being morally and ethically right, accepting diversity and creating an inclusive workplace culture also has real, noticeable advantages (Ojo &Tijani, 2021). Diversity in the workplace fosters creativity, innovation, and adaptability by bringing together people with different backgrounds, experiences, and points of view. Employees from a variety of backgrounds can contribute new insights to problem-solving and foster creativity and innovation within the company when they are empowered and included. Because of this diversity of opinion, businesses are better equipped to adapt to the shifting needs and obstacles of the market. Additionally, studies on inclusive workplaces have shown increased productivity overall, better retention rates, and higher levels of employee engagement. Workers are more likely to be driven, devoted, and focused on their work when they feel appreciated and included. People are more likely to actively participate in the organization's initiatives and offer their ideas in such settings, which fosters improved teamwork and increased collaboration (Catalyst, 2018).

The importance of diversity, equity, and inclusion (DEI) is widely acknowledged, but putting these strategies into practice effectively continues to be difficult, particularly in unique regional contexts like in Sub-Saharan Africa (Adeoye & Oni, 2019). One such practical example is Nigeria. Nigeria takes pride in its rich tapestry of ethnicities, languages, and traditions as a diverse and multicultural country. In addition to creating a sense of community among workers, embracing diversity in the workplace is critical for promoting social progress, economic expansion, and sustainable development in the nation. This example is not only unique to Nigeria but can be generalised to other countries in Africa.

The entrepreneurial team, or the group of founders "chiefly responsible for the strategic decision making and ongoing operations of a new venture" (Klotz et al., 2014, p. 227), is acknowledged by academics and industry professionals as being crucial to the success of new ventures (Lazar et al., 2020). A founder's trust in their team, in particular, is especially important because it has a positive impact on important outcomes at both the team and individual levels. These outcomes include the founder's commitment to the entrepreneurial team (Wang & Wu, 2012), proactive work behaviours, and satisfaction with the team (Chou et al., 2008). Complex knowledge sharing (Chowdhury, 2005), team performance (De Jong et al., 2016), and innovative entrepreneurial team effectiveness and efficiency (Khan et al., 2015). It is crucial to comprehend the elements that contribute to a founder's level of team trust. To deal with a confusing work environment, make logical plans, and produce new results, entrepreneurial leadership places a strong emphasis on coming up with fresh concepts and putting an artistic spin on the organization's procedures (Pauceanu et al., 2021). The term "strategic engagement" refers to a dynamic approach to the various tasks that comprise a business (Wilson, 2012). To integrate fragmented roles, role development and competing core task management are considered (MacLeod et al., 2012). Innovative performance is impacted by an agile workforce. The economic-organizational approach places a strong emphasis on the part that human attitudes and behavioural motivations play in the process of innovation. Companies with the most agile workforces are more likely to innovate, and high skill levels foster creativity and innovation (Franco & Landini, 2022). This study makes the case that studying the triangle formed by agile work teams, strategic engagement, and entrepreneurial leadership in businesses can improve comprehension and remove barriers to the country's economy. Prosperous and long-lasting economic solutions could be deduced by demonstrating how agile work teams, entrepreneurial leadership, and strategic engagement interact and can be leveraged within companies.

Objectives of the chapter

Chapter aims/objectives.

By the end of this chapter the following aims and objectives must be achieved:
- Provide a comprehensive understanding of the importance of diversity in entrepreneurial leadership teams.
- Highlight best practices in inclusive hiring, mentorship, and training programs that contribute to the formation of a diverse leadership team.
- Address concerns and challenges related to building a diverse leadership team, offering solutions to overcome barriers and resistance.
- Emphasize the role of leadership in promoting and sustaining diversity, encouraging the development of leaders who champion inclusive practices.

Focus of the Article

This chapter mostly focus on how to build a diverse entrepreneurial leadership team, the researcher reviewed some literatures related to the topic under study based on the following subtopics below.

Importance of Diversity in Entrepreneurial Leadership Teams.

Innovative thinking is aided by entrepreneurial leadership, which also grabs chances and motivates groups. Leaders with an entrepreneurial mindset are adept at taking calculated risks, solving problems, and communicating clearly. They ensure that businesses stay competitive by fostering growth, innovation, and adaptability. Even in demanding environments, they foster learning, engage staff, and support organizational success. According to Pauceanu et al. (2021) entrepreneurial leadership is progressive leadership that fosters sustainability and innovation. The entrepreneurial leader's keen observation also gives him the exceptional capacity to identify the potential for profit more than others, as he has cultivated a keen sense of grabbing hold of opportunities, paying closer attention to information, analysing it, and making decisions based on this understanding (Amanah et al., 2022a). The ability of managers to lead and be entrepreneurial is essential for an organization's survival in the unpredictable business environment of today. To inspire their teams and shape the future, these leaders need to be creative, skilled, and have relevant experience (Siyal., 2023; Siyal et al., 2023). To steer and invest in opportunities that could help them shape their future image and encourage other employees to pursue their vision, entrepreneurial leaders need to possess relevant experience and skills, particularly personal skills, and creativity (Guberina et al., 2023).

According to Hussein et al. (2023), agility has become increasingly important in response to environmental challenges, competition, and changing customer demands. Agile businesses are excellent at responding to changes in the environment while preserving their processes, people, IT, systems, and resources (Sumukadas & Sawhney, 2004). According to Petermann and Zacher (2020), an agile workforce fosters a dynamic relationship between work, the workplace, and tools by continuously evolving and embracing organizational learning. Organizational agility is recognized as being based on an employee's capacity to identify and successfully navigate dynamic changes in a competitive environment. It would be impossible to implement innovative work approaches without this flexibility (Storme et al., 2020). An agile workforce puts proactive measures ahead of reactive ones in times of crisis. It carefully considers cost, time, and quality when making plans to reduce the need for last-minute preparations (Gedam et al., 2023). These teams actively involve staff members in decision-making while breaking free from conventional approaches to problem-solving. This proactive involvement enhances value for the company and its dedicated workforce by inspiring the development of novel goods and services. For this reason, the diversity of skills is incorporated into the team to ensure success of the business.

Gupta et al. (2004) claim that creating imaginative scenarios is a key component of entrepreneurial leadership. These scenarios are then used to collect and organize a group of people who are committed to the goal. Consequently, this group is driven to investigate and seize chances for strategic value creation (Gupta et al., 2004). Moreover, problem solving, group and interpersonal interactions, and efficient communication and cooperation are the main areas of emphasis for this team-oriented leadership. Entrepreneurial leadership provides team members with direction and support, serving as a "guiding light" for other entrepreneurs. Employee creativity may be greatly stimulated by this effective leadership (Nguyen et al., 2021). Over the last ten years, the startup culture has undergone a complete transformation as most companies and entrepreneurs work tirelessly around the clock to outperform their rival brands, seize market share, and optimize income and profits (Pauceanu et al., 2021). Top leaders engage both internal and external stakeholders proactively through a process known as strategic engagement. The innovative strategic engagement fosters a vibrant, rewarding, and motivated work environment. By integrating staff members into essential management procedures and focusing on their roles and responsibilities within the company, strategic engagement inspires people to go above and beyond and consistently improve their performance (Siyal et al., 2021a; Siyal et al., 2021b; Siyal., 2018; Siyal & Peng., 2018). Employee engagement fosters a natural drive for success and excellence by connecting socially and emotionally with the organization's mission and vision (Odhiambo, 2020). This approach entails involving staff members in important management duties, emphasizing their job descriptions and administrative responsibilities. It impacts workers intellectually, emotionally, and spiritually, igniting their innate drive for success and excellence and motivating them to go above and beyond and excel in their work. Employee engagement strengthens the organization's relationship and advances its goal, vision, and purpose (John, 2023).

According to Ginsburg et al. (2020), strategic engagement plays a crucial role in helping modern organizations succeed by fostering a clear vision and encouraging the pursuit of opportunities to strategically plan and implement employee training programs that will improve employees' long-term abilities, expertise, and knowledge. The role of institutional managers is vital in guiding strategic engagement in a way that aligns with the organization's overall goals, which are always dependent on actively engaged employees, either individually or collectively. This level of engagement heavily depends on staff members to come up with workable solutions, gather relevant data, and enable smooth adaptation to achieve the established company goals as they embrace diversity. Through internal strategic communication, leadership philosophies have a major impact on employee engagement (Jooss et al., 2021). Work engagement can be positively impacted by and associated with flexibility. Breevaart et al. (2016) investigated employee self-strategies and leadership behaviours that are advantageous to the company as well as to the individuals involved. Individuals are motivated and strengthened in their ability to support mutual accountability, skill optimization, enhanced communication, job satisfaction, and value co-creation by this cooperative and goal-aligned approach (Wilson, 2012).

According to Azmy (2021), putting employee engagement into practice may have positive effects on the workforce, like higher job satisfaction, because these elements improve workforce agility. Using employee engagement increased job satisfaction by improving workforce agility for both parties. In addition, politics (Qazi & Bashir, 2022), theology, academia, and business studies were the areas where the strategic engagement was ushered in. Facilitating a collaborative approach between managers and employees to shape their future and align their skills with the organization's goals not only boosts employee motivation but also improves their capacity to make meaningful contributions and add significant value to the business. Both the organization and the people involved win in this situation.

Individuals are motivated and strengthened in their ability to support mutual accountability, skill optimization, enhanced communication, job satisfaction, and value co-creation by this cooperative and goal-aligned approach (Wilson, 2012). According to Azmy (2021), putting employee engagement into practice may have positive effects on the workforce, like higher job satisfaction, because these elements improve workforce agility. Using employee engagement increased job satisfaction by improving workforce agility for both parties. It also improved the productive workforce of the company. Workers frequently pick up new skills, knowledge, and abilities from their peers. The current HR strategy will guarantee the development of a flexible workforce in repeatable situations. This could stand for workers who are enthusiastic about raising employee engagement and dedicated to their work (Azmy, 2021). Sanhokwe and Chinyamurindi (2023) further contended that job engagement encourages adaptability in the workplace to evaluate possible synergies between social and personal resources developed through the work. Thus, an employee's affirmation of themselves as unique individuals and as organizational assets is what is meant by work engagement. It is a resource that, regardless of the working environment, energizes and mobilizes employees' goal-oriented efforts. Subsequently, engagement leads to diversification of skills set within the organisations which is good for any business operations as it enhances productivity. The organization's strategy for employee engagement ought to incorporate several standards. Leadership must consider various focus areas that result in a better understanding of organizational issues and provide solutions strategies through participation as a strategic tool to increase employee satisfaction and motivate them to work; that is, to improve the performance of the organization through the performance of work teams (Jarrar, 2022).

It is imperative that managers and leaders understand that they possess the ability to determine the level of engagement in their workplace (Bannay et al., 2020). It is not the employees who choose to get involved, but the direct manager of the workforce. Managers set expectations, provide guidelines, and allow staff members to participate in order to achieve successes both inside and outside of their immediate work team. The prominence of agile work teams, strategic engagement, and entrepreneurial leadership has increased. The relationship between entrepreneurial leadership and the creation and performance of agile work teams is not well studied. By filling in these gaps, researchers can advance their knowledge of how businesses can effectively manage complexity, encourage creativity, and improve performance in the cutthroat and ever-changing business world of today. The objective of this research is to examine how entrepreneurial leadership influences the creation of agile work teams and to determine if strategic engagement acts as a mediating element in the relationship between these two phenomena by ensuring diversity.

Best Practices in Inclusive Hiring, Mentorship, and Training Programs that Contribute To the Formation of A Diverse Leadership Team.

Mentorship and sponsorship programs that assist underrepresented employees in advancing in their careers are examples of best practices and HR strategies for promoting diverse leadership team (Elegbede, 2019). Systematic performance management that prioritizes impartial standards and fairness can help reduce evaluation bias. Leadership commitment and the establishment of specific diverse leadership team goals that are incorporated into the organization's overarching strategic plan are essential to fostering an inclusive culture (Ojo & Tijani, 2021). Surveys of employee engagement can be used to evaluate the success of diverse leadership team programs and pinpoint areas in need of development. In order to develop awareness and skills for managing diverse teams and creating an inclusive atmosphere, diversity education and training are essential (Adeyeye, 2020). Long-term sustainability of diverse leadership team initiatives also depends on encouraging inclusive leadership practices and diverse leadership representation.

Challenges Related to Building a Diverse Leadership Team, Offering Solutions to Overcome Barriers and Resistance.

Being a leader guarantees that action is strategically directed to enable the desired outcomes, which makes it a crucial entrepreneurial skill. One of the key elements influencing small business enterprises (SMEs") success has been found to be effective leadership (Madanchian et al., 2016b). Abdelkafi and Täuscher (2016) define leadership as an element or technique that inspires a group of people to accomplish a shared goal. Nonetheless, poor, and insufficient leadership skills are the main cause of small and medium enterprises (SME) failure (Razak, 2011). The absence of leadership skills was identified as one of the most important management and technical knowledge problems facing SMEs (Mhlongo, 2021). Lack of a long-term business success vision (sustainable initiatives) in SMEs may be related to poor management abilities brought on by inadequate training and education as well as a lack of business sustainability skills (Ngibe & Lekhanya, 2019). Additionally, it's claimed that SMEs lack the resources and expertise needed to carry out the organizational changes that are required (Singh & Wasdani, 2016). As per the findings of Hashim, Ahmad, and Zakaria (2012), executives are facing greater challenges in effectively leading their companies in the twenty-first century. Leadership is important as an entrepreneurial behaviour because it could assist someone in realizing their own worth in the process. Therefore, it's critical to promote innovation and adjust to changing environments (Mamun, Fazal & Muniady, 2019). It is impossible to establish a single, workable theory of leadership or leadership effectiveness due to the complex and non-linear nature of organizations (Osborn & Marion, 2009).

Entrepreneurial leadership, or the application of leadership to successfully drive a business to success, has been recognized as a crucial competency that business owners can employ to foster competitive and sustainable growth for their enterprises (Lubis, 2017). Leitch and Volery (2017) highlight the importance of understanding the mechanisms that would explain outcomes as well as the cognitive, interpersonal, and social complexity of leadership in SMEs. Leitch and Volery (2017) state that to advance the field's understanding of small businesses, it is imperative to study and comprehend entrepreneurial leadership. One of the challenges that managers of diverse workforces may encounter is accommodating varying work styles and preferences. People from various backgrounds might approach their work in different ways, have different preferences for work schedules, and handle conflict in different ways. To overcome this obstacle, leaders ought to try to establish a workplace that is adaptable and considers various work styles and preferences. This can be accomplished through granting flexible work hours, giving conflict resolution training, and promoting cooperation and teamwork. Wee and Morse (2007). When it comes to workers they perceive as different from themselves, managers may react more negatively than when it comes to workers they perceive as similar. These unfavourable responses may impede the development of the person as well as the organization's potential. These unfavourable behaviours can also include biased hiring practices, stereotypes, unfair work environments, and unequal introductions to the company. (Tran & Sadri, 2002). Jones and George (2009) assert that while striving for the highest performance and the company's business objectives, top executives must have the appropriate mindset while also remembering the significance of the ethical component when managing a diverse workforce. Aghazadeh (2004) also emphasizes that fairness in compensation for employees from different backgrounds should be a top priority for upper management.

Managing a diverse workforce presents many challenges for leaders. All the same, these obstacles can be overcome, and a diverse workforce can turn into a great asset for a company with the appropriate tactics and approach. Leaders can create a work environment that values diversity and fosters cooperation, creativity, and innovation by promoting open and honest communication, cultural sensitivity, inclusivity, equality, and adaptability (Shaban, 2016).

Role of Leadership in Promoting and Sustaining Diversity, Encouraging the Development of Leaders Who Champion Inclusive Practices.

The first article of the 1948 Universal Declaration of Human Rights, which states that "all human beings are born free and equal in dignity and rights," contains the seeds of an inclusive education philosophy. Furthermore, the equal and unalienable right of every student, regardless of disability, to participate in the educational process is emphasized in the Salamanca Declaration (UNESCO, 1994), which was signed by 92 governments and 25 international organizations. A fundamental requirement for this is that educational systems adjust to students' unique needs, skills, and interests. Because inclusive education addresses a wide range of humanitarian, educational, cultural, and particularly social issues like democracy, racism, and social justice, it can be challenging to define the term "inclusion" (Angelidis & Hatzisotiriou, 2013). The goal of creating an inclusive school culture is to create a community that provides equal learning opportunities and fosters safety, acceptance, and cooperation. Thus, it is a general term used to characterize a situation in which all parties engaged in the educational process have access to information, knowledge, and skills in a productive, democratic, and cooperative setting (Hatzisotiriou & Angelidis, 2018). More specifically, an inclusive education system must find the most efficient way to address the issues raised by the diversity of the student body, regardless of gender, race, ethnicity, language, socioeconomic status, religion, mental health, or state of mind, to ensure that every student is appropriately prepared for their adult participation in society. The importance of community, the common good, social justice, and equality is emphasized in research on school leadership.

Since schools and their leadership are active subsystems that together make up the education system, how inclusive education is portrayed in the context of sustainable and systemic school leadership affects the education system and other business sectors. The entire educational system will suffer if the individual subsystems, or school units, lack a vibrant and cooperative culture. Probably the most crucial instrument for establishing inclusive education is school leadership. Furthermore, "the perception of social justice is collective based; however, a particular conceptualization is needed that is based on entrenched social norms giving unique meanings to issues of justice, respect, interpersonal relations, equality, and equity in education," as stated by Oplatka and Arar (2016, pp. 365–366).

Solutions and Recommendations

The study has found the following solutions based on the following themes:

Diversity in Entrepreneurial Leadership Teams

The study revealed that the ability of managers to lead and be entrepreneurial is essential for an organization's survival in the unpredictable business environment of today. To inspire their teams and shape the future, these leaders need to be creative, skilled, and have relevant experience. To steer and invest in opportunities that could help them shape their future image and encourage other employees to pursue their vision, entrepreneurial leaders need to possess relevant experience and skills, particularly personal skills, and creativity (Guberina et al., 2023). Furthermore, problem solving, group and interpersonal interactions, and efficient communication and cooperation are the main areas of emphasis for this team-oriented leadership. Entrepreneurial leadership provides team members with direction and support, serving as a "guiding light" for other entrepreneurs. Employee creativity may be greatly stimulated by this effective leadership (Nguyen et al., 2021). In addition, diversity and entrepreneurship leadership may according to Azmy (2021), putting employee engagement into practice may have positive effects on the workforce, like higher job satisfaction, because these elements improve workforce agility. Using employee engagement increased job satisfaction by improving workforce agility for both parties.

Best Practices for Diverse Leadership

The study finds that mentorship and sponsorship programs that assist underrepresented employees in advancing in their careers are examples of best practices and HR strategies for promoting diverse leadership team (Elegbede, 2019). Also, to develop awareness and skills for managing diverse teams and creating an inclusive atmosphere, diversity education and training are essential (Adeyeye, 2020). Long-term sustainability of diverse leadership team initiatives also depends on encouraging inclusive leadership practices and diverse leadership representation.

Challenges to Building a Diverse Leadership Team.

The absence of leadership skills was identified as one of the most important management and technical knowledge problems facing SMEs (Mhlongo, 2021). Lack of a long-term business success vision (sustainable initiatives) in SMEs may be related to poor management abilities brought on by inadequate training and education as well as a lack of business sustainability skills (Ngibe & Lekhanya, 2019). Additionally, it's claimed that SMEs lack the resources and expertise needed to carry out the organizational changes that are required (Singh & Wasdani, 2016). As per the findings of Hashim, Ahmad, and Zakaria (2012), executives are facing greater challenges in effectively leading their companies in the twenty-first century. Leadership is important as an entrepreneurial behaviour because it could assist someone in realizing their own worth in the process. Therefore, it's critical to promote innovation and adjust to changing environments (Mamun, Fazal & Muniady, 2019). It is impossible to establish a single, workable theory of leadership or leadership effectiveness due to the complex and non-linear nature of organizations (Osborn & Marion, 2009). Managing a diverse workforce presents many challenges for leaders. All the same, these obstacles can be overcome, and a diverse workforce can turn into a great asset for a company with the appropriate tactics and approach. Leaders can create a work environment that values diversity and fosters cooperation, creativity, and innovation by promoting open and honest communication, cultural sensitivity, inclusivity, equality, and adaptability (Shaban, 2016).

Role of Leadership in Promoting and Sustaining Diversity

This study finds that the goal of creating an inclusive school culture is to create a community that provides equal learning opportunities and fosters safety, acceptance, and cooperation. Thus, it is a general term used to characterize a situation in which all parties engaged in the educational process have access to information, knowledge, and skills in a productive, democratic, and cooperative setting (Hatzisotiriou & Angelidis, 2018). More specifically, an inclusive education system must find the most efficient way to address the issues raised by the diversity of the student body, regardless of gender, race, ethnicity, language, socioeconomic status, religion, mental health, or state of mind, to ensure that every student is appropriately prepared for their adult participation in society. The importance of community, the common good, social justice, and equality is emphasized in research on school leadership. Subsequently, entrepreneurship leadership will enable to create diverse team if they are equipped with proper skills and knowledge by the trainers.

Recommendations

Here are the recommendations that the researcher deemed may assist to improve how to build a diverse entrepreneurial leadership team within the organisations:

Dedication to Leadership:

A pronounced and visible commitment to diversity and inclusion should be shown by top leadership. In addition to allocating resources and holding themselves accountable for results, leaders should actively support diversity initiatives. The initiatives include but not limited to equality in hiring procedures, use diverse interview panels, blind hiring, and collaborations with organizations that target underrepresented talent pools as examples of inclusive hiring practices. Moreover, ensure to introduce programs for mentoring and sponsoring; create mentorship and sponsorship programs that connect a range of young, talented individuals with seasoned leaders who can offer advice, encouragement, and support for professional growth. Education and Training; all staff members should receive regular training on diversity, equity, and inclusion, with an emphasis on inclusive leadership techniques, cultural competency, and awareness of unconscious bias. Finally, enhance collaborations and partnerships by joining forces with outside organizations, business associations, and neighbourhood projects that support inclusion and diversity. To increase the impact of diversity initiatives, work together on cooperative projects, exchange best practices, and make use of networks. And eventually development of leadership by ensuring the investment in leadership development initiatives that give present and future leaders' training in diversity and inclusion a high priority. Give leaders the chance to practice inclusive leadership and set a good example.

Future Directions

Even though this preliminary study offers insightful information about how to build a diverse entrepreneurial leadership team in different countries context, there are several directions in which future research could go:

a. **Longitudinal Studies**: These studies can be used to evaluate how building a diverse entrepreneurial team initiatives will affect employee outcomes and organizational performance in the long run.
b. **Comparative Studies**: By contrasting diverse entrepreneurial leadership team strategies and practices across various industries and sectors, one can learn about best practices and sector-specific obstacles.
c. **Comprehensive Research on Intersectionality:** A deeper comprehension of the variety of employee experiences can be obtained by delving deeper into the intricacies of intersectionality and how it affects diverse entrepreneurial leadership team initiatives in different companies.

By filling in these knowledge gaps, academics and professionals can better understand how to build a diverse entrepreneurial leadership team in different workplaces and create evidence-based plans for successfully promoting diversity, equity, and inclusion.

CONCLUSION

The chapter "Building a Diverse Entrepreneurial Leadership Team: An In-Depth Assessment" concludes by highlighting how crucial diversity and inclusion are to the development of prosperous entrepreneurial endeavours. This chapter has demonstrated the many advantages of developing a diverse leadership team by carefully analysing the essential elements and tactics. It has also offered practical suggestions for companies looking to promote diversity within their workforce. Diversity is a strategic asset that stimulates innovation, improves decision-making, and cultivates a resilient and adaptable culture, in addition to being a moral requirement. In an increasingly complex and dynamic business landscape, organizations can outperform competitors, mitigate risks, and unlock new opportunities by leveraging the power of diverse perspectives, backgrounds, and experiences. The importance of leadership commitment, inclusive hiring procedures, sponsorship and mentorship programs, open communication, and ongoing assessment are some of the major topics covered in this chapter. The themes emphasize the comprehensive methodology necessary for constructing and maintaining a varied entrepreneurial leadership group that mirrors the varied requirements and anticipations of interested parties. It's critical to understand that change takes time as organizations set out on this path to increased diversity and inclusion. It calls for commitment, tenacity, and the readiness to face obstacles and get past roadblocks. Nevertheless, there are numerous benefits to assembling a diverse entrepreneurial leadership team, including enhanced creativity, judgment, staff morale, and bottom-line results. The chapter ends by highlighting the fact that diversity is an essential value that should permeate corporate culture rather than merely being a box to be checked. Organizations can make a better, more equitable future for all stakeholders by embracing diversity and promoting an inclusive environment. This will lead to sustainable growth and success in the entrepreneurial landscape.

REFERENCES

Abdelkafi, N., & Täuscher, K. (2016). Business models for sustainability from a system dynamics perspective. *Organization & Environment*, 29(1), 74–96. DOI: 10.1177/1086026615592930

Adeoye, A. O., & Oni, A. A. (2019). Workplace Diversity Management: A Study of Nigerian Organisations. *Ife Psychologia*, 27(2), 138–150.

Adeyeye, A. D. (2020). Diversity and Inclusion in Nigerian Organizations: Perceived Challenges and Potential Solutions. *International Journal of Business and Management*, 15(7), 47–56. DOI: 10.5539/ijbm.v15n7p47

Aghazadeh, S.-M. (2004). Managing workforce diversity as an essential resource for improving organizational performance. *International Journal of Productivity and Performance Management*, 53(6), 521–531. DOI: 10.1108/17410400410556183

Amanah, A. A., Hussein, S. A., & Bannay, D. F. (2022a). Role of proactive behaviour in entrepreneurial alertness: A mediating role of dynamic capabilities. *Problems and Perspectives in Management*, 20(4), 127–137. DOI: 10.21511/ppm.20(4).2022.10

Angelidis, P., & Hatzisotiriou, C. (2013). Inclusive education. Deltio Ekpaidevtikou Provlimatiosmou kai Epikoinonias, 51, 10–14. https://impanagiotopoulos.gr/index.php/component/content/article/9- uncategorised/258-deltio Available from (in Greek)

Azmy, A. (2021). The effect of employee engagement and job satisfaction on workforce agility through talent management in public transportation companies. Media Ekonomi dan Manajemen, 36(2), 212-229. https://doi.org/DOI: 10.24856/mem.v36i2.2190

Bannay, D. F., Hadi, M. J., & Amanah, A. A. (2020). The impact of inclusive leadership behaviours on innovative workplace behaviour with an emphasis on the mediating role of work engagement. *Problems and Perspectives in Management*, 18(3), 479–491. DOI: 10.21511/ppm.18(3).2020.39

Breevaart, K., Bakker, A. B., Demerouti, E., & Derks, D. (2016). Who takes the lead? A multi- source diary study on leadership, work engagement, and job performance. *Journal of Organizational Behavior*, 37(3), 309–325. DOI: 10.1002/job.2041

Catalyst. (2018). Inclusive Environments: A Catalyst for Gender Diversity and Inclusion. https://www.catalyst.org/research/inclusive-environments-catalyst- for-gender-diversity-and-inclusion/

Chen, M. H. (2007). Entrepreneurial leadership and new ventures: Creativity in entrepreneurial teams. [x]. *Creativity and Innovation Management*, 16(3), 239–249. DOI: 10.1111/j.1467-8691.2007.00439.x

Chou, L.-F., Wang, A.-C., Wang, T.-Y., Huang, M.-P., & Cheng, B.-S. (2008). Shared work values and team member effectiveness: The mediation of trustfulness and trustworthiness. *Human Relations*, 61(12), 1713–1742. DOI: 10.1177/0018726708098083

Chowdhury, S. (2005). The role of affect-and cognition-based trust in complex knowledge sharing. *Journal of Managerial Issues*, 17(3), 310–326.

Cox, T. H., & Blake, S. (1991). Managing Cultural Diversity: Implications for Organizational Competitiveness. *The Academy of Management Executive*, 5(3), 45–56.

De Jong, B. A., Dirks, K. T., & Gillespie, N. (2016). Trust and team performance: A meta- analysis of main effects, moderators, and covariates. *The Journal of Applied Psychology*, 101(8), 1134–1150. DOI: 10.1037/apl0000110 PMID: 27123697

Elegbede, T. (2019). Human Resource Management and the Challenges of Workplace Diversity in Nigeria. African Journal of Education. *Science and Technology*, 5(1), 153–162.

Franco, C., & Landini, F. (2022). Organizational drivers of innovation: The role of workforce agility. *Research Policy*, 51(2), 104423. DOI: 10.1016/j.respol.2021.104423

Gedam, V. V., Raut, R. D., Agrawal, N., & Zhu, Q. (2023). Critical human and behavioural factors on the adoption of sustainable supply chain management practices in the context of automobile industry. *Business Strategy and the Environment*, 32(1), 120–133. DOI: 10.1002/bse.3121

Ginsburg, D. B., Law, A. V., Mann, H. J., Palombi, L., Thomas Smith, W., Truong, H. A., Volino, L. R., & Ekoma, J. O. (2020). Report of the 2018–2019 strategic engagement standing committee. *American Journal of Pharmaceutical Education*, 84(1), 7597. Advance online publication. DOI: 10.5688/ajpe7597 PMID: 32292198

Guberina, T., Wang, A. M., & Obrenovic, B. (2023). An empirical study of entrepreneurial leadership and fear of COVID-19 impact on psychological wellbeing: A mediating. effect of job insecurity. PLoS ONE, 18(5), e0284766. https://doi.org/. pone.0284766DOI: 10.1371/journal

Gupta, V., MacMillan, I. C., & Surie, G. (2004). Entrepreneurial leadership: Developing and measuring a cross-cultural construct. *Journal of Business Venturing*, 19(2), 241–260. DOI: 10.1016/S0883-9026(03)00040-5

Hashim, M. K., Ahmad, S. A., & Zakaria, M. (2012). 'A study on leadership style in SMEs', in International conference on Isla mic leadership-2. The Royale Chulan, Kuala Lumpur, September 26-27.

Hatzisotiriou, C., & Angelidis, P. (2018). *European and Multicultural education: From international to school level*. Diadrasi Publishing. (in Greek)

Herring, C. (2009). Does Diversity Pay: Race, Gender, and the Business Case for Diversity. *American Sociological Review*, 74(2), 208–224. DOI: 10.1177/000312240907400203

Hogan, R& R.B. Kaiser, R.B. (2005). What we know about leadership

Hogan, R., & Kaiser, R. B. (2005). What we know about Leadership. *Review of General Psychology*, 9(2), 169–180. DOI: 10.1037/1089-2680.9.2.169

Hussein, S. A., Amanah, A. A., & Kazem, S. A. (2023). Strategic learning and strategic agility: The mediating role of strategic thinking. International Journal of eBusiness and eGovernment Studies, 15(1),1-25. Retrieved from https://sobiad. org/ menu script/index.php/ijebeg/article/view/1369

Jarrar, A. S. (2022). Strategic human resource practices and employee's engagement: Evidence from Jordanian commercial banks. *European Journal of Business & Management Research*, 7(1), 66–72. DOI: 10.24018/ejbmr.2022.7.1.1163

John, E. P. (2023). A study on effect of work engagement in business process organisations. TIJER International Research Journal, 10(2). Retrieved from https:// www. tijer.org/papers/TIJER2302032.pdf

Jones, G., & George, J. (2009). Contemporary Management (6th ed.). New York: McGrawHill Companies, Inc.

Jooss, S., Burbach, R., & Ruël, H. (2021). Examining talent pools as a core talent management practice in multinational corporations. *International Journal of Human Resource Management*, 32(11), 2321–2352. DOI: 10.1080/09585192.2019.1579748

Kalev, A., Dobbin, F., & Kelly, E. (2006). Best practices or best guesses? Assessing the efficacy of corporate affirmative action and diversity policies. *American Sociological Review*, 71(4), 589–617. DOI: 10.1177/000312240607100404

Khan, M. S., Breitenecker, R. J., Gustafsson, V., & Schwarz, E. J. (2015). Innovative entrepreneurial teams: The give and take of trust and conflict. *Creativity and Innovation Management*, 24(4), 558–573. DOI: 10.1111/caim.12152

Klotz, A. C., Hmieleski, K. M., Bradley, B. H., & Busenitz, L. W. (2014). New venture teams: A review of the literature and roadmap for future research. *Journal of Management*, 40(1), 226–255. DOI: 10.1177/0149206313493325

Lazar, M., Miron-Spektor, E., Agarwal, R., Erez, M., Goldfarb, B., & Chen, G. (2020). Entrepreneurial team formation. *The Academy of Management Annals*, 14(1), 29–59. DOI: 10.5465/annals.2017.0131

Leitch, C. M., & Volery, T. (2017). Entrepreneurial leadership: Insights and directions. *International Small Business Journal*, 35(2), 147–156. DOI: 10.1177/0266242616681397

Lubis, R. (2017). Assessing entrepreneurial leadership and the law: Why are these important for graduate students in Indonesia? *The International Journal of the Arts in Society*, 10(02), 41–76.

MacLeod, I., Steckley, L., & Murray, R. (2012). Time is not enough: Promoting strategic engagement with writing for publication. *Studies in Higher Education*, 37(6), 641–654. DOI: 10.1080/03075079.2010.527934

Madanchian, M., Hussein, N., Noordin, F., & Taherdoost, H. (2016). The relationship between ethical leadership, leadership effectiveness, and organizational performance: A review of literature in SMEs context. *European Business and Management*, 2(2), 17–21. DOI: 10.11648/j.ebm.20160202.11

Mamun, A. A., Fazal, S. A., & Muniady, R. (2019). Entrepreneurial knowledge, skills, competencies and performance: A study of micro-enterprises in Kelantan, Malaysia. *Asia Pacific Journal of Innovation and Entrepreneurship*, 13(1), 29–48. DOI: 10.1108/APJIE-11-2018-0067

Mhlongo, T. (2021). 'A systems' thinking approach to entrepreneurial leadership: An analysis of SMES in the Gauteng Province', doctoral dissertation, Durban University of Technology, Durban.

Ngibe, M., & Lekhanya, L. M. (2019). Critical factors influencing innovative leadership in attaining business innovation: A case of manufacturing SMEs in KwaZulu-Natal. *International Journal of Entrepreneurship*, 23(2), 1–20.

Nguyen, P. V., Huynh, H. T. N., Lam, L. N. H., Le, T. B., & Nguyen, N. H. X. (2021). The impact of entrepreneurial leadership on SMEs' performance: The mediating effects of organizational factors. *Heliyon*, 7(6), e07326. DOI: 10.1016/j.heliyon.2021.e07326 PMID: 34195431

Odhiambo, O. J. (2020). Strategic management of HRM: Implications for organizational engagement. *Annals of Contemporary Developments in Management & HR*, 2(3), 1–8. Advance online publication. DOI: 10.33166/ACDMHR.2020.03.001

Ojo, A. S., & Tijani, A. A. (2021). Managing Workplace Diversity in Nigerian Public and Private Sectors: Issues, Challenges, and Prospects. *Journal of Public Administration and Governance*, 11(3), 70–86.

Oplatka, I., & Arar, K. H. (2016). Leadership for social justice and the characteristics of traditional societies: Ponderings of the application of western-grounded models. *International Journal of Leadership in Education*, 19(3), 352–369. https://doi.org/https://doi.org/10.1080/13603124.2015.102846. DOI: 10.1080/13603124.2015.1028464

Osborn, R. N., & Marion, R. (2009). Contextual leadership, transformational leadership and the performance of international innovation seeking alliances. *The Leadership Quarterly*, 20(2), 191–206. DOI: 10.1016/j.leaqua.2009.01.010

Pauceanu, A. M., Rabie, N., Moustafa, A., & Jiroveanu, D. C. (2021). Entrepreneurial leadership and sustainable development– A systematic literature review. *Sustainability (Basel)*, 13(21), 11695. DOI: 10.3390/su132111695

Petermann, M. K. H., & Zacher, H. (2020). Agility in the workplace: Conceptual analysis, contributing factors, and practical examples. *Industrial and Organizational Psychology: Perspectives on Science and Practice*, 13(4), 599–609. DOI: 10.1017/iop.2020.106

Qazi, R. R. K., & Bashir, S. (2022). Strategic engagement as means of conflict prevention: Pakistan's defence diplomacy towards Russia. *Central Asia*, 90(Summer), 1–18. DOI: 10.54418/ca-90.167

Razak, R. A. (2011). Entrepreneurial orientation as a universal remedy for the receding productivity in Malaysian small and medium enterprises: A theoretical perspective. *International Journal of Business and Social Science*, 2(19), 1–9.

Renko, M., El Tarabishy, A., Carsrud, A. L., & Brännback, M. (2015). Understanding and measuring entrepreneurial leadership style. *Journal of Small Business Management*, 53(1), 54–74. DOI: 10.1111/jsbm.12086

Sanhokwe, H., & Chinyamurindi, W. (2023). Work engagement and resilience at work: The moderating role of political skill. *SA Journal of Industrial Psychology*, 49, a2017. DOI: 10.4102/sajip.v49i0.2017

Shaban, A. (2016). Managing and Leading a Diverse Workforce: One of the Main Challenges in Management. *Procedia: Social and Behavioral Sciences*, 230, 76–84. Retrieved May 10, 2023, from. DOI: 10.1016/j.sbspro.2016.09.010

Singh, C., & Wasdani, K. P. (2016). Finance for micro, small, and medium-sized enterprises in India: Sources, and challenges, ADBI Working Paper 581, Asian Development Bank Institute, Tokyo, viewed n.d., from https://www.adb.org/publications/finance-micro- Small and-medium-sized-enterprises-India-sources-and-challenges.

Siyal, S. (2018). Does Leadership lessen turnover of public servants. The moderated mediation effect of leader member exchange and perspective taking [EBSCO open dissertations].

Siyal, S. (2023). Inclusive leadership and work engagement: Exploring the role of psychological safety and trust in leader in multiple organizational context. *Business Ethics, the Environment & Responsibility*, 32(4), 1170–1184. DOI: 10.1111/beer.12556

Siyal, S., Liu, J., Ma, L., Kumari, K., Saeed, M., Xin, C., & Hussain, S. N. (2023). Does inclusive leadership influence task performance of hospitality industry employees? Role of psychological empowerment and trust in leader. *Heliyon*, 9(5), e15507. DOI: 10.1016/j.heliyon.2023.e15507 PMID: 37153410

Siyal, S., & Peng, X. (2018). Does leadership lessen turnover? The moderated mediation effect of leader–member exchange and perspective taking on public servants. *Journal of Public Affairs*, 18(4), e1830. DOI: 10.1002/pa.1830

Siyal, S., Saeed, M., Pahi, M. H., Solangi, R., & Xin, C. (2021). They can't treat you well under abusive supervision: Investigating the impact of job satisfaction and extrinsic motivation on healthcare employees. *Rationality and Society*, 33(4), 401–423. DOI: 10.1177/10434631211033660

Siyal, S., Xin, C., Umrani, W. A., Fatima, S., & Pal, D. (2021). How do leaders influence innovation and creativity in employees? The mediating role of intrinsic motivation. *Administration & Society*, 53(9), 1337–1361. DOI: 10.1177/0095399721997427

Storme, M., Suleyman, O., Gotlib, M., & Lubart, T. (2020). Who is agile? An investigation of the psychological antecedents of workforce agility. *Global Business and Organizational Excellence*, 39(6), 28–38. DOI: 10.1002/joe.22055

Sumukadas, N., & Sawhney, R. (2004). Workforce agility through employee involvement. *IIE Transactions*, 36(10), 1011–1021. DOI: 10.1080/07408170490500997

Thomas, D. A. (2004). Diversity as strategy. *Harvard Business Review*, 82(9), 98–108. PMID: 15449859

UNESCO. (1994). The Salamanca statement and framework for action. In: Final Report of the World Conference on Special Needs Education: Access and Quality, Spain. Salamanca: UNESCO

Wang, C.-J., & Wu, L.-Y. (2012). Team member commitments and start-up competitiveness. *Journal of Business Research*, 65(5), 708–715. DOI: 10.1016/j.jbusres.2011.04.004

Wee, J., & Morse, O. (2007). Juggling People—Secrets for Successful Teams. *Cost Engineering (Morgantown, W. Va.)*, 49(8), 38.

Wilson, C. (2012). Strategic engagement and alignment of corporate talent. *Development and Learning in Organizations*, 26(5), 4–8. DOI: 10.1108/14777281211258626

ADDITIONAL READING

Simba, A., & Thai, M. T. T. (2019). Advancing Entrepreneurial Leadership as a practice in MSME Management and Development []. Journal of Small Business Management, 57(S2), 397–416. https://doi.org/.DOI: 10.1111/jsbm.12481

Tlaiss, H. A., & Kauser, S. (2019). Entrepreneurial Leadership, Patriarchy, gender, and identity in the Arab World: Lebanon in Focus. *Journal of Small Business Management*, 57(2), 517–537. DOI: 10.1111/jsbm.12397

Ximenes, M., Supartha, W. G., Manuati Dewi, I. G. A., & Sintaasih, D. K. (2019). Entrepreneurial leadership moderating high performance work system and employee creativity on employee performance. *Cogent Business & Management*, 6(1), 1697512. DOI: 10.1080/23311975.2019.1697512

KEY TERMS AND DEFINITIONS

Diversity: the act or trait of incorporating or involving individuals with varying genders, sexual orientations, and social and ethnic backgrounds.

Entrepreneurial leadership: is the capacity to positively influence others so they can identify and take advantage of opportunities for entrepreneurship."

Equity: refers to justice and fairness in both the procedure and the outcome. Fair results frequently necessitate resource redistribution and differential treatment in order to create an even playing field for all people and communities.

Inclusive Hiring Practices: procedures created to draw in and keep applicants from a variety of backgrounds are known as inclusive hiring practices. By reducing prejudices and obstacles that may disproportionately affect underrepresented groups, inclusive hiring practices seek to provide fair and equal opportunities for every applicant.

Mentorship Program: wherein a more seasoned person (the mentor) offers direction, counsel, and support to a less seasoned person (the mentee) in order to promote both professional and personal growth. Formal or informal mentoring programs are essential for helping diverse talent advance in their careers.

Chapter 2
Building a Diverse Entrepreneurial Leadership Team

Kiran Thakur
University Canada West, Canada

Badr-un-Nisa Chand
University Canada West, Canada

Saeed Siyal
https://orcid.org/0000-0003-0982-157X
Zhejiang University, China

ABSTRACT

Entrepreneur leaders are visionaries who can transform the organization with their open mindset, flexible approach and learning attitude. Leaders are responsible for identifying the right talent, communicating the vision, empowering the teams, and embracing diversity to outshine. Entrepreneurial teams can significantly impact the organization's performance by bringing collective knowledge together to innovate sophisticated solutions and reduce the risk of uncertainties. This chapter encompasses the concept of diverse entrepreneurial teams, entrepreneurial leadership and its evolution, driving forces responsible for transitioning from traditional to entrepreneurial leadership, tips for building high-performance entrepreneurial teams, entrepreneurial leadership and implications for contemporary organizations.

DOI: 10.4018/979-8-3693-0078-7.ch002

INTRODUCTION

As Small and Medium Enterprises (SMEs) are becoming known for supporting and stabilizing economies worldwide, many studies are now focusing on understanding the role of entrepreneurs and leaders in mobilizing and successfully operating these small businesses (Zhou, 2016; Ireland et al., 2003; Antoncic & Hisrich, 2004; Handfield-jones, 2000). While we do not have an agreed-upon definition for entrepreneurs, in the literature, many keywords have been used to describe them, including pioneers, risk takers, innovators, independent, and visionaries (Perryman, 1982; Stewart, 1989; Lepnurm & Bergh, 1995). According to the researchers, most of the entrepreneurial characteristics described above are inherent/internal parts of individual personalities (McClelland, 1961), just as is the case with leadership. Since there is a vast amount of literature on leadership, leaders have been commonly defined as ambitious, influential, internally motivated, achievement-oriented, honest, and confident individuals (Zaleznik, 1990; Kirkpatrick & Locke, 1991). Leaders do not necessarily operate from a position of authority; their personality traits help them foresee future business direction, lead, motivate, and encourage teams to overcome their weaknesses, and identify their full potential. Although entrepreneurship is a new concept, leadership's roots within management literature can be traced back to 500 BC. This chapter argues that the integration of these two concepts (Entrepreneurship and Leadership) holds utility for entrepreneurial ventures trying to find innovation in collaborative team settings.

Previous studies have noticed that there are clear parallels and common inherent abilities between leaders and entrepreneurs (Cogliser & Brigham, 2004; Roomi & Harrison, 2011) to the extent that some scholars have referred to entrepreneurs as leaders in their work (Vecchio, 2003). This, in turn, has led to the evolution of a new construct, 'entrepreneurial leadership', that focuses on combining entrepreneurial and leadership qualities (a concept we define in detail in the next section of the chapter) (Gupta et al., 2004; Van Zyl & Mathur-Helm, 2007). It is interesting to note that despite an overlap of traits, entrepreneurs often struggle with demonstrating the leadership abilities required to transform their innovative ideas into large-scale business activity (Fernald et al., 2005, p.1) as they mostly work on their own or within small ventures. While entrepreneurial businesses have become popular in recent times, their effectiveness largely depends on entrepreneurial teams improving their leadership characteristics by embracing the entrepreneurial leadership model. Existing studies on the topic indicate that many SMEs fail (at an early stage of business operations) to produce the desired outcomes due to the absence of 'entrepreneurial leadership and resources, such as management skills, competencies, and financial resources' (Gezahegn et al., 2022). It is argued that combining entrepreneurial behaviour (taking initiatives and risks) with effective leadership traits can help entrepreneurial business ventures perform better and become widely successful (Kuratko, 2007; Van Zyl & Mathur-Helm, 2007). This chapter encompasses the concept of diverse entrepreneurial teams, entrepreneurial leadership and its evolution, driving forces responsible for transitioning from traditional to entrepreneurial leadership, tips for building high-performance entrepreneurial teams, entrepreneurial leadership and implications for contemporary organizations.

Literature Review

Literature is replete with studies that have attempted to combine entrepreneurship and leadership studies to provide more detailed accounts of 'entrepreneurial leaders' and their personality traits (Covin & Slevin, 1989; Gonzalez & Guillen, 2002). According to some researchers, the 'entrepreneurial leadership' concept was introduced in response to the outcry by organizations struggling to keep up with the everchanging environmental influences, including technological developments, and the competitive nature of industries (Gezahegn et al., 2022). During the 1980s, organizations focused on developing managers while overlooking leadership or entrepreneurial traits in these individuals (Fernald et al., 2005). Although these managers were effective in getting the tasks done on time while respecting the prescribed procedures outlined by the organizations, they lacked the imagination to foresee the future and what it holds and the creativity required to survive the dynamic nature of business in the face of intense competition (Abubakar et al., 2018). It was for these reasons that a need for individuals with entrepreneurial characteristics and leadership abilities was felt to navigate the businesses successfully, given the complex external and internal environment. The idea of having more entrepreneurs and leaders in the business context was further supported by studies that suggested a positive relationship between a start-up's performance/profitability and the individual characteristics of its entrepreneurs (Horan, 2007; Wood, 2002).

In the beginning, the authors investigated the unique qualities of both leaders and entrepreneurs separately to understand their individual contributions to the field of business. On the one hand, we had studies that engaged closely with leadership behaviour (Gonzalez & Guillen, 2002; Ireland et al., 2003; Siyal, 2023; Siyal et al, 2023; Siyal, 2018). According to these studies, leaders are known for three distinctive characteristics; technical know-how, psycho-emotive ability, and ethical behaviour (Gonzalez & Guillen, 2002). It is asserted that the technical dimension of a leadership role is a powerful determinant of the impact of leaders on their followers. Followers look up to leaders with sound technical knowledge of projects they are engaged with (Gonzalez & Guillen (2002). Hence knowledge of the subject matter helps leaders inspire and influence their followers. The second highlighted leadership quality is their psycho-emotive ability, also referred to as social capital or Emotional

Intelligence – EI (Ireland et al., 2003), in some studies, which enables a leader to manage the project with mutual respect and empathy for the team members. Their study suggests that the greater the leader's ability to create an atmosphere of trust, the better the leader's ability to influence the team. Gonzalez & and Guillen's work argues that if leaders possess the social skills to connect with the team, it will create a climate of trust between leaders and followers. The third quality of leaders is their ethical behavior. Leaders who exhibit moral obligation and have a strong sense of right and wrong achieve the utmost support of their team members (Gonzalez & Guillen, 2002).

On the other hand, there is a vast amount of literature published about entrepreneurs and their unique abilities to add wealth and value to business ventures (Antoncic & Hisrich, 2004). This body of knowledge asserts that the most prominent entrepreneurship qualities include pro-activeness, risk-taking, innovativeness, and creativity (Covin & Slevin, 1989). Since entrepreneurs are visionaries with the ability to foresee the future, they will always be proactive in their pursuit of solutions that can benefit the ventures they are associated with in the long run (Kickul & Gundry, 2002). Entrepreneurs are fearless individuals who are not afraid to take risks. In fact, individuals who like innovation tend to be comfortable with the uncertainty and the risks involved with putting their creative ideas to use (Johannessen et al., 2001; Fillis, 2002; Verhees & Meulenberg, 2004; Im & Workman, 2004). It is because of these innate qualities that entrepreneurs are always considered a source of profit maximization and business expansion for small start-ups (Antoncic & Hisrich, 2004). Ahmed & Harrison (2022) emphasized in their recent research that entrepreneurial leadership is very important in development of teams with in organizations. Santos et al,. (2019) introduced the concept of team entrepreneurial competence, a team level construct representing the level of shared abilities toward entrepreneurial activities within a new venture team. They proposed a multilevel model of the influence of team entrepreneurial competence and team entrepreneurial experience on the cognitive strategies of team members is developed and tested.

Another relatively newer stream of literature has attempted to combine both leadership qualities and entrepreneurial characteristics of individuals to introduce a comprehensive 'entrepreneurial leadership' construct (Gupta et al., 2004). Such studies claim that the two concepts are integrated and complement each other in a way that will provide better utility when studied/investigated together. Since entrepreneurial leadership as a construct has emerged out of the leadership and entrepreneurship stream, in its most simplistic form, it is defined as 'the summative characteristics of [both] the 'entrepreneurship' and 'leadership' concepts' (Van Zyl & Mathur-Helm, 2007, p.17). A previous definition by El-Namaki (1992), asserts that entrepreneurial leadership focuses on 'individual characteristics or behaviors [such as] vision, problem-solving, decision-making, risk-taking, and strategic initiatives' (as cited in Fernald et al., 2005, p.3). Gupta et al. (2004, p.242) extend this definition by highlighting that entrepreneurial leaders are not just visionaries, but they have the capability to assemble and organize a team of people (inspired by their imagination, and creativity) to work alongside them to exploit the opportunities identified by them. In Figure 1. we present this new construct by highlighting how entrepreneurial leadership takes cues from both leadership and entrepreneurship studies. As highlighted in the figure, Entrepreneurial leaders have to take the initiative and risks while ensuring their conduct is ethically justifiable. Similarly, they have to balance their drive for creativity and innovation with their psycho-motive ability to be able to connect with and inspire the teams they are working with.

Figure 1. Relational Framework of Entrepreneurial Leadership derived from Entrepreneurship and Leadership constructs

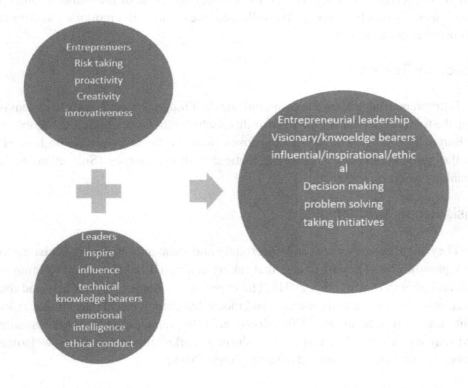

Note. Prepared by the authors

Characteristics of Entrepreneurial Leadership

Entrepreneurial leadership is a distinct leadership style that blends the characteristics and skills of an entrepreneur with those of a leader (Kuratko, 2007). Entrepreneurial leaders are adept at motivating and inspiring their teams. They communicate an enticing vision and motivate individuals to be enthusiastic about their work (Duckworth, 2016). Indeed, aligning business purpose with employee passion can boost employee morale and productivity. Entrepreneurial leadership is critical in finding and generating opportunities for organizational growth. These executives are expert at identifying new markets, diversifying revenue streams, and developing the company (Drucker, 2014). Entrepreneurial executives develop an innovative culture within their organizations. They promote innovative thinking and risk-taking, which creates new goods, services, and processes (Christensen, 2013). This creative attitude assists firms in staying ahead of the competition and meeting changing client needs. The following are some of the most essential traits of entrepreneurial leaders.

Visionary Thinking

Entrepreneurial leaders can communicate their long-term goals and clearly envision the future. They can identify possibilities where others see obstacles (Nambisan & Baron, 2013). They maintain a purpose-oriented attitude by remaining focused on the purpose/intention and staying patient with the journey (Subramaniam & Shankar, 2020).

Risk-Taking & Adaptive

They are at ease with risk and uncertainty and frequently make big decisions to seek possibilities. They recognize that taking calibrated risks can lead to innovation and growth (Sarasvathy, 2001). The experimental nature of their acts and the calculated risk-taking demonstrated and motivated employees to take similar risks (Subramaniam & Shankar, 2020). Moreover, entrepreneurial leaders are versatile and may quickly pivot in response to shifting market conditions. They welcome ambiguity and use it to their advantage (Teece, 2018).

Innovative & Resourcefulness

Entrepreneurial executives promote innovation and creativity in their organizations. They welcome new ideas and constantly seek ways to improve procedures and products (Lumpkin & Dess, 1996). Their learning-oriented approach enables them to listen and pick signals from around them to find opportunities (Subramaniam & Shankar, 2020). They thrive in resource management, formulating creative solutions to limited resources, and successfully leveraging available assets (Alvarez & Barney, 2007).

Resilience & Passion

Entrepreneurial leaders are resilient and adaptable, able to recover from setbacks and learn from failures (Cardon et al., 2011). They are enthusiastic about their businesses and are eager to succeed. Their enthusiasm inspires and motivates their teams (Shane, 2008).

Networking and Relationship Building

They build extensive networks and strong relationships with partners, mentors, and stakeholders, which can be critical for obtaining resources and support (Nahapiet & Ghoshal, 1998). Entrepreneurial leaders keep a people-first mindset, being inclusive, open, pleasant, and thankful. As a result, leaders win the support and trust of their employees and team members (Subramaniam & Shankar, 2020).

Ethical and Social Responsibility

Entrepreneurial leaders focus on consumer expectations and input, leveraging it to drive innovation and commercial decisions. (Blank, 2013). They evaluate the ethical implications of their acts and are socially responsible leaders who understand the societal influence of their endeavours (Tracey et al., 2011).

In today's quickly changing corporate world, these attributes of entrepreneurial leaders are critical for fostering innovation, development, and success. While these characteristics are crucial, effective leadership also necessitates balancing and adapting to each business's unique circumstances and difficulties.

Ethical Entrepreneurial Leadership

In 1982, when Tylenol capsules were tampered with, resulting in several deaths, Johnson & Johnson displayed ethical leadership by recalling 31 million bottles of Tylenol at a cost of millions of dollars. This tragedy prompted the development of tamper-evident packaging and established a new norm for product safety (Cote, 2023). Longenecker et al. (1988) were among the first to develop the concept of entrepreneurial ethics, emphasizing entrepreneurs' tendency to prioritize their interests over those of other stakeholders. The concept of Ethical Entrepreneurial

Leadership combines ethical entrepreneurship and entrepreneurial leadership. This integration is centred on the role of ethics in organizational leadership in order to promote organizational sustainability (Sarmawa, 2020). According to Copeland (2014), leaders must have high moral and ethical standards. The leader is a role model for employees and has a unique opportunity to demonstrate honesty, integrity, and ethics in every significant decision. According to Udo et al. (2017), entrepreneur leadership is defined as leadership that fosters a strong organizational culture, particularly a strong ethical culture.

Not to mention, ethical entrepreneurial leadership is a critical part of corporate management that incorporates ethical concepts into decision-making. It is a management style that emphasizes the importance of ethical behavior and values in achieving company goals. Dwi Widyani (2020) did a study at the Lembaga Perkreditan Desa (LPD) management in Bali, Indonesia; the findings revealed that ethical behavior and entrepreneurial leadership positively impact organizational performance. There are numerous examples of businesses that have demonstrated ethical entrepreneurial leadership. The Body Shop is a cosmetics and skincare brand dedicated to cruelty-free goods and ethical sourcing. They promote worldwide fair trade and community trade activities (Weinstein, 2019). In another example, JetBlue Airlines faced a serious operational catastrophe when a winter storm prompted flight cancellations and passengers were stuck on planes for hours in 2007. JetBlue's CEO, David Neeleman, accepted responsibility for the situation, apologized to consumers, and instituted a customer bill of rights to prevent future mishaps (Cote, 2023). In like manner, Etsy is a website that sells handmade and antique items. The company is dedicated to assisting small businesses and encouraging environmentally friendly practices. They have launched waste reduction, carbon offset, and fair-trade efforts (Terzieva, 2023). Also, Starbucks is well-known for its dedication to ethical coffee bean sourcing. The company works directly with farmers, provides fair prices, and encourages environmentally friendly farming methods. This method has helped coffee producers better their livelihoods while protecting the environment (Cote, 2023). Organizational ethics can boost public trust and lead to a sustainable future (Dwi Widyani, 2020; Siyal & Xin, 2020). Existing studies on the topic indicate that ethical entrepreneurial leadership positively and significantly influences organizational trust, implying that strengthening entrepreneurial leadership ethics can boost organizational trust (Güçe et al., 2012; Engelbrecht et al., 2014; Dwi Widyani, 2020; Sarmawa et al., 2020; Daradkeh, 2023). Hence, it can be argued that ethical principles determine a leader's success in leading an organization (Harrison et al., 2018).

Driving Forces for Transition from Traditional to Entrepreneurial Leadership

Leadership is a dynamic and evolving notion that adapts to the changing landscapes of society, technology, and business (Cortellazzo et al., 2019; Fullan, 2020). Traditional leadership is frequently linked with hierarchical, bureaucratic, and stable companies operating in predictable and stable circumstances. Traditional leaders must be rational, analytical, and consistent in their activities and focus on planning, controlling, and implementing plans based on established norms, processes, and best practices (Gupta et al., 2004). On the other hand, entrepreneurial leadership suits dynamic, innovative, and uncertain firms that function in rapidly changing and complicated contexts. The external and internal driving forces that motivate and enable leaders to alter their thinking, behavior, and abilities from a traditional and hierarchical approach to a more inventive and collaborative one is mentioned here.

Globalization and Dynamic Business Environment

The global economy's interdependence needs leaders who can manage multiple markets, cultures, and regulatory systems. Their agility makes entrepreneurial leaders better equipped for this problem (Deresky, 2017). The rising complexity and uncertainty of the corporate environment necessitate executives to be more adaptive, agile, and resilient to rapid changes and problems (Gupta et al., 2004; Ireland et al., 2003). Leaders must embrace uncertainty and risk as opportunities for learning and progress rather than as threats to be avoided or controlled (Dweck, 2006; Ries, 2011). In addition, rapidly changing consumer preferences and expectations require firms to become more customer-centric and responsive, in line with entrepreneurial leadership concepts (Rajagopal, 2020).

Changing Workforce Dynamics

Younger generations, such as millennials and Gen Z, have distinct leadership expectations. They desire purpose-driven organizations encouraging cooperation and innovation, accelerating the transition to entrepreneurial leadership (Lyons et al., 2015). Since the growing diversity and collaboration in the workplace necessitates leaders to be more inclusive, respectful, and relational in managing their employees' diverse opinions and skills. Leaders must identify their strengths and shortcomings and seek complementary partners to fill in the gaps. They must also recognize the significance of diversity and build an inclusive and respectful atmosphere. They must as well encourage cross-border collaboration by developing shared goals, conventions, and platforms (Page, 2007; Grant et al., 2011).

Technological Advancements

Rapid technological progress has changed traditional company structures, necessitating leaders who understand how to leverage technology for growth and efficiency (Brynjolfsson & McAfee, 2014). Because of the increasing relevance of digitalization and technology in the economy (Siyal et al, 2021), leaders must be more educated, integrative, and strategic in exploiting the potential of digital tools and platforms. Leaders must develop cross-functional fluency and integrative problem-solving skills to manage their businesses' diverse and complex information and knowledge. They must also consider the reactions of other significant stakeholders in the digital ecosystem, such as customers, competitors, and partners (Gupta et al., 2004; Ireland et al., 2003).

Intense Competition

The competitive landscape has shifted dramatically, with disruptive start-ups threatening established businesses. Entrepreneurial leaders are more prepared to deal with competitive threats (Christensen, 1997). The market's increasing desire for innovation and difference necessitates CEOs to be more creative, imaginative, and customer-focused to create value and competitive advantage. Hence, leaders must create and express a clear, compelling future vision that inspires and engages their followers and stakeholders. As part of the innovation process, they must also cultivate a culture of experimentation, feedback, and failure (Sinek, 2009; Kotter, 2012).

Tips for Making Effective Entrepreneurial Leadership Teams

The current business landscape is surrounded by competition, and an effective way for organizations to survive is by engaging- with innovation, creativity, risk-taking, and problem-solving (Zhou, 2016). Entrepreneurial businesses now realize that successful projects require high potential teams, not individual efforts (Beckman, 2006). As a result, a growing number of new ventures are now investing their resources in 'the development of effective leadership teams' (Darling & Leffel, 2010, p. 370). With the concept of entrepreneurial leadership teams receiving attention from the business community, the focus is now on exploring the ways using which effective entrepreneurial teams can be made (Zhou, 2016; Handfield-jones, 2000). Borrowing the insights from existing literature, we outline a few ways of developing high performance entrepreneurial leadership teams.

Enhancing Team Capabilities and Performance Through Action Learning

Creating diverse entrepreneurial teams is important because regardless of the level of creativity and innovation that an individual possesses, they have to rely on an effective team to put their strategic initiatives into practice (Beckman, 2006). Horan, who is the executive director of organizational development for the Walt Disney Company (Asia Specific), in his 2007 paper, shares his experience of developing an entrepreneurial leadership team via an action learning called 'Integrated Leadership Development – ILD.' The program had a dual focus; 1) to develop entrepreneurial leadership ability in individuals recruited from diverse backgrounds through action learning and 2) to explore new business opportunities in newer markets. A team of twenty leaders with high potential was selected to participate in the initiative: Five as trainers and coaches and fifteen as training candidates. Since this was an action learning initiative, instead of coaching them on typical business problems through job rotation or apprenticeship, the company assigned them a real-life high-stakes business opportunity, where achievement of a positive outcome was crucial for the organization. Working on a live project introduced these leaders to many challenges that required them to be proactive and responsive. At the end of the program, emerging leaders reported improved intellectual abilities, critical thinking, and problem-solving skills. At an individual level, the program organizers also noticed a significant change in the behaviour of the entrepreneurial team. At an organizational level, the teams achieved two new business growth opportunities and created a strategic plan for the Indian region (Horan, 2007). Horan's study, despite being useful, focuses on building Entrepreneurial leaders in the context of international firms continuously striving to enter new markets. His work doesn't discuss building diverse teams of leaders but the global team of leaders.

Respect for Individual Personality Differences

Past studies have explored the impact of team composition on the performance of entrepreneurial ventures (Mathieu et al. 2008). It is known from the literature that diversity has been connected with improved creativity, innovation, and problem-solving activity (Williams & O' Reilly, 1998). It is for this reason that the organizations emphasize diversity and inclusion while developing entrepreneurial leadership teams. Although workplace diversity offers many benefits, it also requires organizations to deal with people from different cultural backgrounds and demographics. The work by Kreitner and Kinicki (2004) provides valuable insights for bringing these diverse individuals together and converting them into a team of high achievers to work collectively to pursue the organization's long-term strategy and vision. The individual personalities of entrepreneurs can be noticed in their communication, behaviours, viewpoints on different issues, and interactions with the team members (Morrison, 2000). In order to understand these personality differences, businesses have used personality tools such as the Big Five to make well-informed decisions about the entrepreneurial team composition (Stewart 2006; Bell 2007). It is argued that developing diverse entrepreneurial teams is contingent upon respecting these individuals' unique personalities, cultures, and demographics (Zhou, 2016). The actual task for organizations, then, is to ensure these individuals work collectively in a way where their individual styles are accommodated in the team setting, and they develop mutual respect for each other by putting aside their cultural backgrounds and individual identities to focus on collective organizational goals.

Establishing a Shared Leadership Model

As entrepreneurial leadership teams are developed by combining different leaders, their individual drive for leading the ventures is higher than the regular teams. Organizations need to establish a shared or mutual leadership model that focuses on the division of duties and responsibilities that can be allocated and exchanged between all leaders within a team (Barry, 1991). A similar notion is echoed by Zhou (2016), who stresses that there are multiple sub-roles within a team that require separate leadership attention, and it's in fact a good practice to have people with leadership abilities perform those duties. As opposed to the popular opinion that links leaders' desire for control with conflict, Carson et al. (2007) propose that overall team performance increases if the majority of the members practice leadership behaviour. According to Pearce (2004), the shared leadership model is most appropriate in a team setting where the tasks are unique and interdependent. 'It is unusual for a leading entrepreneur in a team to possess all the required knowledge and skills to effectively lead the team and perform entrepreneurial tasks' (Zhou, 2016y, p.155). Each leader working in the team has different abilities and assigning leadership roles that complement their strengths will boost their commitment to the venture and be beneficial for the overall team performance (Darling & Leffel, 2010; Mehra et al., 2006).

Accountability

Entrepreneurial teams can excel when not bound by various rules and policies (Klotz et al., 2014). To make these teams effective, organizations need to provide them with decision-making power and assign them to loosely structured teams that are not strictly guided by norms and values. As entrepreneurial teams are based on a risk-taking attitude, limiting their freedom to exploit action possibilities or confining them within typical team settings will fail to bring the desired organizational outcomes. These teams take pride in being held responsible for their actions. In the Walt Disney example that we shared earlier, the teams were able to outperform the expectations because they were empowered by assigning an actual business project, given the freedom to face challenges and make decisions that were deemed important but most importantly, due to a sense of accountability for the project and its outcome (Horan, 2007).

Implications for Contemporary Organizations

The shift from traditional to entrepreneurial leadership necessitates a fundamental shift in how leaders think, perform, and interact with others in dynamic, inventive, and uncertain organizations (Kuratko & Hornsby, 1999). Leaders must gain new skills and abilities for entrepreneurial circumstances, such as creativity, vision, risk-taking, learning orientation, and teamwork (Fernald et al., 2005). Alternative sources of education and development that can assist leaders in acquiring and practicing these abilities may be required (Ravet-Brown et al., 2023). Additionally, entrepreneurial qualities, such as critical thinking, inventiveness, and risk management, must be prioritized in leadership development programs (Yukl, 2019). Entrepreneurial leaders must explain their vision in a clear and inspiring manner that appeals to their followers' emotions and ideals. They must include them in co-creating the vision and co-designing the solutions. They must develop trust and commitment by giving information, actively listening, and providing feedback (Sinek, 2009; Kotter, 2012). As entrepreneurial leaders value input from all levels of the business, cross-functional collaboration and open communication become essential (Eisenbeiss et al., 2010).

Indeed, entrepreneurial leaders must recognize the significance of diversity and promote an inclusive and respectful culture. They must foster cross-border collaboration by establishing shared goals, norms, and platforms (Page, 2007; Grant et al., 2011). Further, organizations become more resilient in the face of uncertainty as entrepreneurial leaders improve their ability to pivot, adapt, and exploit opportunities even during difficult times (Sijia et al., 2021). They must approach change and uncertainty with optimism and must-see problems as opportunities for growth and learning. As part of the innovation process, they must encourage experimentation, feedback, and failure (Dweck, 2006; Ries, 2011). Likewise, Companies must deliberately foster a culture of innovation, adaptability, and empowerment.

Furthermore, leaders should guide values and behaviors (Ansari et al., 2014) and should frequently emphasize sustainability and corporate social responsibility in order to reflect changing cultural values and expectations (Espasandn-Bustelo et al., 2010). Entrepreneurial leadership improves organizational sustainability performance, as assessed by the triple bottom line (economic, environmental, and social) (Siyal, Peng & Siyal, 2018; Wang et al, 2022). Entrepreneurial CEOs can improve their firms' economic sustainability by creating value and gaining a competitive edge through innovation and differentiation. They can also improve their organizations' environmental sustainability by reducing waste and emissions, utilizing renewable resources, and implementing green practices. Additionally, they can help their firms' social sustainability by positively impacting their stakeholders, including employees, consumers, suppliers, communities, and society (Pauceanu et al., 2021). While conventional leadership had advantages and was well-suited to a different era, the demands of a dynamic, interconnected world necessitate a more adaptable, innovative, and inclusive leadership style. Companies that successfully use entrepreneurial leadership principles will be better positioned to navigate today's business problems and achieve long-term success.

Entrepreneurial leadership teams provide organizations with a dynamic method of making decisions and solving problems. By bringing together individuals who possess diverse skills, backgrounds, and perspectives, these teams are able to effectively confront complex challenges and capitalize on new opportunities. Through collaboration and collective decision-making, they cultivate innovation, creativity, and adaptability, thereby enabling organizations to maintain competitiveness in rapidly changing markets. Additionally, entrepreneurial leadership teams distribute responsibility and accountability, thereby enhancing risk management and resilience. They also function as platforms for developing leadership skills and providing mentorship, thereby shaping the culture of the organization and promoting strategic alignment across various functional areas. In summary, entrepreneurial leadership teams play a crucial role in driving growth, fostering innovation, and ensuring long-term success in today's dynamic business environment.

CONCLUSION

In conclusion, transitioning from traditional to entrepreneurial leadership requires a significant transformation in mindset and strategy. Building a diverse entrepreneurial leadership team is critical to realizing this transformation's full potential. Leaders may negotiate the difficulties of today's fast-changing corporate scene by adopting attributes such as visionary thinking, flexibility, resilience, networking, innovation, and risk-taking. Furthermore, several variables such as technological advancements, globalization, changing workforce dynamics, intense competition, and changing consumer expectations drive the change towards entrepreneurial leadership. These factors compel firms to adopt a more flexible and forward-thinking leadership style that will allow them to thrive in the 21st-century marketplace.

Furthermore, developing effective entrepreneurial leadership teams necessitates action learning, respect for individual differences, responsibility, and establishing a shared leadership model. Collaboration, communication, and a dedication to learning are essential for success in this dynamic workplace. Simultaneously, ethical considerations are critical in entrepreneurial leadership. Leaders must act with honesty, transparency, and duty toward all stakeholders. Ethical entrepreneurial leadership not only protects the organization's reputation and credibility but also contributes to sustainability. Additionally, the consequences of entrepreneurial leadership for modern businesses are enormous. They include increased innovation, agility, and the ability to capitalize on emerging possibilities. Furthermore, these leadership approaches can build a culture of continuous improvement, employee engagement, and adaptability, which are critical in today's ever-changing corporate environment.

Finally, the shift from traditional to entrepreneurial leadership signifies a fundamental transformation in how businesses run and develop. Organizations can position themselves for success in an increasingly dynamic and competitive environment by assembling diverse entrepreneurial leadership teams, embracing core qualities, and adhering to ethical values. The path to entrepreneurial leadership is a transformative one, with enormous potential for development, innovation, and long-term corporate sustainability.

REFERENCES

Abubakar, L. S., Zainol, F. A., & Binti Wan Daud, W. N. (2018). Entrepreneurial leadership and performance of small and medium sized enterprises: A structural equation modeling approach. *Journal for International Business and Entrepreneurship Development*, 11(2), 163–186. DOI: 10.1504/JIBED.2018.091220

Ahmed, F., & Harrison, C. (2022). Entrepreneurial leadership development in teams: A conceptual model. *International Journal of Entrepreneurship and Innovation*, ●●●, 14657503221143977. DOI: 10.1177/14657503221143977

Alvarez, S. A., & Barney, J. B. (2007). Discovery and creation: Alternative theories of entrepreneurial action. *Strategic Entrepreneurship Journal*, 1(1-2), 11–26. DOI: 10.1002/sej.4

Ansari, S., Bell, J., Iyer, B., & Schlesinger, P. (2014). Educating entrepreneurial leaders. *Journal of Entrepreneurship Education*, 17(2), 31.

Antoncic, B., & Hisrich, R. D. (2004). Corporate entrepreneurship contingencies and organizational wealth creation. *Journal of Management Development*, 23(6), 518–550. DOI: 10.1108/02621710410541114

Barry, D. (1991). Managing the bossless team: Lessons in distributed leadership. *Organizational Dynamics*, 20(1), 31–47. DOI: 10.1016/0090-2616(91)90081-J

Beckman, C. M. (2006). The influence of founding team company affiliations on firm behavior. *Academy of Management Journal*, 49(4), 741–758. DOI: 10.5465/amj.2006.22083030

Bell, S. T. (2007). Deep-level composition variables as predictors of team performance: A meta-analysis. *The Journal of Applied Psychology*, 92(3), 595–615. DOI: 10.1037/0021-9010.92.3.595 PMID: 17484544

Blank, S. (2013). Why the Lean Start-Up Changes Everything. *Harvard Business Review*, 91(5), 63–72.

Brynjolfsson, E., & McAfee, A. (2014). *The second machine age: Work, progress, and prosperity in a time of brilliant technologies*. WW Norton & Company.

Cardon, M. S., Stevens, C. E., & Potter, D. R. (2011). Misfortunes or mistakes?: Cultural sensemaking of entrepreneurial failure. *Journal of Business Venturing*, 26(1), 79–92. DOI: 10.1016/j.jbusvent.2009.06.004

Carson, J. B., Tesluk, P. E., & Marrone, J. A. (2007). Shared leadership in teams: An investigation of antecedent conditions and performance. *Academy of Management Journal*, 50(5), 1217–1234. DOI: 10.2307/20159921

Christensen, C. M. (2013). *The innovator's dilemma: when new technologies cause great firms to fail*. Harvard Business Review Press.

Cogliser, C., & Brigham, K. (2004). The Intersection of Leadership and Entrepreneurship: Mutual Lessons to Be Learned. *The Leadership Quarterly*, 15(6), 771–799. Advance online publication. DOI: 10.1016/j.leaqua.2004.09.004

Copeland, M. K. (2014). The emerging significance of values-based leadership: A literature review. *International Journal of Leadership Studies*, 8(2), 105–135. https://www.regent.edu/acad/global/publi cations/ijls/new/vol8iss2/6-Copeland.pdf

Cortellazzo, L., Bruni, E., & Zampieri, R. (2019). The role of leadership in a digitalized world: A review. *Frontiers in Psychology*, 10, 1938. DOI: 10.3389/fpsyg.2019.01938 PMID: 31507494

Cote, C. (2023, September 14). *4 Examples of Ethical Leadership in Business | HBS Online*. Business Insights Blog. Retrieved September 21, 2023, from https://online .hbs.edu/blog/post/examples-of-ethical-leadership

Covin, J. G., & Slevin, D. P. (1989). Strategic management of small firms in hostile and benign environments. *Strategic Management Journal*, 10(1), 75–87. DOI: 10.1002/smj.4250100107

Daradkeh, M. (2023). Navigating the complexity of entrepreneurial ethics: A systematic review and future research agenda. *Sustainability (Basel)*, 15(14), 11099. DOI: 10.3390/su151411099

Darling, J., & Leffel, A. (2010). Developing the Leadership Team in an Entrepreneurial Venture: A Case Focusing on the Importance of Styles. *Journal of Small Business and Entrepreneurship*, 23(3), 355–371. DOI: 10.1080/08276331.2010.10593490

Deresky, H. (2000). *International management: Managing across borders and cultures*. Pearson Education India.

Drucker, P., & Maciariello, J. (2014). *Innovation and entrepreneurship*. Routledge. DOI: 10.4324/9781315747453

Duckworth, A. (2016). *Grit: The power of passion and perseverance* (Vol. 234). Scribner.

Dweck, C. S. (2006). *Mindset: The new psychology of success*. Random house.

Dwi Widyani, A. A., Landra, N., Sudja, N., Ximenes, M., & Sarmawa, I. W. G. (2020). The role of ethical behavior and entrepreneurial leadership to improve organizational performance. *Cogent Business & Management*, 7(1), 1747827. DOI: 10.1080/23311975.2020.1747827

Eisenbeiss, S. A., Van Knippenberg, D., & Boerner, S. (2008). Transformational leadership and team innovation: Integrating team climate principles. *The Journal of Applied Psychology*, 93(6), 1438–1446. DOI: 10.1037/a0012716 PMID: 19025260

El-Namaki, M. S. S. (1992). Creating a corporate vision. *Long Range Planning*, 25-29(6), 25–29. Advance online publication. DOI: 10.1016/0024-6301(92)90166-Y

Engelbrecht, A. S., Heine, G., & Mahembe, B. (2014). The influence of ethical leadership on trust and work engagement: An exploratory study. *SA Journal of Industrial Psychology*, 40(1), 1–9. DOI: 10.4102/sajip.v40i1.1210

Espasandín-Bustelo, F., Ganaza-Vargas, J., & Diaz-Carrion, R. (2021). Employee happiness and corporate social responsibility: The role of organizational culture. *Employee Relations*, 43(3), 609–629. DOI: 10.1108/ER-07-2020-0343

Fernald, L. W.Jr, Solomon, G. T., & Tarabishy, A. (2005). A New Paradigm: Entrepreneurial Leadership. *Southern Business Review*, 30(2), 1–10. https://digitalcommons.georgiasouthern.edu/sbr/vol30/iss2/3

Fillis, I. (2002). An 'Andalusian dog or a rising star? Creativity and the marketing/entrepreneurship interface. *Journal of Marketing Management*, 18(3-4), 379–395. DOI: 10.1362/0267257022872415

Fullan, M. (2020). The nature of leadership is changing. *European Journal of Education*, 55(2), 139–142. DOI: 10.1111/ejed.12388

Gezahegn, M., Woldesenbet, K., & Hailu, K. (2022). The Role of Entrepreneurial Leadership on MSMEs' Effectiveness: A Systematic Literature Review. Journal of Entrepreneurship & Management 11 (1 & 2), Pp 01-17. http://publishingindia.com/jem/

Goosen, C. J., de Coning, T. J., & Smit, E. M. (2002). Corporate entrepreneurship and financial performance: The role of management. *South African Journal of Business Management*, 33(4), 21–27. DOI: 10.4102/sajbm.v33i4.708

Grant, A. M., Gino, F., & Hofmann, D. A. (2011). Reversing the extraverted leadership advantage: The role of employee proactivity. *Academy of Management Journal*, 54(3), 528–550. DOI: 10.5465/amj.2011.61968043

Greenwich: JAI Press.Wood, E.H. (2002). 'An analysis of the predictors of business performance in small tourism and hospitality firms', *International Journal of Entrepreneurship and Innovation*, 3(3): 201-210.

Güçel, C., Tokmak, İ., & Turgut, H. (2012). The relationship of the ethical leadership among the organizational trust, affective commitment and job satisfaction: Case study of a university. *International Journal of Social Sciences and Humanity Studies*, 4(2), 101–110.

Gupta, V., Macmillan, I. C., & Surie, G. (2004). Entrepreneurial leadership: Developing and measuring a cross-cultural construct. *Journal of Business Venturing*, 19(2), 241–260. DOI: 10.1016/S0883-9026(03)00040-5

Handfield-Jones, H. (2000). How to grow executives. *The McKinsey Quarterly*, 1, 115–123.

Harrison, C. (2014). Entrepreneurial Leadership: A Systematic Literature Review. *International Council for Small Business.World Conference Proceedings.*

Harrison, C., Burnard, K., & Paul, S. (2018). Entrepreneurial leadership in a developing economy: A skill-based analysis. *Journal of Small Business and Enterprise Development*, 25(3), 521–548. DOI: 10.1108/JSBED-05-2017-0160

Horan, J. (2007). Business Driven Action Learning: A Powerful Tool for Building World-Class Entrepreneurial Business Leaders. *Human Resource Management International Digest*, 25(3), 75–80. DOI: 10.1108/hrmid.2008.04416aad.001

Im, S., & Workman, J. P.Jr. (2004). Market orientation, creativity, and new product performance in high-technology firms. *Journal of Marketing*, 68(April), 114–132. DOI: 10.1509/jmkg.68.2.114.27788

Ireland, R. D., Hitt, M. A., & Sirmon, D. G. (2003). A model of strategic entrepreneurship: The construct and its dimensions. *Journal of Management*, 29(6), 963–989. DOI: 10.1016/S0149-2063(03)00086-2

Johannessen, J., Olsen, B., & Lumpkin, G. T. (2001). Innovation as newness: What is new, how new and to whom? *European Journal of Innovation Management*, 4(1), 20–31. DOI: 10.1108/14601060110365547

Kickul, J., & Gundry, L. K. (2002). Prospecting for strategic advantage: The proactive entrepreneurial personality and small firm innovation. *Journal of Small Business Management*, 40(2), 85–97. DOI: 10.1111/1540-627X.00042

Kirkpatrick, S. A., & Locke, E. A. (1991). Leadership: Do traits matter? *The Academy of Management Executive*, ●●●, 48–60.

Klotz, A. C., Hmieleski, K. M., Bradley, B. H., & Busenitz, L. W. (2014). New venture teams: A review of the literature and roadmap for future research. *Journal of Management*, 40(1), 226–255. DOI: 10.1177/0149206313493325

Kotter, J. P. (2007). Leading change: Why transformation efforts fail.

Kreitner, R., & Kinicki, A. (2004). *Organizational Behavior* (6th ed.). McGraw-Hill/Irwin.

Kuratko, D. F. (2007). Entrepreneurial leadership in the 21st century: Guest editor's perspective. *Journal of Leadership & Organizational Studies*, 13(4), 1–11. DOI: 10.1177/10717919070130040201

Kuratko, D. F., & Hodgetts, R. M. (2007). *Entrepreneurship: Theory, Process, Practice* (7th ed.). Thomson/SouthWestern Publishing.

Kuratko, D. F., & Hornsby, J. S. (1999). Corporate entrepreneurial leadership for the 21st century. *Journal of Leadership Studies, 5*(2), 27-39. leadership perceptions and team performance. *The Leadership Quarterly*, 17, 232–245. DOI: 10.1016/j.leaqua.2006.02.003

Lepnurm, R., & Bergh, C. (1995). Small business: Entrepreneurship or strategy? *The Center for Entrepreneurship Review*: 4.

Longenecker, J. G., McKinney, J. A., & Moore, C. W. (1988). Egoism and independence: Entrepreneurial ethics. *Organizational Dynamics*, 16(3), 64–72. DOI: 10.1016/0090-2616(88)90037-X

Lumpkin, G. T., & Dess, G. G. (1996). Clarifying the entrepreneurial orientation construct and linking it to performance. *Academy of Management Review*, 21(1), 135–172. DOI: 10.2307/258632

Lyons, S. T., Schweitzer, L., & Ng, E. S. (2015). How have careers changed? An investigation of changing career patterns across four generations. *Journal of Managerial Psychology*, 30(1), 8–21. DOI: 10.1108/JMP-07-2014-0210

McClelland, D. C. (1961). The achieving society. *Princeton, NJ*: van Nostrand

Mehra, A., Smith, B., Dixon, A., & Robertson, B. (2006). Distributed leadership in teams: the network of

Morrison, A. (2000). Developing a Global Leadership Model. *Human Resource Management*, 39(2-3), 117–131. DOI: 10.1002/1099-050X(200022/23)39:2/3<117::AID-HRM3>3.0.CO;2-1

Nahapiet, J., & Ghoshal, S. (1998). Social capital, intellectual capital, and the organizational advantage. *Academy of Management Review*, 23(2), 242–266. DOI: 10.2307/259373

Nambisan, S., & Baron, R. A. (2013). Entrepreneurship in innovation ecosystems: Entrepreneurs' self–regulatory processes and their implications for new venture success. *Entrepreneurship Theory and Practice*, 37(5), 1071–1097. DOI: 10.1111/j.1540-6520.2012.00519.x

Page, S. E. (2007). *The difference: How the power of diversity creates better groups, firms, schools, and societies*. Princeton University Press.

Pauceanu, A. M., Rabie, N., Moustafa, A., & Jiroveanu, D. C. (2021). Entrepreneurial leadership and sustainable development—A systematic literature review. *Sustainability (Basel)*, 13(21), 11695. DOI: 10.3390/su132111695

Pearce, C. L. (2004). The future of leadership: Combining vertical and shared leadership to transform knowledge work. *The Academy of Management Perspectives*, 18(1), 47–57. DOI: 10.5465/ame.2004.12690298

Perryman, R. (1982). Commentary on research in the field of entrepreneurship. In Kent, C. A., Sexton, D. L., & Vesper, K. H. (Eds.), *The encyclopedia of entrepreneurship* (pp. 377–378). Prentice Hall.

Rajagopal, A. (2020). Transforming entrepreneurial business design: Converging leadership and customer-centric approach. *Journal of Transnational Management*, 25(2), 128–153. DOI: 10.1080/15475778.2020.1734418

Ravet-Brown, T. É., Furtner, M., & Kallmuenzer, A. (2023). Transformational and entrepreneurial leadership: A review of distinction and overlap. *Review of Managerial Science*, ●●●, 1–46.

Ries, E. (2011). *The lean startup: How today's entrepreneurs use continuous innovation to create radically successful businesses*. Currency.

Roomi, M., & Harrison, P. (2011). Entrepreneurial Leadership: What is it and how should it be taught? *International Review of Entrepreneurship*, 9(3), 1–44. http://hdl.handle.net/10547/222995

Santos, S. C., Morris, M. H., Caetano, A., Costa, S. F., & Neumeyer, X. (2019). Team entrepreneurial competence: Multilevel effects on individual cognitive strategies. *International Journal of Entrepreneurial Behaviour & Research*, 25(6), 1259–1282. DOI: 10.1108/IJEBR-03-2018-0126

Sarasvathy, S. D. (2001). Causation and Effectuation: Toward a Theoretical Shift from Economic Inevitability to Entrepreneurial Contingency. *Academy of Management Review*, 26(2), 243–263. DOI: 10.2307/259121

Sarmawa, I. W. G., Widyani, A. A. D., Sugianingrat, I. A. P. W., & Martini, I. A. O. (2020). Ethical entrepreneurial leadership and organizational trust for organizational sustainability. *Cogent Business & Management*, 7(1), 1818368. DOI: 10.1080/23311975.2020.1818368

Shane, S. A. (2008). *The illusions of entrepreneurship: The costly myths that entrepreneurs, investors, and policy makers live by.* Yale University Press.

Sijia, Z., Lingfeng, Y., & Yanling, L. (2021). Entrepreneurial Leadership, Organizational Resilience and New Venture Performance. *Foreign Economics & Management*, 43(03), 42–56.

Sinek, S. (2011). *Start with why: How great leaders inspire everyone to take action.* Penguin.

Siyal, M., Siyal, S., Wu, J., Pal, D., & Memon, M. M. (2021). Consumer perceptions of factors affecting online shopping behavior: An empirical evidence from foreign students in China. [JECO]. *Journal of Electronic Commerce in Organizations*, 19(2), 1–16. DOI: 10.4018/JECO.2021040101

Siyal, S. (2018). Does Leadership lessen turnover of public servants. The moderated mediation effect of leader member exchange and perspective taking [EBSCO open dissertations].

Siyal, S. (2023). Inclusive leadership and work engagement: Exploring the role of psychological safety and trust in leader in multiple organizational context. *Business Ethics, the Environment & Responsibility*, 32(4), 1170–1184. DOI: 10.1111/beer.12556

Siyal, S., Liu, J., Ma, L., Kumari, K., Saeed, M., Xin, C., & Hussain, S. N. (2023). Does inclusive leadership influence task performance of hospitality industry employees? Role of psychological empowerment and trust in leader. *Heliyon*, 9(5), e15507. DOI: 10.1016/j.heliyon.2023.e15507 PMID: 37153410

Siyal, S., Peng, X., & Siyal, A. W. (2018). Socioeconomic analysis: A case of Tharparkar. *Journal of Public Affairs*, 18(4), e1847. DOI: 10.1002/pa.1847

Siyal, S., & Xin, C. (2020). *Public procurement. Global Encyclopedia of Public Administration, Public Policy, and Governance.* Springer International Publishing.

Siyal, S., Xin, C., Umrani, W. A., Fatima, S., & Pal, D. (2021). How do leaders influence innovation and creativity in employees? The mediating role of intrinsic motivation. *Administration & Society*, 53(9), 1337–1361. DOI: 10.1177/0095399721997427

Stewart, A. (1989). *Team entrepreneurship*. Sage.

Stewart, D. W. (2006). Continuing the investigation into personality traits and work-family conflict. Dallas: Poster presented at the *Twenty-First Annual Meeting of the Society for Industrial and Organizational Psychology*.

Subramaniam, R., & Shankar, R. K. (2020). Three mindsets of entrepreneurial leaders. *The Journal of Entrepreneurship*, 29(1), 7–37. DOI: 10.1177/0971355719893498

Terzieva, K. (2023, February 28). The Rise Of Ethical Leadership In Modern Business Enterprises. *Forbes*. https://www.forbes.com/sites/forbescoachescouncil/2023/02/28/the-rise-of-ethical-leadership-in-modern-business-enterprises/?sh=245881b337dd

Tracey, P., Phillips, N., & Jarvis, O. (2011). Bridging institutional entrepreneurship and the creation of new organizational forms: A multilevel model. *Organization Science*, 22(1), 60–80. DOI: 10.1287/orsc.1090.0522

Van Zyl, H. J. C., & Mathur-Helm, B. (2007). Exploring a conceptual model, based on the combined effects of entrepreneurial leadership, market orientation and relationship marketing orientation on South Africa's small tourism business performance. *South African Journal of Business Management*, 38(2), 17–24. DOI: 10.4102/sajbm.v38i2.580

Vargas, G. M., Campo, C. H. G., & Orejuela, H. A. R. (2010). Corporate social responsibility in the context of institutional and organizational change in the Colombian financial sector. *AD-Minister*, (17), 59–85.

Vecchio, R. P. (2003). Entrepreneurship and leadership: Common Trends and Common Threads. *Human Resource Management Review*, 13(2), 303–327. DOI: 10.1016/S1053-4822(03)00019-6

Verhees, J. H. M., & Meulenberg, M. T. G. (2004). Market orientation, innovation, and performance in small firms. *Journal of Small Business Management*, 42(2), 134–154. DOI: 10.1111/j.1540-627X.2004.00102.x

Wang, T., Yu, Z., Ahmad, R., Riaz, S., Khan, K. U., Siyal, S., Chaudhry, M. A., & Zhang, T. (2022). Transition of bioeconomy as a key concept for the agriculture and agribusiness development: An extensive review on ASEAN countries. *Frontiers in Sustainable Food Systems*, 6, 998594. DOI: 10.3389/fsufs.2022.998594

Weinstein, B. PhD. (2019, October 14). Seven Bold Leaders Reveal How Ethical Leadership Is A Boon To Business. *Forbes*. https://www.forbes.com/sites/bruceweinstein/2019/10/14/seven-bold-leaders-reveal-how-ethical-leadership-is-a-boon-to-business/?sh=6b12154e454c

Williams, K. Y., & O'Reilly, C. A. (1998). Demography and diversity in organizations: A review of 40 years of research. In B. Staw & R. Sutton (Eds.), *Research in organizational behavior*, Vol. 20: 77–140.

Zaleznik, (1990). The leadership gap. *Academy of Management Executive*: 7–22.

Zhou, W. (2016). When does shared leadership matter in entrepreneurial teams: The role of personality composition. *The International Entrepreneurship and Management Journal*, 12(1), 153–169. DOI: 10.1007/s11365-014-0334-3

Chapter 3
Creating a Culture of Entrepreneurship in Diverse Teams and Organizations

Surjit Singha
https://orcid.org/0000-0002-5730-8677
Kristu Jayanti College, India

Sateesh Kumar T. K.
https://orcid.org/0000-0002-8406-409X
Kristu Jayanti College, India

M. Biju
https://orcid.org/0000-0001-7358-4199
Kristu Jayanti College, India

ABSTRACT

Entrepreneurship can foster innovation, creativity, and economic growth in diverse teams and organizations. Building an entrepreneurial culture in diverse teams and organizations requires understanding diversity, strategies for overcoming obstacles, developing entrepreneurial skills, and utilizing technology. This chapter examines the significance of entrepreneurship in diverse teams and organizations, the benefits of diversity in entrepreneurship, strategies for building an entrepreneurial culture, developing entrepreneurial skills, overcoming obstacles, and the role of technology in encouraging entrepreneurship.

DOI: 10.4018/979-8-3693-0078-7.ch003

INTRODUCTION

Due to diversity's inherent benefits, entrepreneurship is essential in diverse teams and organizations. When individuals with diverse backgrounds, viewpoints, and experiences collaborate, they offer unique insights and knowledge to stimulate innovation, creativity, and problem-solving (Aluthgama-Baduge & Rajasinghe, 2022). When individuals from diverse backgrounds join, they carry a rich tapestry of ideas, experiences, and cultural influences. This diversity of thought stimulates creativity by exposing team members to novel ideas, unorthodox methods, and alternative perspectives. Cross-pollination of ideas can inspire innovative solutions to complex problems and cultivate a culture of out-of-the-box thinking (Karlsson et al., 2019). Diverse teams are more likely to generate innovative and ground-breaking innovations than homogenous ones. Individuals can challenge the status quo, query presumptions, and identify novel opportunities by combining diverse perspectives. The team's diversity of skills, knowledge, and expertise enables multidisciplinary collaboration in which diverse disciplines and domains intersect to produce innovative solutions (Jones et al., 2020). Diversity broadens the spectrum of concepts generated by a team. Each team member contributes their insights and experiences, allowing for a broader exploration of potential outcomes. Diverse viewpoints nurture a more comprehensive understanding of problems and allow teams to consider a wider range of solutions. This broader spectrum of thoughts increases the likelihood of discovering optimal and original solutions (Aluthgama-Baduge & Rajasinghe, 2022). Effective problem-solving frequently necessitates multifaceted approaches. Diverse teams are better suited to address these obstacles because they possess a diversity of problem-solving approaches and points of view. When confronted with a problem, team members can draw on their varied experiences and implement various analytic frameworks to develop innovative and effective solutions. This collective problem-solving ability enhances the team's capacity to overcome obstacles and adapt to changing conditions. Adapting to a globalized world in the globalized business landscape of the twenty-first century, organizations must comprehend and serve disparate client segments across various markets. Businesses that embrace diversity are better positioned to communicate with and comprehend these diverse markets. By having team members who represent a variety of cultures, dialects, and consumer behaviours, organizations can develop products and services that cater to their customer's specific requirements and preferences (Jones et al., 2020). Diversity in entrepreneurship is advantageous not only for immediate innovation and problem-solving but also for long-term sustainable development. Diverse teams are more adaptable, resilient, and able to navigate difficult obstacles. They are better equipped to recognize emergent trends, react to market shifts, and capitalize on opportunities. By nurturing diversity, organizations can establish a solid foundation for continuous development and adaptability in a business environment that is constantly changing (Salazar et al., 2012). Entrepreneurship is essential in diverse teams and organizations because it capitalizes on diversity's unique characteristics. Diverse teams are better equipped to address complex problems, achieve sustainable development, and prosper in today's globalized world by fostering creativity, spurring innovation, and facilitating a more comprehensive range of ideas (Jones et al., 2020). Historically, entrepreneurial teams consisted primarily of individuals from comparable backgrounds who shared similar experiences and viewpoints. This lack of diversity restricted the variety of ideas, insights, and methods brought to the entrepreneurial process. It also hindered the capacity to meet the requirements and preferences of various consumer segments and markets (Aluthgama-Baduge & Rajasinghe, 2022). Changes in society, heightened awareness, and expanded recognition of the benefits of diversity have altered the entrepreneurial landscape over time. The realization that diverse teams offer distinct advantages in creativity, innovation, problem-solving, and overall business performance has prompted a shift (Jones et al., 2020).

Several factors have contributed to recognizing diversity as a valuable asset in entrepreneurship. First, diverse teams bring together individuals with a wide range of skills, knowledge, and expertise, thereby enhancing the group's collective intelligence. Diverse perspectives and experiences result in a greater variety of ideas, allowing the team to approach problems from a variety of angles and develop more creative solutions. Boder (2006) study found that diverse teams in organizations can effectively harness their collective knowledge and expertise, resulting in notable enhancements in problem-solving, innovation, and decision-making processes. The study highlights the valuable contributions that diverse teams can make to an organization's overall performance and competitiveness, emphasizing the importance of leveraging collective intelligence for improved outcomes.

Diversity among team members is vital for encouraging innovation and non-traditional thought. Introducing team members with varied backgrounds and perspectives fosters a diversity of cultural, social, and cognitive frameworks, stimulating the development of novel ideas and encouraging the adoption of unconventional strategies. Scholarly studies, like Shalley & Perry-Smith (2008), show how essential factors like team evolution, socio-cognitive network centrality, and various external connections are for encouraging creative thinking within a group. Diversity outside of organizational ties contributes a range of viewpoints and expertise from unanticipated sources. In contrast, the centrality of socio-cognitive networks enables the exchange of diverse concepts among team members. Furthermore, the evolution of a team, encompassing alterations in composition and dynamics, promotes diversity of thought and perspective, stimulating innovation and yielding creative results. In today's globalized and multicultural society, diverse teams are better equipped to comprehend and meet the requirements of various client segments. Diverse teams possess a greater comprehension of consumer behaviours, dialects, and cultures, which enables them to develop marketing strategies, products, and services that appeal to a broader range of customers and grant organizations a competitive advantage in the marketplace.

Including diverse teams in the decision-making process is very important, as their unique perspectives facilitate a more thorough assessment of prospective opportunities and risks. Diverse teams employ constructive debates and critical thinking to question presumptions, generating more comprehensive and resilient decisions. There is an increasing acknowledgement of the significance of cultivating inclusive ecosystems in entrepreneurial settings, with the goals of reducing unconscious biases, enhancing the presence of underrepresented groups, encouraging collaboration, and ensuring equal opportunity. With the growing recognition of the drawbacks of homogeneity and the adoption of diversity as a societal value, entrepreneurial endeavours involving diverse teams have transformed, presenting novel opportunities for advancement, expansion, and triumph (Duchek et al., 2019). Promoting an entrepreneurial culture among disparate teams and organizations is critical for long-term success and innovation in the ever-changing business landscape of the twenty-first century. In light of technological advancements and globalization, organizations must adjust by leveraging their teams' innovative thinking, diverse perspectives, and creativity. This chapter delves into the approaches, obstacles, and advantages of fostering an entrepreneurial ethos within heterogeneous teams. It gives organizations valuable perspectives on harnessing diversity as a catalyst for innovation and competitive advantage.

By incorporating principles from diversity management, entrepreneurship, organizational behaviour, and organizational culture, this chapter ties together notions including cognitive diversity, organizational culture, and transformational leadership. This study investigates the impact of transformational leadership on fostering entrepreneurial perspectives and behaviours among diverse teams. Additionally, it analyzes the influence of organizational culture on attitudes towards innovation, creativity, and risk-taking. Furthermore, the chapter delves into the ramifications of cognitive diversity on organizational and team innovation, decision-making, and problem-solving.

The chapter's conceptual framework predates the dynamic relationship among diversity, organizational culture, and entrepreneurship. This instance demonstrates how cultivating an entrepreneurial culture can empower diverse teams to reach their utmost capabilities by promoting innovation, cooperation, and exploring fresh prospects. Moreover, leadership is pivotal in establishing the standard for entrepreneurial conduct and cultivating an all-encompassing atmosphere that appreciates and accepts various viewpoints.

By presenting an exhaustive overview of the strategies and best practices for fostering an entrepreneurial culture in diverse organizations and teams, this chapter seeks to accomplish the same. In addition to delving into the theoretical underpinnings of entrepreneurship, diversity, and organizational culture, this course provides case studies and practical insights that exemplify successful implementation strategies. The chapter investigates many facets of entrepreneurship, encompassing leadership, communication, collaboration, and organizational design (Siyal. (2023); (Siyal et al. (2023)Siyal. (2018); Siyal & Peng. (2018). Its particular emphasis is on how these elements intersect with diversity to foster innovation and confer a competitive edge. The chapter's ultimate objective is to provide readers with the information and resources necessary to cultivate entrepreneurial cultures that flourish in the twenty-first century's dynamic and ever-evolving business environment. The purpose of this chapter is to analyze the significance of entrepreneurship in diverse teams and organizations. This paper shall examine the advantages of diversity within entrepreneurial environments, delineate the historical progression of diversity in entrepreneurship, and deliberate on possible barriers. Furthermore, it will prioritize strategies that foster achievement and inclusivity in various entrepreneurial pursuits.

UNDERSTANDING THE DIVERSITY OF TEAMS AND ORGANIZATIONS

Diversity in teams and organizations goes beyond surface-level characteristics such as race, ethnicity, and gender. It encompasses various attributes and perspectives that individuals bring to the table. Diversity in race and ethnicity recognizes the importance of representing different racial and ethnic backgrounds within teams and organizations. It acknowledges the unique perspectives, experiences, and cultural insights that individuals from diverse racial and ethnic groups bring, enriching the collective knowledge and understanding within the team. Van et al. (2020) state that diversity should be recognized as a catalyst for enhancing organizational performance, encompassing advantages such as improved decision-making, problem-solving, creativity, and innovation, as emphasized by the primary finding in the article. To harness these benefits, organizations should adopt a multifaceted approach. Firstly, they should actively encourage the integration of diverse perspectives and experiences within their teams. Secondly, diversity initiatives should be seamlessly incorporated into broader organizational strategies rather than being isolated efforts. Thirdly, leadership support should extend beyond formal HR practices and include informal actions that promote and champion diversity at all organizational levels. Lastly, establishing standardized accountability systems is vital to ensuring the effective implementation of diversity initiatives. The key takeaway is that organizations can unlock the full potential of diversity by embracing a comprehensive and integrated diversity management strategy and leveraging it as a driving force for synergy and enhanced performance.

Gender diversity refers to individuals across the gender spectrum, including men, women, and those who identify as non-binary or genderqueer. Recognizing and valuing diverse gender identities promotes equal opportunities, challenges gender stereotypes, and fosters a more inclusive and supportive work environment. In their research, Ferrary & Déo (2023) have uncovered a pivotal insight: gender diversity, when present at both middle management and staff levels, positively influences a company's economic performance and enhances its competitive edge. Gender diversity is recognized as a strategic asset that bestows a lasting competitive advantage for the organization, as it generates value rival firms cannot easily replicate. Notably, their study reveals a non-linear relationship marked by a critical mass condition. It indicates that firms within a balanced gender diversity range (with women comprising 40% to 60% of employees) at the middle management and staff tiers tend to achieve greater profitability. Furthermore, the research indicates that companies with predominantly male or female workforces perform at similar levels, underscoring the importance of balanced gender diversity in driving firm performance.

Age diversity acknowledges the value of including individuals from different age groups, from young entrepreneurs to seasoned professionals. Each age group brings distinct perspectives, experiences, and expertise, contributing to intergenerational learning and a well-rounded decision-making process. Kumar (2023) central discovery revolves around the significant influence of top management team (TMT) age demographics on a firm's environmental management (EM) strategy. The research reveals that ageing TMTs are inclined to support beyond-compliance initiatives in environmental management. Their desire for legacy and preference for risk-averse decision-making attributed to this inclination.

Age diversity within the TMT enhances the team's innovative capacity, particularly in addressing compliance-related environmental challenges. The study underscores that ageing TMTs favour strategies beyond mere compliance, whereas age-diverse TMTs excel at developing compliance-oriented initiatives. This discovery illuminates the dynamics of TMT composition and its profound impact on environmental strategy, offering valuable insights for future research.

Socioeconomic diversity emphasizes including individuals from different socioeconomic backgrounds, considering factors such as income, education, and upbringing (Siyal, Peng & Siyal. (2018). By incorporating diverse socioeconomic perspectives, teams and organizations can better understand the needs of various customer segments and develop inclusive solutions that cater to a broader range of individuals. Lee et al. (2023) The central discovery in this study is the presence of a negative perception surrounding the hospitality industry, particularly among

Generation Z employees. Two key factors influence this negative perception: social class background and family expectations. Notably, individuals from lower social-class backgrounds are likelier to hold unfavourable views of the hospitality sector. They are less inclined to consider pursuing careers within it, primarily due to familial expectations. However, an exciting finding emerges when managerial positions are introduced, which mitigates the negative impact on career intentions. It underscores the importance of job titles and advancement opportunities within the hospitality industry as influential factors in shaping career decisions. Furthermore, the study underscores the significance of recognizing social class background as an element of organizational diversity. By addressing these aspects, the hospitality industry can work toward fostering a more inclusive environment and enhancing its recruitment efforts.

Educational, physical ability, cultural, and cognitive diversity are integral to fostering inclusive teams and organizations. Recognizing and valuing these diverse characteristics enriches problem-solving, innovation, and decision-making. Diverse teams offer diverse perspectives and experiences, leading to more comprehensive problem-solving and better-informed decisions. Moreover, entrepreneurship thrives on understanding diverse customer segments, making diverse teams invaluable in identifying market needs and developing products and services that resonate with a broader audience. However, unconscious biases, a lack of representation, and systemic barriers can impede the recruitment and advancement of diverse talent and hinder access to resources (Alexandre-Leclair, 2013). Overcoming these challenges necessitates a concerted effort to promote awareness, implement inclusive practices, and address structural inequalities to create an environment where all individuals, regardless of background, can thrive and contribute to entrepreneurial success.

These examples of successful and diverse entrepreneurship teams and organizations serve as inspiring models for the industry. Cashmere Nicole leads Beauty Bakerie, which offers diverse product lines that celebrate beauty across various skin tones and ethnicities, exemplifying inclusivity in the cosmetics industry. Women Who Code, a global non-profit founded to support women in technology, actively promotes gender diversity and empowerment within the tech sector, providing women with opportunities to excel and contribute to entrepreneurial ventures. Furthermore, Anne Wojcicki, the founder 23andMe, prioritizes diversity in the company's approach to enhancing healthcare outcomes for all populations through personalized medicine and genetics research. These instances underscore the importance of embracing diversity within entrepreneurship, as it fosters innovation, addresses market needs, and creates inclusive and successful ventures that resonate with diverse audiences.

BUILDING A CULTURE OF ENTREPRENEURSHIP
IN DIVERSE TEAMS AND ORGANIZATIONS

A culture of entrepreneurship refers to a set of shared values, beliefs, attitudes, and practices that promote and support entrepreneurial thinking, innovation, and risk-taking within teams and organizations. It is characterized by a mindset of initiative, creativity, adaptability, and a willingness to embrace and learn from failure. A culture of entrepreneurship encourages individuals to take ownership, think critically, and pursue opportunities for growth and innovation. Establish a supportive environment where new ideas are encouraged, and innovation is recognized and rewarded. Encourage team members to explore new possibilities, experiment, and take calculated risks. Value diverse perspectives and encourage open dialogue to foster an inclusive environment. Create opportunities for cross-functional collaboration and knowledge-sharing to enhance creativity and problem-solving. Ensure diverse teams access the necessary resources, tools, and mentorship to pursue entrepreneurial initiatives. Offer training, workshops, and professional development opportunities to enhance entrepreneurial skills and knowledge. Encourage a culture of continuous learning and growth. Emphasize the value of feedback, reflection, and learning from successes and failures (Alexandre-Leclair, 2013). Create a safe space where individuals feel comfortable taking risks and learning from setbacks. Provide autonomy and decision-making authority to team members, allowing them to take ownership of their work and pursue entrepreneurial opportunities. Encourage individuals to think independently, challenge the status quo, and make decisions that drive innovation and growth.

Leaders should communicate a clear vision for fostering entrepreneurship and creating an inclusive environment. They must articulate the importance of diversity, innovation, and risk-taking and lead by example in embracing these principles. Leaders should empower them with the necessary resources, autonomy, and support to pursue entrepreneurial initiatives. Leaders should establish a safe, inclusive space that values and amplifies diverse voices. Leaders should create an environment where team members feel psychologically safe to take risks, share ideas, and express their opinions. It involves actively listening, valuing diverse perspectives, and promoting a culture of mutual respect and trust. Leaders should recognize and reward entrepreneurial thinking and behaviour. Leaders can recognize and reward entrepreneurial thinking and behaviour through acknowledgement, promotions, incentives, or other forms of recognition that reinforce the importance of entrepreneurship and diversity (Félix et al., 2019).

A culture of entrepreneurship promotes the inclusion of diverse perspectives, experiences, and backgrounds. It encourages individuals from different demographic groups to participate, contribute their unique insights, and pursue entrepreneurial opportunities. It increases diversity within teams and organizations, fostering a more inclusive and representative workforce. Kim & Lee (2023) uncover the intricate relationship between organizational diversity and employee dynamics within Korean state-owned enterprises (SOEs). The core finding reveals that the influence of diversity varies depending on the specific dimension under examination. Notably, social category diversity is associated with reduced conflict and enhanced affective commitment among employees, signifying its role in fostering organizational cohesion.

Informational diversity neutralizes conflict and affective commitment, indicating its lack of significant influence in these aspects. Notably, value diversity, which encompasses variations in values and beliefs, links to increased conflict and decreased affective commitment, highlighting the potential challenges of differing core beliefs in the workplace. Moreover, the study highlights that conflict mediates the relationship between value diversity and affective commitment, providing insight into the underlying mechanisms. This research underscores the necessity for a nuanced assessment of diverse dimensions and their distinct effects on organizational dynamics, offering valuable guidance for managing Korean state-owned enterprises (Félix et al., 2019).

Entrepreneurship thrives on innovation, and diversity is crucial in driving innovative thinking and problem-solving. A culture of entrepreneurship that embraces diversity encourages the exploration of different perspectives and approaches, leading to more innovative and creative solutions. West & Sacramento (2023) literature review reveals a fundamental insight into the relationship between creativity, innovation, and the surrounding team and organizational climates. The core finding emphasizes that the environment in which individuals operate plays a significant role in shaping creativity and innovation outcomes, impacting not only individuals but also teams and entire organizations. It underscores the critical importance of cultivating an environment that fosters rather than hinders creative and innovative behaviours. Furthermore, the review presents climate taxonomies and diagnostic tools, providing valuable resources for assessing and enhancing creative climates in practical organizational settings. Lastly, the study highlights the practical implications of understanding and improving creative climates, offers guidance to organizations that promote innovation, and points towards potential areas of future research in this domain.

Diversity within teams and organizations improves decision-making processes by incorporating broader viewpoints and insights. A culture of entrepreneurship that values diversity and inclusivity enables more robust and well-informed decision-making, reducing biases and enhancing the quality of decisions. The core finding of Issa (2023) underscores a positive relationship between gender-diverse boards in European companies and the adoption of clean energy practices. In essence, greater gender diversity on corporate boards correlates with a higher likelihood of using clean energy sources. This alignment with gender socialization and diversity theories suggests that diverse boards contribute to environmentally responsible decision-making. Moreover, the study reveals that environmental, social, and governance (ESG) controversies are moderating, strengthening the link between board gender diversity and clean energy adoption in companies facing such issues. Furthermore, the study confirms adherence to the critical mass theory, indicating that companies with at least three female board members prioritize clean energy. These findings hold robustly across multiple analytical methods, and their implications span stakeholders, policymakers, and managers, emphasizing that board gender diversity can drive clean energy adoption, bolstering company reputation and stakeholder appeal. Policymakers can use these insights to craft diversity-promoting and environmental policies, while managers can make informed choices about board composition and sustainable energy strategies.

A culture of entrepreneurship that embraces diversity creates an inclusive and supportive environment where individuals feel valued, heard, and empowered. It fosters higher levels of employee engagement, satisfaction, and retention. Zeitlin et al. (2023) reveal a central finding: job satisfaction is the dominant predictor of intent to remain employed among both caseworkers of colour and white caseworkers within child welfare organizations. However, the factors affecting job satisfaction differ slightly between these two groups. Age and job stress hold greater significance for caseworkers of colour, whereas white caseworkers are more influenced by work-related burnout.

Additionally, the perception of leadership is pivotal in the intent to remain employed for caseworkers of colour, contrasting with white caseworkers. Furthermore, having a Master of Social Work (MSW) degree predicts retention for white caseworkers but not for caseworkers of colour. These findings underscore the need for tailored retention strategies that account for the unique experiences and influencing factors for workers of colour and white within child welfare organizations. Downey et al. (2015) highlight a significant link between workplace diversity practices and increased employee engagement. Establishing a trusting climate within the organization underpins this relationship. When effectively implemented, diversity practices cultivate employee trust, leading to higher engagement levels. The study reveals that employees' feelings of inclusion influence the strength of the relationship between diversity practices and trust climate. It underscores the dual importance of implementing diversity practices and fostering inclusivity to harness their positive impact on employee engagement fully. This finding holds implications for both theoretical understanding and practical application, emphasizing the pivotal roles of diversity, trust, and inclusion in enhancing workplace well-being. The study also offers recommendations for future research in this domain.

DEVELOPING ENTREPRENEURIAL SKILLS IN DIVERSE TEAMS AND ORGANIZATIONS

Entrepreneurial skills refer to the competencies and capabilities individuals and teams need to identify opportunities, take initiative, innovate, and create value within an entrepreneurial context. Top management teams play a central role in determining the fate of entrepreneurial firms, as highlighted by Eisenhardt (2013) study. It highlights critical insights, emphasizing the importance of factors such as team size and composition, effective decision-making processes, reliance on "simple rules" heuristics, and the dynamic nature of organizational structures. Specifically, the research underscores that larger, more diverse teams with a history of collaboration tend to thrive, particularly in growth markets. Successful teams make prompt strategic decisions, welcome constructive conflict, and nurture positive working relationships. Furthermore, adopting "simple rules" heuristics can guide significant activities and even evolve into the organization's core strategy. Additionally, high-performing top management teams continuously adapt their organizational structures, balancing order and adaptability. In essence, the study highlights the pivotal role of top management teams in shaping the outcomes of entrepreneurial firms and provides valuable insights into the determinants of their success. These skills drive entrepreneurial success and are crucial in diverse teams and organizations.

The ability to recognize and assess potential business opportunities, market gaps, and customer needs. The capacity to generate new and unique ideas, think outside the box, and develop innovative solutions to problems. The willingness to take calculated risks, navigate uncertainties, and persevere in facing challenges and setbacks. The ability to quickly adapt to changing circumstances, embrace new technologies and trends, and adjust strategies as needed. The capability to analyze complex problems, break them into manageable components, and develop practical solutions. The aptitude to work effectively in diverse teams, leverage team members' strengths, and collaborate towards shared goals (Félix et al., 2019). Provide academic opportunities by focusing your seminars, workshops, and training programs on developing entrepreneurial skills. These may include opportunity recognition, creative thinking, risk management, and teamwork. Jones & English (2004) study emphasizes the significance of experiential learning and practical application in entrepreneurship education. By incorporating real-world experiences like internships, business simulations, and case studies, students can enhance their entrepreneurial competencies and be better prepared for the challenges they may face in the entrepreneurial world. The study advocates for a shift from traditional classroom-based learning to a more hands-on approach, enabling students to understand entrepreneurship and acquire the practical skills necessary for success. Ultimately, the study highlights the value of experiential learning in bridging the gap between theory and practice and equipping students with the skills and mindset needed to thrive as entrepreneurs.

Facilitate initiatives and programs that necessitate collaboration between diverse teams. This facilitates the development of entrepreneurial skills through sharing experiences, collaboration, and exposure to various points of view. Kohler (2016) study explores corporate accelerators and their role in facilitating collaboration and innovation between corporations and start-ups. The core finding suggests corporate accelerators serve as platforms for knowledge exchange and resource sharing, benefiting both parties. Start-ups gain access to funding, mentorship, and corporate resources, while corporations gain external innovation, market insights, and access to entrepreneurial talent. The study highlights the advantages of corporate accelerators, including increased innovation, faster time to market, and an enhanced entrepreneurial culture. However, addressing challenges such as cultural differences and effective collaboration is crucial. Overall, corporate accelerators have the potential to drive mutual growth and competitiveness in the business landscape.

Experienced mentors or instructors should partner with team members to assist them in developing entrepreneurial skills. Mentors can provide invaluable insight, advice, and support based on entrepreneurial experiences. Sullivan (2000) study shows that mentoring relationships are an effective support mechanism for entrepreneurial learning. The research emphasizes the importance of continuous learning and knowledge acquisition in the ever-changing and dynamic marketplace. It suggests that traditional volume-driven training programs may not provide immediate relevance to participants, highlighting the value of "just-in-time" support and reflective learning facilitated through mentoring. The study argues that mentors, equipped with suitable skills, knowledge, experience, and access to relevant expertise, can effectively support entrepreneurs by identifying their developmental phases and providing tailored guidance and access to training or other resources. The research also emphasizes the need for further exploration of client-mentor matching and the effectiveness of alternative support programs. Overall, the study concludes that entrepreneurial learning, supported by mentors, is crucial for the survival and growth of small and medium-sized enterprises (SMEs) and suggests that mentoring programs may be more cost-effective and responsive to individual needs compared to upfront prescribed training.

Encourage individuals to experiment with new ideas and methods despite the inherent dangers. Encourage individuals to iterate and improve their entrepreneurial abilities in an environment that embraces failure as a learning and development opportunity. In their study, Zahra et al. (2006) emphasize the interdependence of entrepreneurship and dynamic capabilities. They propose a model that integrates these concepts and highlights their importance for organizational success and competitiveness. The research emphasizes the fundamental connection between entrepreneurship and organizations' ability to adapt and develop. Entrepreneurship catalyzes the development and deployment of dynamic capabilities by recognizing and capitalizing on novel opportunities. By implementing entrepreneurial practices, including innovation and opportunity identification, businesses improve their capacity to adjust and restructure their resources following evolving circumstances. Furthermore, the research emphasizes strategic flexibility, entrepreneurial orientation, and efficient knowledge management when integrating dynamic capabilities and entrepreneurship. Organizations that cultivate an entrepreneurial ethos, adopt a proactive approach to knowledge management, and support strategic flexibility are more aptly positioned to cultivate and exploit dynamic capabilities, ultimately attaining a perpetual competitive edge. In conclusion, the study shows that dynamic capabilities and entrepreneurship go hand in hand. Companies should encourage an entrepreneurial mindset and allocate resources to develop dynamic capabilities to thrive in unstable business environments.

Encourage continuous learning by emphasizing the significance of lifelong learning and personal development. Provide access to resources, such as books, online courses, and industry events, to facilitate acquiring new skills and knowledge. Alenezi (2023) emphasizes the need for a comprehensive and holistic approach to digital transformation in higher education institutions. It recognizes that digital transformation encompasses technological advancements and cultural, procedural, pedagogical, and administrative adjustments. Many stakeholders are involved in the digital processes, each playing a role determined by the specific dimensions and perspectives covered in the digital strategies. The study highlights the complexity of the transformation process and the need for comprehensive approaches in existing literature. It calls for surrogate methods that align with the institution's model, procedures, and user experience, considering internal digital capabilities and future perspectives. Overall, the study emphasizes the significance of reevaluating and reinventing higher education institutions to adapt effectively to the multifaceted impact of technology on various aspects of education.

Training and development are vital for entrepreneurial skills in diverse teams and organizations. Conduct workshops and seminars that emphasize particular entrepreneurial skills. Internal specialists, external educators, or industry experts may conduct these workshops and seminars. Howieson (2003) critically examines the readiness of accounting education to meet the evolving needs and challenges of the accounting profession in the new millennium. The article highlights the changing landscape of accounting practice due to globalization, technological advancements, and shifting regulatory frameworks. It assesses the role of accounting education in preparing future accountants by evaluating curriculum, teaching methods, and assessment practices. Identifying the challenges accounting education faces, such as outdated curricula and gaps in practical experience. The article proposes solutions and recommendations, including curriculum reforms, technology integration (Siyal et al. (2021), and enhanced professional skills development, to bridge the gap between accounting education and the profession's demands.

Through hands-on experience and real-world initiatives, provide opportunities for team members to acquire and develop entrepreneurial skills. Assign challenging assignments that necessitate the application of entrepreneurial thought and problem-solving skills. Ahadi & Jacobs (2017) underscores the pressing need for a more comprehensive exploration of self-organized on-the-job training (S-OJT). It highlights the imperative for additional empirical investigations to deepen our comprehension of this phenomenon. This research effectively categorizes and scrutinizes the existing S-OJT literature, recognizing its potential influence on individuals, teams, and organizations. The study's conceptual framework offers valuable insights into diverse approaches for implementing S-OJT programs, which engage various stakeholders and specialists. This research substantially contributes to the Human Resource Development (HRD) field by illuminating the factors facilitating S-OJT and its implications for training systems, organizational learning, and performance enhancement.

Provide coaching and mentoring programs through which seasoned entrepreneurs or executives within the organization can guide and assist individuals on their path to skill development. Kent et al. (2003) underscore the significant role that mentoring plays in the training and development of small- to medium-sized enterprise (SME) retailers. Conducted in the London Borough of Merton, this research assesses the responses of 40 retailers engaged in the mentoring process. The findings illuminate how mentoring facilitates the transfer of vital information, skills, and expertise while offering flexibility regarding when and where learning occurs. The study culminates in evaluating the project's initial outcomes vis-à-vis its objectives and identifying emerging themes within SME retail management. The research underscores the positive and beneficial impact of mentoring as a training and development approach for SME retailers.

Make available online learning platforms that offer courses and resources on entrepreneurship, innovation, and related skills. These platforms enable team members to learn independently and follow their requirements and interests. Romero-Rodriguez & Montoya (2019) highlight that including entrepreneurial competencies in Massive Open Online Courses (MOOCs) can significantly enhance the attributes of educational innovation and collaborative projects. This research uncovers the positive impact of integrating entrepreneurship-related content into MOOCs, countering criticisms of low completion rates and limited networking capabilities. The study adopts a three-stage approach involving a comprehensive literature review, a quantitative analysis based on participant surveys, and a qualitative examination of interactions within MOOC discussion forums. The findings indicate that MOOCs incorporating entrepreneurship content achieved a relatively higher completion rate of 12.55%, surpassing the literature's average. Moreover, 14.29% of participants recognized opportunities to generate ventures related to the course topics through discussion forums. It underscores the potential of infusing entrepreneurship issues into MOOCs to foster networking and explore business prospects among learners, ultimately contributing to educational innovation.

Entrepreneurial abilities enable teams and organizations to recognize and exploit new opportunities, innovate, and create value. They cultivate a culture of innovation, creating growth and driving new products, services, and business models. Soomro et al. (2021) core finding of this study is that various strategic factors, including personal mastery, transformational leadership, a shared vision, proactivity, and the environment, have a positive and significant impact on both organizational innovation (OI) and organizational learning (OL). Additionally, the research reveals that OI and OL positively and significantly influence organizational performance. These findings provide valuable insights for organizations, highlighting the importance of cultivating these strategic factors to enhance their capabilities, foster innovation, and facilitate learning, ultimately leading to improved organizational performance, particularly in the context of developing countries.

Entrepreneurial skills enhance problem-solving, allowing teams to confront obstacles and adapt to fluctuating market conditions. They encourage a proactive and solution-focused perspective, resulting in more effective problem-solving outcomes. Dullayaphut & Untachai (2013) The core finding of this study is that the four-factor human resource competency model, comprising skills, expertise, problem-solving, and adaptability competencies, is empirically valid and reliable for small and medium enterprises (SMEs) in the upper north-eastern region of Thailand. Through a survey involving 329 SME managers across multiple provinces, the study confirms the applicability of this competency framework. These findings hold significance for SMEs in this region, as they can utilize the validated model to assess and enhance their human resource competencies, ultimately improving their organizational performance and competitiveness.

Entrepreneurial abilities facilitate effective collaboration and cooperation in heterogeneous organizations. They encourage open communication, constructive feedback, and the capacity to capitalize on diverse perspectives and expertise. It contributes to enhanced collaboration and performance. The core finding of this study by Amorim et al. (2020) states that teamwork skills predict entrepreneurial behaviour among K -12 public school teachers. The research involved 367 teachers and identified that teachers with solid teamwork skills were likelier to exhibit entrepreneurial behaviour. Additionally, the study revealed that most participants received teamwork training through their school districts. However, teachers faced barriers to effective teamwork, including time constraints, individual differences, and challenges in collaboration. These findings underscore the importance of teamwork skills in fostering entrepreneurial behaviour among educators and highlight the need to address barriers to effective teamwork in the education sector.

Developing entrepreneurial skills within teams and organizations fosters individual development, learning, and empowerment. It increases employee engagement and satisfaction, thereby increasing motivation and retention. Boonsiritomachai & Sud-On (2022) found that an entrepreneurial attitude among entry-level employees significantly and positively contributes to their work engagement. However, having an entrepreneurial attitude can also divert employee attention regarding the level of commitment to the organization. Interestingly, the research reveals that employees will still commit to an organization if they have engaged with the company, even if they possess a highly entrepreneurial attitude. This study sheds light on the complex relationship between entrepreneurial orientation, work engagement, and organizational commitment, offering insights for organizations seeking to retain entrepreneurial employees while ensuring their commitment.

Entrepreneurial abilities provide teams and organizations with a market advantage. They promote a culture of continuous development and adaptability, allowing teams to adapt to emergent trends rapidly and outperform rivals. Hwang et al. (2020) Organizational innovation capabilities significantly mediate the relationship between entrepreneurial competencies at the individual level and firm performance at the organizational level. While prior research has shown mixed results regarding the direct relationship between entrepreneurial competencies and firm performance, this study highlights the crucial role of organizational innovation capabilities as a mediating factor. The study reveals that the indirect effects of entrepreneurial competencies, channelled through organizational innovation capabilities, are much more robust in influencing competitive advantage than their direct effects. This research underscores the importance of nurturing organizational innovation capabilities to leverage entrepreneurial competencies for sustained competitive advantage. To foster innovation, problem-solving, collaboration, and overall performance, diverse teams and organizations must cultivate entrepreneurial skills. These competencies contribute to organizational growth, competitive advantage, and entrepreneurial and dynamic culture development.

OVERCOMING CHALLENGES IN CREATING A CULTURE OF ENTREPRENEURSHIP IN DIVERSE TEAMS AND ORGANIZATIONS

A reluctance to adopt an entrepreneurial culture may be motivated by apprehension toward the unfamiliar or a preference for conventional work practices. Likewise, teams comprising individuals who fail to completely comprehend the advantages of diversity may underestimate the value of diverse viewpoints and find it challenging to work together despite their differences. Ineffective communication channels or miscommunication may impede the interchange of ideas and the development of a culture that encourages collaboration and innovation. Implicit prejudices and preconceived notions may impede the complete involvement and input of a varied group of team members, thus limiting the capacity for inclusive entrepreneurship. In addition to educating individuals about the value of diversity, enhancing communication channels, and actively combating unconscious biases and stereotypes, addressing these challenges requires nurturing an environment of transparency (Félix et al., 2019; Karlsson et al., 2019).

Leaders must emphasize diversity, inclusion, and entrepreneurial values to cultivate an entrepreneurial culture that thrives in heterogeneous teams and organizations. Leaders should exhibit dedication by prioritizing these principles, correspondingly allocating resources, and setting a good example. Additionally, organizations must implement training initiatives to promote diversity awareness and its benefits. Organizations should encourage team members to value diverse viewpoints and actively participate in cross-cultural education. Promoting inclusive decision-making processes encompassing open dialogue and integrating diverse viewpoints is crucial. Furthermore, it is critical to address implicit biases and stereotypes. By integrating measures such as mentoring programs, unconscious bias training, and diverse recruiting practices, organizations can foster an entrepreneurial culture that flourishes by reducing prejudices and increasing inclusiveness (Félix et al., 2019).

Ensuring effective communication and providing constructive feedback are critical components of fostering an entrepreneurial culture across diverse teams and organizations. Transparent communication channels, including virtual collaboration platforms and routine team meetings, promote open dialogue and exchanging ideas. Active listening fosters a secure atmosphere where team members feel appreciated and empowered to contribute their thoughts and viewpoints. Constructive feedback is paramount in nurturing progress and advancement as it furnishes precise and implementable direction regarding entrepreneurial aptitudes and inclusive conduct. In addition, fostering a culture of perpetual development entails consistently soliciting input from team members via diverse means (e.g., surveys or individual discussions), thereby guaranteeing the continuous adjustment and refinement of communication tactics to align with the ever-changing requirements of the group (Danish et al., 2019; Jones et al., 2020).

Successfully navigating obstacles to foster an entrepreneurial culture within heterogeneous teams and organizations results in many favourable consequences for the performance of both the teams and the associations. To begin with, it stimulates heightened levels of innovation and creativity by utilizing the team's varied experiences and perspectives, resulting in original resolutions to intricate challenges. Additionally, it promotes increased collaboration and cooperation by addressing communication barriers and biases, ultimately leading to enhanced knowledge sharing and the team's overall effectiveness. Moreover, fostering an atmosphere that appreciates diversity and entrepreneurialism enhances employee engagement and satisfaction by providing team members with a sense of inclusion, empowerment, and worth, resulting in heightened motivation and dedication. Additionally, it enhances the organization's adaptability, allowing teams to promptly react to changes in the market and recognize novel prospects for expansion (Félix et al., 2019). Cultivating an entrepreneurial ethos within heterogeneous teams positions them to achieve long-term prosperity by showcasing their capacity for inventive thinking, efficient collaboration, and responsiveness to evolving market conditions, thus conferring a competitive advantage.

THE ROLE OF TECHNOLOGY IN FOSTERING ENTREPRENEURSHIP IN DIVERSE TEAMS AND ORGANIZATIONS

Technology fosters entrepreneurship in diverse organizations and teams by facilitating access to resources, innovation, and collaboration. By utilizing a range of platforms, such as virtual meeting software, project management tools, and cloud-based document sharing, technology facilitates seamless collaboration among teams, regardless of geographical constraints. This fosters the exchange of ideas, knowledge, and practical cooperation. Also, technology makes it easy to get a lot of data, market trends, and industry insights immediately. This lets teams of people from different backgrounds do thorough investigations, make intelligent decisions, and spot new opportunities. Digital marketplaces and platforms facilitate entrepreneurship by providing a venue where people of all backgrounds can exhibit and promote their products or services, promoting equality. Moreover, implementing technology-driven automation improves operational efficiency, enabling entrepreneurs to allocate their time and energy towards strategic pursuits, innovative thinking, and creativity. This, in turn, cultivates an entrepreneurial culture that is dynamic and inclusive of all members of teams and organizations (Jayanna et al., 2024).

Many technological solutions exist to foster entrepreneurship, as demonstrated by various platforms and tools. E-commerce platforms, including but not limited to Shopify, Etsy, and Amazon, allow entrepreneurs to create and oversee virtual storefronts, enabling them to connect with a worldwide clientele irrespective of geographical constraints. Through community support and financial backing, crowdfunding platforms such as Kickstarter and Indiegogo enable entrepreneurs to acquire capital for their ventures. Accelerator and incubator programs utilize technological advancements to facilitate networking, mentorship, and resource provision for entrepreneurs, stimulating their progress and triumph within the technology sector. Virtual collaboration tools, including Slack, Trello, and Google Workspace, enable geographically dispersed team members to engage in project management and communication without interruption. Moreover, using artificial intelligence (AI) and data analytics tools allows entrepreneurs to extract valuable insights about customer behaviour, market trends, and business performance. This empowers them to make well-informed decisions and implement focused strategies. These instances highlight technology's pivotal role in stimulating innovation and entrepreneurship in various industries (Linton & Wei, 2020; Patrício & Fernandes, 2022).

The role of technology in entrepreneurship is crucial in promoting diversity and inclusion, as it eliminates obstacles and broadens prospects for individuals from various backgrounds. Through the provision of equitable access to resources, information, and markets, technology fosters opportunity creation for entrepreneurs who might have otherwise faced conventional obstacles. Furthermore, using technology empowers entrepreneurs to communicate with customers globally, surpassing the constraints imposed by geographical boundaries and expanding the realm in which diverse entrepreneurs can operate. Furthermore, technology enhances inclusion by facilitating the flexibility of remote work and accommodating individuals who face challenges in adapting to conventional work arrangements, such as caregivers and individuals with disabilities. In addition to facilitating virtual collaboration, networking, and mentorship, technological platforms connect entrepreneurs with various origins and areas of expertise. This facilitates intercultural education, cooperation, and the interchange of concepts, ultimately enhancing the entrepreneurial environment with various viewpoints and backgrounds (Linton & Wei, 2020). Several ethical implications must be carefully considered when utilizing technology to promote entrepreneurship. Entrepreneurs must prioritize privacy and data protection by adhering to regulatory requirements and responsibly handling consumer data and personal information. Furthermore, it is critical to resolve the digital divide, given that technology ought to be universally accessible. Establishing measures promoting equal access to technological resources and connectivity prevents individuals from being marginalized. In addition, entrepreneurs must be mindful of the unintentional perpetuation of inequalities resulting from biases in algorithms and data-driven technologies. Vigilance is required to identify and mitigate biases in technological solutions. Moreover, ethical considerations encompass the conscientious and open utilization of data, underscoring the criticality of adhering to ethical protocols throughout data collection, analysis, and application phases in entrepreneurial pursuits (Martin et al., 2019). By placing these ethical considerations at the forefront, entrepreneurs can effectively utilize technology to promote entrepreneurship while maintaining principles of integrity, equity, and inclusiveness.

CONCLUSION

This chapter examined entrepreneurship's significance in diverse teams and organizations. It discussed the history of entrepreneurship in diverse teams, highlighting the transition towards recognizing the value of diversity in driving innovation and expansion. We defined diversity in teams and organizations as the presence of individuals with distinct traits, life experiences, and points of view. The chapter emphasized the advantages of diversity in entrepreneurship, such as increased creativity, innovation, problem-solving, and market responsiveness. In addition, it acknowledged obstacles to diversity and offered solutions for overcoming them. It further provided examples of diverse entrepreneurial teams and organizations that were successful, highlighting their impact and accomplishments. In addition, it explored creating an entrepreneurial culture, developing entrepreneurial skills, and utilizing technology to foster entrepreneurship in diverse teams. Finally, it observed the obstacles, the role of communication, and the consequences of overcoming obstacles in establishing an entrepreneurial culture.

Developing an entrepreneurial culture in diverse teams and organizations is essential for maximizing the potential of individuals and fostering innovation. Organizations can foster a collaborative and innovative environment by embracing diversity, advocating inclusive practices, and developing entrepreneurial skills. It requires a strong commitment from leadership, education, and efforts for continuous improvement. It is essential to overcome obstacles such as resistance to change and biases. Technology fosters entrepreneurship by facilitating access to information, resources, and global markets. However, ethical considerations, such as privacy, data protection, and algorithmic biases, must be considered. Acceptance of diversity and entrepreneurship in teams and organizations contributes to business success, social impact, and sustainable growth.

Numerous implications exist for future research and practice in entrepreneurship in diverse teams and organizations. Additional research can investigate the strategies and interventions that effectively promote diversity and entrepreneurship, considering the unique challenges encountered by various industries, regions, and cultural contexts. In addition, examining the long-term outcomes and effects of diverse entrepreneurship on organizational performance, market competitiveness, and societal transformation would yield valuable insights. Implementing inclusive policies, diversity training programs, and adopting technological tools to foster entrepreneurship and support diverse teams have practical implications. Researchers, policymakers, and business leaders must collaborate to continuously advance the understanding and application of diversity and entrepreneurship in organizations. By actively promoting and embracing diversity, organizations can unlock new opportunities, generate innovation, and contribute to a more inclusive and sustainable future. Fostering an entrepreneurial culture in diverse teams and organizations can foster innovation, creativity, and economic growth. It is essential to overcome barriers to diversity, cultivate entrepreneurial skills, and leverage technology to foster an entrepreneurial culture. Addressing the obstacles that may arise when fostering an entrepreneurial culture in diverse teams and organizations is crucial, as the benefits of diversity in entrepreneurship cannot be overstated. Creating a culture of entrepreneurship in diverse teams and organizations can have enduring effects on economic growth and innovation, which has significant implications for future research and practice.

REFERENCES

Ahadi, S., & Jacobs, R. L. (2017). A review of the literature on structured on-the-job training and directions for future research. *Human Resource Development Review*, 16(4), 323–349. DOI: 10.1177/1534484317725945

Alenezi, M. (2023). Digital learning and digital institution in higher education. *Education Sciences*, 13(1), 88. DOI: 10.3390/educsci13010088

Alexandre-Leclair, L. (2013). Diversity and entrepreneurship. In *Springer eBooks* (pp. 552–558). DOI: 10.1007/978-1-4614-3858-8_461

Aluthgama-Baduge, C., & Rajasinghe, D. (2022). Exploring entrepreneurial diversity: A fascination or frustration? In *Springer eBooks* (pp. 35–45). DOI: 10.1007/978-3-030-87112-3_4

Amorim Neto, R. D. C., Picanço Rodrigues, V., Campbell, K., Polega, M., & Ochsankehl, T. (2020). Teamwork and entrepreneurial behaviour among K-12 teachers in the United States. In *The Educational Forum* (Vol. 84, No. 2, pp. 179–193). Routledge. DOI: 10.1080/00131725.2020.1702748

Boder, A. (2006). Collective intelligence: A keystone in knowledge management. *Journal of Knowledge Management*, 10(1), 81–93. DOI: 10.1108/13673270610650120

Boonsiritomachai, W., & Sud-On, P. (2022). The moderation effect of work engagement on entrepreneurial attitude and organizational commitment: Evidence from Thailand's entry-level employees during the COVID-19 pandemic. *Asia-Pacific Journal of Business Administration*, 14(1), 50–71. DOI: 10.1108/APJBA-03-2021-0101

Danish, R. Q., Asghar, J., Ahmad, Z., & Ali, H. F. (2019). Factors affecting "entrepreneurial culture": The mediating role of creativity. *Journal of Innovation and Entrepreneurship*, 8(1), 14. Advance online publication. DOI: 10.1186/s13731-019-0108-9

Downey, S. N., Van der Werff, L., Thomas, K. M., & Plaut, V. C. (2015). The role of diversity practices and inclusion in promoting trust and employee engagement. *Journal of Applied Social Psychology*, 45(1), 35–44. DOI: 10.1111/jasp.12273

Duchek, S., Raetze, S., & Scheuch, I. (2019). The role of diversity in organizational resilience: A theoretical framework. *Business Research*, 13(2), 387–423. DOI: 10.1007/s40685-019-0084-8

Dullayaphut, P., & Untachai, S. (2013). Development of the measurement of human resource competency in SMEs in the upper north-eastern region of Thailand. *Procedia: Social and Behavioral Sciences*, 88, 61–72. DOI: 10.1016/j.sbspro.2013.08.481

Eisenhardt, K. M. (2013). Top management teams and the performance of entrepreneurial firms. *Small Business Economics*, 40(4), 805–816. https://link.springer.com/article/10.1007/s11187-013-9473-0. DOI: 10.1007/s11187-013-9473-0

Félix, C. B., Aparicio, S., & Urbano, D. (2019). Leadership as a driver of entrepreneurship: An international exploratory study. *Journal of Small Business and Enterprise Development*, 26(3), 397–420. DOI: 10.1108/JSBED-03-2018-0106

Ferrary, M., & Déo, S. (2023). Gender diversity and firm performance: When diversity at middle management and staff levels matter. *International Journal of Human Resource Management*, 34(14), 2797–2831. DOI: 10.1080/09585192.2022.2093121

Howieson, B. (2003). Accounting practice in the new millennium: Is accounting education ready to meet the challenge? *The British Accounting Review*, 35(2), 69–103. DOI: 10.1016/S0890-8389(03)00004-0

Hwang, W. S., Choi, H., & Shin, J. (2020). A mediating role of innovation capability between entrepreneurial competencies and competitive advantage. *Technology Analysis and Strategic Management*, 32(1), 1–14. DOI: 10.1080/09537325.2019.1632430

Jayanna, U. R., Kumar, J. P. S., Aluvala, R., & Rao, B. (2024). The role of technology in entrepreneurship: A comprehensive systematic and bibliometric analysis. *Kybernetes*. Advance online publication. DOI: 10.1108/K-09-2023-1873

Jones, C., & English, J. (2004). A contemporary approach to entrepreneurship education. *Education + Training*, 46(8/9), 416–423. DOI: 10.1108/00400910410569533

Jones, G. B., Chace, B. C., & Wright, J. M. (2020). Cultural diversity drives innovation: Empowering teams for success. *International Journal of Innovation Science*, 12(3), 323–343. DOI: 10.1108/IJIS-04-2020-0042

Karlsson, C., Rickardsson, J., & Wincent, J. (2019b). Diversity, innovation and entrepreneurship: Where are we and where should we go in future studies? *Small Business Economics*, 56(2), 759–772. DOI: 10.1007/s11187-019-00267-1

Kent, T., Dennis, C., & Tanton, S. (2003). An evaluation of mentoring for SME retailers. *International Journal of Retail & Distribution Management*, 31(8), 440–448. DOI: 10.1108/09590550310484115

Kim, S., & Lee, G. (2023). The effects of organizational diversity perception on affective commitment. *Asia Pacific Journal of Public Administration*, 45(2), 160–178. DOI: 10.1080/23276665.2021.2011341

Kohler, T. (2016). Corporate accelerators: Building bridges between corporations and startups. *Business Horizons*, 59(3), 347–357. DOI: 10.1016/j.bushor.2016.01.008

Kumar, A. (2023). Leadership and decision-making: Top management team age demographic and environmental strategy. *Journal of Management & Organization*, 29(1), 69–85. DOI: 10.1017/jmo.2019.91

Lee, L., & Yu, H. (2023). Socioeconomic diversity in the hospitality industry: The relationship between social class background, family expectations and career outcomes. *International Journal of Contemporary Hospitality Management*, 35(11), 3844–3863. Advance online publication. DOI: 10.1108/IJCHM-11-2022-1356

Linton, J. D., & Wei, X. (2020). Research on science and technological entrepreneurship education: What needs to happen next? *The Journal of Technology Transfer*, 46(2), 393–406. DOI: 10.1007/s10961-020-09786-6

Martin, K., Shilton, K., & Smith, J. A. (2019). Business and the ethical implications of technology: Introduction to the symposium. *Journal of Business Ethics*, 160(2), 307–317. DOI: 10.1007/s10551-019-04213-9

Patrício, L. D., & Fernandes, C. (2022). Technology entrepreneurship and innovation: A Systematic literature review. In *EAI/Springer Innovations in Communication and Computing* (pp. 253–284). DOI: 10.1007/978-3-031-17960-0_13

Romero-Rodriguez, L. M., & Montoya, M. S. R. (2019). Entrepreneurship competencies in energy sustainability MOOCs. *Journal of Entrepreneurship in Emerging Economies*, 11(4), 598–616. DOI: 10.1108/JEEE-03-2019-0034

Salazar, M. R., Lant, T. K., Fiore, S. M., & Salas, E. (2012). Facilitating innovation in diverse science teams through integrative capacity. *Small Group Research*, 43(5), 527–558. DOI: 10.1177/1046496412453622

Shalley, C. E., & Perry-Smith, J. E. (2008). The emergence of team creative cognition: The role of diverse outside ties, sociocognitive network centrality, and team evolution. *Strategic Entrepreneurship Journal*, 2(1), 23–41. DOI: 10.1002/sej.40

Siyal, M., Siyal, S., Wu, J., Pal, D., & Memon, M. M. (2021). Consumer perceptions of factors affecting online shopping behavior: An empirical evidence from foreign students in China. [JECO]. *Journal of Electronic Commerce in Organizations*, 19(2), 1–16. DOI: 10.4018/JECO.2021040101

Siyal, S. (2018). Does Leadership lessen turnover of public servants. The moderated mediation effect of leader member exchange and perspective taking [EBSCO open dissertations].

Siyal, S. (2023). Inclusive leadership and work engagement: Exploring the role of psychological safety and trust in leader in multiple organizational context. *Business Ethics, the Environment & Responsibility*, 32(4), 1170–1184. DOI: 10.1111/beer.12556

Siyal, S., Liu, J., Ma, L., Kumari, K., Saeed, M., Xin, C., & Hussain, S. N. (2023). Does inclusive leadership influence task performance of hospitality industry employees? Role of psychological empowerment and trust in leader. *Heliyon*, 9(5), e15507. DOI: 10.1016/j.heliyon.2023.e15507 PMID: 37153410

Siyal, S., & Peng, X. (2018). Does leadership lessen turnover? The moderated mediation effect of leader–member exchange and perspective taking on public servants. *Journal of Public Affairs*, 18(4), e1830. DOI: 10.1002/pa.1830

Siyal, S., Peng, X., & Siyal, A. W. (2018). Socioeconomic analysis: A case of Tharparkar. *Journal of Public Affairs*, 18(4), e1847. DOI: 10.1002/pa.1847

Siyal, S., Xin, C., Umrani, W. A., Fatima, S., & Pal, D. (2021). How do leaders influence innovation and creativity in employees? The mediating role of intrinsic motivation. *Administration & Society*, 53(9), 1337–1361. DOI: 10.1177/0095399721997427

Soomro, B. A., Mangi, S., & Shah, N. (2021). Strategic factors and significance of organizational innovation and organizational learning in organizational performance. *European Journal of Innovation Management*, 24(2), 481–506. DOI: 10.1108/EJIM-05-2019-0114

Sullivan, R. (2000). Entrepreneurial learning and mentoring. *International Journal of Entrepreneurial Behaviour & Research*, 6(3), 160–175. DOI: 10.1108/13552550010346587

Van Knippenberg, D., Nishii, L. H., & Dwertmann, D. J. (2020). Synergy from diversity: Managing team diversity to enhance performance. *Behavioral Science & Policy*, 6(1), 75–92. DOI: 10.1177/237946152000600108

West, M. A., & Sacramento, C. A. (2023). Creativity and innovation: The role of team and organizational climate. In *Handbook of Organizational Creativity* (pp. 317–337). Academic Press., DOI: 10.1016/B978-0-323-91840-4.00024-4

Zahra, S. A., Sapienza, H. J., & Davidsson, P. (2006). Entrepreneurship and dynamic capabilities: A review, model and research agenda. *Journal of Management Studies*, 43(4), 917–955. DOI: 10.1111/j.1467-6486.2006.00616.x

Zeitlin, W., Lawrence, C. K., Armendariz, S., & Chontow, K. (2023). Predicting retention for a diverse and inclusive child welfare workforce. *Human Service Organizations, Management, Leadership & Governance*, 47(1), 9–27. DOI: 10.1080/23303131.2022.2115432

KEY TERMS AND DEFINITIONS

Culture: The shared beliefs, values, customs, traditions, and practices that characterize a particular group of people or society and influence their behaviour and interactions.

Diversity: The presence of a wide range of human differences, including but not limited to race, ethnicity, gender, sexual orientation, age, socioeconomic status, and physical abilities, within a group, organization, or community.

Entrepreneurship: Identifying, creating, and pursuing opportunities to start and manage a business venture, often involving innovation and risk-taking.

Leadership: The ability to inspire, influence, and guide individuals or groups toward achieving common goals, often involving decision-making, communication, and interpersonal skills.

Overcoming Challenges: The process of confronting and addressing obstacles, setbacks, or difficulties in pursuing goals or objectives, often involving resilience, adaptability, problem-solving, and perseverance.

Skills Development: The process of acquiring, enhancing, and applying competencies, knowledge, and abilities through formal or informal learning experiences to improve performance and achieve personal or professional goals.

Technology: Tools, techniques, systems, and processes developed through scientific knowledge and innovation to solve problems, improve efficiency, and create new opportunities in various domains.

Chapter 4
Embracing Multiple Intelligences:
The Future of Leadership in a Changing World

Shivani Dhand
https://orcid.org/0000-0002-4809-1365
Lovely Professional University, India

Kiran Thakur
University Canada West, Canada

Priyanka Chhibber
Lovely Professional University, India

ABSTRACT

Effective leadership in fast-changing environment necessitates a wide range of skills and competencies. The theory of Multiple Intelligences (MI) challenges the traditional conception of intelligence as a single, fixed characteristic. People have distinct forms of intelligence that may be nourished and developed through time. MI can assist leaders in adapting to change, building diverse and inclusive teams, and driving innovation. The leadership of the twentieth century witnessed a shift from one type of intelligence to another due to changing societal needs. Much previous research has attempted to draw out the relationship between MI and leadership performance. This chapter reviews the definitions and models in the field of MI and the connection between MI and leadership. The chapter highlights the leadership shift over time and examples of successful MNCs and SMEs resulting from entre-preneurial leadership in the context of multiple intelligence.

DOI: 10.4018/979-8-3693-0078-7.ch004

INTRODUCTION

Multiple Intelligences (MI) are "the ability to reason and solve problems in more than one way" (Punter, 2016). According to this definition, people using multiple intelligences can synthesize information from several sources by drawing on their own experiences, observing others, and accessing their internal resources. They can combine these pieces into something cohesive and meaningful. One kind of intelligence that is prevalent in various research studies is interpersonal Intelligence (Goleman). Interpersonal intelligence refers to having the social skills necessary for collaboration to achieve shared goals; this would include being able to lift heavy objects or having the creativity necessary for solution generation without putting in a manual effort. Leadership is a complex, multifaceted process that involves a multitude of factors (Siyal., 2023; Siyal et al., 2023; Siyal et al., 2021). However, leadership research has several gaps, especially regarding the role of multiple intelligence. Studies have shown that intelligence and personality traits are essential in leadership: for example, leadership style is strongly correlated with certain personality traits (e.g., openness and agreeableness) (Duckworth et al., 2008). Leadership must involve other factors, including different types of intelligence. In 1983, Gardner developed the multiple Intelligence (MI) theory. Gardner used the data from hundreds of investigations from numerous scientific fields to arrive at his theory. Although he is a member of experimental and psychometric psychology, he does not restrict his supporters to this field.

In contrast, MI theory also considers differential psychology, anthropology- and culture-related neuroscience investigations, and cognitive and developmental psychology (Muhibbin et al., 2020). One aspect of multiple intelligences is verbal-linguistic intelligence, which focuses on speaking, reading, and writing; another is logical-mathematical intelligence, which emphasizes teaching logic, and mathematical concepts, working with numbers, and sorting; and the third is kinesthetic intelligence, which emphasizes drama, creative movement, dance, manipulative, class games, physical education, and sports. The fourth is visual-spatial intelligence, emphasizing graphical representations, flowcharts, visualizations, board games, card games, architecture, and the visual arts. The fifth is musical intelligence, emphasizing singing, music notation, curriculum songs, and musical instruments. The sixth is interpersonal intelligence, emphasizing positive interpersonal environments, conflict management, learning through services, respecting differences, various perspectives, problem-solving, and multicultural education. Finally, seventh is intrapersonal intelligence, emphasizing self-esteem, goal setting, thinking skills, emotional expression, and independent learning (Dabke, 2016). The dynamics of leadership will never end, and this will continue the exploration of the field. This pursuit aims to raise leadership standards both within and outside of organizations.

In response to the industrial revolution, soft leadership skills and digital literacy are one of the challenges facing the world of leadership, among others. The skill gap in multiple intelligence in leadership is the difference between what leaders need to be able to do and what they do; this can be due to several factors, including:

Lack of experience or exposure to the topic
Lacking the basic knowledge of how to proceed
Difficulty with the implementation or how to put the skills into practice

The recent rise of artificial intelligence will significantly impact how businesses are performed. The ability of AI-powered bots to automate day-to-day jobs and perform tasks that humans are too expensive or inefficient to do has led to a growing concern that automation will result in a skill gap in leadership. However, there is reason to believe this could be an opportunity for human advancement. Research shows that multiple intelligence is vital when it comes to effective leadership. Multiple intelligence refers to processing information differently and applying those skills to different situations—which humans often excel at. Multiple intelligence can predict success better than any other factor, including age or education level. It can help leaders understand how their team members work best and adjust their approach accordingly; it can also help them think outside the box by considering new perspectives from different parts of the organization; finally, it can help leaders take risks because they are more likely than others to be successful. Throughout the industry, many examples illustrate the presence of Multiple Intelligence among leaders. Alexander the Great was not only a fantastic military commander but also an excellent speaker who could persuade people with his words alone; Julius Caesar had great physical strength but just was not very good at making speeches, and Abraham Lincoln was a brilliant writer but did not have much interest in public speaking or other aspects of political leadership (such as an organization).

SHOULD LEADERS SHIFT AS THE WORLD IS SHIFTING?

Leadership has been a critical focus of research and discussion in management, but there is a lacuna in the current leadership. Contemporary research suggests that we are entering an age in which the multiple intelligence needed for effective leadership will be more critical than ever. The baby boomer generation is about to retire and replaced by Generation Z, who are digital natives and have grown up with technology. They will have different priorities and attitudes from their predecessors. As humans have evolved, we have become more intelligent. We now live in an age of machine learning and artificial Intelligence (AI), which has made people increasingly dependent on technology rather than each other for many tasks. People will need leaders who can manage other people's emotions, understand how technology works, and make decisions based on data rather than intuition alone. If current trends continue into adulthood—and they seem likely—we may see a shift towards greater gender equality across all fields of work, resulting in more women becoming leaders because traditional gender roles and expectations less tie them down. In the current era, there are several lacunae in leadership. The need for multiple intelligence has been highlighted as an issue for leadership. This chapter will address the dynamics of multiple intelligence in the context of leadership.

MULTIPLE INTELLIGENCES AND LEADERSHIP IN THE EVER-CHANGING WORLD

The literature on multiple intelligence suggests a great deal of overlap between the different types of intelligence. However, there are also some apparent differences in how these intelligence work. Dabrowski (1997) defined the following types of intelligence: general, sensorimotor, visual-spatial, auditory-verbal, inductive reasoning, and reflective reasoning.

Figure 1. Types of Multiple Intelligence.

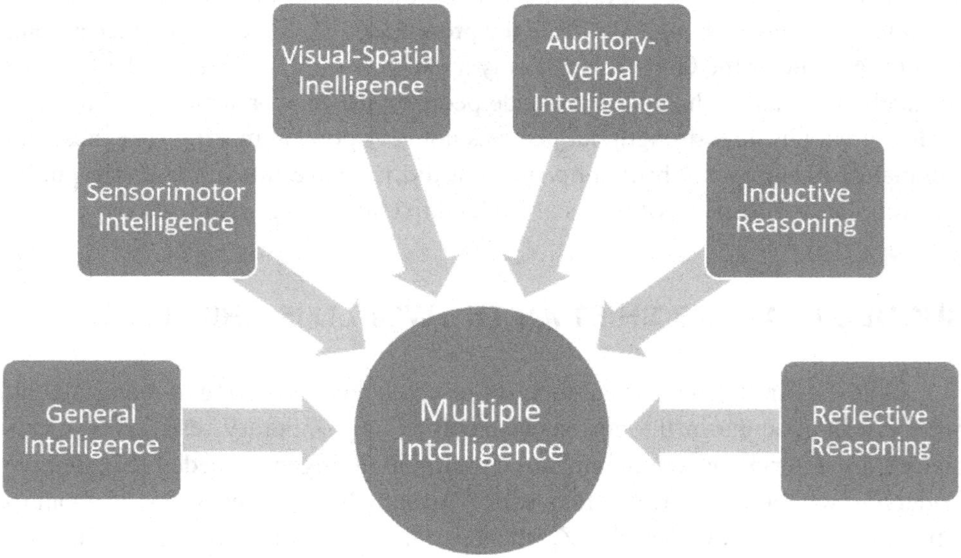

Note. Types of Multiple Intelligence. Source Authors' creation

General Intelligence

General Intelligence (also known as the g factor) refers to the "existence of a broad mental capacity that influences performance on cognitive ability measures" (Cherry, 2023). It is the most commonly studied type of intelligence and includes verbal, numerical, spatial, and mechanical skills. The critical characteristic of general intelligence is its stability over time and its ability to perform well in various domains. In other words, if a person performs well in one type of cognitive task, they are likely to perform well in another task (Jensen, 1999). General Intelligence is greatly heritable, with estimates ranging from 50% to 80% (Deary, Penke, & Johnson, 2010). However, situational factors such as upbringing, education, and diet can also influence the level of Intelligence (Gottfredson, 1997). Children raised in environments that stimulate learning and intellectual curiosity tend to develop higher levels of intelligence than those raised in less engaging environments. General Intelligence is a minimum threshold leaders should possess, but it is not a guarantee for successful leadership.

Sensorimotor Intelligence

Sensorimotor Intelligence is the "cognitive development that occurs during the first two years of life when infants learn to coordinate their sensory perceptions with their motor actions (Piaget, 1952). It encompasses our ability to use the five senses to perceive the world. Information is processed through association with prior knowledge and sensory experiences rather than abstract reasoning or logic. The critical characteristics of sensorimotor intelligence are object permanence and coordination. Object permanence means that humans acknowledge the presence of things even if it is out of sight (Piaget, 1952); this can be very important for leaders to have the ability to identify potential challenges and roadblocks. The other aspect of sensorimotor intelligence is the ability to coordinate; leaders can use this skill to improve team collaboration to achieve goals.

Visual-Spatial Intelligence

Visual-spatial Intelligence refers to the "ability to mentally visualize and manipulate spatial relationships, such as in the context of maps, diagrams, or geometric shapes" (Gardner, 1983). Visual-spatial Intelligence involves mentally representing three-dimensional space using visual cues such as lines or shapes drawn on paper or boards. Understanding and interpreting visual information, such as charts, graphs, and other data visualizations, is essential to visual-spatial intelligence. Leaders with this skill set may be better able to make data-driven decisions and communicate complex information to others clearly and straightforwardly (Nicolson, Fawcett, & Dean, 2001). Furthermore, visual-spatial intelligence leads to creative problem-solving ability (Gardner, 1983). People with this ability can provide solutions to complicated issues. Leaders having visual-spatial intelligence can visualize the data and can provide innovative solutions.

Auditory-Verbal Intelligence

Auditory-verbal Intelligence is "the ability to understand and use spoken language effectively" (Gardner, 1983). It involves processing speech information using words, not just sounds (Wang, 2016). Generally, this type of intelligence is associated with language-related fields, but it can be a game-changer for a leader in various contexts. Auditory-verbal Intelligence is the capacity to communicate effectively with people one-on-one and in groups. Leaders with excellent auditory-verbal intelligence can effectively communicate their opinions and engage teams in fruitful conversations. (Lancaster & Stillman, 2002).

Inductive Reasoning

Inductive reasoning is "the ability to draw general conclusions from specific observations or experiences" (Gardner, 1983). It involves inferring facts from observations or previous experiences based on what would be expected based on those observations (Salovery, 1990). Leaders with high inductive reasoning can make data-driven decisions by analyzing and interpreting complex datasets. In the study by Baumeister and Vohs (2004), leaders who could make decisions based on their observations and experiences were viewed as more effective by their subordinates. This shows that inductive reasoning is a crucial talent for leaders to cultivate.

Reflective Reasoning

It involves introspection by asking oneself questions about internal processes such as emotions or motivation to gain a deeper understanding of a particular situation (Mayer, 1990), the existence of multiple intelligences and their utility for understanding human behavior and cognition (Goleman, 1995; Goleman & Boyatzis, 2002). Van Wart (2008) discovered that leaders who engaged in reflective reasoning were better suited to handle complicated and ambiguous circumstances and were viewed as more effective by their subordinates.

INTERPLAY BETWEEN LEADERSHIP AND DIFFERENT TYPES OF INTELLIGENCE

Literature has suggested that a person's level of one type of intelligence may affect how they use other types of intelligence. Leaders should be flexible to adapt to the changes (Yukl, 2008). Megerian (1996) states that emotional intelligence and leadership qualities are positively correlated. Moreover, according to Hesselbein et al. (1996) and Sims & Lorenzi (1992), interpersonal leadership abilities are becoming increasingly crucial for organizational greatness. The ability to understand and respond to various social settings has been called social Intelligence (Bass, 2001; Zaccaro, 2002). Socially intelligent leaders should be able to identify the talents required for the job, be attuned to complex social cues, and control their behaviour properly to affect the relevant perceptions of other group members (Stogdill, 1948). A business leader needs to become used to the idea that at least three generations are represented in the workforce (Guzman, Stanton, & Stam, 2008). Baby Boomers, Generation X, Generation Y, and Generation Z comprise the current labour force. Generation Z is joining the workforce as Baby Boomers retire. Each of these generations in the workplace brings its own set of values and preferences (Arsenault, 2004; Lancaster & Stillman, 2009). Values, aspirations, perspectives, mindsets, and demography between these generations change significantly. 2000; Zemke, Raines, & Filipczak. One generation will control economic, cultural, and political forces during the "Millennial Moment" in history (Greenberg & Weber, 2008; Howe & Strauss, 2000; Pew Research Centre, 2010). They make up the first millennium generation, born between 1980 and 2000. They comprise the largest generation in the United States, accounting for 24% of the population (US Census Bureau, 2013). Managers at all organizational levels should take the generational cohorts' differences seriously (Lyon et al., 2005). Organizations and managers must know how different generations evaluate leadership (Arsenault, 2004; Lyon et al., 2005; Zemke et al., 2000; Siyal., 2018; Siyal & Peng., 2018)). Organizational leaders must be aware of and comprehend how each generation has a distinct character that manifests in a mentality with various emotions, attitudes, beliefs, preferences, and embodied actions. How a generation leads or wishes to be led differs depending on this attitude (Arsenault, 2004). The majority of experts concur that the characteristics of an effective leader can differ across time and place (Hames & Harvey, 2006; Zaccaro et al., 2004), throughout industries (Stogdill, 1948), and across generations (Baby Boomers, Generation Y, Generation X, and Millennials) (Seider & Gardner,

2009). However, the question of whether specific leadership attributes are timeless remains unanswered.

Given the increasing number of jobs requiring an ability to multitask, employers are not surprised to seek candidates skilled at "multiple intelligences" in their employees. While it may seem like a great idea to hire someone with a good grasp of all sorts of different skills, it is essential to remember that when looking for someone with a particular skill, that person likely has a good handle on all the others. The first thing to remember is that each type of intelligence has its strengths and weaknesses. Some people are better at math than others, and vice versa. Some people are great at spatial reasoning, while others have trouble fitting things into categories and remembering details. Some people are natural leaders—they seem to have an innate ability to lead or inspire others—while others need more practice before becoming influential leaders. An employee who is good at budgeting or time management should also be able to do well on customer service or project management tasks because they will require similar skill sets.

The authors' research found that there is a skill gap in leadership. Leaders are not getting the skills necessary to lead their organizations effectively, and this is not because leaders do not want to get the skills or take on the training but rather because they do not have access to the right resources. Literature shows that when it comes to leadership skills, most people lack the specific knowledge of how to use that general intelligence in a given situation. They do not know what they need to know or how to learn it, and they often find themselves lacking in some way. Leaders with more general intelligence tend to have better leadership skills than those with less—but only up until a certain point. After this point, those with more general intelligence can no longer apply their strengths as effectively as those with less. The skill gap in multiple intelligence in leadership is the inability to employ multiple intelligence skills at once effectively. This can manifest as a lack of ability to recognize, understand, and communicate different types of information (visual, auditory, and kinaesthetic) and share ideas and knowledge with others in a group setting. There is a clear shift of leadership over the period.

LEADERSHIP TRANSFORMATION OVER THE YEARS

The 1980s mark the era of specialist leadership. The specialist leadership model is designed to address the specific needs of organizations. Transformational, transactional, situational, and servant leadership are different types of specialist leadership (Benmira & Agboola 2021). During the 1990s, the generalist leadership model emerged. Generalist leaders can manage various operations that do not require any specialty. For example, Google prefers hiring generalist leaders who can handle complex and diverse projects better. Google has People Innovation Lab to impart training to its leaders. It has a "g2g" (Googler-to-Googler) program, which is an employee-to-employee training program (Wallace & Creelman, 2015). The third era emphasized the importance of multiple intelligence and how leaders can improve their leadership ability by possessing more than one type of intelligence. Other leadership practices were focused on diversity and inclusion initiatives. Leadership today is driven by ambition directing a leader to achieve beyond possibilities. Ambition fuels creativity, innovation and entrepreneurial ability; therefore, it is a most desirable trait of a leader (Marques, 2017). Table 1 summarizes the different eras of leadership from the 1980s to the present, based on the relevant literature review.

Table 1. Changes in Leadership Over the Time

Era (Time)	Changes in Leadership
1980 – 1990	The "specialist" leadership model dominated the first era —the idea that leaders should be experts in a particular field or expertise. Special period of leadership development, as a new generation of leaders arose to take over from the older ones.
1990 – 2000	The second era was marked by the rise of the "generalist" leadership model—the idea that leaders should be skilled at all tasks. They were marked by increased leaders with multiple intelligence, while leaders still used more traditional intelligence.
2000 – 2010	The third era is marked by "multiple intelligences," or expertise in more than one field or specialty. The leadership of the twentieth century was marked by a shift from one type of intelligence to another due to changing societal needs. There was a rise in leadership with multiple intelligence, with more than half of all leaders having this intelligence.
2010 – 2020	This period has brought about another transition period for leadership: an increased focus on diversity and inclusion within organizations, leading to a greater awareness of multiple intelligences among employees and employees. The percentage dropped slightly and then rose again in 2020
2020 - present	Leaders today are as likely to be driven by their ambitions as they are caused by the needs of their organization or team. They are also more likely than ever before to use multiple intelligences in their work: those that involve interpersonal relationships, communication skills, management skills, and so on. In 2040, more than 90% of all leaders are expected to have this type of intelligence.

Note. Yearly Discussion on How Leadership Has Drastically Changed over Time. Source *Authors' creation after relevant literature review.*

There has been an apparent transformation in how leadership is exhibited over these years; a clear shift can be observed from traditional leadership styles to a more flexible one. Leadership styles have evolved into more collaborative, inclusive, and values-driven, complementing growing employee and social needs and expectations.

Figure 2. Characteristics of Leaders from 1990-present

Note. Characteristics of Leaders from 1990-present. Source Authors' creation

ENTREPRENEURIAL LEADERSHIP

To be an entrepreneur, having a good business idea is not enough. It is crucial to be able to implement it and understand how to share that vision with your team and coworkers. An entrepreneurial leader surrounds himself with competent individuals who can aid in bringing the project to life and takes effective ownership of it to ensure its success. Entrepreneurial leadership is a "mindset that focuses organizations on turning problems into opportunities that create economic and social value" (Atwater, 2022). They can positively influence the team and create an ideal work environment to realize organizational objectives. Entrepreneurial leaders possess goal clarity, effective communication skills, and strategic and innovative thinking (Universidad Europea, 2022).

Multiple Intelligences and Successful Entrepreneurial Leadership: Examples from MNCs

MNCs leaders need to use various types of intelligence to tackle the challenges of working in a diverse cultural environment and managing global teams. Linguistic intelligence enables leaders to communicate effectively with stakeholders from diverse language backgrounds, facilitating cooperation and understanding. They could negotiate contracts more effectively, liaise with International Partners and bridge Cultural Obstacles. The success of Apple Inc. is primarily attributable to Steve Jobs' visionary leadership. Jobs possessed great verbal intelligence; he was renowned for effectively explaining Apple's vision and product concepts. His excellent communication abilities contributed to Apple's success by engaging customers, building a solid brand identity, and attracting new business (Isaacson, 2011).

Logical-mathematical Intelligence facilitates data analysis, decision-making, problem-solving, and capitalizing on new opportunities. Under the direction of Jeff Bezos, who possesses a high logical-mathematical intelligence, Amazon.com Inc. achieved fantastic success. Bezos used data-driven decision-making and analytics to drive the company's growth, optimize operations, and innovate in logistics and customer personalization. His analytical approach and strategic use of metrics have contributed significantly to the company's success.

Spatial intelligence helps leaders visualize and develop strategic plans for expanding MNCs' operations in different markets. Tesla Inc. has thrived under the leadership of Elon Musk, his ability to envision and design advanced electric vehicles and renewable energy solutions stems from his spatial intelligence. He has played a vital role in developing Tesla's sleek and efficient vehicle designs, contributing to the company's success and revolutionizing the automotive industry (Vance, 2015).

Interpersonal and intrapersonal intelligence is crucial for building relationships, developing diverse teams, and managing cross-cultural challenges (Van Knippenberg & Schippers, 2007). The Coca-Cola Company has experienced global success with the leadership of Muhtar Kent, known for his strong interpersonal intelligence. His ability to build relationships with stakeholders, including bottlers, employees, and customers, has been instrumental in expanding Coca-Cola's market presence and maintaining solid partnerships worldwide (Edgecliffe-Johnson, 2015).

The success of MNCs relies on leaders who possess multiple intelligences and can effectively leverage them to address the complex challenges of global operations. MNCs may improve their performance, inspire innovation, and navigate the challenges of the global business world by identifying and developing leaders with multiple intelligences.

Multiple Intelligences and Successful Entrepreneurial Leadership: Examples from SMEs

SMEs (small and medium-sized enterprises) are critical to the economy's growth and development. One of the numerous factors influencing the success of SMEs is effective leadership. Leaders with multiple intelligence can boost the performance and outcomes of SMEs. Entrepreneurs possessing linguistic intelligence can adequately express the SME's vision and goals to all stakeholders. Their ability to explain technological innovations in clear and concise language helps build trust and attract support for their ventures.

Moreover, effective communication facilitates collaboration with team members and fosters a positive organizational culture. Innocent Drinks, a successful smoothie and juice company, has been led by founders Richard Reed, Adam Balon, and Jon Wright, who possess solid linguistic intelligence. Their ability to craft compelling brand messaging and engage customers through witty and playful language has been integral to Innocent Drinks' success. During their nascent stage of business, once at their stall, they interviewed customers for their market study. "Should we give up our jobs to make these smoothies?" read a sign over the counter. Customers were instructed to place their empty cups in one of two bins labelled "yes" or "no With only three cups in the "no" bin, the "yes" bin easily won, and they all left their jobs to work full-time at their beverages company (Tucker, 2019).

Logical-mathematical Intelligence enables leaders to analyze market trends, identify business opportunities, and make informed strategic decisions. An exemplary case of logical-mathematical intelligence in an SME leader is demonstrated by Max Levchin, the co-founder and CEO of Affirm, a financial technology company specializing in installment loans and point-of-sale financing. Max's logical-mathematical intelligence is highlighted in his development of Affirm's proprietary underwriting technology. Max utilized his deep data analysis and mathematics knowledge to create a sophisticated algorithmic model that realistically evaluates loan applications (Kauflin, 2021).

Using spatial intelligence, entrepreneurs can visualize the company's physical layout, maximize space usage, and provide a welcoming experience for clients. Leaders with good spatial intelligence can better envisage and conceptualize novel ideas in the creative professions, including design, architecture, and advertising. With the guidance of co-founders Neil Blumenthal, Andy Hunt, Dave Gilboa, and Jeff Raider, who have great visual-spatial intelligence, the eyeglasses brand Warby Parker has achieved exceptional success. Their ability to envision and design fashionable eyewear frames has set the company apart. Their spatial acumen and attention to design details have contributed to Warby Parker's rapid growth and success as a disruptive player in the eyewear industry (Stone, 2012).

Interpersonal and intrapersonal intelligence is crucial for building relationships with employees, customers, and business partners, as well as for self-reflection and self-awareness. Firms in the service industry use effective interpersonal skills to build client relationships, manage teams, and deliver high-quality services. Leaders with strong interpersonal intelligence excel in understanding clients' needs, establishing rapport and effectively communicating insights and recommendations. Patagonia, an outdoor clothing and gear company, has experienced significant success under the leadership of Yvon Chouinard, who possesses strong interpersonal intelligence. His ability to connect with stakeholders and communicate the company's mission has contributed to Patagonia's growth and positive brand reputation. Yvon is known to be unconcerned with when his employees work as long as the job gets done. He favors people that are motivated and engaged above rigid policies. Madhosingh et al., 2022). Ben & Jerry's has thrived under co-founders Ben Cohen and Jerry Greenfield, who have high emotional intelligence. Their ability to empathize with employees, consumers, and social causes has guided the company's commitment to values-based business practices. Their emotional intelligence has fostered a strong sense of purpose, employee engagement, and consumer loyalty, contributing to the success of Ben & Jerry's (Benmelech, 2021).

By recognizing and developing Entrepreneurial leaders with diverse Intelligence, SMEs can enhance their performance, foster innovation, and successfully navigate the challenges of the business landscape. These company examples demonstrate how leaders with different intelligences contribute to the success of SMEs. By leveraging their interpersonal, linguistic, visual-spatial, and emotional intelligence, leaders have played a critical role in shaping these companies' brand identity, customer engagement, innovation, and ethical practices, ultimately driving their success in the competitive world.

DISCUSSION

With time it has been observed that the kind of skill set and intelligence required for the existence or survival of the business two decades ago is not the same as is need of an hour today. Why is it so? It is time which has changed. We all are in the AI world where everything is logically systematic and data-oriented. The kind of followers we had in the early times is different from the current scenario; that is also one of the reasons for the author to write about Multiple Intelligence. Leaders need to be very intelligent to handle difficult situations.MI focuses o self-awareness, self-image, and self-esteem, all contributing to developing leadership. Shortly, it is considered that MI would play a significant role in entrepreneurial leadership. If one leader can understand the intent of MI, he can foster innovation, competency mapping, and employee engagement and fruitfully channel employee behaviour.

RECOMMENDATIONS FOR FUTURE RESEARCH

1) Identify and assess the different types of multiple intelligences required for effective leadership in the current and future changing world. This could be done through literature reviews, interviews with successful entrepreneurs, and self-assessments.
2) Develop training programs focusing on developing multiple intelligences for future leaders. These programs should include modules on emotional intelligence, cultural intelligence, social intelligence, and other relevant areas.
3) Encourage collaboration and teamwork to promote the development of multiple intelligences among leaders. Leaders should be encouraged to work with others from different backgrounds and with different skill sets to develop their multiple intelligence and those of their team members.

4) Provide mentorship opportunities for entrepreneurs. Mentorship can help new leaders develop their multiple intelligence skills by providing guidance and support from experienced leaders.
5) Create a culture of continuous learning and improvement. Leaders must be willing to learn, adapt to the changing world, and be open to feedback and constructive criticism.
6) Identify and recruit entrepreneurial leadership talent from diverse backgrounds and skill sets. The new era of leadership requires leaders with multiple intelligences, and it is essential to identify and nurture talent from different sources.

CONCLUSION

In conclusion, the results are precise: There is a skill gap in leadership that a combination of multiple intelligences can only bridge. The essential skill that any leader must possess is understanding and empathizing with others and managing them effectively. However, thinking creatively, solving problems, and making decisions is also necessary. The study of multiple intelligences has revealed that each individual possesses all of these abilities to varying degrees, which means that every person has the potential to be a great leader. However, it is less likely that someone will naturally possess all of these skills at once than it is for them to possess one or two intelligence more narrowly. This makes sense; if someone has never been able to learn or play an instrument well, it would be unlikely for them ever to become proficient at playing the piano or drums. However, if they have an aptitude for music and an interest in playing an instrument, then learning how to play those instruments might come naturally over time—even with some help from books or online tutorials!

As with any other skill set or talent set, leaders need an understanding of their strengths and weaknesses before they can reach their full potential as leaders—and this requires self-awareness through self-assessments and interviews to know themselves in the better possible way.

The key to embracing multiple intelligences in leadership is recognizing its importance and developing strategies to close the skill gap. By promoting a culture of continuous learning and improvement and investing in developing multiple intelligences, organizations can ensure that their leaders are prepared for the challenges of the future-changing world.

REFERENCES

Ahn, M. J., & Ettner, L. W. (2014). Are leadership values different across generations? A comparative leadership analysis of CEOs v. MBAs. *Journal of Management Development*.

Atwater, E. (2022). What Is Entrepreneurial Leadership? Babson Thought & Action. https://entrepreneurship.babson.edu/entrepreneurial-leadership

Benmelech, E. (2021, August 1). Ben & Jerry's Social Responsibility: ESG Without The G. Forbes. https://www.forbes.com/sites/effibenmelech/2021/08/01/ben--jerrys-social-responsibility-esg-without-the-g/?sh=7068884a3084

Benmira, S., & Agboola, M. (2021). Evolution of leadership theory. *BMJ Leader*, leader-2020.

Bullock, J. B. (2008). Intelligence and leadership: An investigation of multiple intelligences as antecedents to transactional and transformational leadership behaviors.

Cherry, K. (2023). *What Is General Intelligence (G Factor)?* Retrieved from https://www.verywellmind.com/what-is-general-intelligence-2795210

Dabke, D. (2016). Impact of leader's emotional Intelligence and transformational behavior on perceived leadership effectiveness: A multiple source view. *Business Perspectives and Research*, 4(1), 27–40. DOI: 10.1177/2278533715605433

Davis, K., Christodoulou, J., Seider, S., & Gardner, H. E. (2011). The theory of multiple intelligences. *Davis, K., Christodoulou, J., Seider, S., & Gardner, H.(2011). The theory of multiple intelligences. In RJ Sternberg & SB Kaufman (Eds.), Cambridge Handbook of Intelligence*, 485-503.

Deary, I. J., Penke, L., & Johnson, W. (2010). The neuroscience of human intelligence differences. *Nature Reviews. Neuroscience*, 11(3), 201–211. DOI: 10.1038/nrn2793 PMID: 20145623

Edgecliffe-Johnson, A. (2019, January 6). Muhtar Kent: bottling Coca-Cola's secrets for success. Financial Times. https://www.ft.com/content/f8ca0346-0e72-11e9-a3aa-118c761d2745

Eyüp, Y. U. R. T., & Polat, S. (2015). The effectiveness of multiple intelligence applications on academic achievement: A meta-analysis. *Journal of Social Studies Education Research*, 6(1).

Gardner, H. (1995). Reflections on multiple intelligences: Myths and messages. *Phi Delta Kappan*, 77, 200–200.

Gardner, H. (2003). Multiple intelligences after twenty years. *American Educational Research Association, Chicago, Illinois, 21*, 1-15.

Gardner, H. (2010). Multiple intelligences. *New York.-1993*.

Gardner, H. E. (2011). *Frames of mind: The theory of multiple intelligences*. Basic books.

Gottfredson, L. S. (1997). Why g matters: The complexity of everyday life. *Intelligence*, 24(1), 79–132. DOI: 10.1016/S0160-2896(97)90014-3

Hoffman, B. J., & Frost, B. C. (2006). Multiple intelligences of transformational leaders: An empirical examination. *International Journal of Manpower*, 27(1), 37–51. DOI: 10.1108/01437720610652826

Isaacson, W. (2011). *Steve Jobs*. Simon & Schuster.

Jensen, A. R. (1999). The g factor: The science of mental ability. *Psycoloquy*, 10(04), 36–2443.

Kauflin, J. (2021, February 8). Inside The Billion-Dollar Plan To Kill Credit Cards. Forbes. https://www.forbes.com/sites/jeffkauflin/2021/02/08/inside-the-billion-dollar-plan-to-kill-credit-cards/?sh=60e2b98011d9

La Tonya, Y. G. (2012). An examination of Gardner's multiple intelligences of leadership in organizations.

Lancaster, L. C., & Stillman, D. (2009). *When generations collide: Who they are. Why they clash. How to solve the generational puzzle at work*. Harper Collins.

Madhosingh, S. (2022). 4 Key Leadership Lessons from Patagonia Founder, Yvon Chouinard. CEOWORLD Magazine. https://ceoworld.biz/2022/10/14/4-key-leadership-lessons-from-patagonia-founder-yvon-chouinard/

Marques, J. (2017). Leadership and Ambition. In: Marques, J., Dhiman, S. (eds) *Leadership Today*. Springer Texts in Business and Economics. Springer, Cham. DOI: 10.1007/978-3-319-31036-7_20

Matthews, M. D., Hancock, P. A., & Szalma, J. L. (2008). Positive psychology: Adaptation, leadership, and performance in exceptional circumstances. *Performance under stress*, 163-180.

Megerian, L. E., & Sosik, J. J. (1996). An affair of the heart: Emotional Intelligence and transformational leadership. *The Journal of Leadership Studies*, 3(3), 31–48. DOI: 10.1177/107179199700300305

Monteleone, H., & Turner, M. (2016). Managing multicultural teams: The multiple intelligences of a project manager. In *Proceedings of the 40th Australasian Universities Building Education Association Conference (AUBEA 2016)* (pp. 229-239). Central Queensland University.

Muhibbin, A., Fatoni, A., Hidayat, O. T., & Arifin, Z. (2020, November). Transpormation Leadership Based on Local Wisdom in the Multiple Intelligences and the Efforts to Overcome Digital Gap. In *ICSSED 2020: The Proceedings of the 4th International Conference of Social Science and Education, ICSSED 2020, August 4-5 2020, Yogyakarta, Indonesia* (p. 307). European Alliance for Innovation. DOI: 10.4108/eai.4-8-2020.2302531

Nicolson, R. I., & Fawcett, A. J. (1999). Developmental dyslexia: The role of the cerebellum 1. *Dyslexia (Chichester, England)*, 5(3), 155–177. DOI: 10.1002/(SICI)1099-0909(199909)5:3<155::AID-DYS143>3.0.CO;2-4

Palla, K. K. (2022). The Impact of Emotional Intelligence and Multiple Intelligences on Team Performance in the Information Technology Sector.

Piaget, J., & Cook, M. (1952). *No. 5* (Vol. 8). The origins of intelligence in children. International Universities Press.

Rani, J. (2020, December 10). *How Google Trains World-Class Managers*. OpenGrowth. Retrieved June 30, 2023, from https://www.opengrowth.com/resources/how-google-trains-world-class-managers

Sellars, T. (2006). The relationships among multiple intelligences and leadership styles: A study of administrators in Kentucky child care facilities.

Siyal, S. (2018). Does Leadership lessen turnover of public servants. The moderated mediation effect of leader member exchange and perspective taking [EBSCO open dissertations].

Siyal, S. (2023). Inclusive leadership and work engagement: Exploring the role of psychological safety and trust in leader in multiple organizational context. *Business Ethics, the Environment & Responsibility*, 32(4), 1170–1184. DOI: 10.1111/beer.12556

Siyal, S., Liu, J., Ma, L., Kumari, K., Saeed, M., Xin, C., & Hussain, S. N. (2023). Does inclusive leadership influence task performance of hospitality industry employees? Role of psychological empowerment and trust in leader. *Heliyon*, 9(5), e15507. DOI: 10.1016/j.heliyon.2023.e15507 PMID: 37153410

Siyal, S., & Peng, X. (2018). Does leadership lessen turnover? The moderated mediation effect of leader–member exchange and perspective taking on public servants. *Journal of Public Affairs*, 18(4), e1830. DOI: 10.1002/pa.1830

Siyal, S., Xin, C., Umrani, W. A., Fatima, S., & Pal, D. (2021). How do leaders influence innovation and creativity in employees? The mediating role of intrinsic motivation. *Administration & Society*, 53(9), 1337–1361. DOI: 10.1177/0095399721997427

Sternberg, R. J. (2001). Successful Intelligence: A new approach to leadership. *Multiple intelligences and leadership*, 22-41.

Stogdill, R. M., & Shartle, C. L. (1948). Methods for determining patterns of leadership behavior in relation to organization structure and objectives. *The Journal of Applied Psychology*, 32(3), 286–291. DOI: 10.1037/h0057264 PMID: 18867065

Stone, B. (2012). *The rebel sell: Why the culture can't be jammed*. Harper Collins.

Stone, B. (2013). *The everything store: Jeff Bezos and the age of Amazon*. Little, Brown and Company.

Tucker, J. (2019, February 7). Creative entrepreneurs: The story behind Innocent Drinks | Headspace. Headspace. https://www.headspacegroup.co.uk/creative-entrepreneurs-the-story-behind-innocent-drinks/

Universidad Europea. (2022). What is entrepreneurial leadership? Universidad Europea. https://universidadeuropea.com/en/blog/entrepreneurial-leadership/

Van Knippenberg, D., & Schippers, M. C. (2007). Work group diversity. *Annual Review of Psychology*, 58(1), 515–541. DOI: 10.1146/annurev.psych.58.110405.085546 PMID: 16903805

Vance, A. (2015). *Elon Musk: Tesla, SpaceX, and the quest for a fantastic future*. Ecco.

Wallace, W., & Creelman, D. (2015, June 18). *Leading People When They Know More than You Do*. Harvard Business Review. Retrieved June 30, 2023, from https://hbr.org/2015/06/leading-people-when-they-know-more-than-you-do

Wang, Y., Widrow, B., Zadeh, L. A., Howard, N., Wood, S., Bhavsar, V. C., Budin, G., Chan, C., Fiorini, R. A., Gavrilova, M. L., & Shell, D. F. (2016). Cognitive Intelligence: Deep learning, thinking, and reasoning by brain-inspired systems. [IJCINI]. *International Journal of Cognitive Informatics and Natural Intelligence*, 10(4), 1–20. DOI: 10.4018/IJCINI.2016100101

Watson, M., Kuofie, M., & Dool, R. (2018). Relationship between Spiritually Intelligent Leadership and Employee Engagement. *Journal of Marketing Management*, 9(2).

Wilson, S. D. (2004). The relationship between leadership and domains of multiple intelligences.

Wilson, S. D. (2007). A study of multiple intelligences and higher education faculty in the United States. [TLC]. *Journal of College Teaching and Learning*, 4(7). Advance online publication. DOI: 10.19030/tlc.v4i7.1560

Wilson, S. D., & Mujtaba, B. G. (2010). The relationship between leadership and multiple intelligences with the 21st century's higher education faculty. *The Journal of Applied Business and Economics*, 11(3), 106.

Yukl, G. (2008, April). The importance of flexible leadership. In *23rd Annual Conference of the Society for Industrial-Organizational Psychology,* San Francisco, CA.

Zaccaro, S. J. (2001). Organizational leadership and social intelligence. *Multiple intelligences and leadership*, 42-68.

Chapter 5
Entrepreneurial Leadership:
The Best Promoter of Employee Engagement and Innovative Behaviour for Organisational Success

Theresa Obuobisa-Darko
https://orcid.org/0000-0003-4943-4064
Ghana Communication Technology University, Ghana

ABSTRACT

Using the social exchange theory, the paper explains why Entrepreneurial leadership influences employee engagement and employee's innovative behaviour towards organisation success. Findings indicate that entrepreneurial leaders influence employee engagement and employee innovative behaviour because of their People, Learning and Purpose oriented mindset. These enable the leader to influence employees positively and the employees reciprocate by being engaged, thus strive to achieve goals, work with vigour, dedication and absorbed and exhibit innovative behaviour by generating new ideas, promote and implement them for organisation success. The chapter makes a novel theoretical contribution by utilizing social exchange theory to explain the relationship between entrepreneurial leadership, employee engagement and employee's innovative behaviour. A model is developed to guide future empirical studies.

DOI: 10.4018/979-8-3693-0078-7.ch005

INTRODUCTION

With organisational success being dependent on employee behaviour and attitude, leaders of organisations make several changes at the workplace with the onset of the COVID 19 pandemic to meet employees needs. Organisations are adjusting into the "New normal" after the World Health Organization (WHO) declared the end of COVID-19 as a public health energies (World Health Organization, 2023). The organisation's ability to be successful in this "new normal" depends largely on the employees' innovative behaviour.

Innovative behaviour is described as a complex process consisting of behaviours, actions and activities relating to the generation, promotion and implementation of new ideas and processes (Song et al., 2023; Scott & Bruce, 1994; Siyal et al., 2021).Consequently, innovative employees can initiate novel and suitable ideas when performing roles that have been assigned them. With employees' innovative work behaviour being the foundation of organisations' innovation (Wang, 2021) and success (Al-Omari et al., 2019), it is imperative that leaders identify and adopt the most appropriate leadership style to create a conducive environment for employees' innovative behaviour.

Another important contributor to organisation success in addition to employee innovative behaviour is employees due to their unique characteristic, attitude, and behaviour. (Simon, 2011; Liu et al., 2022). Employee Engagement is therefore gaining enormous and critical importance in this post COVID-19 era. Engaged employees have a positive fulfilling work-related state of mind which is characterized by vigour, dedication, and absorption (Schaufeli, et al., 2002, p. 74; Siyal., 2023). Hence, engaged employees employ their cognitive, emotional, and physical energies in performing their roles, making them assets to every organisation. Ensuring employees are engaged therefore seem to be the 'best game plan' for organisational success, post COVID-19 pandemic. However, employee engagement continues to decline post COVID 19 with the current level of engagement in the sub-Saharan Africa being 21%, a gradual decline in employee engagement level (Gullop, 2022) with 63% not engaged and only 20% being engaged (Gallup, 2024). Apart from the decline in employee engagement level, employees not being engaged is costing about 11% of global GDP (Pendell, 2022). These indicators call for research to find an antidote to them. It has been established that leaders significantly influence behaviour and attitude (Ozturk et al., 2021; Rabiul et al., 2023). The question this chapter thus, attempts to answer is, what leadership style should leaders adopt to ensure employees' engagement and innovative behaviour for organisational success post Covid-19?

A leader is an individual who has followers and can influence these followers to voluntarily or involuntarily offer their best to achieve set goals. Leadership is a process not a person with the leader, who is an individual being at the centre of the process and making employees feel valued and involved (Siyal., 2018; Siyal & Peng., 2018) One such contemporary leadership style is Entrepreneurial leadership. Entrepreneurial leadership involves "influencing and directing the performance of group members toward the achievement of organizational goals that involve recognizing and exploiting entrepreneurial opportunities" (Renko et al., 2015, p. 55). Such leaders have three major mind sets- Learning-oriented mind set, People-oriented mind set, and Purpose-oriented mind set which influence how they behave and relate with their subordinates (Subramaniam & Shankar, 2020) and as a result empirical evidence show that they are able to survive in pandemic era (Siwi et al., 2022).

The People-oriented mind set of entrepreneurial leaders, makes them stay inclusive and open; positive and appreciative; which help them gain support and trust of their subordinates. The Learning-oriented mind set, made up of two components: listening and picking signals from all around; and experimenting and risk-taking, make such leaders able to identify opportunities and motivate others to be involved in similar ventures (Subramaniam & Shankar, 2020). Subramaniam and Shankar (2020) opine that the entrepreneurial leader has purpose-oriented mind set. As a result of this mind set, such leaders stay focus on their purpose or intentions and remain patient to achieve their purpose. Again, the Covid 19 pandemic created a high level of uncertainty in the area of job security. However, with these entrepreneurial mindset, ther is empirical evidence that entrepreneurial leadership is negatively linked to work uncertainty (Bilal et al., 2022) and a negative relationship between job insecurity and employee engagement (Yu et al., 2020; Getahun Asfaw & Chang, 2019). Based on these discussions it is argued that entrepreneurial leadership is the "best meddler" for employee engagement and innovative behaviour for organisational success. The chapter attempts to explain how the entrepreneurial leader seem to be the best leader to ensure employees' innovative behaviour and employee engagement for organisational success post COVID-19 pandemic with SET being the underpinning theory.

One of the most influential theories that facilitates the understanding of workplace behaviours is Social Exchange Theory (SET). This theory proposes that all social relationships are rooted within an exchange framework. Social exchange reflects interaction between individuals and how these interactions reinforce the other's behaviour. When employees perceive that their leaders value their inputs and therefore listen, appreciate, remain positive and encourage them to share their unique views, there is improvement in their social exchange relationship which cause them to reciprocate by giving off their best (Obuobisa-Darko & Ameyaw-Domfeh, 2019; Vance, 2006). In this study, the author viewed the leader's behaviour as a reflection of the Learning-oriented mind set, People-oriented mind set, and Purpose-oriented mind-set that encourage innovative behaviour and cause employees to be engaged and consequently feel obliged to reciprocate by putting in their best performance to contribute towards organisational success. This book chapter thus, contributes to knowledge by extending the social exchange theory in the entrepreneurial leadership, employee innovative behaviour and employee engagement literature. The chapter adopts a literature review approach through which information is gathered from textbooks, journal articles and other relevant sources to explain the relationship between innovative behaviour, employee engagement and entrepreneurial leadership in the 21st century post Covid-19 pandemic. The paper proceeds as follows: Following this introduction is the literature review on social exchange theory, employee engagement, and innovative behaviour. This is followed by a description of entrepreneurial leadership and how it relates with employee engagement and employee innovative behaviour. Following this is a description of the relationship between the three main constructs of the chapter: entrepreneurial leadership, employee engagement and employee innovative behaviour. The chapter ends with a conclusion and suggestions for further studies to enhance the understanding of the relationship between different leadership styles, employee engagement and employees' innovative behaviour.

Social Exchange Theory

Social Exchange Theory (SET), a social behaviour theory was first introduced by Homan (1958) and Blau (1964) in psychology and was later extended to management (Cropanzano & Mitchell, 2005). This is one of the theories that significantly facilitate the understanding of individuals' behaviour (Loi et al., 2015). Social exchange is described as "voluntary actions of individuals that are motivated by the returns they are expected to bring and typically do in fact bring from others." (Blau, 1964, p.91). This social exchange reflects the interaction between two persons who are involved in an interaction aimed at a positive outcome (Ali & Khalid, 2017). As a result, these persons compare the potential cost and benefits before performing (Tsui & Kang, 2019; Blau, 1964). The SET therefore helps explain the degree to which an exchange relationship affects the likelihood of one party positively reciprocating or otherwise, the actions of another party (Cropanzano et al., 2017; Cropanzano & Mitchell, 2005). With the basic assumption of the SET being that relationships evolve over time into trusting, loyal, and reciprocal commitments as long as the parties abide by certain "rules" of change (Cropanzano & Mitchell, 2005), people tend to exchange their social behaviour for resources, be it tangible or intangible, and these take place when there are substantial rewards (Lambe et al., 2001). Dominated by the norm of reciprocity, social exchange focuses on socioemotional benefit and limitless obligation (Cropanzano & Mitchell, 2005; Siyal, Peng & Siyal., 2018).

This exchange can take different forms such as friends exchange social approval, traders exchange money and goods and lecturers and other employees exchange time, service, and information for remuneration (Enayat et al., 2022). This exchange relationship therefore involves actions that depends on the rewarding actions of other persons you relate with (Blau, 1964). That is why social cost and rewards determine human behaviour and decision (Cortez & Johnston, 2020).

According to Ritzer (2011), the heart of the Homan SET lies in a set of fundamental propositions which are based on psychological principles. The first proposition is the Success proposition. According to this proposition, for all actions taken by persons, the more often a particular action of a person is rewarded, the more likely the person will perform that action (Homans, 1961). People are likely to repeat what others suggest if the first suggestion works. This behavior that aligns with the success proposition involves three stages: the person's action; a reward received and a repetition of the original action or something similar (Ritzer, 2011). The second proposition is the Stimulus Proposition. According to this proposition, "If in the past the occurrence of a particular stimulus, or set of stimuli, has been the basis for an individual action to be rewarded, then the more similar the present stimuli are to the past ones, the more likely the person is to perform the action, or similar actions (Homans, 1961). This implies if persons involved in an activity are rewarded, they are likely to be involved or engaged in the same or similar situations or actions in the future (Ritzer, 2011). The third proposition is Value Proposition which states that: The more valuable the result of an action, the more probable the action will be repeated (Homans, 1961). Homans explained that if a person perceives a reward for an action or behaviour to be valuable, there is high likelihood to perform that same behaviour than if it were not valued. The fourth proposition is The Deprivation-Satiation Proposition. Enayat et al (2022) used the relationship between a professor and a student to explain this proposition. According to them, when a student first establishes contact with his professor and they arrange for a meeting, the student will sacrifice to honour the appointment. However, after several meetings they may wish to complete what they are doing instead of an unplanned meeting. The fifth proposition is The Aggression-Approval Propositions. This proposition explains that when a person's action does not receive the rewards expected, or receives any form of punishment that was not expected, the person will be angry; likely to exhibit aggressive behaviour, and the results of such behaviour become more valuable to the person (Homans, 1961). The converse is also applicable, in that when the person 's action receives an expected reward, such a person will be happy and more likely to perform the approved behaviour again (Enayat et al., 2022). The last proposition is the Rationality Proposition. According to this proposition, in choosing between alternative actions, a person chooses the one which, as perceived by him at the time, the value (V) of the result, multiplied by the probability (P) of getting the result, is the greatest. (Homans, 1961). That is one's behaviour is influenced by the time, the values placed on the behaviour and the probability of getting the desired outcome.

The foregoing shows that social exchange between individuals or group of individuals is based on the principle of reciprocity. Again, how an individual reacts or reciprocate is influenced by six main principles, that is Success proposition, Stimulus Proposition, Value Proposition, Deprivation-Satiation, Aggression-Approval proposition, and Rationality Proposition.

Employee Innovative Behaviour

Innovation, one of the main research domain for the year 2024 in the area of entrepreneurship (Liguori, 2024), has been conceptualized in different ways by different authors. For instance, it is described as a personality characteristic (Hurt et al., 1977), an output (West, 1987), or as a behaviour (Janseen, 2000; Scott & Bruce, 1994). From the behavioural perspective, employees' Innovative behaviour refers to an extra-role behaviour where employees generate new ideas, promote these ideas continuously and implement them (Choi et al., 2021; Vries et al., 2016). This extra role behaviour thus, is a complex process consisting of behaviours, where the actions and activities relate to the generation, promotion and implementation of these new ideas and processes (Song et al., 2023; Scott & Bruce, 1994). Similarly, Janseen (2000) explain it as a process where the employee intentionally behaves in different ways that result in the creation, introduction, and application of new ideas within a work role, group, or organization, which tends to benefit the individual role performance, the group, or the organization (Janseen, 2000, p 288). An innovative employee is therefore involved in different behaviours within multiple stages where different activities are carried out (Yu et al., 2023). Within these stages they are able to initiate novel and suitable ideas related to processes, producing, or proceeding within the roles performed by the individuals, group or the whole organization (Khan et al., 2021; Scott & Bruce, 1994). Since employees mostly are mostly the first to be aware of challenges and issues that bother on the organisation and its customers, when there exist innovative employees who display innovative behaviour, thus they will generate new ideas to address these challenges and issues.

Innovative behaviour typically involve four major stages: Identification of the problem (problem identification), generation of new novel or adopted ideas to solve the problem (Idea generation), promotion of the ideas generated (seeking support) and lastly, seeking resources to support the implementation of the new idea as well as institutionalising them (Idea implementation) (Scott & Bruce, 1994; Vries et al., 2016). Innovative behaviour is therefore explained as a multi-dimensional, all-embracing construct which captures all forms of behaviour through which employees play a role in the innovation process (De Jong & Den Hartog, 2007) by the generation, promotion, and the implementation of unique ideas meaningful and useful to individual, teams, organization, and society.

It is worth noting that whiles creativity emphasizes on coming up with new and useful ideas (Shalley et al., 2004; De Jong & Den Hartog, 2007), innovation includes the promotion of the idea, product, or practice (Scott & Bruce, 1994) which is beneficial to individuals, teams, organisations, and the society at large (Bledow et al., 2009). The antecedents of innovative behaviour can be put into three major categories: individual, leader-related, and organizational factors (Song et al., 2023). Studies have shown that some individual characteristics that are antecedents to innovative behaviour are: individual personality (Jiang et al., 2022; Ullah et al., 2023), individual's learning orientation (Mutonyi et al., 2022) and individual psychological capital (Kumar et al., 2022), . Besides these individual antecedents, organisational factors such as organisational climate (Xu et al., 2022), talent management (Appau et al., 2021) and internal Communication (Soares et al., 2021) are also antecedents to employees innovative behaviour. In addition, societal factors such as family (Choi et al., 2018) can also influence employees' innovative behaviour. Thus, if there exist an imbalance between work and life activities of the individual it will affect the indiiduals' ability to go through all the four stages of the innovation behaviour process. On the part of leader-related factors, previous research shows how different leadership styles such as authentic leadership (Laguna et al., 2019; Lv et al., 2022), servant leadership (Opoku et al., 2019; Iqbal et al, 2020) affect innovative behaviour. However, how an entrepreneurial leader, one of the contemporary leadership styles, and why it impacts on employee innovative behaviour is limited and even worse post Covid-19 pandemic.

In conclusion, employee innovative behaviour is key towards organisation success. It results in the creation and promotion of unique ideas, products and services or practices which when implemented, positively impact on both the individual and organisation success. Employees go through the process of problem identification, idea generation, seeking support and idea implementation in putting up this behaviour. It should be noted that the successful exhibition of these innovative behaviour depends on the individual, leader related and organisational factors.

Leadership, Entrepreneurship and Entrepreneurial Leadership

The success of organisations depends on the effective application of the skills of leaders, and this is more important in the current emerging economies. Leadership has been conceptualized in different ways by different authors and therefore no decisive definition exists (Yukl, 2002). However, most definitions of leadership depict certain basic elements which include "groups", "influence", and "set goals" (Bryman, 1992). De Jong and Den Hartog (2007) defined leadership as the process of influencing others towards achieving some kind of desired outcome. A more current definition by Northouse (2021) is that leadership is a process whereby an individual influences a group of individuals to achieve a common goal. Leadership is thus conceptualised as a process of influencing, inspiring and supporting others to achieve set goals.

Entrepreneurial leadership, one of the new unique paradigms of leadership, combines entrepreneurship and leadership (Leitch & Volery, 2017; Harrison et al., 2018; Kakabadse et al., 2018)making it a distinct concept (Hoang et al., 2022). Entrepreneurial leadership draws insights from entrepreneurship, which is one's ability to correctly estimate deficiencies and imbalances in the market, explore the opportunities (Kirzner, 1973) and go through the process to influence others, create support and confidence, required to achieve organisational goals (Dubrin, 2022). It involves a process of creation of wealth, enterprise, innovation, change, employment, value, and growth (Morris et al., 2008). Entrepreneurial leadership is therefore suitable for settings that there exist a fast-growing organisation (Vecchio, 2003).

Entrepreneurial leaders influence and direct the performance of group members towards the achievement of organisational goals which involve recognising and exploiting entrepreneurial opportunities (Renko et al., 2015). Thus, these leaders, not only come up with business vision but also possess the competencies and ability to direct and motivate the team members to achieve set target (Renko et al., 2015). additionally, empirical evidence show that, entrepreneurial leaders have positive and significant effect on recognition of entrepreneurial opportunities, innovativeness of students (Ataei et al., 2024), reduces work uncertainty, encourages innovative, impact organisation competitive advantage (Ercantan et al., 2024) business success, digital transformation (Chaniago, 2023; Siyal et al., 2021) and innovation (Hoang et al., 2023, 2024) These, they are able to do because of their three unique characteristics and mind set: Learning-oriented mind set, People-oriented mind set, and Purpose-oriented mind set (Subramaniam & Shankar, 2020). .

Learning orientation is a construct that refers to the extent to which a person is inclined towards learning and improving upon his/her skills and competences. It involves the attitude of managers' considering learning as a key resource for the organisation and understanding the need to unlearn obsolete knowledge and accept new learning (Bontis, et al., 2002). Persons with learning orientation are persistent in learning over a long period to acquire the techniques and required expertise (Jha & Bhattacharyya, 2013). The Learning-oriented mind set of the entrepreneurial leader cause them to listen and pick signals from all around; experiment and take risk which enable them to identify opportunities, and motivate others to support in similar ventures (Subramaniam & Shankar, 2020) to achieve set targets.

Even though creating the appropriate conditions for innovation and learning collectively is cited as one of the greatest challenges of leadership (Yulk, 2009), this is not so in the case of the entrepreneurial leadership. This is because with this learning-oriented mind set, which reflects in the leader's daily activities (Döös et al., 2015), they, as well as their subordinates can learn and acquire the needed innovative skill. This is because learning is not restricted to specific training activities, but rather it is ongoing, and therefore as the leaders' learning mindset is exhibited in their daily activities, they are able to influence their subordinates to also learn. .

People orientation describes the idea of promoting business to protect the lives and health of employees (Yanbin & Chao, 2011). People orientation focuses on treating employees well and recognizing their role in the organisation. This mind set of entrepreneurial leaders reflects in their being open, positive, and appreciative of efforts of the subordinates which help build trust between themselves and their subordinates (Subramaniam & Shankar, 2020). Leaders who have this people-oriented mind set stress on the need to value people, empower and mentor their subordinates (Stone et al., 2004). The entrepreneurial leader again has a Purpose-oriented characteristic. Entrepreneurial leaders, with their purpose-oriented mind set, stay focussed on intention and are patient towards the accomplishment of these intentions (Subramaniam & Shankar, 2020). leaders with this mind set express clearly high levels of goals which gives followers a sense of direction, fulfilment and meaning (Kempster et al., 2011).

As a result of these characteristics, this leadership style can be applied in diverse cultural context such as the Chinese (Qixun, 2024), Indonesia (Chaniago, 2023) and different sectors like banking sector (Djalil et al., 2023), small and medium enterprises (Sipahi Dongul & Artantaş, 2022; Hoang et al., 2022), family business (Wah, 2004; Palalić et al., 2017) as well as new ventures (Yu et al., 2020). The application of the entrepreneurial leadership style can positively affect organisation success (Mishra & Misra, 2017; Sandybayev, 2019; Miao et al., 2019) individual commitment and turnover (Yang et al., 2019), employees' attitude (Kim, et al., 2017) and many other employees' behaviour such as their level of innovation.

The deduction form the afore description is that, leadership involve a process of influencing others towards achieving set goals in the current post Covid 19 pandemic. These goals can best be achieved with an entrepreneurial leadership within the organisation. This is because the entrepreneurial leader correctly identifies deficiencies and imbalances within organisation, create the support and confidence required in individuals and influence these individuals to support them to achieve the set targets. This, they are able to do due to their unique learning, people and purpose oriented mind-set.

Entrepreneurial Leadership and innovative Behaviour

Leaders generally influence employees' work behavior (Yukl, 2002; Yang et al., 2024) and more specifically, their innovative behaviour (Hughes, et al., 2018; Udin, 2024) both through their deliberate actions aiming to stimulate idea generation and application as well as by their more general, daily behavior (De Jong et al., 2007). Researchers have indicated that entrepreneurial leadership has a significant effect on employees' innovative behavior than other leadership styles such as servant leadership or transformational leadership (Newman et al., 2018; Bagheri et al., 2020). This may be because entrepreneurial leaders relate directly to entrepreneurial intentions and actions (Lekutle et al., 2023) which depends on innovation. Again, this phenomenon can be attributed to the unique characteristics and behaviour of the entrepreneurial leader. The entrepreneurial leader sets entrepreneurial goals, identifies and exploits opportunities, takes risk, is proactive and innovative (Kakabadse et al., 2018; Bagheri et al., 2020), has Learning-oriented, People-oriented, and Purpose-oriented mind set (Subramaniam & Shankar (2020) which significantly affect employees' innovative behaviour (Malik et al., 2020; Malibari & Bajaba, 2022). The question then is, why do entrepreneurial leaders influence employee's innovative behaviour even in post COVID-19 pandemic?

Innovative work behaviour involve the production of usable products, processes, or services initiated through the identification of problems to generation of ideas (Al-Omari et al., 2019). this kind of behaviour is exhibited by employees who are motivated to think outside the box, since organisation inclusion practices, the use of diverse workforce increases innovation and change the workplace (Chaudhry et al., 2021). Thus, with entrepreneurial people-oriented mind set, they tend to be open and encourage inclusiveness (Subramaniam & Shankar, 2020). Consequently, their subordinates get the opportunity to be involved in all activities, get motivated to think outside the box and come up with innovative ideas and share these with the leader for implementation. From the theoretical perspective, the social exchange theory can help clarify this relationship. Social exchange tends to engender feelings of obligation, trust, identification (Brown & Michell, 2010), and commitment (Khan & Iqbal, 2020; Mitonga-Monga, 2020). When individuals perceive there exist positive effect of their social exchange relationship with other individuals such as identification with the leader (Gu et al., 2015) and organisational justice (Xu et al., 2016) their behaviour is positively impacted. Hence, the proposition is that there is a high probability that individuals who work with entrepreneurial leaders will perceive themselves as being in a social exchange relationship due to the people-oriented mindset characteristics of the entrepreneurial leader and because of that these employees will be inclined to go beyond their call of duty and get involved in innovative behaviour (Brown & Trevino, 2006; Malibari & Bajaba, 2022; Pinela, et al., 2022).

From the social information processing theory perspective, which proposes that giving time and opportunity to interact, relationships between individuals through communicative behaviour that is valued by the other's culture (Olaniran et al., 2012), the social environment one finds him/herself provides several forms of information which influences the individual's attitude and behaviour (Frazier & Bowler, 2015). One of such is the social environments created by the leadership behaviour, which expresses the values and beliefs of the leader. Thus, given an entrepreneurial leader, who is able to motivate employees (Renko et al., 2015) and open to new ideas (Subramaniam & Shankar, 2020), and employees known to contribute roughly 80% of the new ideas for organizations (Getz & Robinson, 2003), such employees who work with the entrepreneurial leader are encouraged to identify problems, generate new ideas to solve the problem, promote the new ideas and seek for resources to solve the problem, that is the employees put up innovative work behaviour. It can be deduced and concluded from the discussions that the entrepreneurial leaders due to their unique characteristics are able to significantly influence employees' innovative behaviour.

The COVID-19 pandemic has changed people's attitudes and behaviors and as a result, there is the need for leadership style that can help make quick and innovative decisions for their organisation to survive. One of such is the entrepreneurial leaders who are characterised as individuals who with people, learning and purpose mind set. As a result, they are able to motivate, listen, appreciate, take risk and stay focus. With these behavioural characteristics, they are able to influence their subordinates to put up innovative behaviours. These behaviours reflect in the employees willingness to think and generate new ideas and implement them for organisation success.

Employee Engagement

With the COVID-19 pandemic being declared by WHO as no more a public health emergency (World Health Organization, 2023) one of the biggest challenges currently facing organizations is to ensure their success aside having innovative employee work behaviour is how to ensure employee engagement to help revamp and be at a competitive advantage. As a result, both practitioners and researchers are showing much interest in what and how of employee engagement. Notwithstanding the vast interest in employee engagement due to the positive effect it has on organizational success (PratimaSarangi & Nayak, 2018; Bhuvanaiah & Raya, 2014), there is still no universal agreement on its definition (Bailey et al., 2017; Lee et al, 2017). Kahn (1990) defined personal engagement as "harnessing of organisational members' selves to their work roles: in engagement people employ and express themselves physically, cognitively and emotionally during role performances (p. 694)". Similarly, Saks (2006) also referencing Kahn's (1990) definition adopted the behavioural perspective and defined personal engagement as is "a distinct and unique construct that consists of cognitive, emotional, and behavioural components that are associated with individual role performance" (602). Conversely, majority of authors focused on the psychological state engagement which Albrecht (2010) explained as "a positive work-related psychological state characterized by a genuine willingness to contribute to organizational success" (p.5). Like Albrecht's definition, Schaufeli et al (2002) had earlier defined work engagement as "a positive, fulfilling, work-related state of mind that is characterized by vigour, dedication and absorption" (p74). Like Schaufeli et al (2002), Salanova and Schaufeli, (2008) defined employee engagement as positive, fulfilling, work-related state of mind that is characterized by vigour, dedication, and absorption. While vigour refers to a high level of energy and mental toughness displayed at work, dedication describes having a sense of purpose, and absorption referring to being totally engrossed in work such that time passes so fast without you recognising. That explains why Tomlinson (2010) suggests employee engagement consists of three parts – the belief (mental), the feeling (emotion) and, the generation of discretionary effort (behaviour).

Engaged employees' unique characteristics make them work with vision, are dedicated, and have high level of absorption in their work (Schaufeli et al., 2002). While in the view of Maslach et al., (2001) engaged employees are characterized by energy, involvement and efficacy, Pritchard (2008) posit that engaged employees stay, say, and strive towards achieving organisational objectives. The "say" dimension describes how probable an employee is an advocate of the organisation. An employee high in this characteristic, is willing to recommend the organisation to others and speak well of the managers and organisation at large (Pritchard (2008). The "stay" dimension describes the extent to which the employee is committed, loyal and not willing to leave the organisation. That explains why when an organisation's employees are engaged, there is low turnover (McCarthy et al., 2020; Babakus et al., 2017). Engaged employees have "strive" characteristic dimension, which according to Pritchard (2008) describes the extent to which employees are willing to do extra and go over and above the task assigned to ensure organisational success (Pritchard, 2008). Employees high on this are willing to put in the extra to achieve targets. These characteristics reflect in the definition of employee engagement by Lockwood (2007), who defined it as the extent to which employees pledge to do something and do it in the organization, how hard the work and how long they stay on this commitment and pledge. Irrespective of the perspective one looks at employee engagement from, employee engagement reflects in employees' behaviour and attitude.

Ensuring employee engagement has become an important phenomenon in this era of the post Covid 19 pandemic. Organisations need employees who are ready to genuinely willing to support, have a sense of purpose and are ready to stay with the organisation. These characteristics reflect in an engaged employee. Deduction from the different researchers' definition of employee engagement show that engaged employees can be described as individuals who have a positive related mind set and therefore willing to contribute to the organisationby working with vigour, being dedicated abd strong to do extra for the organisation's success.

Entrepreneurial Leadership and Employee Engagement.

Several factors affect employees' engagement which may be external or internal to the organisation (Davis & Van der Heijden, 2023). One of the internal factors that impact employee engagement is leadership style. Extant literature confirms leadership style impact positively on employee engagement (Obuobisa-Darko & Ameyaw-Domfeh, 2019; Islam et al., 2023; Hasan et al., 2023). one leadership style that significantly affect employee engagement is entrepreneurial leadership (Yulivan, 2022; Pinela et al., 2022). The question is why is this so? This relationship can be explained using the SET. This theory postulates that individuals engage in exchange relationships anticipating that they will derive different economic and social benefits (Zhang et al., 2020). it has been established that trust, reputation, and reciprocity are the core elements in determining consumer satisfaction in their exchange relationship (Shiau & Luo, 2012). With employees being the internal customers of any organisation, when the entrepreneurial leader with his people-oriented mind set, is able to build trust among these "internal customers", the subordinates, which cause them to become engaged (Alfes et al., 2016; Bulińska-Stangrecka & Iddagoda, 2020), satisfied and thus, willing to go the extra mile to ensure that targets are met (Alshaabani & Rudnák, 2022; Islam et al., 2020).

From the SET perspective, employees view their commitment to their task as a repayment of how they have been treated (Cropanzano & Mitchell, 2005; Saks, 2006). Employees tend to feel obliged to respond positively and repay the organization, when they receive resources from their organization (Cropanzano & Mitchell, 2005). Since one strategy adopted by individuals to repay their organization is through their level of engagement (Saks, 2006). Engaged employees choose to employ themselves to varying degrees in response to the resources they receive from their organization" (Saks, 2006). Therefore, with the entrepreneurial leaders' unique characteristics as having people-oriented and learning mind set, they tend to be open, appreciative of efforts, listen and accept employees' views, and this builds trustful relationship, cause employees to feel valued and satisfied and therefore ready to reciprocate by showing higher levels of engagement.

The deduction then is that, the adoption of entrepreneurial leadership style causes employees to be engaged and as result ready and genuinely willing to contribute towards the organisation success.

Conclusion, Implication and Future Research Direction

The chapter sought to identify and explain how the entrepreneurial leader is the most appropriate leadership to adopt to ensure innovative behaviour and employee engagement in the current post0covid 19 pandemic organisation, using the SET and a literature review approach. The post covid 19 pandemic has resulted in the need for the introduction innovative ideas, processes and services to ensure organisations progress and survive, since change is only achieved when there is innovation (Chaniago, 2023).

Innovative behavior is considered an essential prerequisite for organizational survival in the current competitive post covid 19 pandemic work environment because innovation impact on organisation success (Janssen, 2000; Tohidi & Jabbari, 2012). Despite this significant contribution towards organisation success it has received very little attention from researchers (De Jong et al., 2007). One significant antecedent to this employee behaviour is entrepreneurial leadership. The entrepreneurial leader can impact on employees' innovative behaviour because these leaders exhibit their entrepreneurial characteristics as they relate with their subordinates and, therefore directly motivate the employees' innovative behaviour (Gupta et al., 2004). The entrepreneurial leaders due to the learning, people and purpose mind set enable them to stay focus, identify opportunities, take risk, stay inclusive, and appreciate which motivate their followers to support (Subramaniam & Shankar, 2020). These characteristics of the entrepreneurial leader thus help their subordinates to generate, promote and realize ideas to address challenges encounter. Additionally, with the the entrepreneurial leader known to exploit opportunities and innovate (Renko et al., 2015) and serve as a role model for their subordinates (Gupta et al., 2004), these subordinates will do same.

With these benefits derived from the entrepreneurial leader and the fact that researchers have indicated that during the covid 19 pandemic entrepreneurial leaders were highly valued qualities to possess (Rotten, 2021) because such leaders brought distinctive value to organisation (Gonzalez-Tejero et al., 2022) by exhibiting such skills as creativity, and entrepreneurial thinking and mindset (Steidle et al., 2024). It is concluded that one of the most suitable leadership style to adopt for organisation success post Covid 19 is the entrepreneurial leadership style.

Engaged employees are important in organisations because, research confirm that engaged employees work harder, more likely to go the extra mile, and are more loyal to their leaders and organisation (Lockwood, 2007). Thus, making engaged employees very important due to the positive effect it has on organisational success (Saks, 2006). With the Covid 19 pandemic having been officially declared as over, and organisation thus expected to adopt to the "New Normal", organisations need to adopt the appropriate style which will encourage employees to be willing to work extra and have a sense of purpose and one such style is the entrepreneurial leader. Thus with the adoption of entrepreneurial leadership style, opportunity for employees to feel valued and take active part in decision will be created. These employees will then reciprocate these positive actions and attitude of the entrepreneurial leader by being engaged and therefore stay, say and work with vigour, dedication and be absorbed in their work for organisational success. It is therefore concluded that, the adoption of entrepreneurial leadership style is the best promoter of employee innovative behaviour and engagement post Covid 19 pandemic for organisational success.

The study concluded that the adoption of entrepreneurial leadership style help ensure employee innovative behaviour and engagement and this has implication for practice and theory. Theoretically, it has been deduced that when employees experience a positive relationship with their leaders and perceive this relationship to be beneficial, they reciprocate by exhibiting innovative behaviour ad work with high levels of dedication, vigour, dedication and strive to achieve set targets. It thus supports and contribute to knowledge in the area of social exchange theory, leadership, employee innovative behaviour and employee engagement.

Practically, with the current levels of competition among organisation, post Covid 19 pandemic, leaders have to ensure employees are engaged to be ready to genuinely and willing to contribute to organisation success by being innovative. Consequently, with the deduction that entrepreneurial leaders are able to ensure this, organisational leaders should adopt the entrepreneurial leadership style and have people, learning and purpose mindset to successfully influence employees to be engaged and develop new innovative ideas, products and services for organisational survival and success. In addition, leader should be given formal training to develop these mind sets to be effective.

For future studies, it is recommended that empirical studies are conducted to confirm the theoretical relationship identified. Again, since different organisational sectors have their unique characteristics, it is recommended that a comparative study is carried out to identify similarities between as well as within counties. also, since context matter in research and Qixun (2024) empirical research after Covid 19 pandemic found that the Chinese has legitimise entrepreneurial leadership but it has been resisted in the African context, it is recommended that studies are carried out in different context using quantitative or mixed method approach.

Figure 1

Conceptual Model

REFERENCE

Al-Omari, M. A., Choo, L. S., & Ali, M. A. M. (2019). Innovative work behavior: A review of literature. *International Journal of Psychosocial Rehabilitation*, 23(2), 39–47.

Albrecht, S. L. (Ed.). (2010). *Handbook of Employee Engagement*. Edward Elgar Publishing. DOI: 10.4337/9781849806374

Alfes, K., Shantz, A., & Alahakone, R. (2016). Testing additive versus interactive effects of person-organization fit and organizational trust on engagement and performance. *Personnel Review*, 45(6), 1323–1339. DOI: 10.1108/PR-02-2015-0029

Alshaabani, A., & Rudnák, I. (2022). *Impact of Trust on Employees' Engagement: The Mediating Role of Conflict Management Climate*. Periodica Polytechnica Social and Management Sciences., DOI: 10.3311/PPso.18154https://

Appau, B. K., Marfo-Yiadom, E., & Kusi, L. Y. (2021). Performance implication of talent management and innovative work behaviour in colleges of education in Ghana. *International Journal of Economics and Business Administration*, 7(1), 1–10.

Ataei, P., Karimi, H., & Zarei, R. (2024). The role of entrepreneurial leadership, intellectual capital, innovativeness culture, and entrepreneurial orientation in entrepreneurial opportunity recognition by students. *Journal of Open Innovation*, 10(2), 100265. DOI: 10.1016/j.joitmc.2024.100265

Babakus, E., Yavas, U., & Karatepe, O. M. (2017). Work engagement and turnover intentions: Correlates and customer orientation as a moderator. *International Journal of Contemporary Hospitality Management*, 29(6), 1580–1598. DOI: 10.1108/IJCHM-11-2015-0649

Bagheri, A., Newman, A., & Eva, N. (2020). Entrepreneurial leadership of CEOs and employees' innovative behavior in high-technology new ventures. *Journal of Small Business Management*, 60(4), 805–827. DOI: 10.1080/00472778.2020.1737094

Bailey, C., Madden, A., Alfes, K., & Fletcher, L. (2017). The meaning, antecedents and outcomes of employee engagement: A narrative synthesis. *International Journal of Management Reviews*, 19(1), 31–53. DOI: 10.1111/ijmr.12077

Bhuvanaiah, T., & Raya, R. P. (2014). Employee engagement: Key to organizational success. *SCMS journal of Indian Management, 11*(4), 61-71.

Bilal, M., Chaudhry, S. A., Sharif, I., Shafique, O., & Shahzad, K. (2022). Entrepreneurial leadership and employee wellbeing during COVID-19 crisis: A dual mechanism perspective. *Frontiers in Psychology*, 13, 800584. DOI: 10.3389/fpsyg.2022.800584 PMID: 35928413

Blau, P. M. (1964). *Exchange and power in social life*. John Wiley and Sons.

Blau, P. M. (1964). Justice in social exchange. *Sociological Inquiry*, 34(2), 193–206. DOI: 10.1111/j.1475-682X.1964.tb00583.x

Bledow, R., Frese, M., Anderson, N., Erez, M., & Farr, J. (2009). A dialectic perspective on innovation: Conflicting demands, multiple pathways, and ambidexterity. *Industrial and Organizational Psychology: Perspectives on Science and Practice*, 2(3), 305–337. DOI: 10.1111/j.1754-9434.2009.01154.x

Bontis, N., Crossan, M., & Hulland, J. (2002). Managing an organizational learning system by aligning stocks and flows. *Journal of Management Studies*, 39(4), 437–469. DOI: 10.1111/1467-6486.t01-1-00299

Brown, M. E., & Mitchell, M. S. (2010). Ethical and unethical leadership. *Business Ethics Quarterly*, 20(4), 583–616. DOI: 10.5840/beq201020439

Brown, M. E., & Treviño, L. K. (2006). Ethical leadership: A review and future directions. *The Leadership Quarterly*, 17(6), 595–616. DOI: 10.1016/j.leaqua.2006.10.004

Bryman, A. (1992). *Charisma and Leadership in Organizations*. Sage.

Bulińska-Stangrecka, H., & Iddagoda, Y. A. (2020). The relationship between inter-organizational trust and employee engagement and performance. *Academy of Management Journal*, 4(1), 8–24.

Chaniago, H. (2023). Investigation of entrepreneurial leadership and digital transformation: Achieving business success in uncertain economic conditions. *Journal of Technology Management & Innovation*, 18(2), 18–27. DOI: 10.4067/S0718-27242023000200018

Chaudhry, I. S., Paquibut, R. Y., & Tunio, M. N. (2021). Do workforce diversity, inclusion practices, & organizational characteristics contribute to organizational innovation? Evidence from the UAE. *Cogent Business & Management*, 8(1), 1947549. DOI: 10.1080/23311975.2021.1947549

Choi, J. N. (2007). Change-oriented organizational citizenship behavior: effects of work environment characteristics and intervening psychological processes. *Journal of Organizational Behavior: The International Journal of Industrial. Journal of Organizational Behavior*, 28(4), 467–484. DOI: 10.1002/job.433

Choi, S. B., Cundiff, N., Kim, K., & Akhatib, S. N. (2018). The effect of work-family conflict and job insecurity on innovative behaviour of Korean workers: The mediating role of organisational commitment and job satisfaction. *International Journal of Innovation Management*, 22(01), 1850003. DOI: 10.1142/S1363919618500032

Choi, W. S., Kang, S. W., & Choi, S. B. (2021). Innovative behavior in the workplace: An empirical study of moderated mediation model of self-efficacy, perceived organizational support, and leader–member exchange. *Behavioral Sciences (Basel, Switzerland)*, 11(12), 182. DOI: 10.3390/bs11120182 PMID: 34940117

Cortez, R. M., & Johnston, W. J. (2020). The Coronavirus crisis in B2B settings: Crisis uniqueness and managerial implications based on social exchange theory. *Industrial Marketing Management*, 88, 125–135. DOI: 10.1016/j.indmarman.2020.05.004

Cropanzano, R., Anthony, E. L., Daniels, S. R., & Hall, A. V. (2017). Social exchange theory: A critical review with theoretical remedies. *The Academy of Management Annals*, 11(1), 479–516. DOI: 10.5465/annals.2015.0099

Cropanzano, R., & Mitchell, M. S. (2005). Social exchange theory: An interdisciplinary review. *Journal of Management*, 31(6), 874–900. DOI: 10.1177/0149206305279602

Davis, A. S., & Van der Heijden, B. I. (2023). Launching the dynamic employee engagement framework: Towards a better understanding of the phenomenon. *Employee Relations*, 45(2), 421–436. DOI: 10.1108/ER-08-2021-0338

De Jong, J. P., & Den Hartog, D. N. (2007). How leaders influence employees' innovative behaviour. *European Journal of Innovation Management*, 10(1), 41–64. DOI: 10.1108/14601060710720546

Djalil, M. A., Amin, M., Herjanto, H., Nourallah, M., & Öhman, P. (2023). The importance of entrepreneurial leadership in fostering bank performance. *International Journal of Bank Marketing*, 41(4), 926–948. DOI: 10.1108/IJBM-11-2022-0481

Döös, M., Johansson, P., & Wilhelmson, L. (2015). Beyond being present: Learning-oriented leadership in the daily work of middle managers. *Journal of Workplace Learning*, 27(6), 408–425. DOI: 10.1108/JWL-10-2014-0077

DuBrin, A. J. (2022). *Leadership: Research findings, practice, and skills*. Cengage Learning.

Emerson, R. M. (1962). Power-dependence relations. *American Sociological Review*, 27(5), 31–41. DOI: 10.2307/2089716

Enayat, T., Ardebili, M. M., Kivi, R. R., Amjadi, B., & Jamali, Y. (2022). A Computational Approach to Homans Social Exchange Theory. *Physica A*, 597, 127263. DOI: 10.1016/j.physa.2022.127263

Ercantan, K., Eyupoglu, Ş. Z., & Ercantan, Ö. (2024). The Entrepreneurial Leadership, Innovative Behaviour, and Competitive Advantage Relationship in Manufacturing Companies: A Key to Manufactural Development and Sustainable Business. *Sustainability (Basel)*, 16(6), 2407. DOI: 10.3390/su16062407

Frazier, M. L., & Bowler, W. M. (2015). Voice climate, supervisor undermining, and work outcomes: A group-level examination. *Journal of Management*, 41(3), 841–863. DOI: 10.1177/0149206311434533

Getahun Asfaw, A., & Chang, C. C. (2019). The association between job insecurity and engagement of employees at work. *Journal of Workplace Behavioral Health*, 34(2), 96–110. DOI: 10.1080/15555240.2019.1600409 PMID: 32874154

Getz, I., & Robinson, A. G. (2003). Innovate or die: Is that a fact? *Creativity and Innovation Management*, 12(3), 130–136. DOI: 10.1111/1467-8691.00276

González-Tejero, C. B., Ulrich, K., & Carrilero, A. (2022). The entrepreneurial motivation, Covid-19, and the new normal. *Entrepreneurial Business and Economics Review*, 10(2), 205–217. DOI: 10.15678/EBER.2022.100212

Gu, Q., Tang, T., & Jiang, W. (2015). Does moral leadership enhance employee creativity? Employee identification with leader and leader-member exchange (LMX) in the Chinese context. *Journal of Business Ethics*, 126(3), 513–529. DOI: 10.1007/s10551-013-1967-9

Gullop (2022). State of the Global Workplace 2022 Report T H E V O I C E O F T H E WORLD'S EMPLOYEES, https://www.gallup.com/workplace/349484/state-of-the-global-workplace

Gullop (2024). State of the Global Workplace 2022 Report T H E V O I C E O F T H E WORLD'S EMPLOYEES, https://www.gallup.com/workplace/349484/state-of-the-global-workplace

Gupta, V., MacMillan, I. C., & Surie, G. (2004). Entrepreneurial leadership: Developing and measuring a cross-cultural construct. *Journal of Business Venturing*, 19(2), 241–260. DOI: 10.1016/S0883-9026(03)00040-5

Harrison, C., Burnard, K., & Paul, S. (2018). Entrepreneurial leadership in a developing economy: A skill-based analysis. *Journal of Small Business and Enterprise Development*, 25(3), 521–548. DOI: 10.1108/JSBED-05-2017-0160

Hasan, A. A., Ahmad, S. Z., & Osman, A. (2023). Transformational leadership and work engagement as mediators on nurses' job performance in healthcare clinics: Work environment as a moderator. *Leadership in Health Services*, 36(4), 537–561. Advance online publication. DOI: 10.1108/LHS-10-2022-0097 PMID: 37093237

Hennessey, B. A. (2015). Creative behavior, motivation, environment and culture: The building of a systems model. *The Journal of Creative Behavior*, 49(3), 194–210. DOI: 10.1002/jocb.97

Hoang, G., Luu, T. T., Du, T., & Nguyen, T. T. (2023). Can both entrepreneurial and ethical leadership shape employees' service innovative behavior? *Journal of Services Marketing*, 37(4), 446–463. DOI: 10.1108/JSM-07-2021-0276

Hoang, G., Luu, T. T., Nguyen, T. T., Du, T., & Le, L. P. (2022). Examining the effect of entrepreneurial leadership on employees' innovative behavior in SME hotels: A mediated moderation model. *International Journal of Hospitality Management*, 102, 103142. DOI: 10.1016/j.ijhm.2022.103142

Hoang, G., Luu, T. T., Nguyen, T. T., Tang, T. T. T., & Pham, N. T. (2024). Entrepreneurial leadership fostering service innovation in the hospitality firms: The roles of knowledge acquisition, market-sensing capability and competitive intensity. *International Journal of Contemporary Hospitality Management*, 36(4), 1143–1169. DOI: 10.1108/IJCHM-08-2022-0969

Hoang, G., Nguyen, H., Luu, T. T., & Nguyen, T. T. (2023). Linking entrepreneurial leadership and innovation performance in hospitality firms: The roles of innovation strategy and knowledge acquisition. *Journal of Service Theory and Practice*, 33(4), 511–536. DOI: 10.1108/JSTP-09-2022-0203

Homans, G. C. (1958). Social behavior as exchange. *American Journal of Sociology*, 63(6), 597–606. DOI: 10.1086/222355

Homans, G. C. (1961). *Social behavior: Its elementary forms*. Harcourt, Brace.

Hughes, D. J., Lee, A., Tian, A. W., Newman, A., & Legood, A. (2018). Leadership, creativity, and innovation: A critical review and practical recommendations. *The Leadership Quarterly*, 29(5), 549–569. DOI: 10.1016/j.leaqua.2018.03.001

Hurt, H. T., Joseph, K., & Cook, C. D. (1977). Scales for the measurement of innovativeness. *Human Communication Research*, 4(1), 58–65. DOI: 10.1111/j.1468-2958.1977.tb00597.x

Iqbal, A., Latif, K. F., & Ahmad, M. S. (2020). Servant leadership and employee innovative behaviour: Exploring psychological pathways. *Leadership and Organization Development Journal*, 41(6), 813–827. DOI: 10.1108/LODJ-11-2019-0474

Islam, M. N., Furuoka, F., & Idris, A. (2020). The impact of trust in leadership on organizational transformation. *Global Business and Organizational Excellence*, 39(4), 25–34. DOI: 10.1002/joe.22001

Islam, T., Khatoon, A., Cheema, A. U., & Ashraf, Y. (2023). How does ethical leadership enhance employee work engagement? The roles of trust in leader and harmonious work passion. *Kybernetes*. ahead-of-print.

Janssen, O. (2000). Job demands, perceptions of effort-reward fairness and innovative work behaviour. *Journal of Occupational and Organizational Psychology*, 73(3), 287–302. DOI: 10.1348/096317900167038

Jha, S., & Bhattacharyya, S. S. (2013). Learning orientation and performance orientation: Scale development and its relationship with performance. *Global Business Review*, 14(1), 43–54. DOI: 10.1177/0972150912466443

Jiang, X., Lin, J., Zhou, L., & Wang, C. (2022). How to select employees to participate in interactive innovation: analysis of the relationship between personality, social networks and innovation behavior. *Kybernetes*, (ahead-of-print).

Kahn, W. A. (1990). Psychological conditions of personal engagement and disengagement at work. *Academy of Management Journal*, 33(4), 692–724. DOI: 10.2307/256287

Kakabadse, N. K., Tatli, A., Nicolopoulou, K., Tankibayeva, A., & Mouraviev, N. (2018). A gender perspective on entrepreneurial leadership: Female leaders in Kazakhstan. *European Management Review*, 15(2), 155–170. DOI: 10.1111/emre.12125

Kempster, S., Jackson, B., & Conroy, M. (2011). Leadership as purpose: Exploring the role of purpose in leadership practice. *Leadership*, 7(3), 317–334. DOI: 10.1177/1742715011407384

Khalid, S., & Ali, T. (2017). An integrated perspective of social exchange theory and transaction cost approach on the antecedents of trust in international joint ventures. *International Business Review*, 26(3), 491–501. DOI: 10.1016/j.ibusrev.2016.10.008

Khan, A. J., & Iqbal, J. (2020). Training and employee commitment: The social exchange perspective. *Journal of Management Sciences*, 7(1), 88–100. DOI: 10.20547/jms.2014.2007106

Khan, M. M., Mubarik, M. S., & Islam, T. (2021). Leading the innovation: Role of trust and job crafting as sequential mediators relating servant leadership and innovative work behavior. *European Journal of Innovation Management*, 24(5), 1547–1568. DOI: 10.1108/EJIM-05-2020-0187

Kim, T., Cha, M., Kim, H., Lee, J. K., & Kim, J. (2017, July). Learning to discover cross-domain relations with generative adversarial networks. In *International conference on machine learning* (pp. 1857-1865). PMLR

Kirzner, I. M. Competition and Entrepreneurship (1973). University of Illinois at Urbana-Champaign's Academy for Entrepreneurial Leadership Historical Research Reference in Entrepreneurship, Available at SSRN: https://ssrn.com/abstract= 1496174

Kumar, D., Upadhyay, Y., Yadav, R., & Goyal, A. K. (2022). Psychological capital and innovative work behaviour: The role of mastery orientation and creative self-efficacy. *International Journal of Hospitality Management*, 102, 103157. DOI: 10.1016/j.ijhm.2022.103157

Laguna, M., Walachowska, K., Gorgievski-Duijvesteijn, M. J., & Moriano, J. A. (2019). Authentic leadership and employees' innovative behaviour: A multilevel investigation in three countries. *International Journal of Environmental Research and Public Health*, 16(21), 4201. DOI: 10.3390/ijerph16214201 PMID: 31671565

Lambe, C. J., Wittmann, C. M., & Spekman, R. E. (2001). Social exchange theory and research on business-to-business relational exchange. *Journal of Business-To-Business Marketing*, 8(3), 1–36. DOI: 10.1300/J033v08n03_01

Lee, Y., Shin, H. Y., Park, J., Kim, W., & Cho, D. (2017). An integrative literature review on employee engagement in the field of human resource development: Exploring where we are and where we should go. *Asia Pacific Education Review*, 18(4), 541–557. DOI: 10.1007/s12564-017-9508-3

Leitch, C. M., & Volery, T. (2017). Entrepreneurial leadership: Insights and directions. *International Small Business Journal*, 35(2), 147–156. DOI: 10.1177/0266242616681397

Lekutle, N. T., Ebewo, P. E., & Shambare, R. (2023). The Effects of Entrepreneurship Leadership on Youth Entrepreneurial Intentions Post-COVID-19: The Case of Gauteng. *Businesses*, 3(4), 569–584. DOI: 10.3390/businesses3040035

Liguori, E. W., Muldoon, J., Ogundana, O. M., Lee, Y., & Wilson, G. A. (2024). Charting the future of entrepreneurship: A roadmap for interdisciplinary research and societal impact. *Cogent Business & Management*, 11(1), 2314218. Advance online publication. DOI: 10.1080/23311975.2024.2314218

Liu, X., Yu, J., Guo, Q., & Li, J. (2022). Employee engagement, its antecedents, and effects on business performance in hospitality industry: A multilevel analysis. *International Journal of Contemporary Hospitality Management*, 34(12), 4631–4652. DOI: 10.1108/IJCHM-12-2021-1512

Lockwood, N. R. (2007). Leveraging employee engagement for competitive advantage: HR's strategic role. SHRM HRMagazine. *Alexandria (Aldershot)*, 52(3), S1–S11.

Loi, R., Lam, L. W., Ngo, H. Y., & Cheong, S. I. (2015). Exchange mechanisms between ethical leadership and affective commitment. *Journal of Managerial Psychology*, 30(6), 645–658. DOI: 10.1108/JMP-08-2013-0278

Lv, M., Jiang, S. M., Chen, H., & Zhang, S. X. (2022). Authentic leadership and innovation behaviour among nurses in China: A mediation model of work engagement. *Journal of Nursing Management*, 30(7), 2670–2680. DOI: 10.1111/jonm.13669 PMID: 35580873

Malibari, M. A., & Bajaba, S. (2022). Entrepreneurial leadership and employees' innovative behavior: A sequential mediation analysis of innovation climate and employees' intellectual agility. *Journal of Innovation & Knowledge*, 7(4), 100255. DOI: 10.1016/j.jik.2022.100255

Malik, S., Awan, T. M., & Nisar, A. (2020). Entrepreneurial leadership and employee innovative behaviour in software industry. *Journal of Business Economics*, 12(1), 63–76.

Maslach, C., Schaufeli, W. B., & Leiter, M. P. (2001). Job burnout. *Annual Review of Psychology*, 52(1), 397–422. DOI: 10.1146/annurev.psych.52.1.397 PMID: 11148311

McCarthy, I. O., Moonesinghe, R., & Dean, H. D. (2020). Association of employee engagement factors and turnover intention among the 2015 US federal government workforce. *SAGE Open*, 10(2), 2158244020931847. DOI: 10.1177/2158244020931847 PMID: 39099646

Miao, Q., Eva, N., Newman, A., & Cooper, B. (2019). CEO entrepreneurial leadership and performance outcomes of top management teams in entrepreneurial ventures: The mediating effects of psychological safety. *Journal of Small Business Management*, 57(3), 1119–1135. DOI: 10.1111/jsbm.12465

Mishra, P., & Misra, R. K. (2017). Entrepreneurial leadership and organizational effectiveness: A comparative study of executives and non-executives. *Procedia Computer Science*, 122, 71–78. DOI: 10.1016/j.procs.2017.11.343

Mitonga-Monga, J. (2020). Social exchange influences on ethical leadership and employee commitment in a developing country setting. *Journal of Psychology in Africa*, 30(6), 485–491. DOI: 10.1080/14330237.2020.1842587

Morris, M. H., Kuratko, D. F., Schindehutte, M., & Spivack, A. J. (2012). Framing the entrepreneurial experience. *Entrepreneurship Theory and Practice*, 36(1), 11–40. DOI: 10.1111/j.1540-6520.2011.00471.x

Mutonyi, B. R., Slåtten, T., & Lien, G. (2020). Empowering leadership, work group cohesiveness, individual learning orientation and individual innovative behaviour in the public sector: Empirical evidence from Norway. *International Journal of Public Leadership*, 16(2), 175–197. DOI: 10.1108/IJPL-07-2019-0045

Newman, A., Herman, H. M., Schwarz, G., & Nielsen, I. (2018). The effects of employees' creative self-efficacy on innovative behavior: The role of entrepreneurial leadership. *Journal of Business Research*, 89, 1–9. DOI: 10.1016/j.jbusres.2018.04.001

Northouse, P. G. (2021). *Leadership: Theory and practice*. Sage publications.

Nunnally, J. C. (1978). *Psychometric theory*. McGraw-Hill.

Obuobisa-Darko, T., & Ameyaw-Domfeh, K. (2019). Leader behaviour to achieve employee engagement in Ghana: A qualitative study, International Journal of Public Leadership. *International Journal of Public Leadership*, 15(1), 19–37. DOI: 10.1108/IJPL-04-2018-0018

Olaniran, B. A., Rodriguez, N., & Williams, I. M. (2012). Social information processing theory (SIPT): A cultural perspective for international online communication environments. In *Computer-mediated communication across cultures: International interactions in online environments* (pp. 45-65). IGI Global.

Opoku, M. A., Choi, S. B., & Kang, S. W. (2019). Servant leadership and innovative behaviour: An empirical analysis of Ghana's manufacturing sector. *Sustainability (Basel)*, 11(22), 6273. DOI: 10.3390/su11226273

Ozturk, A., Karatepe, O. M., & Okumus, F. (2021). The effect of servant leadership on hotel employees' behavioral consequences: Work engagement versus job satisfaction. *International Journal of Hospitality Management*, 97, 102994. DOI: 10.1016/j.ijhm.2021.102994

Palalić, R., Ramadani, V., Dana, L. P., & Ratten, V. (2017). Gender entrepreneurial leadership in family businesses: a case study from Bosnia and Herzegovina. In *Women entrepreneurship in family business* (pp. 208–226). Routledge. DOI: 10.4324/9781315098531-11

Pendell, R. (2022). *The World's $7.8 Trillion Workplace Problem*. Gallup Workplace.

Pinela, N., Guevara, R., & Armijos, M. (2022). Entrepreneurial Leadership, Work Engagement, and Innovative Work Behavior: The Moderating Role of Gender. *International Journal of Economics & Business Administration*, 10(2), 19–40. DOI: 10.35808/ijeba/764

PratimaSarangi, D., & Nayak, B. (2018). Employee engagement and its impact on organizational success–A study in manufacturing company, India. *OSR Journal of Business and Management, 18*(4), 52-57.

Pritchard, K. (2008). Employee engagement in the UK: Meeting the challenge in the public sector. *Development and Learning in Organizations*, 22(6), 15–17. DOI: 10.1108/14777280810910302

Qixun Siebers, L. (2024). Transferring paternalistic entrepreneurial leadership behaviours (PELB): Chinese organisations in sub-Saharan Africa. *International Journal of Cross Cultural Management*, 24(2), 14705958241243171. DOI: 10.1177/14705958241243171

Rabiul, M. K., Karatepe, O. M., Al Karim, R., & Panha, I. M. (2023). An investigation of the interrelationships of leadership styles, psychological safety, thriving at work, and work engagement in the hotel industry: A sequential mediation model. *International Journal of Hospitality Management*, 113, 103508. DOI: 10.1016/j.ijhm.2023.103508

Ratten, V. (2021). COVID-19 and entrepreneurship: Future research directions. *Strategic Change*, 30(2), 91–98. DOI: 10.1002/jsc.2392

Renko, M., El Tarabishy, A., Carsrud, A. L., & Brännback, M. (2015). Understanding and measuring entrepreneurial leadership style. *Journal of Small Business Management*, 53(1), 54–74. DOI: 10.1111/jsbm.12086

Ritzer, G. (2011). Exchange, Networks, and Rational Choice Theories. *Sociological theory*, (8th ed), pp. 416-453.

Saks, A. M. (2006). Antecedents and consequences of employee engagement. *Journal of Managerial Psychology*, 21(7), 600–619. DOI: 10.1108/02683940610690169

Salanova, M., & Schaufeli, W. B. (2008). A cross-national study of work engagement as a mediator between job resources and proactive behaviour. *International Journal of Human Resource Management*, 19(1), 116–131. DOI: 10.1080/09585190701763982

Sandybayev, A. (2019). Impact of effective entrepreneurial leadership style on organizational performance: Critical review. *International Journal of Economics and Management*, 1(1), 47–55.

Schaufeli, W. B., Salanova, M., González-Romá, V., & Bakker, A. B. (2002). The measurement of engagement and burnout: A two sample confirmatory factor analytic approach. *Journal of Happiness Studies*, 3(1), 71–92. DOI: 10.1023/A:1015630930326

Scott, S. G., & Bruce, R. A. (1994). Determinants of innovative behavior: A path model of individual innovation in the workplace. *Academy of Management Journal*, 37(3), 580–607. DOI: 10.2307/256701

Shalley, C. E., Zhou, J., & Oldham, G. R. (2004). The effects of personal and contextual characteristics on creativity: Where should we go from here? *Journal of Management*, 30(6), 933–958. DOI: 10.1016/j.jm.2004.06.007

Simon, S. S. (2011). The essentials of employee engagement in organizations. *Journal of Contemporary Research in Management*, 6(1), 63–72.

Sipahi Dongul, E., & Artantaş, E. (2022). Exploring the link between social work, entrepreneurial leadership, social embeddedness, social entrepreneurship and firm performance: A case of SMES owned by Chinese ethnic community in Turkey. *Journal of Enterprising Communities: People and Places in the Global Economy*, 17(3), 684–707. DOI: 10.1108/JEC-11-2021-0162

Siwi, M. K., Haryono, A., & Nuryana, I. (2022, July). Intellectual Agility and Entrepreneurial Leadership as Innovation Sustainability Business Cooperative in The Covid 19 Pandemic. In Eighth Padang International Conference On Economics Education, Economics, Business and Management, Accounting and Entrepreneurship (PICEEBA-8 2021) (pp. 212-216). Atlantis Press.

Siyal, M., Siyal, S., Wu, J., Pal, D., & Memon, M. M. (2021). Consumer perceptions of factors affecting online shopping behavior: An empirical evidence from foreign students in China. [JECO]. *Journal of Electronic Commerce in Organizations*, 19(2), 1–16. DOI: 10.4018/JECO.2021040101

Siyal, S. (2018). Does Leadership lessen turnover of public servants. The moderated mediation effect of leader member exchange and perspective taking [EBSCO open dissertations].

Siyal, S. (2023). Inclusive leadership and work engagement: Exploring the role of psychological safety and trust in leader in multiple organizational context. *Business Ethics, the Environment & Responsibility*, 32(4), 1170–1184. DOI: 10.1111/beer.12556

Siyal, S., & Peng, X. (2018). Does leadership lessen turnover? The moderated mediation effect of leader–member exchange and perspective taking on public servants. *Journal of Public Affairs*, 18(4), e1830. DOI: 10.1002/pa.1830

Siyal, S., Peng, X., & Siyal, A. W. (2018). Socioeconomic analysis: A case of Tharparkar. *Journal of Public Affairs*, 18(4), e1847. DOI: 10.1002/pa.1847

Siyal, S., Xin, C., Umrani, W. A., Fatima, S., & Pal, D. (2021). How do leaders influence innovation and creativity in employees? The mediating role of intrinsic motivation. *Administration & Society*, 53(9), 1337–1361. DOI: 10.1177/0095399721997427

Soares, M. E., Mosquera, P., & Cid, M. (2021). Antecedents of innovative behaviour: Knowledge sharing, open innovation climate and internal communication. *International Journal of Innovation and Learning*, 30(2), 241–257. DOI: 10.1504/IJIL.2021.117223

Song, J., Jiao, H., & Wang, C. (2023). How work-family conflict affects knowledge workers' innovative behavior: a spill over-crossover-spill over model of dual-career couples. *Journal of Knowledge Management*. ahead-of-print

Steidle, S. B., Glass, C., Rice, M., & Henderson, D. A. (2024). Addressing Wicked Problems (SDGs) Through Community Colleges: Leveraging Entrepreneurial Leadership for Economic Development Post-COVID. *Journal of the Knowledge Economy*, ●●●, 1–26. DOI: 10.1007/s13132-024-01890-4

Stone, A. G., Russell, R. F., & Patterson, K. (2004). Transformational versus servant leadership: A difference in leader focus. *Leadership and Organization Development Journal*, 25(4), 349–361. DOI: 10.1108/01437730410538671

Subramaniam, R., & Shankar, R. K. (2020). Three mindsets of entrepreneurial leaders. *The Journal of Entrepreneurship*, 29(1), 7–37. DOI: 10.1177/0971355719893498

Tohidi, H., & Jabbari, M. M. (2012). The important of innovation and its crucial role in growth, survival and success of organizations. *Procedia Technology*, 1, 535–538. DOI: 10.1016/j.protcy.2012.02.116

Tomlinson, G. (2010). Building a culture of high employee engagement. *Strategic HR Review*, 9(3), 25–31. DOI: 10.1108/14754391011040046

Tsai, J. C. A., & Kang, T. C. (2019). Reciprocal intention in knowledge seeking: Examining social exchange theory in an online professional community. *International Journal of Information Management*, 48, 161–174. DOI: 10.1016/j.ijinfomgt.2019.02.008

Udin, U. (2024). Leadership styles and innovative work behaviour: The role of work engagement. *International Journal of Economics and Business Research*, 28(1), 65–81. DOI: 10.1504/IJEBR.2024.139287

Ullah, I., Hameed, R. M., & Mahmood, A. (2023). The impact of proactive personality and psychological capital on innovative work behavior: evidence from software houses of Pakistan. *European Journal of Innovation Management*. ahead-of-print

Vance, R. J. (2006). Employee engagement and commitment. *SHRM foundation*, *1*, 1-53.

Vecchio, R. P. (2003). Entrepreneurship and leadership: Common trends and common threads. *Human Resource Management Review*, 13(2), 303–327. DOI: 10.1016/S1053-4822(03)00019-6

Vries, H. D., Bekkers, V., & Tummers, L. (2016). Innovation in the public sector: A systematic review and future research agenda. *Public Administration*, 94(1), 146–166. DOI: 10.1111/padm.12209

Wah, S. S. (2004). Entrepreneurial leaders in family business organisations. *Journal of Enterprising Culture*, 12(1), 1–34. DOI: 10.1142/S0218495804000026

Wang, J. (2021). Research on the Influence of Dynamic Work Environment on Employees' Innovative Performance in the Post-epidemic Era–The Role of Job Crafting and Voice Behaviour. *Frontiers in Psychology*, 12, 5948. DOI: 10.3389/fpsyg.2021.795218

West, M. A. (1987). A measure of role innovation at work. *British Journal of Social Psychology*, 26(1), 83–85. DOI: 10.1111/j.2044-8309.1987.tb00764.x

World Health Organization. (2023). Statement on the fifteenth meeting of the IHR (2005) Emergency Committee on the COVID-19 pandemic. *World Heal Organ*.

Xu, A. J., Loi, R., & Ngo, H. Y. (2016). Ethical leadership behavior and employee justice perceptions: The mediating role of trust in organization. *Journal of Business Ethics*, 134(3), 493–504. DOI: 10.1007/s10551-014-2457-4

Xu, Z., Wang, H., & Suntrayuth, S. (2022). Organizational climate, innovation orientation, and innovative work behaviour: The mediating role of psychological safety and intrinsic motivation. *Discrete Dynamics in Nature and Society*, 2022(1), 1–10. DOI: 10.1155/2022/9067136

Yanbin, R., & Chao, S. (2011). Application of the Concept "People-Oriented" to Improve the Working Team Safety Construction. *Procedia Engineering*, 26, 2080–2084. DOI: 10.1016/j.proeng.2011.11.2409

Yang, J., Pu, B., & Guan, Z. (2019). Entrepreneurial leadership and turnover intention of employees: The role of affective commitment and person-job fit. *International Journal of Environmental Research and Public Health*, 16(13), 2380. DOI: 10.3390/ijerph16132380 PMID: 31277473

Yang, Y., & Zhang, X. (2024). A Review of the Influence of Different Leadership Styles on Employees' Initiative Behavior. In SHS Web of Conferences (Vol. 181, p. 01035). EDP Sciences

Yu, S., Gong, X., & Wu, N. (2020). Job insecurity and employee engagement: A moderated dual path model. *Sustainability (Basel)*, 12(23), 10081. DOI: 10.3390/su122310081

Yu, S., Liu, S., Gong, X., Lu, W., & Liu, C. E. (2023). How does deviance tolerance enhance innovative behaviour? The mediating role of cognitive crafting and the moderating role of regulatory focus. *Chinese Management Studies*. ahead-of-print

Yu, Y., Zhang, X., Huang, S., Chen, Z., & Chen, Z. (2020). Entrepreneurial leadership and innovation performance in new ventures: Examining the roles of strategic flexibility and environmental turbulence. *Entrepreneurship Research Journal*, 12(4), 629–652. DOI: 10.1515/erj-2018-0090

Yukl, G. (2002). *Leadership in Organizations* (5th ed.). Prentice-Hall.

Yukl, G. (2009). Leading organizational learning: Reflections on theory and research. *The Leadership Quarterly*, 20(1), 49–53. DOI: 10.1016/j.leaqua.2008.11.006

Yulivan, I. (2022). The Influence of Entrepreneurial Leadership, Work Culture and Organizational Trust on Employee Engagement of Employees in the Ministry of Religious Affairs Republic of Indonesia. *International Journal of Multicultural and Multireligious Understanding*, 8(12), 633–638.

Zhang, Y., Lu, B., & Zheng, H. (2020). Can buzzing bring business? Social interactions, network centrality and sales performance: An empirical study on business-to-business communities. *Journal of Business Research*, 112, 170–189. DOI: 10.1016/j.jbusres.2020.02.034

Chapter 6
Exploring the Nexus of Entrepreneurial Leadership and Innovative Disruption:
A Qualitative Study

Anjali Daisy
https://orcid.org/0000-0003-1207-5002
Loyola Institute of Business Administration, India

ABSTRACT

Grounded in the context of evolving markets and technological advancements, the research seeks to unravel the intricate interplay of entrepreneurial leadership styles and their impact on innovative disruption. Through in-depth interviews with a diverse group of entrepreneurs, executives, and industry experts, the study aims to capture nuanced insights into the strategies, challenges, and outcomes associated with entrepreneurial endeavors in disruptive environments. Employing qualitative research methods, including thematic analysis and participant observation, the research strives to uncover patterns, identify key drivers, and explore the contextual nuances that influence the success or failure of entrepreneurial initiatives amid disruptive forces. The findings of this study are expected to contribute to the theoretical understanding of entrepreneurial leadership and innovation disruption while providing practical implications for business leaders, policymakers, and scholars navigating the ever-changing landscape of modern business ecosystems.

DOI: 10.4018/979-8-3693-0078-7.ch006

INTRODUCTION

In today's fast-paced and dynamic business landscape, the role of entrepreneurial leadership has gained immense significance. Entrepreneurs and leaders alike are constantly seeking ways to innovate, adapt, and drive their organizations forward. They understand that risk and innovation go hand in hand, and mastering this delicate balance is often the key to success. This article delves into the world of entrepreneurial leadership, discussing how it involves navigating uncertainty, fostering innovation. What differentiates a disruption from an ordinary step forward? According to Indeed.com, "disruptive innovation is the idea that the invention of a new product can disrupt an entire market, changing what consumers want out of a business or what employees expect from their employer and vice versa." These are the kinds of significant changes that innovative businesses want to make. And they are the kind that require disruptive leaders who are willing to take risks and think outside the box. If you're a disruptive leader, there are two big risks to watch out for. They can undermine your best efforts, and they're unavoidable. The best you can do is make efforts to minimize their effects. The first big risk of disruptive innovation (creating problems for disruptive leaders) is the chance that your changes might go wrong. "It [disruptive innovation] has to be done constructively, because disruption can destroy value. What we want to do is find a constructive disruption that creates value for our consumers, our communities, and other stakeholders—to build our company and empower our people," says David Taylor, former CEO of Proctor and Gamble. In order to instigate disruption while minimizing risk, Taylor chose to reorganize teams, eliminate layers of management, and create small groups that could take on new projects quickly. These changes have allowed P&G to make strides toward mitigating environmental impact while also keeping risk manageable. No matter how much they try to mitigate risk, disruptive leaders can face resistance from those who are resistant to change. You'll have to handle this resistance in a productive and effective way and avoid alienating those who are concerned about big changes. To be effective with a disruptive leadership style, you'll need to build a lot of trust - first with your board, if you have one, and your senior leadership team, and then with your entire roster of employees. You'll need to clearly communicate your vision so that everyone is in the loop all the time, and allow plenty of time to build consensus and support. Leadership: Your company's senior leaders are smart people who have a lot of experience with what works and what doesn't in business. They will have valid concerns about contradicting proven tactics. Customers: Disruption may not be well-received by customers or other stakeholders if it involves significant changes to products or services that they rely on. Employees: Introducing constant change in the workplace can lead to stress and uncertainty for employees, which leads to poorer performance and turnover. while you're hearing people out, make sure you're really listening. Find ways to mitigate the risks they're concerned about to increase your chances of success with big changes. Disruptive leadership can be an incredibly effective way to drive innovation and bring about positive change in business. By adapting to change and encouraging experimentation disruptive leaders lead their teams to new heights of success.

But it is a risky style that comes with dangers to be addressed, and is not right for every situation. Carefully consider the unique needs and circumstances of your organization before adopting a disruptive leadership style. For more leadership insight, take our quiz to determine your leadership style, read our list of best books on visionary leadership, or consider applying for membership to Fast Company Executive Board, where you'll be surrounded by other innovators making big changes in their industries. As digitization becomes more prevalent, traditional industry boundaries are becoming less defined, prompting companies to undergo reinvention. Today, few companies can afford to remain on the sidelines, and the surge in digital transformation is paralleled by a need for organizational transformation. Despite this widespread shift, only a handful of companies have successfully transformed to emerge as industry leaders in the digital age. Amid the struggles faced by large enterprises, the potential winners are likely to be entrepreneurs and corporate innovators who can adeptly navigate digital disruptions and embody essential leadership traits. This situation poses a significant educational challenge within the realm of innovation management. The question arises: What skills, capabilities, and mindsets must innovators cultivate to excel in the face of these digital challenges? To address this challenge, the Business School at the University of the Aegean in Greece has introduced the "Leadership & Disruptive Innovation" training program. This program is designed to tackle the educational gap by employing a research-driven, practice-oriented didactic model. The primary objectives include helping participants understand the intricacies of leading a new venture amidst continuous digital disruptions and providing real-world experiences to test and enhance their skills, knowledge, and self-confidence. The program employs an innovative combination of coaching, a network of stakeholders, flipped classroom training, and an international field trip. Through these elements, participants have the opportunity to appreciate the complexities of leadership in the face of digital disruptions and engage with relevant leaders in various sectors, including universities, business firms, and government. The initial implementation of the program has garnered high praise, particularly from participants and the media.

Literature Review

In recent years, both entrepreneurship and leadership have undergone significant development and garnered considerable attention (Gartner, 2000; Shane and Venkataraman, 2000; Shane, 2012; Siyal & Peng, 2018; Siyal, 2018; Siyal, 2023; Siyal et al, 2023;2021). While traditionally considered independent fields, scholars have drawn parallels between them, both historically and conceptually (Cogliser and Brigham, 2004). This emerging perspective has led to the exploration of entrepreneurship as a form of leadership, particularly in the context of small business ownership or firm startups (Vecchio, 2003). This integration has given rise to a novel paradigm known as "entrepreneurial leadership," extending beyond the convergence of these fields (Cogliser and Brigham, 2004; Fernald et al., 2005). Entrepreneurial leadership is seen as a crucial element for entrepreneurs to maintain competitiveness in dynamic environments (Fernald et al., 2005). Existing evidence suggests a positive correlation between entrepreneurial leadership and business performance, emphasizing innovation and development, along with a focus on customer and competitor orientation (Van Zyl and Mathur-Helm, 2007). The recognition of the value provided by this form of leadership has sparked a surge in scholarly interest, leading to various definitions proposed by academics. Entrepreneurial leadership is described as a type of leadership that envisions scenarios to assemble and mobilize a committed "supporting cast" for the discovery and exploitation of strategic value creation (Gupta et al., 2004, p. 242). Despite the growing interest and diverse definitions, progress in the field has been hindered by a lack of conceptual development and inadequate tools to measure leaders' entrepreneurial characteristics and behaviors (Renko et al., 2015). While literature has expanded from both empirical and conceptual perspectives on entrepreneurial leadership (e.g., Nicholson, 1998; Swiercz and Lydon, 2002; Cogliser and Brigham, 2004; Gupta et al., 2004; Fernald et al., 2005; Chen, 2007; Renko et al., 2015; Harrison et al., 2016), there remains limited consensus on the precise definition and attributes of entrepreneurial leadership.

Disruptive Innovation and Entrepreneurial Leadership

Over the last two decades, an extensive body of research has emerged to investigate the characteristics and outcomes of disruptive innovation. While scholars may not consistently interpret these innovations in the same way, there is a consensus that they profoundly impact companies, industries, and societies. Notably, much of our understanding of disruptive innovation stems from developed economies, traditionally the primary source of such innovations. This special issue, however, concentrates on disruptive innovations within emerging economies. Disruptive innovation has gained increasing attention across various disciplines, from economics to engineering and technology (Christensen et al., 2018; Si and Chen, 2020; Siyal et al, 2021). This heightened interest is understandable, given the contemporary challenges faced by companies globally, including intense global competition, heightened market volatility, ever-changing consumer demands, and shortened product life cycles. Consequently, disruptive innovation and entrepreneurship based on disruptive innovation are increasingly recognized as strategic approaches for achieving sustainable company growth and competitiveness. Christensen (1997) initially proposed the theory of disruptive innovation, framing it as "disruptive technology." This concept suggests that as these technologies evolve, they gradually surpass dominant technologies in specific markets. It emphasizes that the winning technology may not necessarily be radical or superior, but rather emerges through social, economic, and political negotiation and selection processes. Companies that promptly adopt technologies destined for dominance tend to thrive, while those resisting or slow to adopt are more likely to face failure. The concept of disruptive technology expanded to include broader applications, such as disruptive product innovations and disruptive business model innovations (Christensen and Raynor, 2003; Markides, 2006; Hang et al., 2015). In recent years, disruptive technology and innovation have become integral to the study of entrepreneurship, with a primary application being the increasingly prevalent disruptive innovation technology/disruptive innovation-based entrepreneurial companies. Disruptive innovation is portrayed as a process rather than a mere outcome (Ansari et al., 2016; Christensen, 2006). It typically begins by targeting low-end or new markets, offering products or services with attributes inferior to those valued by mainstream consumers. However, these products still meet the needs of consumers in the low-end or new markets. The products created through disruptive innovation deviate from existing technological trajectories but continuously improve until they align with the needs of mainstream consumers and penetrate the mainstream market (Canham, B. K. 2023). The developmental process of disruptive innovation comprises two stages. In the entry stage, disruptive innovations in low-end or new markets are often overlooked by incumbents. These innovations attract underserved consumers by offering products or services with comparative advantages in specific attributes, avoiding direct competition with incumbents while gaining market space. In the transformation stage, the mainstream attributes of disruptive innovation products or services gradually improve through technological advancements or related processes until they attract mainstream consumers, securing a certain market share. Hoskisson et al. (2000) define emerging economies as low-income, rapid-growth countries relying on economic liberalization for primary growth. Disruptive innovation has played a pivotal role in the rapid growth (Siyal, Peng & Siyal., 2018), especially in countries like China and India, making it a significant focus in emerging economies (Bruton et al., 2013). Theoretical and practical exploration occurs not only in mature economies but also in emerging economies. This special issue aims to present fresh insights into disruptive innovation and innovation-based entrepreneurship in emerging economies, emphasizing research approaches that can transform academic studies on entrepreneurship and disruptive innovation, particularly in the context of emerging economies. Disruptive technology refers to an innovation that displaces an established technology, causing a significant shake-up in the industry or introducing a groundbreaking product that creates an entirely new market Cucino, V., Ferrigno, G., Crick, J., & Piccaluga, A. (2024); Siyal et al., 2021).. In the realm of business theory, a disruptive innovation not only establishes a new market and value network but eventually disrupts existing markets and value networks, displacing leading firms, products, and alliances. Any technology capable of displacing an established one by creating a new industry is deemed disruptive. By reshaping existing markets and creating new ones, disruptive technology provides customers and end-users with unparalleled access, empowerment, convenience, choice, and value. The primary focus of disruptive technology is to challenge established business models and bring about radical transformations in products and services (Evans, 2017). The term "Disruptive Technology" was initially introduced by Joseph Bower, a Harvard Professor, and Clayton Christensen, a businessman, in 1995 through their article titled "Disruptive Technologies: Catching the Wave." They defined disruptive technologies as those fundamentally departing from existing technologies, typically being less complicated, more accessible, and less expensive. Bower and Christensen highlighted the consistent pattern in business where leading companies fail to maintain their dominance when faced with technological or market changes. To stay competitive, these companies must extend their focus beyond satisfying small or emerging markets and concentrate on new technologies meeting the functional demands of mainstream customers (Cheeseman et al., 2020). Clayton Christensen expanded on this concept in his 1997 book, "The Innovator's Dilemma: When New Technologies Cause Great Firms to Fail." The book illustrates how even successful companies that seemingly do everything right can lose their market leadership or fail when new, unexpected competitors emerge and take over the market. Christensen categorized new technologies into two types: sustaining and disruptive. Sustaining technology relies on incremental improvements to an established technology, while disruptive technology, being less refined, often faces performance issues due to its novelty, appeals to a limited audience, and may lack a proven practical application. According to Brand Genetics (2013), large corporations are designed to work with sustaining technologies due to their knowledge of the market, proximity to customers, and established mechanisms for developing existing technology. However, they may struggle to capitalize on the potential efficiencies, cost-savings, or new marketing opportunities presented by low-margin disruptive technologies.

Figure 1. Clayton Christensen's The disruptive triad and entrepreneurship

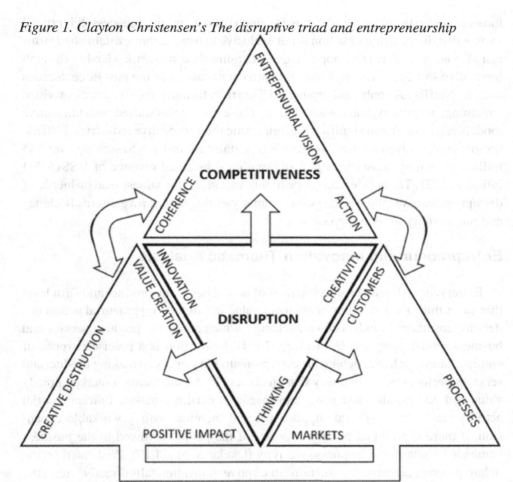

Figure 1 Source: https://doi.org/10.1186/s13731-021-00180-6

Disruptive innovation has emerged as a potent framework for conceptualizing growth driven by innovation, appealing to entrepreneurs, business leaders, and value-centric organizations. An innovation earns the disruptive label when it displaces established market leaders. Clayton Christensen, a prominent figure in this concept, defines disruptive innovation as a process where a product or service initially gains traction in simple applications at the bottom of the market, usually by being more affordable and accessible. Over time, it progressively ascends the market hierarchy, displacing established competitors. Contrary to breakthrough technologies enhancing already good products, disruptive innovations focus on making products and services more accessible and affordable, catering to a broader audience. Disruption occurs when these innovations not only meet the performance expectations of existing customers but also leverage the advantages gained from their initial success. It is crucial to note that disruptive innovation is not exclusive to new entrants; established firms can also adopt a disruptive approach, reaffirming their market leadership through innovative strategies. Examples of disruptive innovations in the past three decades include Netflix, Airbnb, and arguably Uber, transforming the dynamics of video streaming, hospitality, and transportation. These companies started with innovative models and have grown significantly, impacting their respective industries. Netflix, for instance, evolved from an online DVD rental store in 1998 to serving over 145 million streaming subscribers globally, with a substantial revenue of US$15.794 billion in 2021. The accelerating pace of innovation and the widespread influence of disruption are reshaping various value chains, yielding long-term gains in efficiency and productivity for entrepreneurs.

Entrepreneurship Innovation-Thematic Analysis

Entrepreneurship is the development of new relics at the product and firm level that substitutes long-standing with novel value through entrepreneurial action under circumstances of indecision and change, which applies to product, service and business-model prospects (McKelvey, 2004). Innovation is a precise purpose of entrepreneurship; hence defensible entrepreneurship centers on making product and services perform better in a way that customers in the mainstream market already value and address the next generation needs in existing market. Entrepreneurial activity can only be labeled supportable, and therefore satisfy workable expansion, if there is an equal coming together of the people involved in the business value chain, within the business creativity (Okeke et. al., 2019). Predicated on the Schumpeterian „creative destruction" disruptive innovation falls directly within the context of entrepreneurship study. Nevertheless, there is scarcity of investigation in this field that assumes an entrepreneurial view point. There are at least three significant components from entrepreneurship investigation that are not well agreed in the context of disruptive innovation: (1) the sources of opportunity (2) uncertainty in entrepreneurial action and (3) entrepreneurial logic. Entrepreneurial opportunity as a form of disruptive innovation can be term as radical rather than incremental in nature (Shane & Venkataraman, 2000; Eckhardt & Shane, 2003). This relates to product, service, while present-day investigation into disruptive innovation has made a difference between disruptive and sustaining innovation, a significant question has remained unreciprocated: the question of where an opening comes from, i.e., the cradles of entrepreneurial opportunity. Uncertainty is a vital constituent of the entrepreneurial theory of action (McMullen & Shepherd, 2006). Entrepreneurship investigation marks a difference between „risk", which is predictable and comprehensible, and „Knightian uncertainty" (or true uncertainty), which is unpredictable and incomprehensible (Miller, 2007)

Numerous studies, including those by Autio et al. (2014), Chang Chieh Hang et al. (2015a), Kenney (1986), Schumpeter & Opie (1961), Tilmes (2018), and Varis & Littunen (2010), have established strong connections between entrepreneurship and innovation. Schumpeter & Opie (1961) discussed the concept of creative destruction, emphasizing how entrepreneurs unleash disruptive products, services, and processes into the market, challenging and disrupting existing industrial conditions (Autio et al., 2014).The prevalence of disruptive technology, products, and business model innovations has intensified due to the ongoing process of digitalization. This increase has provided entrepreneurs and stakeholders with numerous opportunities, albeit accompanied by risks. The development of disruptive products and business model innovations can open new business opportunities for established entrepreneurs, offering access to untapped markets. However, this development may also lead to reduced market shares and profit margins for established entrepreneurs as competitors, both new and established, introduce their own disruptive products (Kay et al., 2018). A significant challenge for well-established entrepreneurs is coping with the rapid changes in the market brought about by both incumbent and newcomer firms. The continuous activities of these firms, driven by profit motives and organizational objectives, contribute to market dynamism (Andersson & Eriksson, 2018). Disruptive innovation's comprehensive and indiscriminate nature influences market variations, affecting entrepreneurs and firms in diverse ways. The impact extends to the means of value creation, customer preferences, and the overall market landscape (Bleicher & Stanley, 2016; Kagermann, 2015; Loebbecke & Picot, 2015). Therefore, enhancing entrepreneurs' knowledge about disruptive technology, product, and business model innovation becomes crucial (Chang Chieh Hang et al., 2015a). Technological change and innovations have significantly improved the productivity and efficiency of entrepreneurs. As per Christensen (1997), technological changes can be either sustaining or disruptive. Sustaining innovations support existing business practices and technological standards, whereas disruptive innovations focus on reshaping markets, industries, and enterprises. Disruptive technology and innovation literature often emphasize the displacement of long-established businesses to favor the entry of new players into the market. Disruptive innovations offer new businesses the opportunity for seamless market entry and domination, while established businesses must adapt their strategies to keep pace with evolving market trends or face displacement (Feder, 2018). Considering the pivotal role of business and entrepreneurs in any economy, managing the versatility of evaluating and utilizing opportunities brought about by disruptive technologies and business model innovation is of utmost importance. Existing empirical evidence and studies exploring the major disruptive technologies and the entrepreneurial competencies influencing successful implementation are limited. Consequently, this study aims to scrutinize the major disruptive innovations and competencies employed by entrepreneurs and firms to achieve entrepreneurial and business objectives. The study seeks to ascertain how disruptive innovation can provide a competitive advantage for business entrepreneurs and delineate the importance and benefits entrepreneurs and companies derive from embracing disruptive innovation.

Hardman et al. (2013) defines disruptive innovation as innovations that are so different that their establishment in the market disrupts the pre-existing system. Their work was centered around the ability of new technologies to penetrate the market, that is, whether or not a technology is potentially disruptive. Existing literature highlight historical case studies of successful technologies which provided seven characteristics of disruptive technologies at the stage of market penetration (Pathak, M. D., Kar, B., & Panda, M. C. 2022). A three-part criterion to define disruptive technologies was proposed by the authors which include relation of disruption to manufacturers and infrastructure while innovation must provide more than the equivalence of service to the end-users. These seven characteristics gotten as a review of successful historic technologies where then used to as a yardstick to measure the possibility of emerging technologies which include battery-electric and hydrogen fuel cell vehicles and the result was similar to what was seen during the review of other historic innovations in terms of market penetration challenges, but it also identified more prominent ways to aid higher market penetration of the technologies. In (Guo et al., 2018), the authors consider disruptive innovation as challenging, especially when it comes to assessment. In other to address the issue, a multidimensional measurement framework was presented. The framework considered three aspects to disruptive innovation which includes market place dynamics, external environments, and technological features, and it was tested using three different innovations to ascertain the viability of the framework. Hence, the study provides perceptions when it comes to product launch and resource allocation regarding disruptive innovation potentials even though a larger sample size was not considered in testing the framework. Chang Chieh Hang et al. (2015a) consider disruptive innovations and entrepreneurial opportunities with an emphasis on the importance and opportunities of disruptive innovation in both emerging and advanced economies. A case study showcasing how entrepreneurs have undertaken disruptive innovations for customers of low-end and new markets was provided. According to Brattstr et al. (2018) considers strength and weakness in innovation by highlighting the importance of innovation auditing; they believed that the audit framework that exists are not sufficient because they lack significant trends which include openness, servitization, and digitalization; hence they proposed a revised innovation audit framework which comprises of these trends.

A significant aspect of technological innovation that has evolved drastically and has also become an essential practice is the concept of disruptive innovation theory which was propagated by Christensen in 1997. The disruptive innovation theory has brought about a noteworthy influence on management practices in various organizations as well as sufficient stimulated debate within the academia (Yu & Hang, 2010). Five-dimensional factors that drive disruption include cost, quality, customers, regulation, and resources. In 2003, Christensen and Raynor replaced the term disruptive technology with disruptive innovation this was because they broadened the use of the theory to include both technological and non-technological products, services and business models innovation like online businesses education, discount department stores (Yu & Hang, 2010); Markides, (2006) argued that technological innovations were diverse from business model innovations and requested a better way of categorization within the sphere of disruptive innovation.

In the background of disruption, innovation and technology can be referred to as a transformation that makes existing processes, services, or products futile. Whilst disruptive innovation is defined as the commercial introduction of product or service Simms, C., McGowan, P., Pickernell, D., Vazquez-Brust, D., & Williams, A. (2022) that disrupts activities of existing services in an industry or system. Disruptive innovation can occur at various levels such as industry segment, industry structure, and social system. Millar et al. (2018) defined disruptive technology as a technology with the possibility to create disruptive innovation at any of the levels of disruptive innovation. Disruptive technologies are those technologies that deliver standards different from the conventional type of technologies; they are initially inferior to those technologies especially in terms of performance which is of utmost importance to the consumers (Yu & Hang, 2010).

Nagy et al., (2016) highlight and addresses three vital questions regarding innovations that forestall academics from helping managers find out if a new technology is a disruptive innovation to their organization. These questions include the meaning of disruptive innovation, how disruptive innovation can be disruptive to some and yet supporting to others, finally how disruptive innovations can be identified before a disruption occurs. They further proposed a heuristic to determine whether an innovation could be disruptive through the relative nature characteristics of the innovation. Reinhardt & Gurtner, (2018) discussed the overlooked role of embeddedness in the disruptive innovation theory, defining embeddedness as the degree to which a product is anchored in the social, market, and technological system of the user. They highlight embeddedness as a tool that would help understand the dynamics of disruptive innovations as a significant moderator that complements the theory. Considering disruptive innovation in low-income context, Nogami & Veloso, (2017) analyzed the concept of disruptive innovation in the low-income market. A theoretical review of disruptive innovation was done, and several challenges such as low income, budget instability which endangers financial planning. Solutions to penetrate low-income markets that include simplicity, the convenience of use and low prices was suggested. (Chang Chieh Hang et al., 2015a) considering disruptive innovations as essential in both developed and developing economies calls for a better understanding of opportunities provided by these disruptions. A study which shows how ambitious consumers from the low-end market and emerging industries have welcomed innovative technologies.

Major Disruptive Innovation Utilized by Entrepreneurs

Internet-of-things

The term *"Internet of Things"* was invented by Kevin Ashton in 1999 (Ashton, 2009). The idea is to make it easier for everyone to connect to all things through the Internet. This means, in theory, all cars, retailers, ticket providers and even the living spaces would compulsorily be linked to the internet, allowing more business to be automated in effect. In return, this will require more artificial system development based on intelligence. Investments are being pushed into IoT (Al-Fuqaha et al., 2015) so it can become the standard, and examples of such companies running with this (Atzori et al., 2010) include Intel. The disruptive potential of the IoT is possibly making it connect each of our devices to the Internet (Gasiorowski-Denis 2016). Though there are concerns concerning this development such as the rapid demand for the use of the internet, network and data security. Therefore, measures should be taken preceding the progress of IoT in specific countries in order to understand all these issues.

Cloud computing

This is can be defined as an action whereby the process is stored and maintained on the internet. NIST describes cloud computing as a model that enables a common pool of programmable computing resources to be accessible widely, flexibly, efficiently and quickly provided and released with minimal management effort and interaction." (Mell & Grance, 2011). Since its emergence, a number of fields have been disrupted and the computer service environment has changed constantly. Spotify, a service that downloads songs, revolutionised music consumption with the advent of IoT. The use of Spotify, however, includes the use of cloud computing to preserve its user data (Metz, 2016). Cloud enables global users to use the social service. For other purpose, such as training, storage and business purposes, more data will be available. But there are still concerns. For starters, protection and confidentiality of cloud computing information. Research should therefore be undertaken to deal with the problem.

Blockchain

It is the major feature that led to Bitcoin 's success, originally written as Block Chain. Lou Carlozo states the blockchain is a decentralized database archive that is publicly available and often updated. This transaction was made publicly and experts considered it difficult to corrupt. Instead Lou reiterates the concept of Blockchain by describing it as a database of business records carried out in chains. A major reason this technology is very successful is because it provides financial transactions without a third - party intermediary being involved in the transaction. The Bitcoin's volatile function generates a disruptive technology which is the distributed ledger system.

This is different from the current online payment where the banking or other payment methods are supposed to intervene. It is recorded that more than 24 countries currently participate in blockchain study at the 2016 World Economic Forum, and that more than 25000 blockchain patents have been filed since 2013. The disruptive effect of blockchain is evident with over 1.4 billion investments for technology in the past three years. Recently, however, Blockchain was discussed and used in other areas. In addition to its current primary use of bitcoins, the development of IoT and Artificial Intelligence suggests that the potential of blockchain would spread to other areas. There are more discussions elsewhere. The challenge, however, is that a great deal of cooperation between the financial service provider, government and developer is necessary for security purposes for future work to ensure that the distributed headline is done correctly.

Bitcoin

In 2008, the paper "*Bitcoin A Peer-to-Peer Electronic Cash System*" was published by Satoshi Nakamoto launching the Bitcoin phenomenon globally (Satoshi Nakamato, 2013). It was subsequently revealed publicly, where the name is a pseudonym to the Bitcoin creator, which may consist of one person or group (Segendorf, 2014). It is a digital money transaction, cryptocurrency, that does not have a Central Authority or an issuer (Reid and Harrigan 2013). Their cryptocurrency nature means that they use the encryption which, in turn, makes a secure transaction possible, without third parties. Many experiments have been carried out since its induction. In a Forbes article (Bovaird, 2017) the total market cap of Bitcoin reached $100 billion. Google's findings of the searches related to its name show the major promise of Bitcoin. The Google Trends results of Bitcoin searches on 11 November 2017 demonstrated that search growth has risen by more than 300 per cent since 11 October 2015 with the buzz revolving around 4IR. In his article, Marc Andreessen pointed out that Bitcoin has many advantages, such as micropayment and anti-spam capability (Andreessen, 2014). The perturbing innovation feature of Bitcoin led to the creation of another perturbing innovation called Blockchain, covered in the next paragraph. A peer-reviewed journal called Ledger, which primarily discussed cryptocurrency and Bitcoin, was published in the year. However, several Bitcoin concerns, including privacy and safety risks during application use should be discussed.

Entrepreneurial Competencies Adopted for the Achievement of a Successful Disruptive Innovation

Competencies to create, promote or sustain disruptive innovations usually are not linear; there is no single strategy for how they are implemented or how they function.

Leapfrogging mindset

Leading disruptive innovation requires a strategy such as leapfrogging. This strategy involves achieving a new or different thing that makes a significant step forward. Leapfrog mindset is a strategy adopted by entrepreneurs to beat the market leaders (existing incumbents) in the business environment by engaging in a massive leap of intelligence that brings in extraordinary growth and an increase in profit. This is a strategy that assumes that a market challenger will bypass the market leader and takes over the non-existing consumers and eventually the existing consumers of the market leader. For the market challenger to gain great strides, the market challenger must have game-changing knowledge and technology that is better in every way possible to that of its competitors. adopt a strong commitment to create breakthroughs and add new levels of value to the market (Kaplan, 2012; Mike, 2019; Serradell- López, 2019).

Boundary pushing

This is very vital to an entrepreneur that works with different people who have diverse talents. This leads to the development of creative problem-solving skills. This involves the continuous push of the limits of their team member to broaden their mind to create new opportunities (Mike, 2019; Serradell-López, 2019).

Data-intuition integration

Entrepreneurs require data to make vital decisions. In most cases, robust and rigid data in the event of disruption are not usually available for them to take decisions. However, they have to use all available information from various sources and use impulses to comfortably find answers to existing opportunities. (Mike, 2019; Serradell-López, 2019).

Adaptive planning

It calls for incredible levels of insecurity. It is also a way to achieve efficiency through repeating corrective actions. We understand them, and then we change hypotheses and methods in the same way. Whether these results are large or terrible, they will usually get closer to the leap, as the result is generally new perceptions. These new perceptions shape our future activities, which are inevitably better adapted to market needs. (Mike, 2019; Serradell-López, 2019).

Savoring surprise

Disruptive innovation is an unexpected process that might include technological advances, customer feedback, business trends, political and supervisory movements, and other usually unexpected events and planned changes. Most businesses believe surprises should be avoided. Entrepreneurs who view surprises as an unavoidable part of the procedure are best prepared to use them as an analytical tool to make them the most active and effective organizations to capitalize on unexpected events. Based on this increasingly disruptive competitive environment, entrepreneurs that are able to differentiate themselves and their organizations must gain new capabilities (Serradell-López, 2019). Also, the introduction of virtual collaborations, technological convergence, integration into a universal hierarchy and the development of online communities are some strategies required by entrepreneurs in the company that may be employed to incorporate disruptive innovation (Allen, 2018). (Denning, 2013).

Gemici & Alpkan (2015) noted the practical effects of new technology for the company's members. One strategy that is identified is the management of both traditional and new technology business models, and best of all if traditional and disruptive business models differ in their costs and revenue structures. The authors suggested that business leaders should react with flexibility in their strategy plans to disruptive innovations, taking into account all external and internal factors. In today's fast-paced business landscape, disruptive technologies and innovative business models are reshaping industries, challenging traditional norms, and creating new opportunities for growth and success. Embracing these transformative forces has become essential for companies striving to stay competitive and relevant in the digital age. This article explores the concept of disruptive technologies and business models, their impact on various industries, and how companies can harness their potential for sustainable growth and long-term success.

Understanding Disruptive Technologies

Disruptive technologies are innovations that fundamentally transform the business landscape by replacing established methods and systems with more efficient, cost-effective, and scalable alternatives. These technologies often introduce ground-breaking concepts that challenge existing paradigms, compelling organizations to adapt or face the risk of becoming obsolete. One of the defining characteristics of disruptive technologies is their ability to scale rapidly, allowing them to serve a broad range of markets and applications. Additionally, they are typically more accessible and affordable compared to traditional solutions Haider, M., Shannon, R., Moschis, G. P., & Autio, E. (2023)., which facilitates their widespread adoption and integration. This transformative impact is evident across various sectors; for instance, blockchain technology has revolutionized data security and transparency, while artificial intelligence has driven advancements in automation and data analytics. By disrupting the status quo, these technologies not only prompt businesses to rethink their strategies but also drive a culture of continuous innovation and improvement. Companies must navigate the challenges and opportunities presented by such disruptions, adopting agile and adaptive approaches to harness their full potential and maintain a competitive edge in an ever-evolving market.

Examples of Disruptive Technologies

Several technologies have disrupted industries, transforming the way business is conducted. One notable example is "Blockchain", which revolutionized data security and transparency in financial services, supply chain management, and other sectors. Another powerful disruptor is "Artificial Intelligence", driving advancements in automation, customer service, and data analytics across various industries. Several technologies have profoundly disrupted industries, reshaping business operations and methodologies. One prominent example is **Blockchain**, a decentralized ledger technology that has revolutionized data integrity and transparency across financial services, supply chain management, and other sectors. Blockchain's immutable ledger and consensus algorithms enhance data security, reduce fraud, and enable real-time transaction verification, creating trustless systems where intermediaries are minimized. This technology facilitates **smart contracts**, which automate and enforce contractual agreements without the need for traditional enforcement mechanisms.

Another significant disruptor is **Artificial Intelligence (AI)**, which encompasses a range of technologies including **machine learning**, **natural language processing (NLP)**, and **computer vision**. AI drives advancements in automation by employing algorithms that enable machines to learn from data and perform tasks that typically require human intelligence. In customer service, AI-powered **chatbots** and **virtual assistants** provide instant support and personalized experiences, leveraging NLP to understand and respond to user inquiries. In data analytics, AI utilizes **predictive analytics** and **deep learning** to uncover insights and trends from large datasets, facilitating data-driven decision-making and strategic planning. These technologies collectively enhance operational efficiency, optimize processes, and create new value propositions, fundamentally altering traditional business models and driving industry-wide transformation.

The Role of Disruption in Business

Disruption serves as a powerful catalyst for innovation, fundamentally altering the business landscape by compelling organizations to reevaluate and transform their strategies, products, and services. As disruptive technologies and market shifts challenge conventional business practices, companies are driven to seek out and implement creative solutions to address evolving consumer demands and preferences. This process of adaptation is not merely a response to change but a proactive approach that fosters a culture of innovation and continuous growth. The essence of disruption lies in its ability to challenge the status quo. Traditional business models often rely on established procedures and incremental improvements. However, when faced with disruptive forces—such as new technologies, shifting market trends, or evolving consumer behaviors—these conventional approaches may no longer suffice. Disruption forces organizations to abandon outdated methods and explore novel ways of operating. This shift necessitates a fundamental rethinking of how businesses approach their value propositions, operational processes, and customer engagement strategies. One of the most significant impacts of disruption is its ability to stimulate creative problem-solving. For instance, when a disruptive technology like blockchain or artificial intelligence enters the market, it introduces new possibilities and challenges existing norms. Companies must innovate to harness these technologies effectively, often leading to the development of new products, services, or business models. This environment of constant change and competition encourages businesses to think outside the box and explore unconventional solutions that may not have been considered under more stable conditions. The drive for innovation brought about by disruption also contributes to a culture of continuous improvement. In a rapidly changing business environment, complacency can be detrimental. Companies that embrace disruption are more likely to foster an organizational culture that values experimentation, learning, and agility. Hussain, M., Rasool, S. F., Xuetong, W., Asghar, M. Z., & Alalshiekh, A. S. A. (2023). This mindset encourages employees to contribute new ideas, challenge existing practices, and seek ways to enhance organizational performance. By integrating innovation into their core values, businesses can remain competitive and responsive to market dynamics. Moreover, disruption often leads to the creation of entirely new market segments and opportunities. As traditional industries are disrupted, new niches and demands emerge, providing fertile ground for entrepreneurial ventures and innovative solutions. For example, the rise of the gig economy, driven by digital platforms and apps, has created new opportunities for freelance work and on-demand services. Companies that can identify and capitalize on these emerging trends are better positioned to gain a competitive edge and achieve sustainable growth. embracing disruption also comes with its challenges. Organizations must navigate the uncertainties and risks associated with adopting new technologies and shifting their operational paradigms. This requires not only strategic foresight but also a robust change management framework to guide the transition. Effective leadership, clear communication, and stakeholder engagement are crucial for managing the impact of disruption and ensuring a smooth adaptation process. disruption plays a pivotal role in driving innovation within businesses. By challenging conventional approaches and pushing organizations to rethink their strategies and operations, disruption fosters a culture of creativity and continuous improvement. Companies that successfully navigate the challenges of disruption and leverage its opportunities are more likely to thrive in an increasingly dynamic and competitive marketplace. The ongoing drive for innovation and growth driven by disruptive forces underscores the need for businesses to remain agile, forward-thinking, and responsive to the ever-evolving landscape of their industries.

Traditional vs. Disruptive Business Models

Traditional business models focus on stability and incremental improvements, while disruptive business models prioritize agility and adaptability. Disruptive companies are more willing to take risks and embrace uncertainty, aiming for significant breakthroughs rather than gradual progress. This fundamental shift allows them to capture untapped markets and gain a competitive edge. The distinction between traditional and disruptive business models illustrates how different approaches to business operations and strategies can profoundly impact an organization's success and market position. Traditional business models, characterized by their focus on stability and incremental improvements, stand in stark contrast to disruptive models that prioritize agility, innovation, and significant breakthroughs. Understanding these differences is crucial for organizations seeking to navigate today's dynamic and competitive landscape.

Traditional Business Models are often built on established practices and incremental enhancements. These models emphasize stability, predictability, and efficiency, focusing on optimizing existing processes and leveraging established revenue streams. Companies operating under traditional models typically invest in refining their core products or services and gradually improving operational efficiencies to maintain a competitive edge. This approach often involves significant investments in physical infrastructure, long-term planning, and risk aversion. Traditional business models are generally designed to minimize disruptions and maintain steady growth by adhering to proven strategies and industry norms. A hallmark of traditional business models is their emphasis on **incremental innovation**. Changes and improvements are made gradually, with a focus on refining existing products or services rather than completely overhauling them. For example, a company manufacturing consumer electronics might focus on adding incremental features to its existing product lines rather than developing entirely new technologies. This approach is effective in maintaining existing market share and catering to well-established consumer needs but may fall short in rapidly evolving markets where agility and innovation are critical.

Disruptive business models challenge conventional approaches by introducing radical changes that significantly alter market dynamics. These models often leverage new technologies or innovative practices to create entirely new markets or redefine existing ones. Disruptive business models are characterized by their focus on **agility, scalability**, and **adaptability**. Companies employing disruptive models are more willing to embrace uncertainty and take calculated risks to achieve substantial breakthroughs. They prioritize rapid experimentation, customer-centric design, and the development of novel solutions that address unmet needs or create new opportunities.

A key feature of disruptive business models is their ability to deliver **transformative value**. This can involve leveraging cutting-edge technologies such as artificial intelligence, blockchain, or the Internet of Things (IoT) to create new products or services that fundamentally change consumer expectations. For instance, companies like Netflix and Uber have disrupted traditional industries by introducing innovative business models that leverage digital platforms and data analytics to offer more convenient and personalized services. Netflix's subscription-based streaming model replaced traditional cable TV, while Uber's ride-sharing platform transformed personal transportation. **Scalability** is another crucial aspect of disruptive business models. Unlike traditional models that may rely on physical assets and fixed costs, disruptive models often utilize digital platforms and cloud-based solutions that allow for rapid scaling and global reach. This scalability enables companies to reach broader markets and adapt quickly to changing consumer demands. **Customer-centricity** is also a hallmark of disruptive business models. Disruptive companies often focus on delivering exceptional customer experiences by leveraging data and technology to personalize their offerings and enhance engagement. This approach contrasts with traditional models that may prioritize operational efficiencies over customer satisfaction. adopting a disruptive business model comes with its own set of challenges. Companies must navigate **uncertainty** and **risk**, as disruptive strategies often involve significant investments in new technologies or business processes. Additionally, managing the transition from a traditional to a disruptive model requires effective change management, clear communication, and a willingness to embrace a culture of innovation and experimentation. while traditional business models emphasize stability and incremental improvement, disruptive models focus on agility, scalability, and transformative value. Organizations that can effectively leverage disruptive business models are better positioned to thrive in today's fast-paced and evolving market environment, capturing new opportunities and driving substantial growth.

Identifying Disruptive Opportunities

Market research is essential for identifying potential disruptive opportunities. Understanding consumer behavior, preferences, and pain points can reveal unmet needs that innovative technologies could address. Additionally, analyzing market trends and emerging technologies can help companies stay ahead of the curve. Staying competitive requires continuous monitoring of industry trends and competitor actions. By studying successful disruptive ventures and learning from their strategies, companies can identify gaps in the market and develop unique value propositions. Fostering a culture of innovation involves empowering employees to think creatively, take calculated risks, and share their ideas openly. Encouraging cross-functional collaboration and providing resources for experimentation can yield groundbreaking results. Adopting agile business strategies enables companies to respond quickly to market changes and consumer demands. By embracing flexibility and adaptability, businesses can pivot their models to leverage disruptive technologies effectively. Introducing disruptive technologies can face resistance from employees and stakeholders accustomed to traditional methods. Transparent communication, education, and involving all stakeholders in decision-making can mitigate resistance and foster buy-in. Disruptive environments can be unpredictable, requiring businesses to prepare for various scenarios. Scenario planning, risk assessments, and contingency strategies help companies navigate uncertainty and make informed decisions. Market research is a pivotal element in identifying and capitalizing on potential disruptive opportunities, as it offers a comprehensive understanding of consumer behavior, preferences, and pain points. By delving into these aspects, businesses can uncover unmet needs that innovative technologies or new business models could address, thus positioning themselves to seize emerging opportunities before their competitors. Analyzing market trends and keeping abreast of emerging technologies are crucial for staying ahead of the curve, allowing companies to anticipate shifts in consumer demands and adapt their strategies accordingly. This proactive approach helps in identifying nascent trends that could evolve into significant disruptions, giving companies a competitive edge.

Equally important is the continuous analysis of competitors and industry trends. Staying competitive requires vigilant monitoring of both direct competitors and broader industry movements. By studying successful disruptive ventures, companies can gain insights into effective strategies and innovative practices that can be emulated or adapted to fit their unique context. This involves not only tracking competitors' actions but also analyzing their responses to disruptive changes and learning from their successes and failures. Understanding how leading players are navigating disruption can reveal market gaps and opportunities for differentiation, enabling companies to develop unique value propositions that resonate with evolving consumer expectations. Embracing disruption necessitates a fundamental shift in how business models are approached and adapted. Creating a culture of innovation is essential for fostering an environment where disruptive ideas can thrive. (Ahmed, F., & Harrison, C. (2022, This involves empowering employees to think creatively, take calculated risks, and openly share their ideas. Encouraging cross-functional collaboration and providing resources for experimentation can yield groundbreaking results, as diverse perspectives and collaborative efforts often lead to innovative solutions. A culture that values and supports experimentation enables organizations to explore new possibilities and refine their approaches in response to market feedback and technological advancements. Adopting agile business strategies is another critical aspect of effectively embracing disruption. Agile methodologies emphasize flexibility and adaptability, allowing companies to respond swiftly to market changes and evolving consumer demands. This approach enables businesses to pivot their models, iterate on their strategies, and leverage disruptive technologies more effectively. By integrating agile principles, companies can enhance their responsiveness and resilience in the face of uncertainty, ensuring they remain competitive in a rapidly changing environment. Navigating the challenges and risks associated with disruption requires careful planning and management. One of the primary challenges is overcoming resistance to change, which can arise from employees and stakeholders accustomed to traditional methods. To address this, transparent communication is essential. Educating stakeholders about the benefits of disruptive technologies and involving them in the decision-making process can mitigate resistance and foster buy-in. Effective change management practices ensure that the transition to new technologies or business models is smooth and well-received, minimizing disruptions to ongoing operations.

Managing uncertainty in disruptive environments involves preparing for various scenarios and developing robust contingency strategies. Disruptive environments are often unpredictable, necessitating scenario planning and risk assessments to navigate potential challenges. Companies must anticipate different possible outcomes and devise strategies to address them, ensuring they are equipped to handle unexpected developments. This proactive approach to risk management enables businesses to make informed decisions and maintain stability amidst uncertainty. conducting thorough market research, analyzing competitors and industry trends, fostering a culture of innovation, adopting agile strategies, and managing challenges and risks are all integral to successfully navigating and leveraging disruptive opportunities. By understanding and anticipating market shifts, encouraging innovative thinking, and being adaptable in the face of change, companies can effectively embrace disruption, create new value propositions, and achieve sustained growth in a rapidly evolving business landscape.

Case Studies: Successful Disruption Stories

Netflix: Revolutionizing the Entertainment Industry

Netflix fundamentally disrupted the entertainment industry with its innovative approach to content delivery and consumption. By introducing an online streaming platform, Netflix challenged the traditional cable TV model, which was based on scheduled programming and linear channel bundles. Instead, Netflix offered a more flexible, on-demand viewing experience that allowed users to access a vast library of content anytime, anywhere, and on any device with internet connectivity. This shift from physical media and scheduled broadcasts to digital streaming represented a significant transformation in how audiences engage with entertainment. A key aspect of Netflix's disruption was its strategic use of data analytics. The company leverages sophisticated algorithms to analyze viewer preferences and behavior, which enables it to provide highly personalized content recommendations. This data-driven approach not only enhances user experience by suggesting relevant shows and movies based on individual viewing habits but also drives engagement and retention by keeping viewers hooked on content tailored to their interests. Netflix's recommendation engine became a cornerstone of its strategy, differentiating it from traditional cable providers who lacked similar capabilities for personalized content delivery. In addition to its data analytics prowess, Netflix's investment in producing original content played a crucial role in its rise to dominance. The company ventured into creating its own films and series, which allowed it to offer exclusive content not available on other platforms. This move not only attracted new subscribers but also helped build a strong brand identity and fostered a loyal customer base. Notable successes such as "House of Cards," "Stranger Things," and "The Crown" demonstrated Netflix's ability to create high-quality, engaging content that resonated with global audiences. By investing in original programming, Netflix not only reduced its reliance on external content providers but also set itself apart as a major content creator and distributor in the entertainment industry.

Netflix's approach to content production and distribution exemplifies how leveraging technology and data can disrupt traditional industries. Its success in transforming the entertainment landscape highlights the power of innovation in reshaping consumer behavior and industry standards. The platform's model of subscription-based streaming, combined with personalized recommendations and exclusive original content, revolutionized how people consume media and set new benchmarks for the entertainment sector. As a result, Netflix not only emerged as a dominant force in the market but also paved the way for other digital streaming services, further accelerating the shift away from traditional cable TV and redefining the future of entertainment.

Tesla: Transforming the Automotive Market

Tesla's electric vehicles disrupted the automotive industry, pushing for sustainable and eco-friendly transportation. Their innovative approach to design, performance, and battery technology transformed the perception of electric cars worldwide.

CONCLUSION

Exploring the nexus between entrepreneurial leadership and innovative disruption unveils how transformative changes are effectively driven and managed within industries. Entrepreneurial leadership, marked by visionary thinking, strategic risk-taking, and a relentless drive for innovation, is essential in navigating the complex landscape of disruptive technologies and market shifts. Leaders who excel in this role anticipate and embrace disruptive forces, leveraging them to gain a strategic advantage. They are adept at challenging existing paradigms, managing uncertainty, and fostering a culture that encourages creativity and agility. Disruptive innovation, characterized by the introduction of groundbreaking technologies or business models, fundamentally alters industry practices by offering more efficient, scalable, and accessible alternatives to traditional methods. Technologies such as artificial intelligence, blockchain, and digital platforms exemplify this transformative impact, creating new market opportunities and redefining consumer expectations. The synergy between entrepreneurial leadership and innovative disruption is pivotal for harnessing the potential of these changes. Visionary leaders identify and exploit disruptive opportunities, orchestrating strategic adjustments to integrate these innovations into their organizations. They cultivate an environment that supports experimentation, continuous learning, and creative problem-solving, which is crucial for adapting to rapid technological advancements and shifting market dynamics. Effective management of disruptive change involves strategic risk assessment and planning, balancing the rewards of innovation with the uncertainties it brings. Additionally, transformational change driven by entrepreneurial leaders often requires reconfiguring business models and processes to align with new market realities, ensuring that innovation is seamlessly embedded within organizational operations. Engaging stakeholders—including employees, customers, and partners—is also critical in managing disruption. Transparent communication and collaborative approaches help secure buy-in and facilitate smooth transitions, ensuring that the benefits of innovation are maximized while mitigating potential resistance. Overall, the interplay between entrepreneurial leadership and innovative disruption underscores the importance of dynamic leadership in shaping industry futures. Organizations that successfully integrate these elements are better positioned to navigate the complexities of disruption, capitalize on emerging opportunities, and maintain competitive advantages. As industries continue to evolve rapidly, leveraging entrepreneurial leadership to drive and manage innovative disruption will be crucial for achieving sustained success and growth.

REFERENCES

Ahmed, F., & Harrison, C. (2022, September). Innovation strategies of SMEs' entrepreneurial leaders: evidence from Pakistan. In *British Academy of Management Annual Conference 2022: Reimagining Business and Management as a Force for Good*. British Academy of Management.

Alsharif, N. Z. (2019). Disruptive innovation in pharmacy: An urgent call! *American Journal of Pharmaceutical Education*, 84(9), 1–10.

Andrevski, G., & Ferrier, W. J. (2019). Does it pay to compete aggressively? Contingent roles of internal and external resources. *Journal of Management*, 45(2), 1–50. DOI: 10.1177/0149206316673718

Arabeche, Z. (2020). Profil du dirigeant, Entrepreneuriat et performance: Cas de l'Algérie. *Al-riyada for Business Economics Journal*, 6(1), 139–156.

Aroyeun, T. F., Adefulu, A. D., & Asikhia, O. U. (2018). Effect of competitive aggressiveness on competitive advantage of selected small and medium scale enterprises in Ogun State Nigeria. *European Journal of Business and Management*, 10(35), 125–135.

Avram, B. (2019). Airlines customer segmentation in the hyper-competition era. *Expert Journal of Marketing*, 7(2), 137–143.

Boukella, M. (1996). *Les industries agro-alimentaires en Algérie: politiques, structures et performances depuis l'indépendance* (Vol. 19). CIHEAM, Cahiers Options Méditerranéennes.

Bourbouze, A. (2001). Le développement des filières lait au Maghreb; Algérie, Maroc, Tunisie: Trois images, trois stratégies différentes. *Agroligne*, 44, 1–14.

Brennan, N. M., Subramaniam, N., & van Staden, C. J. (2019). Corporate governance implications of disruptive technology: An overview. *The British Accounting Review*, 51(6), 1–15. DOI: 10.1016/j.bar.2019.100860

Caner, T., Bruyaka, O., & Prescott, J. E. (2016). Flow signals: Evidence from patent and alliance portfolios in the US biopharmaceutical industry. *Journal of Management Studies*, 55(2), 232–264. DOI: 10.1111/joms.12217

. Canham, B. K. (2023). Navigating complexity in an Internet of Things era: A case study of entrepreneurial leadership in a Silicon Valley IoT Startup.

Charreire, S., & Durieux, F. (1999). *Explorer et tester, Méthodes de recherche en management*. Dunod.

Chemma, N., & Arabeche, Z. (2018). Mutations and movements: What winning strategy in a turbulent environment? A comparison of two Algerian actors settled in the light of their behaviour and attitudes. *Moroccan Journal of Research in Management and Marketing*, 18, 78–98.

Chen, J., Chen, T., Chen, T. W., & Chen, M. J. (2019). Rock the boat: Competitive repertoire rhythm and interfirm rivalry. *Academy of Management Journal*, 22(1), 1–6.

Chen, M. J., & Miller, D. (2015). Reconceptualizing competitive dynamics: A multidimensional framework. *Strategic Management Journal*, 36(5), 758–775. DOI: 10.1002/smj.2245

Cherfaoui, A. (2003). Essai de diagnostic stratégique d'une entreprise publique en phase de transition, Master of science,62, Centre international deshautes études agronomiques méditerranéennes de. France: Montpellier.

Cucino, V., Ferrigno, G., Crick, J., & Piccaluga, A. (2024). Identifying entrepreneurial opportunities during crises: A qualitative study of Italian firms. *Journal of Small Business and Enterprise Development*, 31(8), 47–76. DOI: 10.1108/JSBED-04-2023-0159

D'Aveni, R. A., Dagnino, G. B., & Smith, K. G. (2010). The age of temporary advantage. *Strategic Management Journal*, 31(13), 1371–1385. DOI: 10.1002/smj.897

Dinesh, K. K., & Sushil, N. A. (2019). Strategic innovation factors in startups: Results of a cross-case analysis of Indian startups. *Journal for Global Business Advancement*, 12(3), 449–470. DOI: 10.1504/JGBA.2019.10022956

Flor, M. L., Cooper, S. Y., & Oltra, M. J. (2018). External knowledge search, absorptive capacity and radical Innovation in high technology firms. *European Management Journal*, 36(2), 183–194. DOI: 10.1016/j.emj.2017.08.003

Haider, M., Shannon, R., Moschis, G. P., & Autio, E. (2023). How has the covid-19 crisis transformed entrepreneurs into sustainable leaders? *Sustainability (Basel)*, 15(6), 5358. DOI: 10.3390/su15065358

Hammoud, K., & Abdallah, J. (2019). Empirical analysis on strategy and hyper - competition with Smes. Proceeding of the international management conference. Academy of Economic Studies, 13(1), 951–960.

Hanson, K. T., & Tang, V. T. (2020). Perspectives on disruptive innovations and Africa's services sector. In Arthur, P., Hanson, K., & Puplampu, K. (Eds.), *Disruptive technologies, innovation and development in Africa*. International Political Economy Series. Palgrave Macmillan. DOI: 10.1007/978-3-030-40647-9_12

Hassan, S., Mir, A. A., & Khan, S. J. (2023). Digital entrepreneurship and emancipation: Exploring the nexus in a conflict zone. *International Journal of Emerging Markets*, 18(10), 4170–4190. DOI: 10.1108/IJOEM-07-2021-1076

Hughes-Morgan, M., Kolev, K., & Macnamara, G. (2018a). A meta-analytic review of competitive aggressiveness research. *Journal of Business Research*, 85, 73–82. DOI: 10.1016/j.jbusres.2017.10.053

Hughes-Morgan, M., Kolev, K., & Mcnamara, G. (2018b). A meta-analytic review of competitive aggressiveness research. *Journal of Business Research*, 85, 73–82. DOI: 10.1016/j.jbusres.2017.10.053

Hussain, M., Rasool, S. F., Xuetong, W., Asghar, M. Z., & Alalshiekh, A. S. A. (2023). Investigating the nexus between critical success factors, supportive leadership, and entrepreneurial success: Evidence from the renewable energy projects. *Environmental Science and Pollution Research International*, 30(17), 49255–49269. DOI: 10.1007/s11356-023-25743-w PMID: 36764994

Indrianti, Y., Abdinagoro, S. B., & Rahim, R. K. (2024). A resilient Startup Leader's personal journey: The role of entrepreneurial mindfulness and ambidextrous leadership through scaling-up performance capacity. *Heliyon*, 10(14), e34285. DOI: 10.1016/j.heliyon.2024.e34285 PMID: 39113945

Jamak, A. B. S. A., Ali, R. M. M., & Ghazali, Z. (2014). A breakout strategy model of Malay, Malaysian Indigenous, micro-entrepreneurs. *Procedia: Social and Behavioral Sciences*, 109, 572–583. DOI: 10.1016/j.sbspro.2013.12.509

Kaci, M., & Sassi, Y. (2007). *Industrie laitière et des corps gras, fiche sous sectorielle, rapport ED pme*.

Kiduff, G. J. (2019). Interfirm relational rivalry: Implications for competitive strategy. *Academy of Management Review*, 44(41), 775–799. DOI: 10.5465/amr.2017.0257

. Kim, C. W., & Mauborgne, R. (2015). Blue ocean strategy. Boston Massachusetts: Harvard business review press.

Le, P. B., & Lei, H. (2018). The effects of innovation speed and quality on differentiation and low-cost competitive advantage: The case of Chinese firms. *Chinese Management Studies*, 12(2), 305–322. DOI: 10.1108/CMS-10-2016-0195

Leavy, B. (2018). Value innovation and how to successfully incubate "blue ocean" initiatives. *Strategy and Leadership*, 46(3), 10–20. DOI: 10.1108/SL-02-2018-0020

Lehmann-Ortega, L., Musikas, H., & Schoettl, J.-M. (2017). (Ré)inventez votre Business Model - 2e éd. Dunod.

Lehmann-Ortega, L., & Schoettl, J.-M. (2005). From buzzword to managerial tool: the role of business model in strategic innovation. In CLADEA Retrieved from: http://www.businessmodelcommunity.com/fs/root/8jvaa-businessmodelsantiago.pdf

Linyiru, B. M., & Ketyenya, R. P. (2017). Influence of competitive aggressiveness on performance of state corporations in Kenya. *International Journal of Entrepreneurship*, 2(1), 1–14.

Liu, W., Liu, R., Chen, H., & Mboga, J. (2020). Perspectives on disruptive technology and innovation: Exploring conflicts, characteristics in emerging economies. *International Journal of Conflict Management*, 31(3), 313–331. DOI: 10.1108/IJCMA-09-2019-0172

Markides, C. (1997). Strategic innovation. *Sloan Management Review*, 39(3), 9–23.

Pathak, M. D., Kar, B., & Panda, M. C. (2022). Chaos and complexity: Entrepreneurial planning during pandemic. *Journal of Global Entrepreneurship Research*, 12(1), 1–11. DOI: 10.1007/s40497-022-00306-4

Simms, C., McGowan, P., Pickernell, D., Vazquez-Brust, D., & Williams, A. (2022). Uncovering the effectual-causal resilience nexus in the era of Covid-19: A case of a food sector SME's resilience in the face of the global pandemic. *Industrial Marketing Management*, 106, 166–182. DOI: 10.1016/j.indmarman.2022.08.012

Siyal, M., Siyal, S., Wu, J., Pal, D., & Memon, M. M. (2021). Consumer perceptions of factors affecting online shopping behavior: An empirical evidence from foreign students in China. [JECO]. *Journal of Electronic Commerce in Organizations*, 19(2), 1–16. DOI: 10.4018/JECO.2021040101

. Siyal, S. (2018). Does Leadership lessen turnover of public servants. The moderated mediation effect of leader member exchange and perspective taking [EBSCO open dissertations].

Siyal, S. (2023). Inclusive leadership and work engagement: Exploring the role of psychological safety and trust in leader in multiple organizational context. *Business Ethics, the Environment & Responsibility*, 32(4), 1170–1184. DOI: 10.1111/beer.12556

Siyal, S., Liu, J., Ma, L., Kumari, K., Saeed, M., Xin, C., & Hussain, S. N. (2023). Does inclusive leadership influence task performance of hospitality industry employees? Role of psychological empowerment and trust in leader. *Heliyon*, 9(5), e15507. DOI: 10.1016/j.heliyon.2023.e15507 PMID: 37153410

Siyal, S., & Peng, X. (2018). Does leadership lessen turnover? The moderated mediation effect of leader–member exchange and perspective taking on public servants. *Journal of Public Affairs*, 18(4), e1830. DOI: 10.1002/pa.1830

Siyal, S., Peng, X., & Siyal, A. W. (2018). Socioeconomic analysis: A case of Tharparkar. *Journal of Public Affairs*, 18(4), e1847. DOI: 10.1002/pa.1847

Siyal, S., Xin, C., Umrani, W. A., Fatima, S., & Pal, D. (2021). How do leaders influence innovation and creativity in employees? The mediating role of intrinsic motivation. *Administration & Society*, 53(9), 1337–1361. DOI: 10.1177/0095399721997427

Chapter 7
Institutional Environment and Sustainability in Entrepreneurship Ecosystems

José G. Vargas-Hernandez
https://orcid.org/0000-0003-0938-4197
Tecnológico Nacional de México, ITS Fresnillo, Mexico

Francisco J. Gonzàlez-Àvila
Tecnológico Nacional de México, ITS Fresnillo, Mexico

Omar C. Vargas-González
https://orcid.org/0000-0002-6089-956X
Tecnológico Nacional de México, Ciudad Guzmán, Mexico

Selene Cstañeda-Burciaga
https://orcid.org/0000-0002-2436-308X
Universidad Politécnica de Zacatecas, Mexico

Omar A. Guirette-Barbosa
https://orcid.org/0000-0003-1336-9475
Universidad Politécnica de Zacatecas, Mexico

ABSTRACT

This study analyzes the implications of institutional environment and sustainability on entrepreneurship ecosystems. It is assumed in a complex, uncertain and turbulent institutional environmental sustainability affects the development of national, regional, and local entrepreneurship ecosystems. The method employed is the meta-

DOI: 10.4018/979-8-3693-0078-7.ch007

analysis and reflective based on the theoretical, conceptual, and empirical review of the literature. It is concluded that the institutional environmental sustainability influences the national, regional, and local entrepreneurship ecosystems.

INTRODUCTION

There are not studies to analyze the entrepreneurship intention to develop entrepreneurship ecosystems in a knowledge intensive, innovative, and digitalized environment and sustainable entrepreneurship ecosystems. Entrepreneurship ecosystems is affected by the organizational environment in which the ecosystem operates (Mustafa *et al.*, 2019; Ghosh *et al.*, 2021; Piccolo *et al.*, 2021).

The entrepreneurship ecosystem has been a contextual turn in organizational and entrepreneurship studies drawing attention to forces in local environments in specific boundary conditions environmental munificence. Entrepreneurship ecosystems theory differentiates from systems theory because this one is less concerned with the ecological relationships between the organisms and the environment. The resulting theoretical contributions and empirical evidence of the entrepreneurship ecosystems and initiatives are underdeveloped and with differences among the spatial and environmental sustainability differences (Cao & Shi, 2020).

It should be noted that the theory of business ecosystems has not yet been able to provide a complete explanation of how organizational strategies are developed and organized in companies that are located in environments that demonstrate different types of environmental sustainability and that can influence the decisions made by the company. Such as in cases of resource -poor, unmunificent and without any access to local knowledge, investments, etc. (Xu & Dobson, 2019; Siyal, 2023; Siyal, 2018; Siyal & Peng, 2018).

The individual environment in entrepreneurship ecosystems theory creates opportunities to expand the explanatory power of micro-foundations of strategic foundations beyond the predominant macro-dynamics focus that do not explain the connectivity between entrepreneurship, ecosystems, capital ventures. The probability of opportunistic or craftsman entrepreneurship success to external environment influencing profitability, survival and scalability in entrepreneurship ecosystems and entrepreneurship ventures.

Since the declarations for institutional sustainability science developed during the 1990s a variety of programs have been developed at institutional sustainability science at academic and research institutions. *and Corporate Change*, 28, 4, 941–959. The limited analysis on university entrepreneurship to science commercialization activities and specific issues such as the operating agents in entrepreneurship actions in sub-optimal institutional environments to drive commercialization activities, engaging in regions with strategies *bypassing institutional mandates* (Johnson *et al.*, 2019; Lucas & Fuller, 2017; Pugh *et al.*, 2018).

Entrepreneurship ecosystem analysis and studies on corporate entrepreneurship, global entrepreneurship, venture financing, entrepreneurship cognition, social entrepreneurship and sustainability, women minority entrepreneurship, family business, entrepreneurial education, etc., are only some of the relevant topics (Kansheba, & Wald, 2020).

For policy to just attract anchor firms and create a supportive entrepreneurship institutional environment ensures the sustainable flow of knowledge in the entrepreneurship ecosystem. The Austrian entrepreneurial ecosystem involving a young generation in entrepreneurial activities in a friendly environment with government institutions promoting the establishment and expansion of new business. Austrian government supports an entrepreneurial friendly institutional environment in the establishment and expansion of business (Rezaei *et al.*, 2014, GEM, 2018)

Research is interested in study the influence focusing on the systematic, turbulent, complex and uncertain nature of entrepreneurship ecosystem and entrepreneurship ventures concepts and their interrelations with other contextual elements recognized as a community of stakeholders creating entrepreneurship environments reinforced by entrepreneurship policymaking (Cao & Shi, 2020). Research on entrepreneurship relationship between individual and organizational actors and their environments have effects on the entrepreneurship initiatives.

Research and science policy making at academic and scientific research institutions promote reforms on the sustainability science with new styles of scientific activities which have had limited impact due to lack of capacities to accomplish task-consuming tasks related to modes of ethical and transdisciplinary research. The entrepreneurship ecosystem concept becomes a reference out of the seminal work of Isenberg (2011) as a cost-effective strategy to stimulate economic prosperity reacting to policy failures to withdrawn of entrepreneurship, lacking clear objectives, depreciation as a career and supported self-sustained entrepreneurship, omitting causal paths.

Hybrid academic and extra-academic collaborative and participative institutional sustainability research programs have been established at academic and research institutions with promising results in integrating sustainability issues through experiential learning, developing methodologies, and fostering collaboration partnerships with other stakeholders.

Transdisciplinary institutional sustainability science research engages fellowships and professorships in initiatives at academic and research institutions making relevant contributions but rarely are connected to institutional transformation and reform processes despite that several institutional initiatives have been launched to overcome the fragmentation, such as global networks to broaden community building such as European Sustainability Science Group (ESSG) (Brousseau *et al.*, 2012).

The analysis of implications between the turbulent, complex and uncertain institutional environmental sustainability influences the entrepreneurship ecosystems is carried out through the meta-study of the institutional environment and sustainability as variables. First, it is analyzed the institutional environment followed by the sustainability. Finally, some conclusions are offered.

INSTITUTIONAL ENVIRONMENT

The term ecosystem created by Tansley (1935) refers to the interactive nature between organisms and their environment. It also refers to a biological community group (Acs *et al.*, 2017). Now a business ecosystem can be understood as the set of organizations, institutions and even processes that are connected to each other, either formally or informally, which come together to mediate organizational performance in the local environment. An entrepreneurship ecosystem is defined as the composition of mutually dependent but coordinated factors forming a creative environment for entrepreneurship. Entrepreneurship ecosystem is a bundle of organized factors and actors interacting to develop favorable environments towards entrepreneurship activities as a natural output (Stam, 2015).

The concepts related to entrepreneurship contexts preceded entrepreneurship ecosystems including the concepts of entrepreneurship ecosystem environments, systems. Entrepreneurial communities, triple helix, infrastructure and so on Lyons *et al.*, 2012). Supporting environmental sustainability is indispensable for the business ecosystem in the form of natural resources.

On the other hand, the conditions of the business framework at the macro level reflect the entrepreneurial ecosystem as an exogenous environment, which allows an analysis of the impact of the context on the creation of new companies, taking into account policy conditions, infrastructure, financing programs, government policies and programs, as well as research and development transfer, in addition to taking into account issues related to education and training, and other social and cultural issues. Institutions affect individual entrepreneurship behavior and entrepreneurship activity and both influence the institutional environment overcoming its limitations (Lucas & Fuller, 2017).

The institutional framework affects the quality of institutions and the entrepreneurship ecosystem operationalized with a generic and a specific entrepreneurship indicator covering institutional environment (Boudreaux & Nikolaev, 2019; Webb *et al.*, 2019). Agent behavior in entrepreneurship action toward science commercialization activities manifests in the institutional mandates, in some cases manifesting institutional support to challenge institutional environment toward a systemic approach to entrepreneurship under conditions of limited institutional mandates (Klingbeil *et al.*, 2019).

The Global Entrepreneurship Monitor (GEM) Database is a large survey research on entrepreneurship ecosystems supported by a theoretical framework used to capture heterogenic, reliable, and comparable data on entrepreneurship environments and activities (Content *et al.* 2020; Hechavarria & Ingram, 2019). Entrepreneurship activities are superior at competitive levels in developed economy environments that in less competitive economies where the entrepreneurial spirit is encapsulated in structures of lower quality of entrepreneurship ecosystem (Ali, *et al.* 2015).

The growth of business ecosystems in complex and uncertain environments requires the support of stakeholders and all participating and active agents. Likewise, it is possible to recognize that an entrepreneurial ecosystem is made up of various elements, whether social, business or human, and that, in order to develop optimally, it is necessary to have support to grow in a turbulent, complex and uncertain environment that requires the cohesive support of the active agents. Complexity of entrepreneurship environment system us subject to transformational forces (Fredin & Lidén, 2020).

Evolutionary stages of entrepreneurship ecosystems environment in emerging and developed economies have not well researched (Guerrero *et al.* 2020). Organizational business growth is the result of a strong economic environment with increasing job opportunities, the interests on business and relationships among entrepreneurship activities and regional and local economic development. Environmental sustainability enablers such as disruptive ecological shifts and regulatory activities, led to the formation of local eco entrepreneurship ecosystem.

The complexity of organizational meso level influences the regional entrepreneurship ecosystems and environments through the alignment of elements between the individual activities at the micro level and the formal and informal institutions that create the rules at regional macro level. The traditional entrepreneurship ecosystems approach is related to an interconnected set of entrepreneurship stakeholders acting in regional environments and fostering engagement to contribute to prosperous regional economy (Bischoff, 2021).

Entrepreneurs take a self-starting an active approach spotting environmental sustainability opportunities and using vision, creativity, resourcefulness, and resilience leading to innovation and entrepreneurship initiatives conducting individuals to be more innovative and entrepreneurial and achieve better results on entrepreneurship ecosystems performance (Nsereko *et al.,* 2018). Entrepreneurship initiative is related to better environmental sustainability and ecosystems conditions as demonstrated by the empirical results.

Individuals have different personal characteristics to behave different in developing entrepreneurship initiatives and activities to develop individual behaviors and abilities to seize opportunities, acknowledge the environments and its effects on exploitation. The entrepreneurship ecosystem environment determines the occurrence of entrepreneurship influenced by a reciprocal relationship supported by the entrepreneurship behavior (Bischoff, 2021). Entrepreneurship skills and abilities creating opportunities to be used in environments to match personality traits.

The taxonomy of entrepreneurship environments shows the differences between the entrepreneurship ecosystems acknowledging the impact of the different factors influencing the entrepreneurship initiative. The connection between entrepreneurship ecosystems and entrepreneurship initiatives with the individual characteristics of entrepreneurs provide insights about differences between regions considered as external environments of organizational entrepreneurship initiatives with different combinations of elements and processes.

Environments affect the embedded entrepreneurial initiative dynamics with nexus between entrepreneurship ecosystems and entrepreneurship initiatives entangle with the individual characteristics of entrepreneurs. An elitist approach to the entrepreneurship ecosystem taxonomy considers that entrepreneurship environment is more influential in educated people while is not relevant for individuals who pursue entrepreneurship initiatives as a survival.

Other dimensions considered are the media and educational and financial institutions as essential in entrepreneurship ecosystem environments (Fellnhofer & Mueller, 2018; Krueger, 2017; Lehner & Harrer, 2019). Opportunistic entrepreneurs are highly skilled at analyzing the organizational environment, due to their management experience, education and the various sources of financing they can access.

An entrepreneurship ecosystem environment is friendlier in developing and emerging economies. The regional entrepreneurship ecosystems diversity of views suggests specific offerings inherent to multi-level involving and static elements that creates optimal environments for entrepreneurial actions and dynamic elements embodied in spillover impacts (Audretsch *et al.*, 2015). Focus on entrepreneurship ecosystems in a changing environment is a viable path. Internal factors, entrepreneurship, and the environment nurture the success of enterprise.

End-user entrepreneurship firms participate in ecosystems to access to resources, knowledge, technology, etc. that they may not be able to acquire and supporting the environment for applied research and innovation, new entrepreneurial practices and activities aimed to increase the initiatives for competitive advantages, the attractiveness and competitiveness of the territory (Siyal et al, 2021). Entrepreneurship ecosystems in developing countries find it difficult to survive in competitive environments which requires assessing the factors stressing the dimensions to promote entrepreneurships (Anwar ul Haq *et al.*, 2014).

Incubators disseminate concrete ideal of meaningful entrepreneurship in an uncertain and complex environment. Incubators develop an entrepreneurship culture influencing the mindset of entrepreneurs in a community with efficient startups enable to scale up fast in which time is crucial factor in uncertain environment.

Favorable environmental sustainability factors and external entrepreneurship culture motivate to undertake entrepreneurial venture, and start a new business influenced by feasibility and desirability resulting from the environmental sustainability factors knowledge. Entrepreneurship and knowledge are related to specific requirements in places, environments, and times to seize entrepreneurship opportunities and initiatives. Entrepreneurship ecosystems gain capabilities to achieve success in external environments as the primary source of businesses (Lehner & Harrer, 2019). Organizational networks of entrepreneurship ecosystems count on information regarding on environmental sustainability opportunities and threats.

Knowledge and technology transfer in the intellectual human capital improves the innovation activities of an organizational digitalized environment (Popkova *et al.*, 2021). Entrepreneurship ecosystems can explore and exploit different types of digital technologies to promote the creation and growth of new capital ventures which have a complementary crucial role to manage mechanisms for competitiveness by being pioneers, imitate followers, and facilitate digital disruptions in dynamic environments through transformative digital practices and activities.

Entrepreneurship ecosystem landscapes are determined by the environments and policies. Entrepreneurship ecosystems present different patterns in a dense landscape identified with entrepreneurship determinants of initiatives in each environment which are stimulated and promoted by entrepreneurship policies influencing the entrepreneurial action for growth (Pita *et al.*, 2021). Entrepreneurship policies develop a support system and cultural and social environments affecting the intentions to become entrepreneurship. Policymaking in conducive entrepreneurship ecosystem environment is expected to favor entrepreneurship ventures (Malen & Marcus 2017).

A regulative environment, institutional cognitive patterns and social normative systems local geographic communities have an influence on corporate social action. Qualitative grounded theory analysis may catalyze environmental sustainability regulatory changes toward the formation of the entrepreneurship ecosystem aimed to low-resourced eco entrepreneurship. Regulatory responses to environmental sustainability changes and shifts in the natural and regulatory environments enable the eco entrepreneurship development and venture creation activities. Regulatory enablement dimensions shift conditions to favor venture building (Juma, *et al.* 2023)

Design and implementation of supporting policymaking towards a global entrepreneurship leads local economies to manage entrepreneurship ecosystems despite the structural differences in local development and environments, expanding the action space and leveraging internal perspectives among the different realities (Guerrero, *et al.*, 2020; Kansheba, & Wald, 2020; Acs *et al.* 2017).

It should be noted that the organizational environment is changing due to the formulation and implementation of various policies aimed at the promotion and development for the adoption of new innovative digital technologies within the business ecosystems, which has generated digital entrepreneurship activities, causing a new business competitiveness (Zahra et al., 2023). This innovative shift in the entrepreneurship ecosystem environment gives rise to the concept of artificial intellectual capital (Popkova & Sergi, 2020; Ferraris *et al.*, 2020a, b). Intellectual capital and entrepreneurship ecosystems at organizational level boosting performance of new ventures but ignoring the facilitation in technological environments.

SUSTAINABILITY

The concept of entrepreneurship ecosystems is defined by Cohen (2006) the interconnected group of actors in the local geographic community who are committed to sustainable development by supporting and facilitating of new sustainable ventures. The entrepreneurship processes in building an ecosystem are affected by the interconnection of the external and internal conditions which maximize the creation, production, and development of sustainable entrepreneurship (Stam, 2015).

Integration and institutional sustainability issues declarations in academic and research institutions have been developed at international, national, and local scales. Institutional sustainability science as a function incorporates issues research, teaching and services and cross-institutional actions. Functions of entrepreneurship ecosystems such as creating, discovering and exploiting entrepreneurship opportunities are centered in the entrepreneur as the core agent and actor in building, developing and sustaining the ecosystem.

Emotional development is an essential capacity of entrepreneurship to strengthen self-esteem and moral autonomy leading to make the best decisions from among several options that require evaluation processes of social responsibility and commitment to global sustainability (Del Solar, 2010). Global sustainability is aligned with the agenda to tackle societal changes inducing individuals to get involved in sustainable entrepreneurship and enable transitions for competitive positions (Volkmann *et al*, 2021). The increasing pressures of societal changes such as poverty and inequality, climate change (UN report, 2021), are a priority to integrate traditional approaches to profit seeking with sustainable and human-centric perspectives. The static approach to entrepreneurship ecosystems ignores their origins, stimulus, and the self-sustained processes.

The global community is challenged by scarcity of natural resources, environmental sustainability, climate change, etc., leading to productive entrepreneurship practices and activities to find opportunities to foster a strategy of sustainable orientation behaviors. Another declaration at the global scale on the establishment of institutional sustainability science in 2002 is the Ubuntu Declaration on Education, Science and Technology for Sustainable Development signed by academic institutions (Van der Leeuw *et al.*, 2012).

Entrepreneurship policies may place relevance on the exploitation of entrepreneurship environments leading to create a transition to sustainable entrepreneurship ecosystems (O'Shea *et al.,* 2021). The cultural attributes of ecosystems environments must contribute to sustainable organizations and to develop economic and non-economic benefits (Volkmann *et al.* 2021). It is possible to highlight that sociointercultural management combines values in the masculinity-femininity cultural dimension, which would be related to sustainability (Siyal, Peng & Siyal., 2018).

The development, adoption and implementation of socio-intercultural entrepreneurship strategies foster interaction, encounter and exchange between different cultures, addressing the varied needs of people. These strategies promote inclusive, equitable and active participation of people, organizations and communities in economic growth, social advancement and environmental sustainability. To create a framework that highlights the importance of continuous growth and development of organizations, the dimensions of entrepreneurship ecosystems (EES) are employed.

Funding institutional sustainability research projects among academic and research institutions at different levels, and the establishment of advisory boards to provide reports on the best practices and develop quality management standards, lead to institutional transdisciplinary sustainability research transformations, and change through organizing sustainable assessment systems. The empirical results stress the self-sustaining entrepreneurship ecosystems development in opposition to the limited support provided by the subsistence model grounded on founded resources. Among the research results, factors contributing to create more attractive places of entrepreneurship ecosystem concept to sustain organizational business emphasize a systemic overview to give preponderance of the constituted elements interacting (Brito & Leitão, 2020)

An institution is the turbulent, complex and uncertain whole guiding and sustaining individual identity. Incentive and reward systems of the research institutions and the collaboration mode with industry is relevant in establishing social benefits which are insufficient and require implementing the multi-stakeholder collaborations to solve interconnected and complicated institutional sustainability concerns and issues in local and regional communities. The use of alternative micro-level data sources my inhibit and capture the regional dynamic processes to sustain innovation and entrepreneurship ecosystems (Feldman & Lowe, 2015; Strangler & Bell-Masterson, 2015).

Discussion of the external environment and the entrepreneurship ecosystem environment formalized by Cohen (2006) integrating the community to support entrepreneurship for sustainable growth synergizing the activities as the result of creating value for the stakeholders. Intangible assets of a firm, among others, culture, knowledge, skills, reputation, innovativeness, etc., cannot be replaced to improve the sustainable value of the entrepreneurship ecosystems (Pearson *et al.*, 2015). Entrepreneurship in a risk adverse culture characterizes the emerging phase with limited capital and few supportive specialized organizations leading to the development of elements in domestic and global markets while the networks get dense enhancing the entrepreneurial culture.

During the sustained stage of entrepreneurial development leading to decline in venture capital, education and others supportive elements. The decline stage of entrepreneurial development is due to the tendency of institutions to disappear such as markets, financial capital, networks and other supporting organizations that attract and produce resources such as capital and human capital. The entrepreneurship ecosystem must be sustainable and adaptable to adjust to the turbulences, differing in evolving over time and influencing entrepreneurship initiatives depending on the individual perceptions of the environment and place where they are embedded (Acs, *et al.* 2017).

Emerging institutional research networks could design and implement far-reaching sustainability assessment systems of integrated academic and research institutions to monitor and evaluate usage of water, energy and other material, issues of research, education, etc. (Brousseau *et al.*, 2012). Assessment and appraisal systems are a significant force for the institutional integration of institutional sustainability research in academic and research institutions.

Networks live to expectations of long-term transdisciplinary institutional sustainability research relying in structural changes in funding and reforms in training and careers in academic and research institutions. Entrepreneurial ecosystems is sustained by the entrepreneurial structural conditions, which facilitates or hinders the emergence and launching of new businesses ventures (GEM, 2021).

Entrepreneurship-led spin-offs firms have the tendency to be located in clustering proximity to the incubator to utilize social, employees and business networks to have access to resources, knowledge, human capital needed to start and growth binding the locations and entrepreneurship ecosystems in required social support required to sustain their entrepreneurship ventures while avoiding to disrupt family ties enabling spouses to work and continue bringing income into the household. The human capital theory sustains that high levels of human capital including knowledge, skills and social capital assisting to engaging in new ventures tend to achieve better performance in serial entrepreneurship.

However, regional spin-offs generate aspects within their region that stimulate the emergence of a network of business ecosystems, which allow the growth of entrepreneurial companies to be sustained. Individuals and institutions that create a networking group to represent institutional sustainability science is an emerging institutional arrangement with potential implications in society over a long-term period (Brousseau *et al.*, 2012). The ecosystem infrastructure uses the open and collaborative nature of digital entrepreneurship ecosystems in which the cooperation of actors takes place on community objectives in sustainable development (George *et al.*, 2021).

Digital ecosystems and entrepreneurship ecosystems frameworks consist of biotic entities, users and agencies, and abiotic components digital infrastructure and digital platforms framework. The digital entrepreneurship framework has differences between the protected user privacy and agencies sets the conditions for sustainable digital entrepreneurship ecosystems, encouraging competition, securing digital infrastructure and increase platform efficiency (Song, 2019).

Digital technologies should be strategically implemented and exploited in entrepreneurship ecosystems to achieve and sustain competitive advantages. Digital technologies sustain and promote entrepreneurial ecosystems defined by an environment triggering changes through exploration and exploitation of digital technologies (Autio *et al.*, 2018; Elia *et al.*, 2020). Digital technologies create and sustain entrepreneurship ecosystems in dynamic interactions with different motivations and goals to manage business and undertake entrepreneurship practices and activities.

Similarly, heterogeneous results are recognized within business innovation systems, this within institutional environments suitable for productive business innovation. Likewise, individual agents are fundamental for the maintenance and creation of entrepreneurial ecosystems (Alvedalen & Boschma (2017). Sustainable orientation of entrepreneurship innovation ecosystems explores market opportunities to support and benefit the greater good and provide solutions to societal problems by sustaining the communal natural environment (Gregori *et al.*, 2021). The environmental sustainability and societal challenges require entrepreneurship ecosystems with turbulent, complex and uncertain knowledge recombination leading through high-growth orientation and productive entrepreneurship innovation ecosystems.

Entrepreneurial ecosystems have significant differences in innovation levels capturing the causal relationships between policies and innovation, performance, capacities, environment, and sustainability of entrepreneurship. *Technology Transfer*, 44, 2, 313– 325. Technological innovation ecosystem brings the sustainable orientation of entrepreneurship innovation ecosystem. Technology of the greener, socially inclusive, and economically viable solutions in serial entrepreneurship ecosystems linking innovation sustainability to business model (Caputo *et al.*, 2021; Pizzi *et al.*, 2020).

Sustainable orientation management in entrepreneurship ecosystems conduiting innovation ecosystem (EIE) performance and focusing on developed economies where is rewarded (Audretsch and Belitski, 2017, 2020; Stam, 2015; Guerrero *et al.*, 2021; Spigel *et al.*, 2020; Bacq & Alt, 2018). The general management knowledge sustains a process that goes forth and back between self-realization and tangible skills development from new activities and followed by regrouping of individuals based on tacit knowledge to enable self-realization (Spigel, 2022). The sustainable orientation management has effects on the quality and quantity of entrepreneurship innovation ecosystems in addressing the United Nations Sustainable Development Goals (SDGs) (United Nations, 2015).

Sustainable orientation management draws on social entrepreneurship activity defined as the source of solutions to certain illnesses of modern societies (Bacq & Janssen, 2011) and from the definition of sustainable entrepreneurship ecosystems as identification, creation, and exploitation of opportunities to create goods and services that sustain the natural and communal environment to provide development gains (Volkmann, *et al.* 2019). Likewise, it is possible to recognize that social entrepreneurship activities in developing countries have an important support from those agents that promote social change, both in political aspects, as well as in the media itself, with which an attempt is made to address various problems of poverty and social inequality. Various social organizations and networks support the contribution of social entrepreneurs to society.

Sustainable and social entrepreneurship literature analyzes the institutional quality and legal reforms (Sarma & Sanwar, 2017; Chowdhury *et al.*, 2019; Audretsch *et al.*, 2022a, 2022b, 2022c). Institutional quality is related to the sustainable orientation management of entrepreneurship innovation ecosystems (EIE) actors and entrepreneurship innovation ecosystems (EIE) performance., conducive to productive entrepreneurial activity. Sustainable orientation management entrepreneurship shapes performance of the entire entrepreneurship innovation ecosystems (EIE) at different institutional quality levels. The diminishing marginal returns to sustainable orientation management are higher in societies with quality of institutions for productive entrepreneurship.

On the other hand, within the quality of entrepreneurial innovation ecosystems (EIE), several empirical evidences show that quality is fundamental within these ecosystems; being that, existing research is complemented with respect to the productive orientation of entrepreneurial ecosystems (Audretsch, *et al.* 2023). Therefore, the correct choice of management behaviors of sustainable orientation, as well as their possible combinations, is essential, which is aimed at maximizing productive business innovation ecosystems.

However, the research on entrepreneurial ecosystems (EIEs) arises from shaping the productive and growth orientation, derived from the entrepreneurial activity that is based on the management of sustainable orientation, as well as the institutional quality to achieve the United Nations Sustainable Development Goals (SDGs) (Audretsch, *et al.* 2023). It should be noted that, although the sustainable orientation management and the quality of business innovation ecosystems shape their quality, they are not an indication of their quantity and visibility.

Sustainable orientation and entrepreneurship innovation ecosystem performance is moderated by institutional quality (Sarma & Sanwar, 2017). Likewise, productive entrepreneurship benefits from the sustainable orientation of the business innovation ecosystem; this has a direct impact on the growth and improvement of social problems, since creative solutions are generated, thus achieving a sustained improvement through entrepreneurship that integrates this type of objectives. The mechanisms of entrepreneurship innovation ecosystems driving the relationship between the sustainable orientation and the performance needs to be explained and analyzed. The supportive conditions for entrepreneurship hold to lead to ecosystems with available venture capital as the attribute for technology innovation clusters required for the sustainable growth and development of clusters (Malecki, 2011).

On the other hand, workers have a great potential to drive companies to compete in the global market, due to their capacity for innovation; therefore, it is necessary to attract and retain qualified human talent, through the generation of a sustainable entrepreneurial ecosystem, which helps workers to become entrepreneurs and work in scaleup companies. Capacity building measures in emerging research networks can be scaled and integrated in transdisciplinary sustainability research transformations and reforms at the level of academic and scientific institutions. Although there are not simple solutions to challenges posed by sustainable science institutions but to strengthen disciplines and methods in workshops and training to support interdisciplinary and transdisciplinary institutional sustainability research.

CONCLUSION

This study analyzes the implications of institutional environment and sustainability on entrepreneurship ecosystems, concluding that the institutional environmental sustainability influences the national, regional, and local entrepreneurship ecosystems.

Findings on entrepreneurship ecosystems adds value to knowledge as the most strategic resource to improve top management as an extension of resources based view in a changing technological turbulent environment in sustainable entrepreneurship ecosystems. The most critical dimensions of entrepreneurship ecosystems are human resource development, finance, support, and networking, which can be verified in different environments and developed supported by entrepreneurial development policies formulated on the needs of organizational development of industry sectors. Environmental sustainability, technological, social, and moral support are critical factors in entrepreneurship culture.

Entrepreneurial ecosystems support heterogenous, dynamic, and responsive entrepreneurship activities to buffer organizations against technological changes in a changing global organizational environment. Environmental sustainability entrepreneurship ecosystem place-based explains the differences in diverse places and changes over time for which entrepreneurship is responsible. Peripheral places of entrepreneurship ecosystems struggle with the lack of economic resources, social and cultural critical thinking leading to lag the more advanced entrepreneurship environments.

The environmental sustainability challenges forces entrepreneurship to become more innovative and competitive. The entrepreneurship involved in initiatives takes time to build a sustainable entrepreneurship economy. The entrepreneurship ecosystem development requires institutional ability to create external links and to build cooperation within institutions for a sustainable entrepreneurship ecosystem. Self-sustaining ecosystem development and sustainable entrepreneurship ecosystems combine components to support the processes. Motivations into entrepreneurship are accompanied by different types of knowledge development creating a self-sustained loop of entrepreneurship recycling within the ecosystem.

The spin-off process leads to the creation of a self-sustaining critical mass of new firms supporting organizations to attracts and develop venture capital. Transformation of entrepreneurship ecosystems into a self-sustained systems reduces the short-term results by promoting entrepreneurship culture to improve entrepreneurship initiative.

More developed economies tend to possess better environments for entrepreneurship ecosystems development, the necessary encouragement to entrepreneurship in terms of infrastructures, governmental programs, funding support, market openness, education, research, and development, etc. National and regional institutional quality and sustainable orientation in entrepreneurship innovation ecosystem (EIE) performance requires further research. Regional entrepreneurship ecosystem does not focus in sustaining the veracity but on the influence on regional change and stability.

Finally, it is possible to recognize the important relationship between sustainable orientation and productive entrepreneurship, since it is possible to reduce marginal returns not observed in other performance outcomes, such as the visibility of business innovation ecosystems. Therefore, the impact of sustainable orientation management shapes productive entrepreneurship conditional on organizational development itself.

Future research on serial entrepreneurship and the concept of sustainability is emerging in the scientific field despite that the literature is silent. Further research development is required on entrepreneurship environment related to entrepreneurship initiatives.

REFERENCES

Acs, J. Z., Stam, E., Audretsch, D. B., & O'Connor, A. (2017). The lineages of the entrepreneurial ecosystem approach. *Small Business Economics*, 2017(49), 1–10. DOI: 10.1007/s11187-017-9864-8

Ali, A., Espinosa, J., Hart, M., Kelley, D., & Levie, J. (2015). *Leveraging Entrepreneurial Ambition and Innovation: A Global Perspective on Entrepreneurship, Competitiveness and Development.* Available online: http://www3.weforum.org/docs/WEFUSA_

Alvedalen, J., & Boschma, R. (2017). A critical review of entrepreneurial ecosystems research: Towards a future research agenda. *European Planning Studies*, 25(6), 887–903. DOI: 10.1080/09654313.2017.1299694

Anwar ul Haq, M., Usman, M., Hussain, N., & Anjum, Z.-Z. (2014). Entrepreneurial activity in China and Pakistan: A GEM data evidence. *Journal of Entrepreneurship in Emerging Economies,* 6(2), 179–193.

Audretsch, D., & Moog, P. (2022a). Democracy and entrepreneurship. *Entrepreneurship Theory and Practice*, 46(2), 368–392. DOI: 10.1177/1042258720943307

Audretsch, D. B., & Belitski, M. (2017). Entrepreneurial eco-systems in cities: Establishing the framework conditions. *The Journal of Technology Transfer*, 42(5), 1030–1051. DOI: 10.1007/s10961-016-9473-8

Audretsch, D. B., & Belitski, M. (2020). The role of R&D and knowledge spillovers in innovation and productivity. *European Economic Review*, 123, 103391. DOI: 10.1016/j.euroecorev.2020.103391

Audretsch, D. B., Belitski, M., Caiazza, R., & Desai, S. (2022c). The role of institutions in latent and emergent entrepreneurship. *Technological Forecasting and Social Change*, 174, 121263. DOI: 10.1016/j.techfore.2021.121263

Audretsch, D. B., Belitski, M., & Guerrero, M. (2023). Sustainable orientation management and institutional quality: Looking into European entrepreneurial innovation ecosystems. *Technovation*, 124, 102742. DOI: 10.1016/j.technovation.2023.102742

Audretsch, D. B., Eichler, G. M., & Schwarz, E. J. (2022b). Emerging needs of social innovators and social innovation ecosystems. *The International Entrepreneurship and Management Journal*, 18(1), 217–254. DOI: 10.1007/s11365-021-00789-9

Audretsch, D. B., Kuratko, D. F., & Link, A. N. (2015). Making sense of the elusive paradigm of entrepreneurship. *Small Business Economics*, 45(4), 703–712. DOI: 10.1007/s11187-015-9663-z

Autio, E., Nambisan, S., Thomas, L. D., & Wright, M. (2018). Digital affordances, spatial affordances, and the genesis of entrepreneurial ecosystems. *Strategic Entrepreneurship Journal*, 12(1), 72–95. DOI: 10.1002/sej.1266

Bacq, S., & Alt, E. (2018). Feeling Capable and Valued: A Prosocial Perspective on the Link between Empathy and Social Entrepreneurial Intentions. *Journal of Business Venturing*, 33(3), 333–350. DOI: 10.1016/j.jbusvent.2018.01.004

Bacq, S. & Janssen, F. (2011). The multiple faces of social entrepreneurship: a review of definitional issues based on geographical and thematic criteria. *Entrepreneurship & Regional Development*, Taylor & Francis Journals, vol. 23(5-6), pages 373-403, June. DOI: DOI: 10.1080/08985626.2011.577242

Bischoff, K. A. (2021). study on the perceived strength of sustainable entrepreneurial ecosystems on the dimensions of stakeholder theory and culture. *Small Business Economics*, 56(3), 1121–1140. DOI: 10.1007/s11187-019-00257-3

Boudreaux, C. J., & Nikolaev, B. (2019). Capital is not enough: Opportunity entrepreneurship and formal institutions. *Small Business Economics*, 53(3), 709–738. DOI: 10.1007/s11187-018-0068-7

Brito, S., & Leitão, J. (2020). Mapping and defining entrepreneurial ecosystems: A systematic literature review. *Knowledge Management Research and Practice*, 19(1), 21–422. DOI: 10.1080/14778238.2020.1751571

Brousseau, E., Dedeurwaerdere, T., & Siebenhüner, B. (2012). *Reflexive Governance for Global Public Goods*. MIT Press. DOI: 10.7551/mitpress/9780262017244.001.0001

Cao, Z., & Shi, X. (2020). A systematic literature review of entrepreneurial ecosystems in advanced and emerging economies. *Small Business Economics*, ●●●, 2020.

Caputo, A., Pizzi, S., Pellegrini, M. M., & Dabić, M. (2021). Digitalization and business models: Where are we going? A science map of the field. *Journal of Business Research*, 123, 489–501. DOI: 10.1016/j.jbusres.2020.09.053

Chowdhury, F., Audretsch, D. B., & Belitski, M. (2019). Institutions and entrepreneurship quality. *Entrepreneurship Theory and Practice*, 43(1), 51–81. DOI: 10.1177/1042258718780431

Cohen, B. (2006). Sustainable valley entrepreneurial ecosystems. *Business Strategy and the Environment*, 15(1), 1–14. DOI: 10.1002/bse.428

Content, J., Bosma, N., Jordaan, J., & Sanders, M. (2020). Entrepreneurial ecosystems, entrepreneurial activity and economic growth: New evidence from European regions. *Regional Studies*, 2020(54), 1007–1019. DOI: 10.1080/00343404.2019.1680827

Del Solar, S. (2010). *Emprendedores en el aula. Guía para la formación en valores y habilidades sociales de docentes y jóvenes emprendedores*. Fondo Multilateral de Inversiones del Banco Interamericano de Desarrollo.

Elia, G. *et al.* (2020) Digital entrepreneurship ecosystem: how digital technologies and collective intelligence are reshaping the entrepreneurial process *Technol. Forecast. Soc. Change*

Feldman, M., & Lowe, N. (2015). Triangulating Regional Economies: Realizing the Promise of Digital Data. *Research Policy*, 44(9), 1785–1793. DOI: 10.1016/j.respol.2015.01.015

Fellnhofer, K., & Mueller, S. (2018). I want to be like you!: The influence of role models on entrepreneurial intention. *Journal of Enterprising Culture*, 26(02), 113–153. DOI: 10.1142/S021849581850005X

Ferraris, A., Giudice, M. D., Grandhi, B., & Cillo, V. (2020a). Refining the relation between cause-related marketing and consumers purchase intentions: A cross-country analysis. *International Marketing Review*, 37(4), 651–669. DOI: 10.1108/IMR-11-2018-0322

Ferraris, A., Santoro, G., & Pellicelli, A. C. (2020b). Openness of public governments in smart cities: Removing the barriers for innovation and entrepreneurship. *The International Entrepreneurship and Management Journal*, 16(4), 1259–1280. DOI: 10.1007/s11365-020-00651-4

Fredin, S., & Lidén, A. (2020). Entrepreneurial ecosystems: Towards a systemic approach to entrepreneurship? *Geografisk Tidskrift*, 120(2), 87–97. DOI: 10.1080/00167223.2020.1769491

GEM (2018). *Global Entrepreneurship Monitor*. Institut für Internationales Management, Austria – Europe.

GEM (2021) Entrepreneurial Framework Conditions (EFCs). Available at: https://www.gemconsortium.org/wiki/1154 (accessed June 11, 2021).

George, G., Merrill, R. K., & Schillebeeckx, S. J. D. (2021). Digital sustainability and entrepreneurship: How digital innovations are helping tackle climate change and sustainable development. *Entrepreneurship Theory and Practice*, 45(5), 999–1027. DOI: 10.1177/1042258719899425

Ghosh, S. K., Chaudhuri, R., Chatterjee, S., & Chaudhuri, S. (2021). Adoption of AI-integrated CRM system by Indian industry: From security and privacy perspective. *Information and Computer Security*, 29(1), 1–24. DOI: 10.1108/ICS-02-2019-0029

Gregori, P., Holzmann, P., & Schwarz, E. J. (2021). My future entrepreneurial self: Antecedents of entrepreneurial identity aspiration. *Education + Training*, 63(7/8), 1175–1194. DOI: 10.1108/ET-02-2021-0059

Guerrero, M., Liñán, F., & Cáceres-Carrasco, F. (2020). The influence of ecosystems on the entrepreneurship process: A comparison across developed and developing economies. *Small Business Economics*, ●●●, 2020.

Guerrero, M., Liñán, F., & Cáceres-Carrasco, F. R. (2021). The influence of ecosystems on the entrepreneurship process: A comparison across developed and developing economies. *Small Business Economics*, 57(4), 1733–1759. DOI: 10.1007/s11187-020-00392-2

Hechavarria, D., & Ingram, A. (2019). Entrepreneurial ecosystem conditions and gendered national-level entrepreneurial activity: A 14-year panel study of GEM. *Small Business Economics*, 53(2), 431–458. DOI: 10.1007/s11187-018-9994-7

Isenberg, D. (2011). *The Entrepreneurship Ecosystem Strategy as a New Paradigm for Economic Policy: Principles for Cultivating Entrepreneurships*. Babson. Available online: http://www.wheda.com/uploadedFiles/Website/About_Wheda/BabsonEntrepreneurshipEcosystemProject.pdf (accessed on 5 November 2020).

Johnson, D., Bock, A. J., & George, G. (2019). Entrepreneurial dynamism and the built environment in the evolution of university entrepreneurial ecosystems. *Industrial and Corporate Change*, 28(4), 941–959. DOI: 10.1093/icc/dtz034

Juma, N., Olabisi, J., & Griffin-EL, E. (2023). External enablers and entrepreneurial ecosystems: The brokering role of the anchor tenant in capacitating grassroots ecopreneurs. *Strategic Entrepreneurship Journal*, 17(2), 372–407. Advance online publication. DOI: 10.1002/sej.1462

Kansheba, M., & Wald, A. (2020). Entrepreneurial ecosystems: A systematic literature review and research agenda. *Journal of Small Business and Enterprise Development*, 27(6), 943–964. DOI: 10.1108/JSBED-11-2019-0364

Klingbeil, C., Semrau, T., Ebbers, M., & Wilhelm, H. (2019). Logics, leaders, lab coats: A multi- level study on how institutional logics are linked to entrepreneurial intentions in academia. *Journal of Management Studies*, 56(5), 929–965. DOI: 10.1111/joms.12416

Krueger, N. F. (2017). Entrepreneurial intentions are dead: Long live entrepreneurial intentions. In Brännback, M., & Carsrud, A. (Eds.), *Revisiting the entrepreneurial mind. International studies in entrepreneurship* (Vol. 35). Springer. DOI: 10.1007/978-3-319-45544-0_2

Lehner, O. M., & Harrer, T. (2019). Crowd funding revisited: A neo-institutional field-perspective. *Venture Capital*, 21(1), 75–96. DOI: 10.1080/13691066.2019.1560884

Lucas, D. S., & Fuller, C. S. (2017). Entrepreneurship: Productive, unproductive, and destructive— relative to what? *Journal of Business Venturing Insight*, 7, 45–49. DOI: 10.1016/j.jbvi.2017.03.001

Lyons, T. S., Alter, T. R., Audretsch, D., & Augustine, D. (2012). Entrepreneurship and community: The next frontier of entrepreneurship inquiry. *Entrepreneurship Research Journal*, 2(1), 1–26. DOI: 10.2202/2157-5665.1064

Malecki, E. J. (2011). Connecting local entrepreneurial ecosystems to global innovation networks: Open innovation, double networks and knowledge integration. *International Journal of Entrepreneurship and Innovation Management*, 14(1), 36–59. DOI: 10.1504/IJEIM.2011.040821

Malen, J., & Marcus, A. A. (2017). Promoting clean energy technology entrepreneurship: The role of external context. *Energy Policy*, 102(3), 7–15. DOI: 10.1016/j.enpol.2016.11.045

Mustafa, S. Z., Chatterjee, S., & Kar, A. K. (2019). Securing IoT devices in Smart Cities of India: From ethical and enterprise information system management perspective. *Journal of Enterprise Information System*, 15(4), 585–615.

Nsereko, I., Balunywa, W., Munene, J., Orobia, L., & Muhammed, N. (2018). Personal initiative: Its power in social entrepreneurial venture creation. *Cogent Bus. Manag.*, 5(1), 1443686. DOI: 10.1080/23311975.2018.1443686

O'Shea, G., Farny, S., & Hakala, H. (2021). The buzz before business: A design science study of a sustainable entrepreneurial ecosystem. *Small Business Economics*, 2021(56), 1097–1120. DOI: 10.1007/s11187-019-00256-4

Pearson, J., Pitfield, D., & Ryley, T. (2015). Intangible resources of competitive advantage: Analysis of 49 Asian airlines across three business models. *Journal of Air Transport Management*, 47(C), 179–189. DOI: 10.1016/j.jairtraman.2015.06.002

Piccolo, R., Chatterjee, S., Chaudhuri, R., & Vrontis, D. (2021). Enterprise social network for knowledge sharing in MNCs: Examining the role of knowledge contributors and knowledge seekers for cross-country collaboration. *Journal of International Management*, 27(1), 303–327.

Pita, M., Costa, J., & Moreira, A. C. (2021). Entrepreneurial Ecosystems and Entrepreneurial Initiative: Building a Multi-Country Taxonomy. *Sustainability (Basel)*, 2021(13), 4065. DOI: 10.3390/su13074065

Pizzi, S., Corbo, L., & Caputo, A. (2020). Fintech and SMEs sustainable business models: Reflections and considerations for a circular economy. *Journal of Cleaner Production*. Advance online publication. DOI: 10.1016/j.jclepro.2020.125217

Popkova, E. G., & Sergi, B. S. (2020). Human capital and AI in industry 4.0. Convergence and divergence in social entrepreneurship in Russia. *Journal of Intellectual Capital*, 21(4), 565–581. DOI: 10.1108/JIC-09-2019-0224

Popkova, E. G., Sergi, B. S., Rezaei, M., & Ferraris, A. (2021). Digitalisation in transport and logistics: A roadmap for entrepreneurship in Russia. *International Journal of Technology Management*, 87(1), 7–28. DOI: 10.1504/IJTM.2021.118887

Pugh, R., Lamine, W., Jack, S., & Hamilton, E. (2018). The entrepreneurial university of the region: What role for entrepreneurship departments? *European Planning Studies*, 26(9), 1835–1855. DOI: 10.1080/09654313.2018.1447551

Rezaei, S., Goli, M., & Dana, L.-P. (2014). Beyond legal entrepreneurship: The case of Austria. *International Journal of Entrepreneurship and Small Business*, 21(2), 202–215. DOI: 10.1504/IJESB.2014.059473

Sarma, S. & Sanwar A. S., (2017). Civic entrepreneurial ecosystems: Smart city emergence in Kansas City, *Business Horizons*, Elsevier, vol. 60(6), pages 843-853. Handle: DOI: DOI: 10.1016/j.bushor.2017.07.010

Siyal, M., Siyal, S., Wu, J., Pal, D., & Memon, M. M. (2021). Consumer perceptions of factors affecting online shopping behavior: An empirical evidence from foreign students in China. [JECO]. *Journal of Electronic Commerce in Organizations*, 19(2), 1–16. DOI: 10.4018/JECO.2021040101

Siyal, S. (2018). Does Leadership lessen turnover of public servants. The moderated mediation effect of leader member exchange and perspective taking [EBSCO open dissertations].

Siyal, S. (2023). Inclusive leadership and work engagement: Exploring the role of psychological safety and trust in leader in multiple organizational context. *Business Ethics, the Environment & Responsibility*, 32(4), 1170–1184. DOI: 10.1111/beer.12556

Siyal, S., & Peng, X. (2018). Does leadership lessen turnover? The moderated mediation effect of leader–member exchange and perspective taking on public servants. *Journal of Public Affairs*, 18(4), e1830. DOI: 10.1002/pa.1830

Siyal, S., Peng, X., & Siyal, A. W. (2018). Socioeconomic analysis: A case of Thar-parkar. *Journal of Public Affairs*, 18(4), e1847. DOI: 10.1002/pa.1847

Song, A. K. (2019). The digital entrepreneurial ecosystem—A critique and recon-figuration. *Small Business Economics*, 53(3), 569–590. DOI: 10.1007/s11187-019-00232-y

Spigel, B. (2022). Examining the cohesiveness and nest-edness entrepreneurial ecosystems: Evidence from British FinTechs. *Small Business Economics*, 59(4), 1381–1399. DOI: 10.1007/s11187-021-00589-z

Spigel, B., Kitagawa, F., & Mason, C. (2020). A manifesto for researching entrepreneur-ial ecosystems. *Local Economy*, 35(5), 482–495. DOI: 10.1177/0269094220959052

Stam, E. (2015). Entrepreneurial Ecosystems and Regional Policy: A Sym-pathetic Critique. *European Planning Studies*, 2015(23), 1759–1769. DOI: 10.1080/09654313.2015.1061484

Strangler, D., & Bell-Masterson, J. (2015). *Measuring an Entrepreneurial Ecosys-tem*. Kauffman Foundation.

Tansley, A. G. (1935). The use and abuse of vegetational concepts and terms. *Ecol-ogy*, 16(3), 284–307. DOI: 10.2307/1930070

UN report (2021). United Nations report. Report of the Secretary-General on the Work of the Organization (A/76/1, seventy-sixth session). United Nations.

United Nations (2015). *Transforming Our World: The 2030 Agenda for Sustainable Development*. Resolution Adopted by the General Assembly on 25 September 2015, 42809, 1-13. https://doi.org/DOI: 10.1007/s13398-014-0173-7.2

Van der Leeuw, S., Wiek, A., Harlow, J., & Buizer, J. (2012). How much time do we have? Urgency and rhetoric in sustainability science. *Sustainability Science*, 7(S1), 115–120. DOI: 10.1007/s11625-011-0153-1

Volkmann, C., Fichter, K., Klofsten, M., & Audretsch, D. (2021). Sustainable entre-preneurial ecosystems: An emerging field of research. *Small Business Economics*, 56(3), 1047–1055. DOI: 10.1007/s11187-019-00253-7

Volkmann, C., Fichter, K., Klofsten, M., & Audretsch, D. B. (2019). Sustainable entrepreneurial ecosystems: An emerging field of research. *Small Business Eco-nomics*, ●●●, 1–9. DOI: 10.1007/s11187-019-00253-7

Webb, J. W., Khoury, T. A., & Hitt, M. A. (2019). The influence of formal and infor-mal institutional voids on entrepreneurship. *Entrepreneurship Theory and Practice*, 104225871983031. Advance online publication. DOI: 10.1177/1042258719830310

Xu, Z., & Dobson, S. (2019). Challenges of building entrepreneurial ecosystems in peripheral places. *Journal of Entrepreneurship and Public Policy*, 8(3), 408–430. DOI: 10.1108/JEPP-03-2019-0023

Zahra, S. A., Liu, W., & Si, S. (2023). How digital technology promotes entrepreneurship in ecosystems. *Technovation*, 119, 102457. DOI: 10.1016/j.technovation.2022.102457

Chapter 8
Interpretations of Entrepreneurial Leadership Across Cultures:
Implications for Cross-Cultural Leadership Development

Ancia Katjiteo
https://orcid.org/0000-0001-5704-2728
University of Namibia, Namibia

ABSTRACT

Entrepreneurial leadership is shaped by cultural influences, presenting diverse interpretations across different societies. This chapter examines the multifaceted nature of entrepreneurial leadership through a cultural lens and explores its implications for cross-cultural leadership development. Drawing on established cultural dimensions proposed by scholars like Hofstede and Trompenaars. Through case studies from various countries, the chapter illustrates the cultural nuances in entrepreneurial leadership practices.

INTRODUCTION

Thus, entrepreneurial leadership is described as the processes of leading complex and dynamic organisations in accordance with the current challenges of the global environment (Fernald et al., 2005; Renko, 2017; Zijlstra, 2024). This style of the leaders is characterized by several entrepreneurship qualities such as; creativity,

DOI: 10.4018/979-8-3693-0078-7.ch008

willingness to take risks, and focus on opportunities (Clark and Bradley, 2024; Islam and Asad, 2024). Culture influences entrepreneurial leadership in a considerable way since the nature and intensity of exposure to the manifestation of the leadership style differ from one culture to another. Every culture gives birth to its own template in deploying entrepreneurial leadership based on the norms, values and relations in the culture.

It is possible to state that culture plays a crucial role in the formation of the patterns of values, convictions, and attitudes that are the key to understanding the contours of the entrepreneurial leadership (Clark & Bradley, 2024; Fernald et al., 2005; Islam & Asad, 2024; Roomi & Harrison, 2011; Zijlstra, 2024). It therefore becomes pertinent to underscore the relationship between culture and entrepreneurial leadership because the world has become a global village and intercultural interaction in the business domain and the market is rather frequent. Economic liberalization has brought about cultural homogenization and thus integration of countries and societies around the world. Therefore, to top executive and entrepreneurs, cultural competencies that contribute to the effectiveness of their businesses are imperative.

This chapter focuses on the complex dynamics between entrepreneurship leadership and culture in the case of the business owning entrepreneurs. It intends to see the ways in which, and the extent to which, the concept of entrepreneurial leadership is translated and practiced, recognising the nuances and differences that exist. However, the chapter will also for the consequences that has been brought about by cultural diversity on leadership development outcomes. As organizations develop their operations internationally, they must deal with different cultures which can present different attitudes toward business and power. Hence, it is essential for the organizations to develop training interventions that assist the leaders and employees in the organizations to develop the competencies required in the leader in the multicultural organization. These programs should aim to also establish the degree to which culture impacts entrepreneurial leadership in a bid to enhance successful cultural leadership initiatives.

The Purpose of the Chapter

The purpose of this chapter is to present the culture-entrepreneurial leadership relationship and to explore the dynamics of cultural environment on leadership and development of cross-cultural leadership. To present a clear understanding of how and in what ways entrepreneurial leadership is being perceived and enacted cross culturally with the intention to assist in identifying and explaining practical executive leadership capabilities in multicultural organisations.

Research Objectives

- To use culture as a variable in order to examine the external influences on the leadership behaviour of entrepreneurs.
- To examine the implications that culture has on leadership development in business-owning entrepreneurs.
- To evaluate how organizations develop effective training programs to enhance entrepreneurial leadership competencies in multicultural settings?

Research Questions

- How does culture influence the interpretation and practice of entrepreneurial leadership across different cultural contexts?
- What are the implications of cultural diversity on leadership development outcomes for business-owning entrepreneurs?
- How can organizations develop effective training programs to enhance entrepreneurial leadership competencies in multicultural settings?

CULTURAL DIMENSIONS OF ENTREPRENEURIAL LEADERSHIP

Cultural factors of entrepreneurial leadership focus on, how cultural belief systems affect the leadership and entrepreneurial processes. According to Hofstede (2001) and House et al., (2004), power distance for instance describes how societies embrace and tolerate contracts of power; societies with high power distance are likely to embrace autocratic leaders, while those with low power distance are likely to embrace more democratic leaders. Power distance also influences leadership, where cultures that tolerate a large level of power distance encourage entrepreneurs to have their vision and act independently, while cultures with a low tolerance for power distance want entrepreneurs to implement their authority in a way that is acceptable on a collective level (Hofstede, 2001; House et al., 2004). Uncertainty avoidance is the level of society's anxiety about the future and its attitudes of uncertainty and risk in terms of the level of tolerance for ambiguity and the emphasis on, for example, schedules, plans, and rituals (Hofstede, 2001; House et al., 2004). Also, the masculinization versus feminization dimension also affects leadership, where assertiveness and competitiveness and dominant in the masculine cultures and aggressive and result-oriented leadership in feminine cultures are nurtured, empathy and cooperation and care leads to more inclusive leadership (Hofstede, 2001; Trompenaars & Hampden-Turner, 1997) There is also the dimension of long/

short-term orientation that specifies the emphasis on planning for future outcomes and perseverance in working towards them in people of long-term oriented cultures and the immediacy of accomplishment and flexibility in people of short-term oriented cultures can influence leaders' strategic management. Last but not the least, cultural beliefs affect both expressiveness and formidableness of leadership, and the manner of sharing the vision as well as delegating or motivating individuals and teams (Siyal et al., 2021; Siyal., 2023; Siyal & Peng., 2018). Knowledge of those dimensions serves to define the framework where businesspersons and managers operate, as well as to provide insights on how best to act and achieve better results in otherwise homogenized overseas locations (Hofstede, 2001; Trompenaars & Hampden-Turner, 1997)

Scholars such as Gerrt Hofstedent, Fons Trompenaars and many others have acknowledged the differences in entrepreneurial leadership across different cultural settings and cultural dimensions. Understanding cultural dimensions can best explain the underlaying cultural beliefs, norms and orientations that affect leadership practices and behaviours. Geert Hofstede come up with cultural dimensions that are seen as the foundation of cross-cultural research and are used in this chapter as frameworks to explore cultural foundations of leadership. Geert Hofstede's dimensions include Individualised-collectivism, Power Distance, Uncertainty Avoidance and Masculinity-Femininity (Hofstede, 2001; House et al., 2004).

The Individualism-Collectivism dimension has to do with people's placement of their own personal objectivity and autonomy at a higher priority compared to the aims of the whole group and preservation of group collectivism (cohesion). In countries that are branded by collectivism, such as numerous East Asian nations, entrepreneurial leadership may place a weight on the importance of cooperation, the development of agreement, and loyalty to the group of people. Causing East Asian entrepreneurial leaders to be more loyal to their group (enterprises). In most cases these are family businesses passed on from generations (Cahya & Semnani, 2024; Hofstede, 2001;.Nguyen, 2020; Pauluzzo et al.., 2018; Stoudemire, 2024; Trompenaars & Hampden-Turner, 1997).

Power Distance dimension is also known as the power gap, it is the willingness of less powerful members of society in accepting or anticipate an uneven allocation of power in society. Many Middle East countries have a large power gap, in these countries entrepreneurial leaders may opt for a more authoritarian and hierarchical role. On the other side, in places line Scandinavian countries that have a lower power distance entrepreneurial leaders would be more egalitarian and participatory (Nguyen, 2020; Pauluzzo et al.., 2018; Stoudemire, 2024). The Uncertainty Avoidance dimension looks at ambiguity and uncertainty, and how much people are threatened by ambiguity and uncertainty. To void of ambiguity and uncertainty people endeavour to reduce their danger by setting stringent rules, formalities, and rituals. These societies place a high value on warding off uncertainty, an example of these is Japan. Japan entrepreneurial leaders place a high priority on predictability, stability and risk reduction and thus always work towards achieving this (Hofstede, 2001; House et al., 2004). On the other hand, other entrepreneurial leaders would be more open ambiguity and uncertainty. An example of this would be entrepreneurial leaders from the United States of America, they are more experimental and risk-taking, and have a low tendency to shun uncertainty. They are not afraid of the unknown but are always eager to thrive on it as it may bring entrepreneurial success (Cahya & Semnani, 2024; Hofstede, 2001; House et al., 2004; Pauluzzo et al.., 2018; Stoudemire, 2024).

Accorsing to Hofstede, (2001) and Trompenaars & Hampden-Turner (1997), the Masculinity-Femininity dimension is what entrepreneurial leaders can display in their leadership. Masculinity related to extent which culture places value on assertiveness, competition, and success. While femininity places its importance on caring, quality of life, and collaboration. In cultures that are more masculine like in the United States, entrepreneurial leaders may demonstrate a more forceful and achievement driven behaviour. On the hand in culture that are more feminine like Nordic nations, they may place more importance on interpersonal relationships, social responsibility, and work-life balance (Nguyen, 2020; Pauluzzo et al.., 2018; Stoudemire, 2024).

Fons Trompenaars' Cultural Dimensions Offer Additional Insights into How Cultural Orientations Shape Entrepreneurial Leadership Styles

Fons Trompenaars' cultural dimensions consist of these three dimensions, the Universalism-Particularism, the neutral-affective dimension, and the Specific-defuse dimension. Universalism-Particularism, universalistic cultures adhere to standards, principles and norms that are applicable everywhere, while particularistic cultures place an emphasis on context, relationship, and situational judgement. In cultures that are more universalistic entrepreneurial leaders place great emphasis on justice, meritocracy and consistency, an example of this is Germany. On the other hand, cultures that are more particularistic place greater emphasis on personal relationships known as guanxi and flexibility to individual settings. an example of this would be China (Siyal et al; 2023; Hampden-Turner & Tromprenaars, 1997; Helfrich, 2024; Smith et al., 1996; Tromprenaars, 1996; Tromprenaars et. al., 2004; Trompenaars

& Woolliams, 2024a; Trompenaars & Woolliams, 2024b; Trompenaars & Woolliams, 2024c).

The neutral-affective dimension shows the degree to which citizens feel free to express their feelings (affective) or keep their feeling in check (neutral). In cultures such as Italy entrepreneurial leaders are affective, they can easily express their emotions, passion, and charisma, while in countries like Japan, an entrepreneurial leader has to maintain calmness, professionalism and restraint in their behaviour (Tromprenaars, 1996; Tromprenaars et. al., 2004; Trompenaars & Woolliams, 2024a; Trompenaars & Woolliams, 2024b; Trompenaars & Woolliams, 2024c).

Specific-Diffuse is also known as diffuse differentiation. It refers to the way people compartmentalise their private and public lives, as opposed to not integrating them. In the United States is easy for entrepreneurial leaders to separate the personal and prefessional lives. Higher priority is placed on connections that would bring about a task to completion. In other cultures, like Saudi Arabia, there is no separation with personal life and professional life. Personal and professional ties create loyalty, trust, and reciprocity (Smith et al., 1996; Tromprenaars, 1996; Tromprenaars et. al., 2004; Trompenaars & Woolliams, 2024a; Trompenaars & Woolliams, 2024b; Trompenaars & Woolliams, 2024c)

When organisational leaders take all these cultural variances into consideration, they can acquire more in-depth knowledge of the ways in which cultural orientations affect entrepreneurial leadership style and modify their strategies effectively. It makes it easier to do business successfully beyond boarders. For entrepreneurial leaders to be effective in today's global economy they have to embrace cultural diversity and finding ways to use cultural insights.

On this account, it is imperative to look at Geert Hofstede and Fons Trompenaars' cultural dimensions since the former came up with a wide framework for analysis of how cultures influence the behaviour of individuals in organizations. Using Hofstede's model one can gain a general insight into how cultural factors affects manager and leadership practices, while Trompenaars' model gives a more detailed understanding on how cultural values impact on relationship between people and in organization. Both structures are compatible and as a result provide a strong foundation for understanding cross-cultural leadership and understanding how cultural values affect entrepreneurial actions, as well as leadership outcomes (Smith et al., 1996; Tromprenaars, 1996; Tromprenaars et. al., 2004; Trompenaars & Woolliams, 2024).

Hofstede's cultural dimensions are useful due to their teachings that provide systematic framework for the cross-national comparisons of culture values. As for the Hofstede's corporate culture parameters which include Power Distance, Individualism/Collectivism and Uncertainty Avoidance; enshrine the cultural attitudes to authority, self-organization and unpredictability, respectively. Such dimensions are significant because they make it easier for leaders and entrepreneurs to adapt to cultural practices and be more effective in their endeavours. This knowledge is vital when developing culturally sensitive leadership intervention plans and also for enhancing the communication between persons of different cultures (Hofstede, 2001; House et al., 2004).

The following aspects of leadership have been derived from the dimensions suggested by Hofstede and Trompenaars; The Hofstede's dimensions can help a leader learn about cultural values that may impact the teams, its decision-making, and conflicts. For example, it is evident that leaders in the high-Power Distance cultures will require applying more power distance, in contrast to the leaders in low Power Distance cultures who will have to apply more equal power distance. In general, Trompenaars' dimensions like Universalism vs. Particularism or Neutral vs. Affective could be useful to find some clues as to how to act in case of we differing in relations or emotions. Awareness of these cultural differences helps the leaders to come up with the right approach towards the team and make the right plan thus helping them to achieve their goal of leading multinational teams and prosper in the international markets (Tromprenaars, 1996; Tromprenaars et. al., 2004; Trompenaars & Woolliams, 2024).

Figure 1. Conceptual framework: Culturally Adaptive Entrepreneurial Leadership (CAEL) Framework

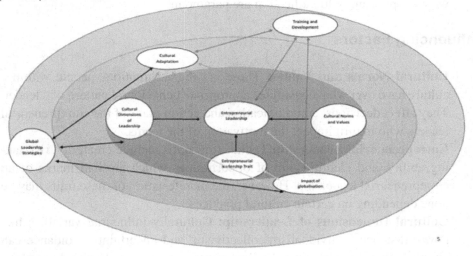

The explain the CAEL Framework it is important to differentiate the mapping of the framework elements. **Entrepreneurial Leadership** is identified as the element at the center of the model. Surrounding this central node are the three primary influencing factors: **Cultural norms and values, Entrepreneurial Leadership Traits** and **Cultural Dimensions of Leadership**. These factors are linked to different satellite nodes to the central node by arrows to indicate how they affect entrepreneurial leadership. In order to show the dynamic nature of these interactions, a layer is placed around the influencing factors which represents the **Cultural Adaptation of Leadership Styles** and the **Impact of Globalisation** as well as arrows that show the interactions between these dynamic elements, the central node and the influencing factors. Last but not the least on the outermost layer, the **effects** or the **Outcomes** namely the **Training and Development** and the **global leadership strategies** are placed to show the final output or the final condition of the Leadership interacting with Culture, and the connection line ties this final output again to the dynamic interactions and of course the entrepreneurial leadership.

The Culturally Adaptive Entrepreneurial Leadership (CAEL) Framework is meant to identify how cultural environments affect entrepreneurial leadership and to inform about the effective approaches to leadership in a culturally diverse environment. The framework encompasses of the following:

Core Concept: Entrepreneurial Leadership

- Entrepreneurial Leadership incorporates the process of leading in the entrepreneurship environment, where aspects such as innovation, risk taking as well as opportunity identification are paramount.

Influencing Factors

- **Cultural Norms and Values:** These are the assumptions people within a culture have over what constitutes appropriate behavioural pattern of a leader. They affect decisions, communication and action plans of the entrepreneurial leaders who in turn impact the motivation of the teams.
- **Entrepreneurial Leadership Traits:** Key skills include creativity, risk taking ability, and identification of opportunities which are hall marks of an entrepreneurial leadership. However, the manifestation of these traits may be done depending on certain cultural practices.
- **Cultural Dimensions of Leadership:** Culturally influential variables like power distance, individualism-collectivism, and uncertainty avoidance can greatly influence how leadership is practised and received around the globe (Hofstede, 2001; House et al., 2004).

Dynamic Interactions

- **Cultural Adaptation of Leadership Styles:** Managers have to properly navigate their leadership to suit the culture area they find themselves in. This calls for cultural sensitivity and adaptability, since leadership behaviours which work well in one culture might not be as effective in another culture.
- **Impact of Globalization:** Globalization affects leadership in that; it enhances multiplicity of cultures and in most instances results in standardization of leadership practices. But it does stress the need to preserve cultural differences and to adjust the management model to the specific national environment.

Outcomes

- **Training and Development:** Thus, the framework puts stress on the leadership training programmes aimed at the elaboration of cultural competencies and providing leaders with effective tools to manage multicultural contexts.
- **Global Leadership Strategies:** According to this framework, organisations should encourage leadership strategies that are globally best compatible, which would permit the leader to work in other cultures.

Overall Understanding

The CAEL Framework helps identify and describe the specifics of how culture influences entrepreneurial leadership and gives a set of instructions on how to build leadership skills in multicultural and global environments. It stresses cultural contingency noting that leadership relates to culture and should therefore be sensitive to it. This framework is particularly useful in today's world where top managers function in the global environment and are called to design measures that would be appropriate for the cultural context and effective from the global perspective.

Process of Cases Chosen for Discussion

Selection process

Figure 2. Case study selection process

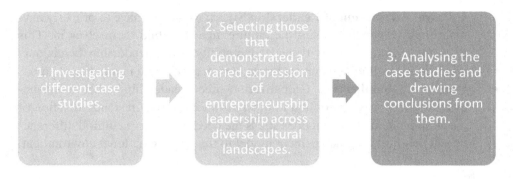

Figure 1 shows the selection process of how case studies were selected. A series of case studies were investigated that demonstrated a varied expression of entrepreneurial leadership across diverse cultural landscapes. Examples were drawn from strong economies such as the United States, China, India, Germany, Japan, South Korea, Brazil, Sweden, France, Nigeria, South Africa, Canadian and Mexico.

Case Studies

The selection of these case studies was made in view of their typical representation of the impact of culture on entrepreneurial leadership in diverse industries and geographic locations.

1. United States: Innovation Profile of Silicon valley
    *   **Cultural Nuances:** Risk-taking culture, promotion based on past performance, encouraging of radical ideas and innovation.
    *   **Impact on Leadership Behaviours:** Managers never shy away from risk but rather seek to find ways of implementing better strategies in their organisation.
    *   **Organizational Dynamics:** It also includes versatile and loose organizational structures which foster flexibility and fast decision-making.
    *   **Decision-Making Process:** Tends to be dual shaded, involves cooperation and multiple cycles, appreciates individuals' responding to changes quickly.
2. China: Alibaba's Visionary Leadership
    *   **Cultural Nuances:** Exchange of favours, Confucianism, win-win approach.

- **Impact on Leadership Behaviours:** People in this culture combine idea of relations with idea of planning, and always respect the authority.
- **Organizational Dynamics:** High levels of bureaucracy buttressed by the interconnection of tactical and strategic choices, as well as relationship management.
- **Decision-Making Process:** Strategising over several years with regard to relationships with other cultures and individual, usually with approval from organisational leaders.

3. India: Infosys's Values-Driven Leadership
- **Cultural Nuances:** Policing focuses on harmony, obedience, and spirituality.
- **Impact on Leadership Behaviours:** In the present study, in synthesized narratives, leaders were revealed to prioritize ethics, transparency and engage employees.
- **Organizational Dynamics:** Stress is on the institution of structured hierarchical participation in community development projects.
- **Decision-Making Process:** Decisions are made and evaluated with regard to traditional value and ethical concerns in terms of consequences.

4. Germany: Family Business Leadership of Mittelstand
- **Cultural Nuances:** Patience, accountability and this aspect of a business being a steward and a responsible member of society.
- **Impact on Leadership Behaviours:** Holders value order, predictability and everybody's agreement on decisions taken.
- **Organizational Dynamics:** Small businesses that may be owned by a family and emphasize on continuing with the traditional ways that they use in relating with the people in the community.
- **Decision-Making Process:** Decisions are taken in the long-run and can be reached after a lot of consultation and consensus within the family and the leadership.

5. Japan: The Kaizen Leadership Position
- **Cultural Nuances:** 'Management of change', better known as continuing improvement (Kaizen), focus on the details and always obey orders from the superior.
- **Impact on Leadership Behaviours:** Leaders emphasize on finer changes, betterment and the group synergies.
- **Organizational Dynamics:** Clearly defined procedures accompanied by a major focus on cooperation and consecutive improvements.
- **Decision-Making Process:** Decisions are made with due terms of quality and quantitative aspects, as well as with the utilization of feedback and improving organization.

6. South Korea: The Samsung Technology leadership of chaebols
   - **Cultural Nuances:** On the organisational culture, one will find such peculiarities as hierarchy, Confucianism, and innovation.
   - **Impact on Leadership Behaviours:** Managers continue to dominate the organizations and at the same time encourage dedication to technology and internationalization strategies.
   - **Organizational Dynamics:** Decision making centralized with most responsibility lying at the headquarters and with special emphasis on the concepts of innovation and internationalization.
   - **Decision-Making Process:** Another interesting aspect regards the fact that strategic choices are still oriented by tradition and competitive claims.
7. Brazil: Reflecting on the Leadership Practices of Grandeur: The Case of Natura
   - **Cultural Nuances:** Looking at the main themes, corporate social responsibility can be summed up by the so called three Rs: Respect, Responsibility and Relationships.
   - **Impact on Leadership Behaviours:** Managers pay attention to what is right and wrong and ways of creating business value sustainably.
   - **Organizational Dynamics:** Effective working relationships, environment, conservation of renewable resources and the social context.
   - **Decision-Making Process:** It has ethical standards for decision-making and also involves stakeholders in the process taking into account sustainability and impacts of the community.
8. Sweden: IKEA's Democratic Leadership
   - **Cultural Nuances:** Some of the values are getting a consensus, equality and inclusion.
   - **Impact on Leadership Behaviours:** Managers bring and maintain culture of decentralization and collaboration throughout the organizations.
   - **Organizational Dynamics:** In a decentralised structure more focus is placed on participating and decision-making employees.
   - **Decision-Making Process:** All committees operate on the basis of the consensus, which signifies that there is free flow of information and all members of an organization get involved in the decision-making.
9. France: The Greatest Visionary Leadership Present in L'Oréal
   - **Cultural Nuances:** Greek, PowerPoint graphics and flair.
   - **Impact on Leadership Behaviours:** Head of the department are work on the conception of innovations, brand initiative, and close attention to the elegance level.

- **Organizational Dynamics:** Stressing on the aspect of creativity and keeping the brand look and feel. Appealing to the target audience and focusing on the simplicity of the advertising material.
- **Decision-Making Process:** The strategic choices are of an innovative nature and are a result of a focus on a firm's image as a robust and fashion forward company.

10. Nigeria: Another issue, the visionary leadership is illustrated with the inspected in the Dangote Group.
    - **Cultural Nuances:** Technology development through innovation and resistance to adversity.
    - **Impact on Leadership Behaviours:** Managers remain flexible and show a desire to be the first to innovate while maintaining explicit attention financial stakes.
    - **Organizational Dynamics:** Vitality of the Organizational culture and the organization's devotion to Adaptation, progress, and societal usefulness.
    - **Decision-Making Process:** Strategic choices relate to community requirements and economic possibilities for the future perspective.

11. Sweden: The Disruptive Leadership Provided by Spotify
    - **Cultural Nuances:** The principle of collaboration, non-discrimination, and access to information.
    - **Impact on Leadership Behaviours:** Managers support the ideas of innovation, equal rights, and customer-orientation.
    - **Organizational Dynamics:** Uncomplicated structure that helps creativity and teamwork.
    - **Decision-Making Process:** Decision making is guided by an ideology, which seeks to make music available to as many people as possible and to allow the creation of as much music as is possible.

12. South Africa: The Ethical Leadership Position of Nando's
    - **Cultural Nuances:** Application of communities, realism and social justice".
    - **Impact on Leadership Behaviours:** Managers pay attention to community relations and being an excellent corporate citizen.
    - **Organizational Dynamics:** Ethical issues and community participation taking into consideration cultural values of the south African community.
    - **Decision-Making Process:** It is driven by cultural and social values and erred on the positive side where social justice is the order of the day.

13. Japan: Uniqlo's Innovative Leadership

- **Cultural Nuances:** Workmanship, closeness to perfection and manner in dealing with the customers.
- **Impact on Leadership Behaviours:** Those that practice leadership pay close attention to quality that is given to their products, satisfaction of customers as well as improvement.
- **Organizational Dynamics:** A focus on the accuracy of activities on the one hand along with personalized changes to the offering in a more rigid process architecture on the other hand.
- **Decision-Making Process:** It is in this line that decisions are made to deliver services and products in a most professional way with an emphasize on the quality and timely delivery that suits the customers.

14. Canada: Shopify's Empowerment Leadership
- **Cultural Nuances:** Equality, equity, and solidarity.
- **Impact on Leadership Behaviours:** They underscore the importance of promoting trust, decentralisation and support to the initiatives of an entrepreneurial nature.
- **Organizational Dynamics:** Organizational culture that is most inclusive and supportive with a large amount of freedom given to individuals.
- **Decision-Making Process:** They are made with the focus on creativity, people's involvement, and value for multiculturalism.

15. Mexico: Grupo Bimbo: Leadership That Survives Troubled Times
- **Cultural Nuances:** Family orientation, collectivism, and resistance.
- **Impact on Leadership Behaviours:** Leaders are flexible, and stakeholders are more strategic and concerned with the distant future, corporate social responsibility.
- **Organizational Dynamics:** Family-centred and proactive approach is used because of strong Mexican cultural identities imposed on the individuals.
- **Decision-Making Process:** It follows a major decision-making criterion of community responsibility and relevance with an intent to produce sustainable development.

The case studies have been selected to give an understanding of how the cultural profile influences both, entrepreneurial leadership and organizational processes globally. They show how culture shapes interaction patterns, behavioural processes, and concepts of authority that are manifest in organisations. For instance, risk taking in Silicon Valley is good because it covers product development and quickness while guanxi and Confucianism in Alibaba frame its strategic behaviour in China. Infosys shows that Indian ethics are applied in ethical leadership in organizations, while the Mittelstand shows how family leadership is done sustainably in Germany.

Another idea stems from Toyota that is trying to apply Kaizen that means 'continual improvement,' while the concept of chaebol is linked to the hierarchical and innovative organization style of Korean companies. Sustainability Leadership in Natura – Brazil, IKEA's people's power in Sweden, and L'Oreal's beauty in France: Culture and business success. The Dangote Group's success in Nigeria, Spotify's disruption in Sweden, Nando's ethical leadership in South Africa, Uniqlo's emphasis on craftsmanship in Japan, Shopify's enablement in Canada and Grupo Bimbo's community involvement in Mexico also depict how culture influences many forms of leadership and management.

Discussion

1. How does culture influence the interpretation and practice of entrepreneurial leadership across different cultural contexts?

Culture thus is found to influence business leadership in the spectrum of how leadership directives are perceived and executed. This influence can be observed across various cultural dimensions. This influence can be observed across various cultural dimensions:

- **Cultural Norms and Values:** Cultural Norms and Values: It just occur the necessity to explain that leaders and their actions are always influenced by cultural values. Thus, for instance, the degree of Power Distance, as illustrated by the Saudi Arabia, is a lot higher as compared to the defined norms of civilised societies. This can be evidenced by the charbol system of South Korea in which the leaders of a company such as Samsung embark on innovation yet practice tight hierarchical authority (Smith et al., 1996). On the other hand, in Sweden, leadership tends to be collectivist and decentralised as envisaged by IKEA's decentralised organisational structure that pockets for employee activism and decision making through consensus (Trompenaars & Woolliams, 2024a).

- **Leadership Traits and Behaviour:** Culture traits, for instance, the extent to which the particular culture reflects Individualism or Collectivism, constrains the characteristics that are expected from leaders. As observed in countries such as the United States, people embrace specific cultural dimensions where leaders strive towards the vision and personal agency or concept analogous to creativity found in Silicon Valley of Northern California (Nguyen, 2020). On the other hand, civilised cultures such as those in China value people's loyalty to the collective whilst harbouring no individuality and this is well illustrated by the implementation of guanxi and Confucianism in Alibaba's management (Hofstede, 2001; Trompenaars & Hampden-Turner, 1997).

- Decision-Making Processes: People's decisions are influenced through their Cultural Uncertainty Avoidance attitude. The High uncertainty avoidance cultures such as Japan make the leaders to aim at avoiding risks and seeking stability, something that is seen at Toyota through the kaizen management that advocates for minor improvements accompanied by quality (Hofstede, 2001; House et al., 2004; Pauluzzo et al., 2018). On the other hand, as per Hofstede (2001)'s dimension where the USA has low Uncertainty Avoidance, leaders are free to explore and are ready to take risks, which is compatible with Silicon Valley culture (Hofstede, 2001; House et al., 2004; Stoudemire, 2024).

- **Communication Styles:** Culture entertains leaders through the ways they get to exhibit themselves. For example, when discussing, 'affective culture', Italian leaders would demonstrate emotions and passion, on the same note, passion and emotions are minimized in 'neutral' cultures, for instance, Japanese leaders remain calm and professional (Trompenaars & Woolliams, 2024b). This poses a considerable concern to leaders whom it changes the way they supervise their subordinates and communicate their goals and objectives.

2. What are the Implications of Cultural Diversity on Leadership Development Outcomes For Business-Owning Entrepreneurs?

Below are the manners through which cultural diversity impacts leadership development outcomes:

- Cultural Intelligence Enhanced: Leaders get to up their cultural intelligence since they are exposed to different contexts in other cultures. It's an essential feature when running teams from different cultural background and operating in a world economy. For instance, Infosys in India wants to develop ethical management skills and community participation. This presents how cultural intelligence seeks to moderate business across the globe which is depicted by the following promises.

- Flexible Leadership Styles: In the multicultural workplace, the leaders should adopt versatile ways of leadership so that the two can be harmonized to accommodate the evolving culture. For instance, a leadership style of Alibaba reflects both Hofstede's power distance, where flexibility is made toward both traditional and modern ways of business, as well as having a long term orientation, respect of hierarchy and the flexibility is made toward both vertical and very long term views on the business (Hofstede, 2001; House et al., 2004; Nguyen, 2020).

- Challenges of Training: The creation of highly effective training interventions in a multisystems environment is a very challenging endeavour. It has to address requirements of different cultures, for example in leadership, which is seen at the Brazilian Natura that focused on sustainable development as well as purity of business (Hofstede, 2001; House et al., 2004; Pauluzzo et al., 2018; Siyal., 2018).

- Innovation and Creativity: Culture might bring in diversity when it comes to thinking or ideas in dealing with an existing challenge. For example, Spotify's leaders work toward creating an environment where there is creativity and gender egalitarianism; and therefore, there is an emergence of new innovations in the music market.

3. How Can Organizations Develop Effective Training Programs to Enhance Entrepreneurial Leadership Competencies In Multicultural Settings?

Effective training programs can, however, be developed in organizations if they employ the following strategies as provided for in the CAEL Framework:

- Cultural Awareness Training: It is suggested that such programs should be made flexible and should contain cultural attitude and behavioural leadership. For instance, the power distance index or individualism/collectivism possibly could be familiar as offering a framework of the relative freedom of strategic management leaders in applying the strategy in various cultural places (Helfrich, 2024; Hofstede, 2001; House et al., 2004).

- Use of Case Studies and Real-Life Examples: Application reflects cultural factors based on samples from other cultures to provide applicability to leadership. For instance, a glance at the Toyota's Kaizen strategy, as well as the sustainability activities founded on Natura, might provide suitable real-life examples of the use of different cultural concepts.

- Interactive Learning Practices: Simulations and role-playing were useful in engaging participants to proliferate cultural sensitivity. This very aspect can be noticed in Uniqlo, as its strategic direction is to constantly innovate and meet the needs of the customer, the primary activity being strongly interactive and based on feedback. For example, the experience of facilities that have downsized as a result of converting to lean production systems has been inquired about in surveys commissioned by Pauluzzo et al. (2018).

- Expertise Locally-Based and Mentorship: Local cultural informants or tutors are incorporated in the training process in order to avail a more specific approach. For instance, leaders in the Mexican Giants such as Grupo Bimbo get important information and or understanding regarding cultural values of their people and engagement in social activities during their operations (Hofstede, 2001; House et al., 2004; Stoudemire, 2024).
- Continuous Feedback and Adaptation: online feedback loop should be easily recognizable in time-honored training processes. This means that the training programs should be dynamic so as to meet the current change in a multiculture environment. It assisted leaders like those at Shopify where the aspect of power and idea encouragement was recommended in a diversified context (Cahya et al, 2024; Hofstede, 2001; House et al., 2004).
- Discuss the Soft Skills: Promoting soft skills like empathy and flexibility increases the competence of leaders in addressing issues to do with cultural diversity. For instance, when IKEA employments relationship management and the equality participation at the workplace is its key strategy, that is a perfect illustration of how interpersonal skills is a characteristic of leadership (Trompenaars & Woolliams, 2024b).

Recommendations for Policy and Practice in Enhancing Entrepreneurial Leadership Across Cultures

1. Cultivate Specific Cultural Sensitivity Education

Policy Recommendation: Management development programs should include cultural competency as one of the measures that are required to be implemented in organizations. The intention cannot be anything but facilitating the development of cultural awareness in these leaders.

Practice Recommendations:
- Curriculum Design: Offer the cultural dimensions theories such as Hofstede and Trompenaars and show how culture is a factor in the different case studies that depict actual scenarios of how culture affects leadership.
- Interactive Training: Levelling activities that involve behaviours, concepts, issues and relations that leaders must learn through practice prior to experiencing them in real live situations.
- Expert Involvement: This might be done with 'local cultural" experts or better still involving a consultant who has had work experience in particular regions or cultures as appropriate.

2. Culturally Adaptive Leadership Styles

Policy Recommendation: Organizations should foster the cultivation of cultural sensitive leadership styles so as to enable an organization to respond appropriately to various cultures.

Practice Recommendations:
- Leadership Development Programs: Develop training sessions that target on the aspect of flexibility and adaptability of leadership procedures. For instance, training leaders for changing their behaviour in relation to a number of cultural variables that have consideration for elements such as Power Distance and the extent to which a culture favours the individualist or collectivist tendency (Hofstede, 2001; House et al., 2004; Nguyen, 2020).
- Mentorship: Pair leaders with individuals who know about the multicultural environment organization and how to handle it for practical purposes.

3. Establish Inclusive Decision-Making Processes

Policy Recommendation: Ensure that the decision making is grounded in the organisational structure to ensure that they are sound, they involve other people and are culturally sensitive.

Practice Recommendations:
- Collaborative Decision-Making: Make sure that the decisions arrived at are as inclusive as is possible after being made by a selection of the workforce cross section. For example, IKEA's approach of consensus-building and involving its employees may become an erudite example of steps on inclusion of the decision-making process.
- Cultural Sensitivity: Managers should be educated on feature recognition and appreciation of various communication diverse and choices in decision making processes. For instance: Power distance vs. Low power Distance cultures.

4. International Management Strategies

Policy Recommendation: The cultural sensitisation and adjustment within different global settings of strategies of international management.

Practice Recommendations:

- Formulating the Strategy: Formulate management techniques where cultural factors are embraced i. e. Long-term/Short-term perspective or Universalism/Particularism.
- Constant Readjustment: Review and revitalize international them from time to time due to new cultural trends, but also due to feedback from international operations.

5. Case Studies and Real-World Applications: They all point towards providing an enriching leadership training to the employees.

Policy Recommendation: The leadership training courses should be adjusted in a way that it will provide more possibilities to use cases and examples in order to present the influence of cultural diversity on the modern leadership.

Practice Recommendations:

- Case study integration: This theory can be supported by different examples from different countries: for example, Alibaba using the guanxi system in China, or Toyota using the Kaizen system in Japan.
- Practical experience: Make certain that leader development programs encompass first-hand, practical, overseas project or assignment that will help the leader use team management, cross cultural experience.

6. Multicultural Organizational Practice That is Integral to Functional Work

Policy Recommendation: On the organizational level, hierarchy should adopt and promote cultural diversity where it should foster, support and advance a positive corporate culture.

Practice Recommendations:

- Diversity Initiatives: Activities suggesting Institution's commitment to Diversity and inclusion. This is in terms of diversity as epitomized in the hiring strategies that are typical of differentiated cultures.
- Community Engagement: Interact with the cultures within these regions to be conversant with such expectations and include them in the company's practice as in the practice applied by Natura on sustainability as recommended by Pauluzzo et al. (2018).

7. Regular appraisals and assessment on the trainings and development programmes.

Policy Recommendations: Once in a while check the relevance and the effectiveness of the leadership training and development programs in any culture.

Practice Recommendations:
- Feedback Mechanisms: Finally, there should be constructed channels through which leaders can provide their opinions on the effectiveness of the training programs and the other possible enhancements that may be carried out.
- Updating Programs: From time to time, alter the information and approaches of the training according to revised cultural tendencies as well as newly developed practices of leadership (as cited in Helfrich, 2024; Stoudemire, 2024).

CONCLUSION

Culture as a contingency factor for entrepreneurial leadership is crucial in today's intensely globalized business setting to foster the creation of suitable minority lead innovations. Cultural dimensions by Geert Hofstede and Fons Trompenaars significantly help in identifying how the culture of a society looks like in as much as it supports or fits the leadership styles and decisions made. Hofstede's dimensions of Power Distance, Individualism vs. Collectivism, and Uncertainty Avoidance present how leaders deal with power, organise goals in order of relative importance and how they estimate risk in various cultures. Trompenaars' dimensions like Universalism vs Particularism or Neutral vs Affective describe how such cultural orientations in the broad spectrum influence organisational relationships and muted portrayal of emotions in leaders.

The cultural dimensions with relation to change discussed so far take on a comparative and practical tone in case studies that include the role of guanxi in Alibaba in China, Toyota's Kaizen in Japan, and values-based leadership in Infosys in India. These examples illustrate reasons why cultural sensitivity and flexibility is important for leadership.

Specifically, organisations will have to operate with a general cultural competence training, culturally sensitive modes of leadership, and practices of culturally sensitive decision-making to do justice to and work in multicultural environments. Moreover, better strategies regarding the leadership on international level resulted by the cultural intelligence as well as more enhanced practical training with actual scenarios can significantly enhance the quality of leadership program. Cultural diversity should be integrated more in the organizational practices and the training programs could be assessed more frequently so that the value of leadership development remains significant. Such recommendations, if adopted, will have provided the leaders with favourable inoculation for a multiplicity of cultures, resulting in increased innovation, cooperation and success in the global markets. In addition to increasing leadership capability, the approval and application of cultural dimensions can also help an organisation in the development of a better and more effective culture.

REFERENCES

Cahya, P., & Semnani, D. A. (2024). Navigating Cross-Cultural Communication in International Business Negotiations: Insights and Strategies for Effective Negotiation Outcomes. *Kampret Journal*, 3(2), 72–79.

Clark, D. R., & Bradley, K. J. (2024). Entrepreneurial leadership: Putting the "U" in team. *Business Horizons*, 67(2), 183–198. DOI: 10.1016/j.bushor.2023.11.004

Fernald, L. W., Solomon, G. T., & Tarabishy, A. (2005). A new paradigm: Entrepreneurial leadership. *Southern Business Review*, 30(2), 1–10.

Hampden-Turner, C., & Trompenaars, F. (1997). Response to geert hofstede. *International Journal of Intercultural Relations*, 21(1), 149–159. https://www.researchgate.net/publication/348109177. DOI: 10.1016/S0147-1767(96)00042-9

Helfrich, H. (2024). Description and Classification of Cultures. In *Cross-Cultural Psychology* (pp. 53–66). Springer Berlin Heidelberg., DOI: 10.1007/978-3-662-67558-8_5

Hofstede, G. (2001). *Culture's consequences: Comparing values, behaviors, institutions and organizations across nations*. Sage publications. www.googlescholar.com

House, R. J. (2004). *Culture, leadership, and organizations: The GLOBE study of 62 societies*. Sage. www.googlescholar.com

Islam, T., & Asad, M. (2024). Enhancing employees' creativity through entrepreneurial leadership: Can knowledge sharing and creative self-efficacy matter? *VINE Journal of Information and Knowledge Management Systems*, 54(1), 59–73. DOI: 10.1108/VJIKMS-07-2021-0121

Nguyen, T. T. (2020). A Cultural Comparison Based on Entrepreneurial Personality: Case Comparison Between Finland and Vietnam. https://urn.fi/URN:NBN:fi:amk-2020091220392

Pauluzzo, R., Shen, B., Pauluzzo, R., & Shen, B. (2018). Culture and Its Dimensions: General Implications for Management. *Impact of Culture on Management of Foreign SMEs in China*, 91-138. https://doi.org/DOI: 10.1007/978-3-319-77881-5_4

Renko, M. (2017). Entrepreneurial leadership. *Forthcoming in" Nature of Leadership", 3rd edition. Edited by David V. Day and John Antonakis. SAGE Publications.* https://ssrn.com/abstract=2977744

Roomi, M. A., & Harrison, P. (2011). Entrepreneurial leadership: What is it and how should it be taught? http://hdl.handle.net/10547/222995

Siyal, S. (2018). Does Leadership lessen turnover of public servants. The moderated mediation effect of leader member exchange and perspective taking [EBSCO open dissertations].

Siyal, S. (2023). Inclusive leadership and work engagement: Exploring the role of psychological safety and trust in leader in multiple organizational context. *Business Ethics, the Environment & Responsibility*, 32(4), 1170–1184. DOI: 10.1111/beer.12556

Siyal, S., Liu, J., Ma, L., Kumari, K., Saeed, M., Xin, C., & Hussain, S. N. (2023). Does inclusive leadership influence task performance of hospitality industry employees? Role of psychological empowerment and trust in leader. *Heliyon*, 9(5), e15507. DOI: 10.1016/j.heliyon.2023.e15507 PMID: 37153410

Siyal, S., & Peng, X. (2018). Does leadership lessen turnover? The moderated mediation effect of leader–member exchange and perspective taking on public servants. *Journal of Public Affairs*, 18(4), e1830. DOI: 10.1002/pa.1830

Siyal, S., Xin, C., Umrani, W. A., Fatima, S., & Pal, D. (2021). How do leaders influence innovation and creativity in employees? The mediating role of intrinsic motivation. *Administration & Society*, 53(9), 1337–1361. DOI: 10.1177/0095399721997427

Smith, P. B., Dugan, S., & Trompenaars, F. (1996). National culture and the values of organizational employees: A dimensional analysis across 43 nations. *Journal of Cross-Cultural Psychology*, 27(2), 231–264. DOI: 10.1177/0022022196272006

Stoudemire, T. (2024). Diversity Done Right: Navigating Cultural Difference to Create Positive Change In the Workplace. John Wiley & Sons. www.booksgoogle.com.na

Svensson, F., & Molén, S. (2024). Unravelling the mystery of municipal employer branding-An exploratory case study of employer branding strategies in a Swedish public organisation. https://hdl.handle.net/2077/79595

Trompenaars, F. (1996). Resolving international conflict: Culture and business strategy. *Business Strategy Review*, 7(3), 51–68. DOI: 10.1111/j.1467-8616.1996.tb00132.x

Trompenaars, F. (2021). A trans-cultural leadership paradigm. In *Transformative Strategies* (pp. 180–197). Routledge., https://www.taylorfrancis.com/chapters/edit/10.4324/9780429274381-13/trans-cultural-leadership-paradigm-fons-trompenaars DOI: 10.4324/9780429274381-13

Trompenaars, F., & Hampden-Turner, C. (1997). *Riding the Waves of Culture: Understanding Diversity in Global Business*. McGraw-Hill. www.googlescholar.com

Trompenaars, F., & Woolliams, P. (2024). Career Developing/Supporting Cultures. In *New Approaches to Recruitment and Selection* (pp. 79–82). Emerald Publishing Limited. DOI: 10.1108/978-1-83797-759-820241016

Trompenaars, F., & Woolliams, P. (2024). Leadership Free of Cultural Bias. In *New Approaches to Recruitment and Selection* (pp. 75–77). Emerald Publishing Limited., DOI: 10.1108/978-1-83797-759-820241015

Trompenaars, F., & Woolliams, P. (2024). Seeking to Make Assessment Free of Cultural Bias. In *New Approaches to Recruitment and Selection* (pp. 19–29). Emerald Publishing Limited., DOI: 10.1108/978-1-83797-759-820241005

Zijlstra, P. H. (2014). *When is entrepreneurial leadership most effective* (Master's thesis, University of Twente). https://purl.utwente.nl/essays/66030

KEY TERMS AND DEFINITIONS

Adaptability: The capacity to adjust and thrive in changing or diverse environments.

Case studies: In-depth analyses of real-world examples or scenarios to illustrate principles, theories, or phenomena in context.

Cross-cultural leadership development: The process of developing leadership skills and competencies to effectively navigate and lead in diverse cultural contexts.

Cultural dimensions: Fundamental aspects of culture, such as individualism-collectivism, power distance, and uncertainty avoidance, which influence behaviour and attitudes.

Cultural diversity: The presence of a variety of cultural backgrounds, perspectives, and practices within a group or organization.

Cultural intelligence: The ability to understand and adapt to different cultural contexts, behaviours, and communication styles.

Cultural nuances: Subtle or intricate aspects of culture that may influence perceptions, values, and behaviours.

Entrepreneurial leadership: The leadership style characterized by innovation, risk-taking, and the ability to create and capitalize on opportunities.

Globalization: The interconnectedness and integration of economies, cultures, and societies on a global scale.

Leadership behaviours: Observable actions and characteristics exhibited by leaders in guiding and influencing others.

Chapter 9
Prospects of Green Entrepreneurship Development:
A Review of Literature Using R–Software

Manoj Kumar Mishra
https://orcid.org/0000-0003-1857-9076
FMS, Marwadi University, Rajkot, India

Akanksha Upadhyaya
JIMS Rohini Sector-5 Delhi, India

ABSTRACT

The development of business products and practices that have the potential to generate profits while also improving the environment is an urgent task that must be completed as soon as possible. The objective of the study is to investigate the possibilities for the continued growth of environmentally responsible business ventures. The word cloud method was utilized in the current study to analyze the keywords from the earlier studies. In addition, a tree map, a word count table, and a correlation between entrepreneurship and other variables could be observed. This conceptual research paper makes use of various secondary sources of published literature. This study highlighted a number of different facets that had been investigated in earlier studies. It has been discovered that the word "entrepreneurship" is now frequently used in conjunction with "green" and "sustainability." It will be useful for future investigations because it is possible to understand previously observed trends in greater detail.

DOI: 10.4018/979-8-3693-0078-7.ch009

1. INTRODUCTION

The environment is deteriorating as a direct result of the many different business practices. The development of business products and practices that have the potential to generate profits while also improving the environment is an urgent matter that requires immediate attention (Baah, et.al., 2020; Kim et.al., 2021). The purpose of this project is to investigate the viability of eco-friendly business ventures among younger generations.

Text analysis will be used in order to evaluate the possibilities and viability of environmentally conscious business ventures. The future generations would like to make a profit, but not at the expense of the degradation of the environment. The development of both society and the economy can benefit from environmentally conscious business practices. Therefore, the utilization of environmentally friendly business practices is required in order to restore the natural world and its luxuries. Finding solutions to environmental problems and assessing their severity are at the heart of green entrepreneurship. This form of entrepreneurship contributes to the construction of an innovative business opportunity that will help to repair the damage done to the environment while also improving its overall condition. Green entrepreneurship, in its most basic form, helps to improve the economic situation of the nation by bridging the gap between financially sustainable practices and environmentally sound practices (Sengupta et. al., 2018; Vedula et. al., 2022).

According to Lotfi (2018), the utilization of environmentally conscious business practices is required in order to restore the natural world and its associated luxuries. The primary goal of green entrepreneurship is to ascertain environmental needs and assess existing environmental damage. Green entrepreneurs are drivers of change Green entrepreneurship extends beyond the narrow technology-based aspects of running a business, despite the fact that its roots are primarily in A level technological innovation, such as the reduction of pollution, the adoption of clean production processes, and the optimization of resource use. It has the potential to foster a subculture of changes in one's day-to-day life and to instigate the use of environmentally friendly products on a societal level. This, in turn, helps not only in the generation of employment but also in the improvement of the environment through the adoption of environmentally friendly practices. The studies conducted in the entrepreneurship are mainly emphasized on the economic development of nation due to employment generation. The past of sustainable development was not explore much in this field so the present study using the green entrepreneurship concept try to make this development sustainable for the future.

2. REVIEW OF LITERATURE

Banerjee and Dutta (2017) previously acknowledged this when they determined that treaties, laws, and regulations should be created to support green practice in our enterprises by making it required while also rewarding voluntary green entrepreneurship. This was done in order to eliminate or reduce harmful consequences on society and nature. In spite of the fact that people all over the world are working hard to protect the natural environment so that it can support a more robust and robust eco system, many businesses that are associated with greenwashing have remained unconcerned despite the fact that some ethical businesses are still working on developing effective ways to reduce their environmental footprints. However, in order to achieve sustainable development, it is necessary to implement green policies, procedures, and programs that are led by strong leadership that is committed to achieving sustainability (Siyal. 2023; Siyal. 2018; Siyal & Peng. 2018). This is because reorienting the workforce on the critical need to reintegrate environmental success metrics into existing financial indices is a prerequisite for achieving sustainable development. According to (Zhaojoun et al. 2017), proponents of the green economy (also known as eco-concerned capitalisms) naturally find fulfilment in the accomplishment of their own personal aspirations. This is true in spite of the challenges that may arise in the process of making green products and services available to consumers. This gives the impression that they are energized and cannot be stopped in any way. As a consequence of this, stringent environmental rules that define acceptable behaviour for citizens are likely to be enacted so as to prevent environmental-opportunist businesses from unfairly benefiting from the green market.

Horisch et al. (2017) argue that because the need to cater for numerous pastimes, which include marketers' very own fee reorientation and ideals, is what caused the genuine ardour for brand new environmentally friendly ventures, which sets out to take advantage of growing opportunities with inside the surroundings, then particular advantages ought to be available to environmentally friendly marketers for such entrepreneurial endeavors. (Merkajiw et al. 2019) argue that even though innovation structures can be accomplished at exceptional stages of a company's lifestyles cycle, new corporations generally tend to incur excessive prices on research and development (R&D) in addition to training of personnel. On the other hand, antique installed companies have a tendency to be green in this regard due to economies of scale enjoy and received reputation. In spite of the fact that there is an initial challenge in the technological existence cycle on the subject of market entry, research has shown that environmentally responsible business is more likely to be successful in the long run when compared to conventional companies.

In his article "Overburdening the Planet's Biocapacity," Demuth (2014) makes the argument that companies' unsustainable business practices are causing an excessive amount of waste that is far superior to what may be thoroughly absorbed through the biosphere, which in turn overburdens the capacity of the planet's biosphere. In the meantime, the problem of climate change does not any longer recognize geographical barriers, and as a result, whenever it strikes, it influences whatever is in the character's rage at a particular point in time. In other words, humanity has exceeded its allotted ecological assets as a result of careless ecological footprints within the direction of commercial enterprise activities. These ecological footprints were caused by the activities of commercial enterprises. It is therefore impossible to understate the role that business owners play in providing long-term solutions to environmental problems that are caused by business practices that are not environmentally friendly.

Environmentally conscious innovation and environmentally conscious promotion have a significant bearing on the overall performance of groups. Because the market for environmentally friendly goods is expanding at such a rapid rate all over the world, business owners have to be able to quickly identify promising new markets and employ strategies that are suited to meeting the expectations and prerequisites of customers. Both public and private organizations are concerned about the environment and are in agreement that green advertising needs to turn into the norm in developing countries like India and that green corporations and green advertising offer an opportunity to support sustainable development (Hasan & Ali, 2015; Garg 2015).

3. RESEARCH METHOD

The use of research methodologies aides in the comprehensive resolution of research agendas. It is possible to interpret it as a technological know-how of reading how scientific studies are carried out. [Citation needed] In it, we take a look at the various processes that are followed by a researcher in his studies, each of which is supported with argumentation in the back of it. "the strategy or architectural design by which the researcher maps out an approach to problem-finding or problem-solving," this is how the authors define research methodology. The vast majority of the articles were obtained from Google scholar, ScienceDirect, and other essential databases pertaining to environmentally conscious business practices and sustainability. These papers were submitted to and published in a variety of management journals. Here, 114 research papers were included, out of which one was deemed suitable for use in this investigation. R-software is used to assist in the process of conducting a qualitative analysis of the existing body of research. The R software, which assists in word clouding, text search, data mining, and assists in establishing correlations between text and terms. R-software is used to assist in the process of conducting a qualitative analysis of the existing body of research. The R software, which assists in word clouding, text search, data mining, and assists in establishing correlations between text and terms.

"R Studio" is a piece of software that, among other things, gives users the ability to organize and conduct analysis on text documents, PDFs, files, papers, spreadsheets, bibliographical data, and web pages. There has been an analysis of the articles' quality from multiple perspectives, and they are all available in a variety of formats. The results obtained through the use of the R software will be interpreted and presented in the following part of the research. R is a programming language that can be used for statistical computing as well as graphics, and RStudio is an Integrated Development Environment (IDE) for R. It is available in two distinct formats, which are: The RStudio Desktop application is a traditional desktop application, whereas the RStudio Server application is a web-based application that runs on a remote server.

4. ANALYSIS AND INTERPRETATION

Figure 1.

The resulted figure of word cloud is created in R- studio. Various words are shown in the diagram. The highlight terms are more in frequency. Sustainable, business, green, social and environmental are few frequent occurring words. It is found sustainable, green environment and social are the most associated word with entrepreneurship. So, the correlation of this term with entrepreneurship will be also be high.

Figure 2.

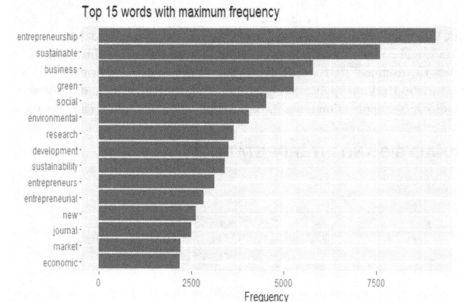

The above figure highlights the words which have been used most frequently in the previous studies related to entrepreneurship. The histogram of words shows the word entrepreneurship was most frequently used with sustainable and green in terms of its use in the study.

Table 1. Most frequent word

WORDS	COUNT
entrepreneurship	9096
sustainable	7593
business	5785

continued on following page

Table 1. Continued

WORDS	COUNT
green	5260
social	4518
environmental	4055
research	3638
development	3515
sustainability	3412
entrepreneurs	3130
entrepreneurial	2834
new	2636
journal	2504
market	2213
economic	2203
management	2127
innovation	1874
also	1850
model	1689
environment	1671
opportunities	1503
study	1492
value	1288
international	1276
knowledge	1263

The above table highlights the exact number of times each word has appeared in the previous studies. The words like entrepreneurs, green and sustainable are leading the table. But few noticeable words are social and economic as well.

Figure 3.

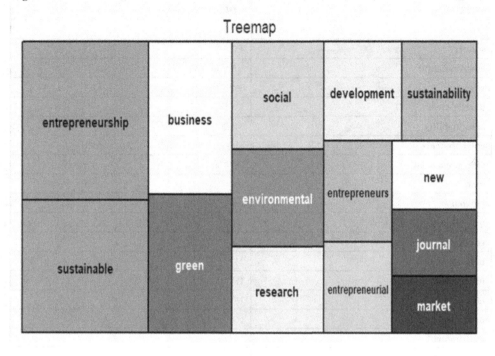

The above figure highlights that the words visible In the tree map has appeared most frequently in the previous studies. Although the diagram lists various words. This shows the relation of word entrepreneurship with green, sustainable and social.

Table 2. Correlation value with the word 'entrepreneurship'

word	correlation
sustainable	0.65
review	0.64
society	0.63
economic	0.62
social	0.61

The word entrepreneurship has correlation with various words. Here 0.6 is considered as moderate corelation. Therefore, entrepreneurship is moderately correlated with the words mentioned in the table.

5. IMPLICATIONS OF THE STUDY

After conducting an in-depth evaluation and analysis of the previous research and literature, it has become abundantly clear that the fields of sustainability, business, and entrepreneurship have been extensively researched. Studies have been conducted on green entrepreneurship under a variety of guises, including sustainable business, social business, sustainability management, and others. The spirit of entrepreneurship can contribute to the betterment of society. The promotion of a sustainable economy is at the heart of green entrepreneurship, which has a close relationship with societal development. It has also changed the way in which society views businesses and the ways in which we can save the planet by introducing a variety of environmentally friendly solutions that also have the capacity to boost the economy. In addition, the shift is getting even more pronounced.

Entrepreneurs now have the opportunity to engage in business endeavors that will have a beneficial effect on the surrounding environment as a result of green entrepreneurship, which made this possibility possible. It is possible to develop society and boost the economy all at the same time through the practice of green entrepreneurship. Despite the common perception that business ownership is solely for the purpose of generating profits, environmentally conscious business owners can make a significant contribution to both society and the environment by adopting environmentally conscious business practices. It is self-evident that business owners have altered the ways in which they think and behave when deciding their offerings in the market and focusing on sustainability as well as this, and it is also self-evident that these changes have occurred. Studies have shortcomings, and conducting research based on secondary sources has many drawbacks, some of which are outlined in the following paragraphs:

I.   Length of Time: The subject matter discussed in the research has a broader scope than the subject matter discussed in the project report, which was not possible to discuss in such a brief period of time as two months.

II. Reliability and Accuracy - Because a significant portion of the data comes from secondary sources, the reliability and accuracy of the information has a tendency to suffer.

III. Difficulty in removing data from the system as a result of the lockdown.

This research can be used to gain a quantitative understanding of the previous literature and reviews. Through the utilization of a word cloud, this will make it easier for future researchers and academicians to comprehend all of the previous studies. It gives a specific count of the number of significant words that have been researched.

6. CONCLUSION

- An increasing trend towards green entrepreneurship can be observed. Adaptation and acceptance of green entrepreneurship is being encouraged within entrepreneurs.
- The word entrepreneurship is now repeatedly used with green, sustainability as well.
- Green entrepreneurship is a win-win situation for both entrepreneurs and environmentalists.
- It basically bridges the gap by helping entrepreneurs earn profit, make money while taking care of the environment and nature to greater extend.
- Green entrepreneurship not only helps the society but also have a contribution to economy.
- However, to have a shift towards the green economy for the sustainable future, it is important to have sustainable orientation and sustainable education among the younger entrepreneurs.
- This will lead to offer a better living place to the coming generation not only in India but in the globe.
- Green entrepreneurship have a role in social development but in economic development as well.

7. FUTURE SCOPE IN THE RESEARCH

On the subject of how young people feel about environmentally conscious business practices, an in-depth study can be carried out. Research can also be done on the propensity of members of generation Z or millennials to engage in environmentally conscious business practices.

REFERENCES

Abd Rahman, A., Nezakati, H., Ho, J. A., & San Ong, T. Integrating operations, human resource, marketing, and accounting and finance perspectives in sustainable supply chain research. *Achieving Sustainable Supply Chain through the Creation of Economic Growth, Environmental Protection and Social Progress*, 1.

Ahmad, N. H., Halim, H. A., Ramayah, T., & Rahman, S. A. (2015). Green entrepreneurship inclination among Generation Y: The road towards a green economy. *Problems and Perspectives in Management*, (13, Iss. 2 (contin.)), 211–218.

Alonso, M. A. P., Garcia, J. C. S., & Pinto, M. J. C. (2018). The Impact of Cultural Attitudes Toward Environmental Issues on the Green Entrepreneurship Entry Level: A Comparative Study of Three European Countries. In *Eurasian Business Perspectives* (pp. 217–232). Springer. DOI: 10.1007/978-3-319-67913-6_15

Alwakid, W., Aparicio, S., & Urbano, D. (2021). The influence of green entrepreneurship on sustainable development in Saudi Arabia: The role of formal institutions. *International Journal of Environmental Research and Public Health*, 18(10), 5433. DOI: 10.3390/ijerph18105433 PMID: 34069588

Baah, C., Opoku-Agyeman, D., Acquah, I. S. K., Issau, K., & Abdoulaye, F. A. M. (2020). Understanding the influence of environmental production practices on firm performance: A proactive versus reactive approach. *Journal of Manufacturing Technology Management*, 32(2), 266–289. DOI: 10.1108/JMTM-05-2020-0195

Choudhary, S., & Patil, N. (2015). Green entrepreneurship: Role of entrepreneurs in energy economics in Nepal. *Annual Research Journal of Symbiosis Centre for Management Studies*, 3(1), 166–175.

Chygryn, O. (2017). Green entrepreneurship: EU experience and Ukraine perspectives. *Centre for Studies in European Integration Working Papers Series*, (6), 6-13.

del Mar Alonso-Almeida, M., & Álvarez-Gil, M. J. (2018). Green Entrepreneurship in Tourism. In *The Emerald Handbook of Entrepreneurship in Tourism, Travel and Hospitality*. Emerald Publishing Limited. DOI: 10.1108/978-1-78743-529-220181027

Farinelli, F., Bottini, M., Akkoyunlu, S., & Aerni, P. (2011). Green entrepreneurship: The missing link towards a greener economy. *Atdf Journal.*, 8(3/4), 42–48.

Jabik, B. B., & Bawakyillenuo, S. (2016). Green entrepreneurship for sustainable development in Ghana: A review. *GHANA SOCIAL SCIENCE*, 13(2), 96.

Jain, T. K. Towards the Theory of Green Entrepreneurship. Available at *SSRN* 3284935. 2018 Nov 15.

Jeevan, P. (2014). Green Entrepreneurship-A Conceptual Framework. In *National Conference on Change and Its Contemporary Social Relevance-Department of Social Work, SIMS, 27th September.*

Johnsen, C. G., Olaison, L., & Sørensen, B. M. (2018). In. *Organization Studies*, 39(2-3), 397–415. DOI: 10.1177/0170840617717551

Kaim, M. (2020). The development of green entrepreneurship in the modern world economy. *Center for Studies in European Integration Working Papers Series*, (16), 14-25.

Kaur, M. (2020). GREEN ENTREPRENEURSHIP INDIA PERSPECTIVE. *New Horizons in Commerce, IT &. Social Sciences*, ●●●, 10.

Kim, G., Humble, J., Debois, P., Willis, J., & Forsgren, N. (2021). *The DevOps handbook: How tcreate world-class agility, reliability, & security in technology organizations*. IT Revolution.

Lotfi, M., Yousefi, A., & Jafari, S. (2018). The effect of emerging green market on green entrepreneurship and sustainable development in knowledge-based companies. *Sustainability (Basel)*, 10(7), 2308. DOI: 10.3390/su10072308

Luca, B. (2008). *Innovating for Sustainability: Green Entrepreneurship in personal mobility* (1st ed.). Routledge.

Makki, A. A., Alidrisi, H., Iqbal, A., & Al-Sasi, B. O. (2020). Barriers tGreen Entrepreneurship: An ISM-Based Investigation. *Journal of Risk and Financial Management*, 13(11), 249. DOI: 10.3390/jrfm13110249

Melay, I., & Kraus, S. (2012). Green entrepreneurship: Definitions of related concepts. *Int. J. Strateg. Manag.*, 12, 1–2.

Mirjana Radoviʹc-Markoviʹc 1,2,* and BrankŽivanoviʹc (2019), Sustainability, 11, 6826; DOI: 10.3390/su11236826

E.I. Nikolaou, An evaluation of the prospects of green entrepreneurship development using a SWOT analysis, Department of Logistics, Technological Education Institution of Chalkida, Greece, Vol. 18, No. 1, February 2011.

Pacheco, D. F., Dean, T. J., & Payne, D. S. (2010). Escaping the green prison: Entrepreneurship and the creation of opportunities for sustainable development. *Journal of Business Venturing*, 25(5), 464–480. DOI: 10.1016/j.jbusvent.2009.07.006

Porter, M. E., & van der Linde, C. (1995). Toward a new conception of the environment competitiveness relationship.

Schumpeter, J. (1934). The theory of economic development. Cambridge, MA: Harvard University Press. Shapira, P., Gök, A., Klochikhin, E., & Sensier, M. (2014). Probing green industry enterprises in the UK: a new identification approach. *Journal of Technological Forecasting and Social Change*, 85, 93–104.

Sengupta, S., Sahay, A., & Croce, F. (2018). Conceptualizing social entrepreneurship in the context of emerging economies: An integrative review of past research from BRIICS. *The International Entrepreneurship and Management Journal*, 14(4), 771–803. DOI: 10.1007/s11365-017-0483-2

Setyawati, I., Purnomo, A., Irawan, D. E., Tamyiz, M., & Sutiksno, D. U. (2018). A visual trend of literature on Ecopreneurship research overviewed within the last twdecades. *Journal of Entrepreneurship Education*, 21(4), 1–7.

Shamroukh, W. (2016, January). Green Entrepreneurship. *Conference on Environment and Alternative Power*.

Sharda, A., Goel, A., Mishra, A., & Chandra, S. (2015). Green entrepreneurship in India: global evaluation, needs analysis, and drivers for growth. In *Entrepreneurial Ecosystem* (pp. 261–282). Springer. DOI: 10.1007/978-81-322-2086-2_11

Simatupang, T. M., Schwab, A., & Lantu, D. C. (2015). Introduction: Building Sustainable Entrepreneurship Ecosystems. [Editorial]. *International Journal of Entrepreneurship and Small Business*, 26(4), 389–398.

Siscan, Z., & Kaim, M. (2020). Green entrepreneurship in the Republic of Moldova and European circular economy trend.

Siyal, S. (2018). Does Leadership lessen turnover of public servants. The moderated mediation effect of leader member exchange and perspective taking [EBSCopen dissertations].

Siyal, S. (2023). Inclusive leadership and work engagement: Exploring the role of psychological safety and trust in leader in multiple organizational context. *Business Ethics, the Environment & Responsibility*, 32(4), 1170–1184. DOI: 10.1111/beer.12556

Siyal, S., & Peng, X. (2018). Does leadership lessen turnover? The moderated mediation effect of leader–member exchange and perspective taking on public servants. *Journal of Public Affairs*, 18(4), e1830. DOI: 10.1002/pa.1830

Soenarto, S., Rahmawati, R., Suprapti, A. R., Handayani, R., & Sudira, P. (2018). Green Entrepreneurship Development Strategy Based on Local Characteristic tSupport Power Eco-Tourism Continuous at Lombok. *Journal of Tourism & Hospitality (Los Angeles, Calif.)*, 7(06), 2167–0269. DOI: 10.4172/2167-0269.1000394

Stadnyk, V., Krasovska, G., Pchelianska, G., & Holovchuk, Y. (2021). Determinants of "green entrepreneurship" competitive strategies implementation in the agro-industrial sector of Ukraine. []. IOP Publishing.]. *IOP Conference Series. Earth and Environmental Science*, 628(1), 012032. DOI: 10.1088/1755-1315/628/1/012032

Suudin, H., & Brown, D. A. (2017). Greening the black box: Integrating the environment and management control systems. Journal of Accounting. *Accounting, Auditing & Accountability Journal*, 30(3), 620–642. DOI: 10.1108/AAAJ-03-2014-1649

Tamvada, J. P. (2015). The spatial distribution of self-employment in India: Evidence from semiparametric geoadditive models. *Regional Studies*, 49(2), 300–322. DOI: 10.1080/00343404.2013.779656

Tan, K. L., Suhaida, S., & Leong, Y. P. (2013, June). Self-Efficacy and green entrepreneurship. []. IOP Publishing.]. *IOP Conference Series. Earth and Environmental Science*, 16(1), 012119. DOI: 10.1088/1755-1315/16/1/012119

Tee, M., Abdulahi, R., Din, J., Abdulahi, S., & Wu, L. (2017). Green SD Adoption using knowledge management facilitation – Motivational perspective. *Journal of Theoretical and Applied Information Technology*, 5(17), 4291–4301.

Vedula, S., Doblinger, C., Pacheco, D., York, J. G., Bacq, S., Russo, M. V., & Dean, T. J. (2022). Entrepreneurship for the public good: A review, critique, and path forward for social and environmental entrepreneurship research. *The Academy of Management Annals*, 16(1), 391–425. DOI: 10.5465/annals.2019.0143

Yousuf, N. A., Awang, H., & Iranmaneseh, M. (2017). Determinants and outcome of environmental practices in Malaysian construction projects. *Journal of Cleaner Production*, 156(17), 345–354. DOI: 10.1016/j.jclepro.2017.04.064

Zhaojun, Y., Jun, S., Yali, Z., & Ying, W. (2017). Green, Green, It's Green: A Triad Model of Technology, Culture, and Innovation for Corporate Sustainability. *Sustainability*, 9, 1–23.

Chapter 10
The Dragon's Approach:
Entrepreneurial Leadership in the Chinese Cultural Context

Mohamad Zreik
https://orcid.org/0000-0002-6812-6529
Sun Yat-sen University, China

ABSTRACT

This chapter examines entrepreneurial leadership in the context of China's distinct sociocultural environment, taking into account the country's rapid economic development and robust entrepreneurial spirit. At first, it provides an overview of China's history, government, and economy. Then, it delves into how "guanxi" and "mianzi"—two concepts central to Chinese culture—influence the way business leaders in China operate. Key aspects of Chinese entrepreneurial leadership are presented, and the chapter discusses how these elements match up with or differ from globalized notions. As an added bonus, it provides techniques of measuring these factors in a Chinese setting. Insights from Chinese business success stories are provided as the chapter finishes. Leaders in today's increasingly globalized world can benefit from gaining a deeper appreciation for the cultural nuances of China's entrepreneurial leadership setting.

1. INTRODUCTION

This chapter explores the intriguing topic of entrepreneurial leadership in the context of China's distinctive and rich sociocultural environment. China's rapid economic development and reputation for a vibrant entrepreneurial culture provide

DOI: 10.4018/979-8-3693-0078-7.ch010

an attractive prism through which to study and learn about entrepreneurial leadership across cultures.

The chapter begins by describing in detail the complex terrain of China. It focuses on the cultural, economic, and sociopolitical contexts in which entrepreneurial leadership in China is exercised. The chapter then delves into a thorough analysis of how traditional Chinese philosophies, societal conventions, and certain cultural notions influence the way entrepreneurial leadership is understood and carried out in China. The chapter then delves into the finer points of the Chinese concept of entrepreneurial leadership, analyzing the ways in which it may parallel or deviate from Western notions of the same.

An efficient method of quantifying these factors, especially in the Chinese cultural setting, is also outlined in this chapter. The chapter concludes with a collection of intriguing Chinese case studies and success stories, each of which offers actionable advice that may benefit entrepreneurs at any stage of their careers.

It is hoped that the readers will be able to effectively modify their leadership styles and strategies to meet cultural expectations in China by having a deep awareness of the cultural intricacies of entrepreneurial leadership in China. Organizational success in today's multicultural and globalized environment can be substantially aided by developing leaders who can effectively work across cultural boundaries (Caligiuri et al., 2020).

There are a number of important reasons why an appreciation for China's entrepreneurial leadership is essential in today's international business environment. To begin, China's growing economy and status as the world's second largest make it a major role on the international stage (Zreik, 2023). Understanding China's distinctive leadership style, which is heavily impacted by the country's deep cultural traditions and values, is crucial for companies and executives that want to do business in or with China.

Second, there are valuable lessons to be learned from the Chinese model of entrepreneurial leadership that can be applied in other societies. Understanding how to build trust, keep the peace, and create a solid foundation for your business network can benefit from the Chinese emphasis on 'guanxi' or relationships, and 'mianzi' or face/reputation (Tse & Tsang, 2021).

In addition, the Chinese way of leading by example in business incorporates both traditional and contemporary ideas and methods (Zhu et al., 2019). Recognizing this combination will help gain a deeper appreciation for how classical ideas might be integrated into 21st-century management practices. It also sheds light on the ways in which many cultures have developed their own distinct perspectives on effective corporate leadership.

Finally, as organizations become increasingly international in scope, entrepreneurial leadership can be found anywhere in the world (Amit & Zott, 2020). More and more often, leaders and organizations must operate in multiethnic settings. In certain situations, it can be helpful to have a deeper familiarity with China's cultural backdrop in order to better strategize and communicate with Chinese counterparts.

2. OVERVIEW OF CHINA'S LANDSCAPE

2.1. Cultural Landscape

China has a rich cultural history that spans millennia, with traditions, philosophies, and rituals that continue to shape all aspects of modern life. The ancient philosophies of China, particularly Confucianism, Taoism, and Buddhism, are the foundation upon which modern Chinese society is built (Smith, 2021; Angle, & Tiwald, 2017).

Perhaps the most dominant world view, Confucianism stresses the value of education, obedience to authority, and social peace (Truong, Hallinger, & Sanga, 2017). As a result, 'guanxi' or relationship-building becomes increasingly important in all spheres of life, including business. Mianzi, which literally means "keeping one's face," is another pervasive Confucian principle in Chinese culture (Liu & Stening, 2016).

The ideals of Taoism are peace and harmony with all aspects of life (Wang, Wong, & Yeh, 2016). In the workplace, this idea stresses the need of executives keeping their cool and rolling with the punches as the corporate landscape constantly shifts.

The idea of collectivism, moreover, reflects the influence of these philosophies. Chinese culture, in contrast to the individualism of many Western countries, places a premium on the collective over the person. This cultural aspect is highly influential in Chinese decision-making and leadership (Chen, Xiao, & Zhao, 2021).

There is considerable regional variation in China's cultural environment. There are 56 officially recognized ethnic groups, and because of the country's size and geography, there are also significant regional distinctions in language, customs, and traditions (Zhu & Grigoriadis, 2022).

2.2. Economic Landscape

The development of China's economy has been nothing short of spectacular. Since Deng Xiaoping's economic reforms in the late 1970s, China has gone from being an agrarian economy to an industrial powerhouse and one of the world's top economies (Zreik, 2021). Today, it possesses the world's largest economy when measured in terms of purchasing power parity and the second largest when measured in terms of nominal GDP (Freeman, 2023).

The market-oriented reforms that opened the Chinese economy to international investment and private entrepreneurship while maintaining strong state control resulted in a distinctive mix of state-owned enterprises (SOEs) and private enterprises. This mixed economic approach, sometimes known as "socialism with Chinese characteristics," has allowed China to thrive and flourish rapidly (Bingmeng, 2018).

The role of the private sector, where entrepreneurial leadership is most visible, is growing in importance to China's economy. It's a major factor in economic growth, job creation, and new ideas. Particularly in the technology sector, Chinese entrepreneurial leadership has shown its strength and promise with the growth of global giants like Alibaba, Tencent, and Baidu.

China's 2013 Belt and Road Initiative shows the country's desire to expand its economic clout by creating new channels of commerce and collaboration with nations around the world (Al Shaher & Zreik, 2022).

While China's economic expansion has brought many benefits, it has also brought serious problems like income disparity, pollution, and a rapidly graying population. Chinese business executives who take on these issues will face both difficulties and possibilities.

The background of entrepreneurial leadership in China can only be understood by having a firm grasp on the country's economic landscape. It sheds light on the factors—opportunities, threats, and dynamics—that influence business owners' choices and moves.

3. CHINESE PHILOSOPHIES AND SOCIETAL NORMS IMPACTING LEADERSHIP

3.1. Influence of Confucianism

One of China's most influential philosophies is Confucianism, which takes its name from the ancient philosopher Confucius. Business and leadership are only two areas where its teachings continue to have a significant impact on modern China after more than two millennia.

Virtue, social order, and peaceful interactions are valued highly in Confucianism. It promotes admirable qualities like kindness, justice, propriety, sagacity, and honesty. Fairness, deference to authority, ethical behavior, and concern for the well of the group are all examples of leadership attributes (Siyal, 2023; Siyal et al, 2023; Siyal et al, 2021; Han, 2013).

Leadership arrangements in Chinese businesses are strongly influenced by Confucianism, which places a premium on hierarchy and obedience to superiors. Leaders are tasked with guiding their followers toward a more moral and peaceful existence by preserving ethical standards and serving as positive role models. They construct a paternalistic style of leadership in exchange for deference and compliance.

The concept of 'guanxi' is central to Confucianism and has profound implications for leadership. Relationships and networks among people are emphasized. Cultivating 'guanxi' can help leaders succeed in corporate talks, make better decisions, and resolve conflicts (Nie & Lämsä, 2015). It promotes a more inclusive and holistic style of leadership by urging its practitioners to consider the needs of a wide range of interested parties.

'Mianzi,' which literally translates to "face," is another fundamental Confucian term that stands for a person's reputation and social status in society. 'Mianzi' is a quality that must be nurtured and developed in a leader. It suggests that superiors should not publicly reprimand or humiliate their employees for fear of 'losing face.' It's an incentive for leaders to prove their worth by acting in a trustworthy manner (Yuan, Chia, & Gosling, 2023).

3.2. Influence of Taoism

Taoism, another major Chinese philosophy, differs greatly from Confucianism but has had an equal, if not greater, impact on establishing Chinese social norms, particularly the importance of entrepreneurial leadership. The Tao is the fundamental truth or reality behind the universe, and the Tao-Chi philosophy stresses naturalness, simplicity, spontaneity, and harmony with the Tao.

Leaders that follow Taoist ideals tend to be more malleable, resilient, and adaptive. Leaders are urged to be flexible and responsive to changes in the business environment by the emphasis placed on going with the flow, or 'wu wei' (effortless action) in the ideology (Burkett, 2018).

Taoism also emphasizes a harmony between polarities, or 'Yin and Yang.' This idea emphasizes the importance of striking a balance between seemingly opposed forces in order to achieve peace and stability (Wang, 2021). In the realm of leadership, this can mean striking a good balance between, say, firmness and compassion, or between micromanagement and broad delegating, or between continuity and fresh ideas.

Chinese leaders are also influenced by the Taoist value of self-deprecation. Leaders should be modest and self-effacing, striving to influence followers not via coercion but through example, cultivating a positive work atmosphere and inspiring teamwork.

Finally, the Taoist value of achieving balance with the natural world has implications for eco-friendly management practices. This outlook inspires CEOs to think about how their actions will affect the natural world and to seek out solutions that don't harm it.

3.3. Importance of "Guanxi" and "Mianzi"

'Guanxi' and 'Mianzi' are two important notions in Chinese culture that have a substantial impact on social relationships, including business and leadership. The word "guanxi" may mean "relationships" in English, but in Chinese it has broader connotations. It is the embodiment of a sophisticated web of interpersonal connections and power structures that aids in commercial and other transactions. Leaders who practice 'guanxi' recognize the value of cultivating and nurturing positive relationships with those both inside and outside the company (Wong, Wong, & Wong, 2014). A CEO with 'guanxi' can more easily access resources, mediate disputes, and advance their company's goals. In summary, 'guanxi' is a crucial part of the Chinese perspective on entrepreneurial leadership since it promotes trust, cooperation, and mutual advantages.

In the social environment, a person's "face" (or "mianzi") is representative of their reputation, dignity, and prestige. In Chinese culture, losing one's 'mianzi' can result in a significant drop in status and respect (Leung et al., 2011). Leaders in the entrepreneurial sphere are counted on to advise their teams on how to avoid public humiliation and criticism. In a similar vein, leaders earn "mianzi" through excelling in their roles, fulfilling their goals, and keeping moral and societal standards. A leader's 'mianzi' affects their capacity to inspire and win over their followers and other interested parties (Zhang & Baker, 2008).

Both 'guanxi' and 'mianzi' are based on mutual trust and respect. In the same way that they work to cultivate and nurture their own 'guanxi' and 'mianzi,' leaders are supposed to recognize and value those of their subordinates.

One must be familiar with the concepts of 'guanxi' and 'mianzi' in order to function well in the Chinese business environment. Successful business navigation in the Chinese cultural setting requires an understanding of these ideas, which impact communication, decision-making, and leadership approaches.

4. THE CHINESE CONSTRUCT OF ENTREPRENEURIAL LEADERSHIP

4.1. Key Dimensions

There is a deep interplay between cultural, philosophical, and sociopolitical factors that shape the core features of Chinese entrepreneurial leadership. The three main dimensions are as follows:

Relationship-Oriented Leadership: The Chinese term 'guanxi,' which means 'relationship capital,' is the inspiration for this factor (Velez-Calle, Robledo-Ardila, & Rodriguez-Rios, 2015). Successful Chinese business leaders place a premium on networking both inside and outside of their companies. They value these connections as essential tools for advancing the company's mission. In the Chinese setting, economic transactions, effective issue solving, and fruitful discussions are generally facilitated by relationships based on trust and mutual respect. Success in business is typically facilitated by a leader's ability to tap into their 'guanxi' network for the purpose of securing resources, gaining allies, and boosting morale.

Face-Saving Leadership: In Chinese culture,'mianzi,' often known as "face," is extremely important. 'Mianzi' means caring about one's own and others' respect and honor when in a position of leadership (Guan & Ploner, 2020). To safeguard their own "mianzi," leaders work hard to impress with their knowledge, honesty, and adherence to established norms. They do what they can to protect their team members' "mianzi" by being encouraging, not publicly criticizing them, and praising their efforts. This method promotes an atmosphere of mutual regard and peace in the workplace, which in turn boosts morale and productivity (Zreik, 2022).

Paternalistic Leadership: This Confucian approach to leadership has the boss acting more like a father figure to his subordinates (Chen et al., 2014). Leaders who adopt a paternalistic stance are authoritative and caring. They establish their power by providing specific instructions and enforcing strict rules, but they also genuinely care about their colleagues' well-being. They expect loyalty and respect from their staff despite making judgments that aren't always popular. This method has the potential to increase loyalty and dedication among workers, which in turn can improve the organization's effectiveness.

These dimensions help to define a model of entrepreneurial leadership in China that is uniquely suited to the country's history, society, and economy. Anyone hoping to do business with Chinese entrepreneurs and businesses would benefit from gaining a deeper understanding of these factors.

While there are certain connections between the Chinese and more Western conceptions of entrepreneurial leadership, there are also notable variations. Individualism, assertiveness, and transformative leadership are frequently stressed in globalized leadership theories, which are often characterized by Western-centric attitudes (Goh, 2009). Leaders are counted on to instill a sense of shared purpose in their followers while also encouraging creative problem solving and taking calculated risks. The team also places a premium on its members being self-sufficient and developing their own ideas. While cultivating connections is essential for global leadership, it does not have the same weight or nuance that 'guanxi' has in China.

Chinese culture, heavily inspired by ideologies such as Confucianism and Taoism, emphasizes paternalistic leadership, harmonious interpersonal interactions ('guanxi,' or "personal connections"), and the preservation of reputation and dignity ('mianzi,' or "personal pride"). Respect for tradition, social harmony, and hierarchical institutions is maintained alongside an appreciation for innovation and motivation. Leadership is viewed as more than just a method to achieve organizational goals; it is also a position with moral and societal obligations (Lin, 2011).

This contrast demonstrates how leadership concepts vary greatly from one culture to the next. It's possible that the nuances of leadership in a country like China are lost in the broader backdrop provided by international constructs. For successful cross-cultural leadership and cooperation, an appreciation of these distinctions is essential. It stresses the significance of understanding cultural differences and adjusting one's leadership style accordingly.

4.2. Methods of Measurement in Chinese Context

To assess entrepreneurial leadership in China, one must negotiate the intricate web of cultural, economic, sociopolitical, and geographical aspects that influence leadership styles and practices. Indigenous ideas like 'guanxi' and 'mianzi' and their impact on leadership styles need to be comprehended.

Culturally sensitive evaluation measures are useful for gauging the level of entrepreneurial leadership among Chinese students. These resources need to accommodate for differences in cultural practices, norms, and values. Measures of a leader's sensitivity to mianzi, their alignment with Confucian and Taoist ideals, and their capacity to develop and maintain 'guanxi' are all possible components of a leadership assessment instrument in China.

Common methods of gathering information about leadership styles include surveys and questionnaires (Siyal, 2018; Siyal & Peng, 2018; Long, 2017). These, however, require careful design to ensure cultural acceptability in a Chinese environment. The questions should demonstrate familiarity with traditional values and social mores in China.

The leadership styles of Chinese entrepreneurs can be better understood through observational research as well. The dynamics of 'guanxi' cultivation, face-saving techniques, and paternalistic leadership styles can be captured in such research.

Furthermore, case studies, such as the successes and failures of well-known Chinese business executives, can serve as valuable resources. These analyses can shed light on the ways in which cultural values shape leadership styles in China and provide useful instances of their implementation.

Finally, input from subordinates, peers, and other interested parties can provide useful insights about a leader's performance in a Chinese setting. To evaluate a leader's effectiveness in these areas and in the complex Chinese business environment, 360-degree feedback is invaluable (Winston & Fields, 2015).

Researchers, corporate executives, and educators can acquire a more nuanced and accurate knowledge of entrepreneurial leadership in the Chinese setting by employing culturally sensitive measurement methodologies. Leadership training and international cooperation can both benefit from this.

5. CASE STUDIES AND SUCCESS STORIES

5.1. Review of Successful Entrepreneurial Leadership in China

Understanding the theoretical principles of leadership can be aided by looking at examples of effective entrepreneurial leadership in China. Many prominent businesspeople in China have emerged from the country's thriving startup scene. These individuals have successfully navigated China's distinct sociocultural environment to leave an indelible imprint on the country and the world.

Take Jack Ma, one of the founders of Alibaba Group, as an example. His distinctive blend of relationship-centered, face-saving, and paternalistic leadership approaches is illustrative of Chinese entrepreneurial leadership. The success of Alibaba can be attributed in large part to Ma's ability to cultivate powerful 'guanxi' networks (Greeven, 2014). As a result of his efforts to protect 'mianzi,' as seen by his public acclaim for his staff and his dedication to maintaining the respect of all parties involved, an atmosphere of mutual respect and cooperation has emerged. Employee loyalty and dedication have flourished under his paternalistic leadership style, which mixes authority with charity.

Success stories abound, and Pony Ma, founder of Tencent, one of the world's largest technology giants, is no exception. Pony Ma's method of leadership exemplifies the power of classical Chinese thought. His low-key approach to leadership is a reflection of the Taoist principle of 'wu wei' (effortless action), which he adheres to (Leavy, 2016).

Furthermore, Xiaomi's creator, Lei Jun, is emblematic of a new breed of Chinese business leaders who respect both local customs and international best practices (Steenkamp, 2017). Jun approaches leadership with a blend of traditional Chinese values like 'guanxi' and 'mianzi' and Western ones like encouraging experimentation, taking risks, and giving employees a voice. His skill at fusing together seemingly disparate aspects has propelled Xiaomi to the forefront of the technology industry worldwide.

These studies provide concrete examples of how prominent Chinese business executives integrate many facets of leadership into their methods and decisions. They stress the relevance of 'guanxi' and 'mianzi,' the impact of traditional ideas, and the capability to tailor Western business practices to the Chinese market. Future business leaders and entrepreneurs might benefit much from studying these examples of exemplary leadership in the Chinese cultural environment.

5.2. Analysis of Common Themes and Strategies

Several similar themes and tactics have been crucial to the success of Chinese business leaders, as evidenced by a review of case studies and success stories. One recurring idea is how important 'guanxi' is in Chinese business. Successful Chinese business leaders place a premium on cultivating mutually beneficial partnerships at all levels of their operations. They recognize the value of these connections for securing funding, building a loyal customer base, and advancing the company's mission.

Second, they have an ingrained notion of "mianzi" in their approaches to leadership. These officials are well-aware of the weight that one's reputation carries in Chinese culture. To safeguard their own "mianzi," they exert effort to appear capable, honest, and respectful. At the same time, they aid their coworkers in keeping face, which contributes to an overall more pleasant and productive workplace.

A third point is that many effective Chinese leaders have a paternalistic style of leadership that originates in Confucianism. They strike a nice mix between being authoritative and warm and caring for the well-being of their staff. This two-pronged strategy promotes dedication and loyalty, which in turn improves team output and keeps businesses afloat.

Successful Chinese business executives often show an impressive capacity for transformation. These leaders, inspired by Taoism, can adapt quickly to the ever-changing conditions of the market and the commercial world. They've managed to strike a good balance between remaining true to their traditions and being receptive to new ways of doing things.

Last but not least, these leaders share a special blend of traditional Chinese cultural values and global ideas of entrepreneurship. While they recognize the value of 'guanxi,''mianzi,' and other ancient practices, they are also open to adopting more Western values such as creativity, independence, and risk-taking. They are successful in both the domestic and international commercial environments because to their diversified strategies.

These shared elements and methods shed light on what it takes to be an effective business leader in the Chinese culture. Leaders may benefit themselves and their organizations by learning about and adapting to the nuances of doing business in China.

5.3. Practical Implications and Lessons Learned

For business leaders, entrepreneurs, and scholars interested in cross-cultural leadership, the practical consequences and lessons acquired from studying entrepreneurial leadership in the Chinese cultural context can be beneficial.

One takeaway is the significance of recognizing and valuing the cultural setting in which one operates. Concepts like 'guanxi' and 'mianzi' and ideologies like Confucianism and Taoism have substantial sway over leadership techniques in China (King, 2018). Leaders who want to do well in this setting should make an effort to learn about and accommodate for these cultural differences.

The importance of healthy relationships is another takeaway. Chinese business executives place a premium on 'guanxi,' which may be a crucial asset in the global marketplace. Investing in relationships can make commercial transactions, issue solving, and negotiations go more smoothly in any culture.

One further important lesson is the value of face-saving measures (or "mianzi"). Leaders should protect their own and others' honor at all costs. This method has the potential to promote an atmosphere of mutual regard and cooperation at work, strengthen team bonds, and boost productivity.

Furthermore, the paternalistic style of leadership prevalent in China demonstrates the significance of striking a harmony between authority and kindness. A strong sense of loyalty and dedication can be fostered by leaders who demonstrate their authority while also displaying real concern for the well-being of their staff.

Finally, leading Chinese business figures show how vital it is to be flexible. They have a flexible approach and are ready to adapt to new market and business conditions. In a commercial world where things are always shifting, the ability to adapt quickly can be invaluable.

6. CONCLUSION

This chapter has provided a comprehensive exploration of the meaning and practice of entrepreneurial leadership in the context of contemporary China. In order to better understand the Chinese viewpoint on entrepreneurial leadership, a brief overview of China's history, economics, and political structure was provided.

It then discussed how cultural norms and traditional Chinese philosophies like Confucianism and Taoism inform this view.

The Chinese concepts of 'guanxi' (relationships) and 'mianzi' (face or reputation) were highlighted as crucial to effective entrepreneurial leadership in China. The chapter discussed how 'guanxi' strengthens a leadership approach that places a premium on building and sustaining connections, and how 'mianzi' provides the foundation for a leadership approach that places a premium on upholding dignity and integrity. The authoritarian style of leadership at the period was widely understood to have its roots in Confucian values.

Then, the most salient features of Chinese entrepreneurial leadership were discussed, alongside instances illustrating where they matched or differed from their Western counterparts. The best ways to evaluate these elements while also accounting for the Chinese cultural context were investigated. Analyzing common themes and strategies used by successful Chinese business executives in the context of a number of case studies and success stories shed light on the applicability of these traits.

Leadership qualities such as cultural sensitivity and adaptability cannot be overstated. Culture and history shape a society's leadership style, making it unique to each group. Recognizing cultural differences, accepting cultural nuances, and adapting leadership styles are all essential for effective cross-cultural collaboration and leadership. According to the results of these research, CEOs can be at their most effective in both domestic and international business settings when they find a happy medium between upholding traditional values and embracing new, more universal ones.

Appreciating Chinese entrepreneurial leadership contributes to the conversation of global business in a number of ways. As one of the world's largest economies and a country with a well-earned reputation for invention and initiative, China has a significant impact on international trade. A deeper understanding of Chinese entrepreneurial leadership styles can help ensure the success of partnerships and joint ventures between Chinese and international businesses.

Furthermore, lessons can be learned by business owners and managers anywhere from these observations. The entrepreneurial spirit of China has much to teach the rest of the world about putting others first, building trust, and finding a healthy balance between authority and compassion. They are a useful reminder that leadership includes understanding of social and moral responsibilities, acquaintance with cultural norms, and the ability to connect effectively with others.

REFERENCES

Al Shaher, S., & Zreik, M. (2022). Sino-Iranian Relations: More Cooperation Despite Sanctions. *resmilitaris, 12*(2), 637-649.

Amit, R., & Zott, C. (2020). *Business model innovation strategy: Transformational concepts and tools for entrepreneurial leaders*. John Wiley & Sons.

Angle, S. C., & Tiwald, J. (2017). *Neo-Confucianism: A philosophical introduction*. John Wiley & Sons.

Bingmeng, H. (2018). An Analysis of the Anti-socialist Nature of Neo-liberalism. *International Critical Thought*, 8(1), 28–45.

Burkett, T. (2018). *Zen in the Age of Anxiety: Wisdom for Navigating Our Modern Lives*. Shambhala Publications.

Caligiuri, P., De Cieri, H., Minbaeva, D., Verbeke, A., & Zimmermann, A. (2020). International HRM insights for navigating the COVID-19 pandemic: Implications for future research and practice. *Journal of International Business Studies*, 51, 697–713. PMID: 32836500

Chen, M., Xiao, J. Z., & Zhao, Y. (2021). Confucianism, successor choice, and firm performance in family firms: Evidence from China. *Journal of Corporate Finance*, 69, 102023. DOI: 10.1016/j.jcorpfin.2021.102023

Chen, X. P., Eberly, M. B., Chiang, T. J., Farh, J. L., & Cheng, B. S. (2014). Affective trust in Chinese leaders: Linking paternalistic leadership to employee performance. *Journal of Management*, 40(3), 796–819.

Freeman, A. (2023). The 60-year downward trend of economic growth in the industrialized countries of the world. *The Japanese Political Economy*, 1-23.

Goh, J. W. P. (2009). 'Parallel leadership in an "unparallel" world'—Cultural constraints on the transferability of Western educational leadership theories across cultures. *International Journal of Leadership in Education*, 12(4), 319–345.

Greeven, M. J. (2014). The Alibaba Group and Jack Ma. In *Handbook of East Asian Entrepreneurship* (pp. 380–390). Routledge.

Guan, S., & Ploner, J. (2020). The influence of cultural capital and mianzi (face) on mature students' orientation towards higher education in China. *Compare: A Journal of Comparative Education*, 50(1), 1–17.

Han, P. C. (2013). Confucian leadership and the rising Chinese economy: Implications for developing global leadership. *Chinese Economy*, 46(2), 107–127.

King, A. Y. (2018). *China's great transformation: Selected essays on Confucianism, modernization, and democracy*. The Chinese University of Hong Kong Press.

Leavy, B. (2016). The next wave of global disruption and the role of China's entrepreneurs. *Strategy and Leadership*, 44(3), 27–37.

Leung, T. K. P., Chan, R. Y. K., Lai, K. H., & Ngai, E. W. (2011). An examination of the influence of guanxi and xinyong (utilization of personal trust) on negotiation outcome in China: An old friend approach. *Industrial Marketing Management*, 40(7), 1193–1205.

Lin, L. H. (2011). Cultural and organizational antecedents of guanxi: The Chinese cases. *Journal of Business Ethics*, 99(3), 441–451. DOI: 10.1007/s10551-010-0662-3

Liu, T. Q., & Stening, B. W. (2016). The contextualization and de-contextualization of Confucian morality: Making Confucianism relevant to China's contemporary challenges in business ethics. *Asia Pacific Journal of Management*, 33(3), 821–841. DOI: 10.1007/s10490-015-9415-2

Long, S. (2017). *Exploring which leadership styles are effective with millennial employees* (Doctoral dissertation, Walden University).

Nie, D., & Lämsä, A. M. (2015). The leader–member exchange theory in the Chinese context and the ethical challenge of guanxi. *Journal of Business Ethics*, 128, 851–861.

Siyal, S. (2018). Does Leadership lessen turnover of public servants. The moderated mediation effect of leader member exchange and perspective taking [EBSCO open dissertations].

Siyal, S. (2023). Inclusive leadership and work engagement: Exploring the role of psychological safety and trust in leader in multiple organizational context. *Business Ethics, the Environment & Responsibility*, 32(4), 1170–1184.

Siyal, S., Liu, J., Ma, L., Kumari, K., Saeed, M., Xin, C., & Hussain, S. N. (2023). Does inclusive leadership influence task performance of hospitality industry employees? Role of psychological empowerment and trust in leader. *Heliyon*, 9(5). PMID: 37153410

Siyal, S., & Peng, X. (2018). Does leadership lessen turnover? The moderated mediation effect of leader–member exchange and perspective taking on public servants. *Journal of Public Affairs*, 18(4), e1830.

Siyal, S., Xin, C., Umrani, W. A., Fatima, S., & Pal, D. (2021). How do leaders influence innovation and creativity in employees? The mediating role of intrinsic motivation. *Administration & Society*, 53(9), 1337–1361.

Smith, R. J. (2021). *Fortune-tellers and philosophers: Divination in traditional Chinese society*. Routledge.

Steenkamp, J. B. (2017). *Global brand strategy: World-wise marketing in the age of branding*. Springer.

Truong, T. D., Hallinger, P., & Sanga, K. (2017). Confucian values and school leadership in Vietnam: Exploring the influence of culture on principal decision making. *Educational Management Administration & Leadership*, 45(1), 77–100.

Tse, T., & Tsang, L. T. (2021). Reconceptualising prosumption beyond the 'cultural turn': Passive fashion prosumption in Korea and China. *Journal of Consumer Culture*, 21(4), 703–723.

Velez-Calle, A., Robledo-Ardila, C., & Rodriguez-Rios, J. D. (2015). On the influence of interpersonal relations on business practices in Latin America: A comparison with the Chinese guanxi and the Arab Wasta. *Thunderbird International Business Review*, 57(4), 281–293.

Wang, H. (2021). *Contemporary Daoism, organic relationality, and curriculum of integrative creativity*. IAP.

Wang, S. Y., Wong, Y. J., & Yeh, K. H. (2016). Relationship harmony, dialectical coping, and nonattachment: Chinese indigenous well-being and mental health. *The Counseling Psychologist*, 44(1), 78–108.

Winston, B., & Fields, D. (2015). Seeking and measuring the essential behaviors of servant leadership. *Leadership and Organization Development Journal*, 36(4), 413–434.

Wong, Y. T., Wong, S. H., & Wong, Y. W. (2014). A study of subordinate-supervisor guanxi in Chinese joint ventures. In *Confucian HRM in greater China* (pp. 90–103). Routledge.

Yuan, L., Chia, R., & Gosling, J. (2023). Confucian virtue ethics and ethical leadership in modern China. *Journal of Business Ethics*, 182(1), 119–133.

Zhang, H., & Baker, G. (2008). *Think like Chinese*. Federation Press.

Zhu, J., & Grigoriadis, T. N. (2022). Chinese dialects, culture & economic performance. *China Economic Review*, 73, 101783.

Zhu, W., Zheng, X., He, H., Wang, G., & Zhang, X. (2019). Ethical leadership with both "moral person" and "moral manager" aspects: Scale development and cross-cultural validation. *Journal of Business Ethics*, 158, 547–565.

Zreik, M. (2021). Europe: An attractive region for Chinese investment. *Journal of the Belarusian State University.International Relations*, 1, 51–61.

Zreik, M. (2022). "Rethinking China's Leadership through an Analysis of the Belt and Road Initiative "Information & Security. *International Journal (Toronto, Ont.)*, 52, 81–100.

Zreik, M. (2023). From Boom to Bust: A Study of China's Economy in the Wake of COVID-19 Outbreak in H1 2020. *BRICS Journal of Economics*, 4(1), 147–171. DOI: 10.3897/brics-econ.4.e101050

KEY TERMS AND DEFINITIONS

Adaptability: The ability to adjust to new conditions and changes in the environment, a crucial trait for leaders in dynamic and rapidly evolving markets like China.

Belt and Road Initiative (BRI): A global development strategy adopted by China involving infrastructure development and investments in various countries, aimed at enhancing trade and economic growth.

Collectivism: A cultural value that emphasizes the importance of the group over the individual, prevalent in many Asian cultures, including China.

Confucianism: A philosophical system based on the teachings of Confucius, emphasizing values such as respect for authority, filial piety, and the importance of education and moral development.

Cultural Sensitivity: The awareness and respect of cultural differences, essential for effective leadership and communication in a multicultural environment.

Entrepreneurial Leadership: The ability to lead and innovate within a business environment, characterized by a focus on vision, risk-taking, and the ability to inspire and mobilize others toward achieving entrepreneurial goals.

Ethical Leadership: A leadership style characterized by guiding subordinates with principles of fairness, integrity, and ethical behavior, aligned with Confucian values.

Face-Saving: Efforts made to maintain one's dignity and reputation in social and business interactions, critical in Chinese culture to avoid public embarrassment.

Guanxi: A Chinese term meaning "relationships" or "connections," which refers to the network of personal and professional relationships that are essential for business success in China.

Hierarchy: A system of organization in which people or groups are ranked one above the other according to status or authority, significantly influencing Chinese business practices.

Mianzi: A Chinese concept translating to "face" or "reputation," reflecting the importance of maintaining one's social standing and honor in interpersonal interactions and business dealings.

Paternalistic Leadership: A leadership style that combines strong authority and control with concern and care for employees, often seen in Confucian-influenced cultures.

Relationship-Oriented Leadership: A leadership approach that prioritizes building and maintaining strong interpersonal relationships, often facilitated by guanxi in the Chinese context.

Socialism with Chinese Characteristics: A political and economic model adopted by China that integrates socialist principles with elements of market capitalism, allowing for private enterprise alongside state control.

Taoism: A Chinese philosophy and spiritual tradition emphasizing living in harmony with the Tao (the fundamental nature of the universe), simplicity, spontaneity, and non-action (wu wei).

Compilation of References

Abd Rahman, A., Nezakati, H., Ho, J. A., & San Ong, T. Integrating operations, human resource, marketing, and accounting and finance perspectives in sustainable supply chain research. *Achieving Sustainable Supply Chain through the Creation of Economic Growth, Environmental Protection and Social Progress*, 1.

Abdelkafi, N., & Täuscher, K. (2016). Business models for sustainability from a system dynamics perspective. *Organization & Environment*, 29(1), 74–96. DOI: 10.1177/1086026615592930

Abubakar, L. S., Zainol, F. A., & Binti Wan Daud, W. N. (2018). Entrepreneurial leadership and performance of small and medium sized enterprises: A structural equation modeling approach. *Journal for International Business and Entrepreneurship Development*, 11(2), 163–186. DOI: 10.1504/JIBED.2018.091220

Acs, J. Z., Stam, E., Audretsch, D. B., & O'Connor, A. (2017). The lineages of the entrepreneurial ecosystem approach. *Small Business Economics*, 2017(49), 1–10. DOI: 10.1007/s11187-017-9864-8

Adeoye, A. O., & Oni, A. A. (2019). Workplace Diversity Management: A Study of Nigerian Organisations. *Ife Psychologia*, 27(2), 138–150.

Adeyeye, A. D. (2020). Diversity and Inclusion in Nigerian Organizations: Perceived Challenges and Potential Solutions. *International Journal of Business and Management*, 15(7), 47–56. DOI: 10.5539/ijbm.v15n7p47

Aghazadeh, S.-M. (2004). Managing workforce diversity as an essential resource for improving organizational performance. *International Journal of Productivity and Performance Management*, 53(6), 521–531. DOI: 10.1108/17410400410556183

Ahadi, S., & Jacobs, R. L. (2017). A review of the literature on structured on-the-job training and directions for future research. *Human Resource Development Review*, 16(4), 323–349. DOI: 10.1177/1534484317725945

Ahmad, N. H., Halim, H. A., Ramayah, T., & Rahman, S. A. (2015). Green entrepreneurship inclination among Generation Y: The road towards a green economy. *Problems and Perspectives in Management*, (13, Iss. 2 (contin.)), 211–218.

Ahmed, F., & Harrison, C. (2022, September). Innovation strategies of SMEs' entrepreneurial leaders: evidence from Pakistan. In *British Academy of Management Annual Conference 2022: Reimagining Business and Management as a Force for Good*. British Academy of Management.

Ahmed, F., & Harrison, C. (2022). Entrepreneurial leadership development in teams: A conceptual model. *International Journal of Entrepreneurship and Innovation*, ●●●, 14657503221143977. DOI: 10.1177/14657503221143977

Ahn, M. J., & Ettner, L. W. (2014). Are leadership values different across generations? A comparative leadership analysis of CEOs v. MBAs. *Journal of Management Development*.

Al Shaher, S., & Zreik, M. (2022). Sino-Iranian Relations: More Cooperation Despite Sanctions. *resmilitaris, 12*(2), 637-649.

Albrecht, S. L. (Ed.). (2010). *Handbook of Employee Engagement*. Edward Elgar Publishing. DOI: 10.4337/9781849806374

Alenezi, M. (2023). Digital learning and digital institution in higher education. *Education Sciences*, 13(1), 88. DOI: 10.3390/educsci13010088

Alexandre-Leclair, L. (2013). Diversity and entrepreneurship. In *Springer eBooks* (pp. 552–558). DOI: 10.1007/978-1-4614-3858-8_461

Alfes, K., Shantz, A., & Alahakone, R. (2016). Testing additive versus interactive effects of person-organization fit and organizational trust on engagement and performance. *Personnel Review*, 45(6), 1323–1339. DOI: 10.1108/PR-02-2015-0029

Ali, A., Espinosa, J., Hart, M., Kelley, D., & Levie, J. (2015). *Leveraging Entrepreneurial Ambition and Innovation: A Global Perspective on Entrepreneurship, Competitiveness and Development*. Available online: http://www3.weforum.org/docs/WEFUSA_

Al-Omari, M. A., Choo, L. S., & Ali, M. A. M. (2019). Innovative work behavior: A review of literature. *International Journal of Psychosocial Rehabilitation*, 23(2), 39–47.

Alonso, M. A. P., Garcia, J. C. S., & Pinto, M. J. C. (2018). The Impact of Cultural Attitudes Toward Environmental Issues on the Green Entrepreneurship Entry Level: A Comparative Study of Three European Countries. In *Eurasian Business Perspectives* (pp. 217–232). Springer. DOI: 10.1007/978-3-319-67913-6_15

Alshaabani, A., & Rudnák, I. (2022). *Impact of Trust on Employees' Engagement: The Mediating Role of Conflict Management Climate*. Periodica Polytechnica Social and Management Sciences., DOI: 10.3311/PPso.18154https://

Alsharif, N. Z. (2019). Disruptive innovation in pharmacy: An urgent call! *American Journal of Pharmaceutical Education*, 84(9), 1–10.

Aluthgama-Baduge, C., & Rajasinghe, D. (2022). Exploring entrepreneurial diversity: A fascination or frustration? In *Springer eBooks* (pp. 35–45). DOI: 10.1007/978-3-030-87112-3_4

Alvarez, S. A., & Barney, J. B. (2007). Discovery and creation: Alternative theories of entrepreneurial action. *Strategic Entrepreneurship Journal*, 1(1-2), 11–26. DOI: 10.1002/sej.4

Alvedalen, J., & Boschma, R. (2017). A critical review of entrepreneurial ecosystems research: Towards a future research agenda. *European Planning Studies*, 25(6), 887–903. DOI: 10.1080/09654313.2017.1299694

Alwakid, W., Aparicio, S., & Urbano, D. (2021). The influence of green entrepreneurship on sustainable development in Saudi Arabia: The role of formal institutions. *International Journal of Environmental Research and Public Health*, 18(10), 5433. DOI: 10.3390/ijerph18105433 PMID: 34069588

Amanah, A. A., Hussein, S. A., & Bannay, D. F. (2022a). Role of proactive behaviour in entrepreneurial alertness: A mediating role of dynamic capabilities. *Problems and Perspectives in Management*, 20(4), 127–137. DOI: 10.21511/ppm.20(4).2022.10

Amit, R., & Zott, C. (2020). *Business model innovation strategy: Transformational concepts and tools for entrepreneurial leaders*. John Wiley & Sons.

Amorim Neto, R. D. C., Picanço Rodrigues, V., Campbell, K., Polega, M., & Ochsankehl, T. (2020). Teamwork and entrepreneurial behaviour among K-12 teachers in the United States. In *The Educational Forum* (Vol. 84, No. 2, pp. 179–193). Routledge. DOI: 10.1080/00131725.2020.1702748

Andrevski, G., & Ferrier, W. J. (2019). Does it pay to compete aggressively? Contingent roles of internal and external resources. *Journal of Management*, 45(2), 1–50. DOI: 10.1177/0149206316673718

Angelidis, P., & Hatzisotiriou, C. (2013). Inclusive education. Deltio Ekpaidevtik-ou Provlimatiosmou kai Epikoinonias, 51, 10–14. https://impanagiotopoulos.gr/index.php/component/content/article/9- uncategorised/258-deltio Available from (in Greek)

Angle, S. C., & Tiwald, J. (2017). *Neo-Confucianism: A philosophical introduction.* John Wiley & Sons.

Ansari, S., Bell, J., Iyer, B., & Schlesinger, P. (2014). Educating entrepreneurial leaders. *Journal of Entrepreneurship Education*, 17(2), 31.

Antoncic, B., & Hisrich, R. D. (2004). Corporate entrepreneurship contingencies and organizational wealth creation. *Journal of Management Development*, 23(6), 518–550. DOI: 10.1108/02621710410541114

Anwar ul Haq, M., Usman, M., Hussain, N., & Anjum, Z.-Z. (2014). Entrepreneurial activity in China and Pakistan: A GEM data evidence. *Journal of Entrepreneurship in Emerging Economies,* 6(2), 179–193.

Appau, B. K., Marfo-Yiadom, E., & Kusi, L. Y. (2021). Performance implication of talent management and innovative work behaviour in colleges of education in Ghana. *International Journal of Economics and Business Administration*, 7(1), 1–10.

Arabeche, Z. (2020). Profil du dirigeant, Entrepreneuriat et performance: Cas de l'Algérie. *Al-riyada for Business Economics Journal*, 6(1), 139–156.

Aroyeun, T. F., Adefulu, A. D., & Asikhia, O. U. (2018). Effect of competitive aggressiveness on competitive advantage of selected small and medium scale enterprises in Ogun State Nigeria. *European Journal of Business and Management*, 10(35), 125–135.

Ataei, P., Karimi, H., & Zarei, R. (2024). The role of entrepreneurial leadership, intellectual capital, innovativeness culture, and entrepreneurial orientation in entre-preneurial opportunity recognition by students. *Journal of Open Innovation*, 10(2), 100265. DOI: 10.1016/j.joitmc.2024.100265

Atwater, E. (2022). What Is Entrepreneurial Leadership? Babson Thought & Action. https://entrepreneurship.babson.edu/entrepreneurial-leadership

Audretsch, D. B., & Belitski, M. (2017). Entrepreneurial eco-systems in cities: Establishing the framework conditions. *The Journal of Technology Transfer*, 42(5), 1030–1051. DOI: 10.1007/s10961-016-9473-8

Audretsch, D. B., & Belitski, M. (2020). The role of R&D and knowledge spillovers in innovation and productivity. *European Economic Review*, 123, 103391. DOI: 10.1016/j.euroecorev.2020.103391

Audretsch, D. B., Belitski, M., Caiazza, R., & Desai, S. (2022c). The role of institutions in latent and emergent entrepreneurship. *Technological Forecasting and Social Change*, 174, 121263. DOI: 10.1016/j.techfore.2021.121263

Audretsch, D. B., Belitski, M., & Guerrero, M. (2023). Sustainable orientation management and institutional quality: Looking into European entrepreneurial innovation ecosystems. *Technovation*, 124, 102742. DOI: 10.1016/j.technovation.2023.102742

Audretsch, D. B., Eichler, G. M., & Schwarz, E. J. (2022b). Emerging needs of social innovators and social innovation ecosystems. *The International Entrepreneurship and Management Journal*, 18(1), 217–254. DOI: 10.1007/s11365-021-00789-9

Audretsch, D. B., Kuratko, D. F., & Link, A. N. (2015). Making sense of the elusive paradigm of entrepreneurship. *Small Business Economics*, 45(4), 703–712. DOI: 10.1007/s11187-015-9663-z

Audretsch, D., & Moog, P. (2022a). Democracy and entrepreneurship. *Entrepreneurship Theory and Practice*, 46(2), 368–392. DOI: 10.1177/1042258720943307

Autio, E., Nambisan, S., Thomas, L. D., & Wright, M. (2018). Digital affordances, spatial affordances, and the genesis of entrepreneurial ecosystems. *Strategic Entrepreneurship Journal*, 12(1), 72–95. DOI: 10.1002/sej.1266

Avram, B. (2019). Airlines customer segmentation in the hyper-competition era. *Expert Journal of Marketing*, 7(2), 137–143.

Azmy, A. (2021). The effect of employee engagement and job satisfaction on workforce agility through talent management in public transportation companies. Media Ekonomi dan Manajemen, 36(2), 212-229. https://doi.org/DOI: 10.24856/mem.v36i2.2190

Baah, C., Opoku-Agyeman, D., Acquah, I. S. K., Issau, K., & Abdoulaye, F. A. M. (2020). Understanding the influence of environmental production practices on firm performance: A proactive versus reactive approach. *Journal of Manufacturing Technology Management*, 32(2), 266–289. DOI: 10.1108/JMTM-05-2020-0195

Babakus, E., Yavas, U., & Karatepe, O. M. (2017). Work engagement and turnover intentions: Correlates and customer orientation as a moderator. *International Journal of Contemporary Hospitality Management*, 29(6), 1580–1598. DOI: 10.1108/IJCHM-11-2015-0649

Bacq, S. & Janssen, F. (2011). The multiple faces of social entrepreneurship: a review of definitional issues based on geographical and thematic criteria. *Entrepreneurship & Regional Development,* Taylor & Francis Journals, vol. 23(5-6), pages 373-403, June. DOI: DOI: 10.1080/08985626.2011.577242

Bacq, S., & Alt, E. (2018). Feeling Capable and Valued: A Prosocial Perspective on the Link between Empathy and Social Entrepreneurial Intentions. *Journal of Business Venturing*, 33(3), 333–350. DOI: 10.1016/j.jbusvent.2018.01.004

Bagheri, A., Newman, A., & Eva, N. (2020). Entrepreneurial leadership of CEOs and employees' innovative behavior in high-technology new ventures. *Journal of Small Business Management*, 60(4), 805–827. DOI: 10.1080/00472778.2020.1737094

Bailey, C., Madden, A., Alfes, K., & Fletcher, L. (2017). The meaning, antecedents and outcomes of employee engagement: A narrative synthesis. *International Journal of Management Reviews*, 19(1), 31–53. DOI: 10.1111/ijmr.12077

Bannay, D. F., Hadi, M. J., & Amanah, A. A. (2020). The impact of inclusive leadership behaviours on innovative workplace behaviour with an emphasis on the mediating role of work engagement. *Problems and Perspectives in Management*, 18(3), 479–491. DOI: 10.21511/ppm.18(3).2020.39

Barry, D. (1991). Managing the bossless team: Lessons in distributed leadership. *Organizational Dynamics*, 20(1), 31–47. DOI: 10.1016/0090-2616(91)90081-J

Beckman, C. M. (2006). The influence of founding team company affiliations on firm behavior. *Academy of Management Journal*, 49(4), 741–758. DOI: 10.5465/amj.2006.22083030

Bell, S. T. (2007). Deep-level composition variables as predictors of team performance: A meta-analysis. *The Journal of Applied Psychology*, 92(3), 595–615. DOI: 10.1037/0021-9010.92.3.595 PMID: 17484544

Benmelech, E. (2021, August 1). Ben & Jerry's Social Responsibility: ESG Without The G. Forbes. https://www.forbes.com/sites/effibenmelech/2021/08/01/ben--jerrys-social-responsibility-esg-without-the-g/?sh=7068884a3084

Benmira, S., & Agboola, M. (2021). Evolution of leadership theory. *BMJ Leader*, leader-2020.

Bhuvanaiah, T., & Raya, R. P. (2014). Employee engagement: Key to organizational success. *SCMS journal of Indian Management, 11*(4), 61-71.

Bilal, M., Chaudhry, S. A., Sharif, I., Shafique, O., & Shahzad, K. (2022). Entrepreneurial leadership and employee wellbeing during COVID-19 crisis: A dual mechanism perspective. *Frontiers in Psychology*, 13, 800584. DOI: 10.3389/fpsyg.2022.800584 PMID: 35928413

Bingmeng, H. (2018). An Analysis of the Anti-socialist Nature of Neo-liberalism. *International Critical Thought*, 8(1), 28–45.

Bischoff, K. A. (2021). study on the perceived strength of sustainable entrepreneurial ecosystems on the dimensions of stakeholder theory and culture. *Small Business Economics*, 56(3), 1121–1140. DOI: 10.1007/s11187-019-00257-3

Blank, S. (2013). Why the Lean Start-Up Changes Everything. *Harvard Business Review*, 91(5), 63–72.

Blau, P. M. (1964). *Exchange and power in social life*. John Wiley and Sons.

Blau, P. M. (1964). Justice in social exchange. *Sociological Inquiry*, 34(2), 193–206. DOI: 10.1111/j.1475-682X.1964.tb00583.x

Bledow, R., Frese, M., Anderson, N., Erez, M., & Farr, J. (2009). A dialectic perspective on innovation: Conflicting demands, multiple pathways, and ambidexterity. *Industrial and Organizational Psychology: Perspectives on Science and Practice*, 2(3), 305–337. DOI: 10.1111/j.1754-9434.2009.01154.x

Boder, A. (2006). Collective intelligence: A keystone in knowledge management. *Journal of Knowledge Management*, 10(1), 81–93. DOI: 10.1108/13673270610650120

Bontis, N., Crossan, M., & Hulland, J. (2002). Managing an organizational learning system by aligning stocks and flows. *Journal of Management Studies*, 39(4), 437–469. DOI: 10.1111/1467-6486.t01-1-00299

Boonsiritomachai, W., & Sud-On, P. (2022). The moderation effect of work engagement on entrepreneurial attitude and organizational commitment: Evidence from Thailand's entry-level employees during the COVID-19 pandemic. *Asia-Pacific Journal of Business Administration*, 14(1), 50–71. DOI: 10.1108/APJBA-03-2021-0101

Boudreaux, C. J., & Nikolaev, B. (2019). Capital is not enough: Opportunity entrepreneurship and formal institutions. *Small Business Economics*, 53(3), 709–738. DOI: 10.1007/s11187-018-0068-7

Boukella, M. (1996). *Les industries agro-alimentaires en Algérie: politiques, structures et performances depuis l'indépendance* (Vol. 19). CIHEAM, Cahiers Options Méditerranéennes.

Bourbouze, A. (2001). Le développement des filières lait au Maghreb; Algérie, Maroc, Tunisie: Trois images, trois stratégies différentes. *Agroligne*, 44, 1–14.

Breevaart, K., Bakker, A. B., Demerouti, E., & Derks, D. (2016). Who takes the lead? A multi- source diary study on leadership, work engagement, and job performance. *Journal of Organizational Behavior*, 37(3), 309–325. DOI: 10.1002/job.2041

Brennan, N. M., Subramaniam, N., & van Staden, C. J. (2019). Corporate governance implications of disruptive technology: An overview. *The British Accounting Review*, 51(6), 1–15. DOI: 10.1016/j.bar.2019.100860

Brito, S., & Leitão, J. (2020). Mapping and defining entrepreneurial ecosystems: A systematic literature review. *Knowledge Management Research and Practice*, 19(1), 21–422. DOI: 10.1080/14778238.2020.1751571

Brousseau, E., Dedeurwaerdere, T., & Siebenhüner, B. (2012). *Reflexive Governance for Global Public Goods*. MIT Press. DOI: 10.7551/mitpress/9780262017244.001.0001

Brown, M. E., & Mitchell, M. S. (2010). Ethical and unethical leadership. *Business Ethics Quarterly*, 20(4), 583–616. DOI: 10.5840/beq201020439

Brown, M. E., & Treviño, L. K. (2006). Ethical leadership: A review and future directions. *The Leadership Quarterly*, 17(6), 595–616. DOI: 10.1016/j.leaqua.2006.10.004

Bryman, A. (1992). *Charisma and Leadership in Organizations*. Sage.

Brynjolfsson, E., & McAfee, A. (2014). *The second machine age: Work, progress, and prosperity in a time of brilliant technologies*. WW Norton & Company.

Bulińska-Stangrecka, H., & Iddagoda, Y. A. (2020). The relationship between inter-organizational trust and employee engagement and performance. *Academy of Management Journal*, 4(1), 8–24.

Bullock, J. B. (2008). Intelligence and leadership: An investigation of multiple intelligences as antecedents to transactional and transformational leadership behaviors.

Burkett, T. (2018). *Zen in the Age of Anxiety: Wisdom for Navigating Our Modern Lives*. Shambhala Publications.

Cahya, P., & Semnani, D. A. (2024). Navigating Cross-Cultural Communication in International Business Negotiations: Insights and Strategies for Effective Negotiation Outcomes. *Kampret Journal*, 3(2), 72–79.

Caligiuri, P., De Cieri, H., Minbaeva, D., Verbeke, A., & Zimmermann, A. (2020). International HRM insights for navigating the COVID-19 pandemic: Implications for future research and practice. *Journal of International Business Studies*, 51, 697–713. PMID: 32836500

Caner, T., Bruyaka, O., & Prescott, J. E. (2016). Flow signals: Evidence from patent and alliance portfolios in the US biopharmaceutical industry. *Journal of Management Studies*, 55(2), 232–264. DOI: 10.1111/joms.12217

Cao, Z., & Shi, X. (2020). A systematic literature review of entrepreneurial ecosystems in advanced and emerging economies. *Small Business Economics*, ●●●, 2020.

Caputo, A., Pizzi, S., Pellegrini, M. M., & Dabić, M. (2021). Digitalization and business models: Where are we going? A science map of the field. *Journal of Business Research*, 123, 489–501. DOI: 10.1016/j.jbusres.2020.09.053

Cardon, M. S., Stevens, C. E., & Potter, D. R. (2011). Misfortunes or mistakes?: Cultural sensemaking of entrepreneurial failure. *Journal of Business Venturing*, 26(1), 79–92. DOI: 10.1016/j.jbusvent.2009.06.004

Carson, J. B., Tesluk, P. E., & Marrone, J. A. (2007). Shared leadership in teams: An investigation of antecedent conditions and performance. *Academy of Management Journal*, 50(5), 1217–1234. DOI: 10.2307/20159921

Catalyst. (2018). Inclusive Environments: A Catalyst for Gender Diversity and Inclusion. https://www.catalyst.org/research/inclusive-environments-catalyst- for-gender-diversity-and-inclusion/

Chaniago, H. (2023). Investigation of entrepreneurial leadership and digital transformation: Achieving business success in uncertain economic conditions. *Journal of Technology Management & Innovation*, 18(2), 18–27. DOI: 10.4067/S0718-27242023000200018

Charreire, S., & Durieux, F. (1999). *Explorer et tester, Méthodes de recherche en management*. Dunod.

Chaudhry, I. S., Paquibut, R. Y., & Tunio, M. N. (2021). Do workforce diversity, inclusion practices, & organizational characteristics contribute to organizational innovation? Evidence from the UAE. *Cogent Business & Management*, 8(1), 1947549. DOI: 10.1080/23311975.2021.1947549

Chemma, N., & Arabeche, Z. (2018). Mutations and movements: What winning strategy in a turbulent environment? A comparison of two Algerian actors settled in the light of their behaviour and attitudes. *Moroccan Journal of Research in Management and Marketing*, 18, 78–98.

Chen, J., Chen, T., Chen, T. W., & Chen, M. J. (2019). Rock the boat: Competitive repertoire rhythm and interfirm rivalry. *Academy of Management Journal*, 22(1), 1–6.

Chen, M. H. (2007). Entrepreneurial leadership and new ventures: Creativity in entrepreneurial teams. [x]. *Creativity and Innovation Management*, 16(3), 239–249. DOI: 10.1111/j.1467-8691.2007.00439.x

Chen, M. J., & Miller, D. (2015). Reconceptualizing competitive dynamics: A multidimensional framework. *Strategic Management Journal*, 36(5), 758–775. DOI: 10.1002/smj.2245

Chen, M., Xiao, J. Z., & Zhao, Y. (2021). Confucianism, successor choice, and firm performance in family firms: Evidence from China. *Journal of Corporate Finance*, 69, 102023. DOI: 10.1016/j.jcorpfin.2021.102023

Chen, X. P., Eberly, M. B., Chiang, T. J., Farh, J. L., & Cheng, B. S. (2014). Affective trust in Chinese leaders: Linking paternalistic leadership to employee performance. *Journal of Management*, 40(3), 796–819.

Cherfaoui, A. (2003). Essai de diagnostic stratégique d'une entreprise publique en phase de transition, Master of science,62, Centre international deshautes études agronomiques méditerranéennes de. France: Montpellier.

Cherry, K. (2023). *What Is General Intelligence (G Factor)?* Retrieved from https://www.verywellmind.com/what-is-general-intelligence-2795210

Choi, J. N. (2007). Change-oriented organizational citizenship behavior: effects of work environment characteristics and intervening psychological processes. *Journal of Organizational Behavior: The International Journal of Industrial. Journal of Organizational Behavior*, 28(4), 467–484. DOI: 10.1002/job.433

Choi, S. B., Cundiff, N., Kim, K., & Akhatib, S. N. (2018). The effect of work-family conflict and job insecurity on innovative behaviour of Korean workers: The mediating role of organisational commitment and job satisfaction. *International Journal of Innovation Management*, 22(01), 1850003. DOI: 10.1142/S1363919618500032

Choi, W. S., Kang, S. W., & Choi, S. B. (2021). Innovative behavior in the workplace: An empirical study of moderated mediation model of self-efficacy, perceived organizational support, and leader–member exchange. *Behavioral Sciences (Basel, Switzerland)*, 11(12), 182. DOI: 10.3390/bs11120182 PMID: 34940117

Choudhary, S., & Patil, N. (2015). Green entrepreneurship: Role of entrepreneurs in energy economics in Nepal. *Annual Research Journal of Symbiosis Centre for Management Studies*, 3(1), 166–175.

Chou, L.-F., Wang, A.-C., Wang, T.-Y., Huang, M.-P., & Cheng, B.-S. (2008). Shared work values and team member effectiveness: The mediation of trustfulness and trustworthiness. *Human Relations*, 61(12), 1713–1742. DOI: 10.1177/0018726708098083

Chowdhury, F., Audretsch, D. B., & Belitski, M. (2019). Institutions and entrepreneurship quality. *Entrepreneurship Theory and Practice*, 43(1), 51–81. DOI: 10.1177/1042258718780431

Chowdhury, S. (2005). The role of affect-and cognition-based trust in complex knowledge sharing. *Journal of Managerial Issues*, 17(3), 310–326.

Christensen, C. M. (2013). *The innovator's dilemma: when new technologies cause great firms to fail*. Harvard Business Review Press.

Chygryn, O. (2017). Green entrepreneurship: EU experience and Ukraine perspectives. *Centre for Studies in European Integration Working Papers Series*, (6), 6-13.

Clark, D. R., & Bradley, K. J. (2024). Entrepreneurial leadership: Putting the "U" in team. *Business Horizons*, 67(2), 183–198. DOI: 10.1016/j.bushor.2023.11.004

Cogliser, C., & Brigham, K. (2004). The Intersection of Leadership and Entrepreneurship: Mutual Lessons to Be Learned. *The Leadership Quarterly*, 15(6), 771–799. Advance online publication. DOI: 10.1016/j.leaqua.2004.09.004

Cohen, B. (2006). Sustainable valley entrepreneurial ecosystems. *Business Strategy and the Environment*, 15(1), 1–14. DOI: 10.1002/bse.428

Content, J., Bosma, N., Jordaan, J., & Sanders, M. (2020). Entrepreneurial ecosystems, entrepreneurial activity and economic growth: New evidence from European regions. *Regional Studies*, 2020(54), 1007–1019. DOI: 10.1080/00343404.2019.1680827

Copeland, M. K. (2014). The emerging significance of values-based leadership: A literature review. *International Journal of Leadership Studies*, 8(2), 105–135. https://www.regent.edu/acad/global/publi cations/ijls/new/vol8iss2/6-Copeland.pdf

Cortellazzo, L., Bruni, E., & Zampieri, R. (2019). The role of leadership in a digitalized world: A review. *Frontiers in Psychology*, 10, 1938. DOI: 10.3389/fpsyg.2019.01938 PMID: 31507494

Cortez, R. M., & Johnston, W. J. (2020). The Coronavirus crisis in B2B settings: Crisis uniqueness and managerial implications based on social exchange theory. *Industrial Marketing Management*, 88, 125–135. DOI: 10.1016/j.indmarman.2020.05.004

Cote, C. (2023, September 14). *4 Examples of Ethical Leadership in Business | HBS Online*. Business Insights Blog. Retrieved September 21, 2023, from https://online .hbs.edu/blog/post/examples-of-ethical-leadership

Covin, J. G., & Slevin, D. P. (1989). Strategic management of small firms in hostile and benign environments. *Strategic Management Journal*, 10(1), 75–87. DOI: 10.1002/smj.4250100107

Cox, T. H., & Blake, S. (1991). Managing Cultural Diversity: Implications for Organizational Competitiveness. *The Academy of Management Executive*, 5(3), 45–56.

Cropanzano, R., Anthony, E. L., Daniels, S. R., & Hall, A. V. (2017). Social exchange theory: A critical review with theoretical remedies. *The Academy of Management Annals*, 11(1), 479–516. DOI: 10.5465/annals.2015.0099

Cropanzano, R., & Mitchell, M. S. (2005). Social exchange theory: An interdisciplinary review. *Journal of Management*, 31(6), 874–900. DOI: 10.1177/0149206305279602

Cucino, V., Ferrigno, G., Crick, J., & Piccaluga, A. (2024). Identifying entrepreneurial opportunities during crises: A qualitative study of Italian firms. *Journal of Small Business and Enterprise Development*, 31(8), 47–76. DOI: 10.1108/JSBED-04-2023-0159

D'Aveni, R. A., Dagnino, G. B., & Smith, K. G. (2010). The age of temporary advantage. *Strategic Management Journal*, 31(13), 1371–1385. DOI: 10.1002/smj.897

Dabke, D. (2016). Impact of leader's emotional Intelligence and transformational behavior on perceived leadership effectiveness: A multiple source view. *Business Perspectives and Research*, 4(1), 27–40. DOI: 10.1177/2278533715605433

Danish, R. Q., Asghar, J., Ahmad, Z., & Ali, H. F. (2019). Factors affecting "entrepreneurial culture": The mediating role of creativity. *Journal of Innovation and Entrepreneurship*, 8(1), 14. Advance online publication. DOI: 10.1186/s13731-019-0108-9

Daradkeh, M. (2023). Navigating the complexity of entrepreneurial ethics: A systematic review and future research agenda. *Sustainability (Basel)*, 15(14), 11099. DOI: 10.3390/su151411099

Darling, J., & Leffel, A. (2010). Developing the Leadership Team in an Entrepreneurial Venture: A Case Focusing on the Importance of Styles. *Journal of Small Business and Entrepreneurship*, 23(3), 355–371. DOI: 10.1080/08276331.2010.10593490

Davis, K., Christodoulou, J., Seider, S., & Gardner, H. E. (2011). The theory of multiple intelligences. *Davis, K., Christodoulou, J., Seider, S., & Gardner, H.(2011). The theory of multiple intelligences. In RJ Sternberg & SB Kaufman (Eds.), Cambridge Handbook of Intelligence*, 485-503.

Davis, A. S., & Van der Heijden, B. I. (2023). Launching the dynamic employee engagement framework: Towards a better understanding of the phenomenon. *Employee Relations*, 45(2), 421–436. DOI: 10.1108/ER-08-2021-0338

De Jong, B. A., Dirks, K. T., & Gillespie, N. (2016). Trust and team performance: A meta- analysis of main effects, moderators, and covariates. *The Journal of Applied Psychology*, 101(8), 1134–1150. DOI: 10.1037/apl0000110 PMID: 27123697

De Jong, J. P., & Den Hartog, D. N. (2007). How leaders influence employees' innovative behaviour. *European Journal of Innovation Management*, 10(1), 41–64. DOI: 10.1108/14601060710720546

Deary, I. J., Penke, L., & Johnson, W. (2010). The neuroscience of human intelligence differences. *Nature Reviews. Neuroscience*, 11(3), 201–211. DOI: 10.1038/nrn2793 PMID: 20145623

del Mar Alonso-Almeida, M., & Álvarez-Gil, M. J. (2018). Green Entrepreneurship in Tourism. In *The Emerald Handbook of Entrepreneurship in Tourism, Travel and Hospitality*. Emerald Publishing Limited. DOI: 10.1108/978-1-78743-529-220181027

Del Solar, S. (2010). *Emprendedores en el aula. Guía para la formación en valores y habilidades sociales de docentes y jóvenes emprendedores*. Fondo Multilateral de Inversiones del Banco Interamericano de Desarrollo.

Deresky, H. (2000). *International management: Managing across borders and cultures*. Pearson Education India.

Dinesh, K. K., & Sushil, N. A. (2019). Strategic innovation factors in startups: Results of a cross-case analysis of Indian startups. *Journal for Global Business Advancement*, 12(3), 449–470. DOI: 10.1504/JGBA.2019.10022956

Djalil, M. A., Amin, M., Herjanto, H., Nourallah, M., & Öhman, P. (2023). The importance of entrepreneurial leadership in fostering bank performance. *International Journal of Bank Marketing*, 41(4), 926–948. DOI: 10.1108/IJBM-11-2022-0481

Döös, M., Johansson, P., & Wilhelmson, L. (2015). Beyond being present: Learning-oriented leadership in the daily work of middle managers. *Journal of Workplace Learning*, 27(6), 408–425. DOI: 10.1108/JWL-10-2014-0077

Downey, S. N., Van der Werff, L., Thomas, K. M., & Plaut, V. C. (2015). The role of diversity practices and inclusion in promoting trust and employee engagement. *Journal of Applied Social Psychology*, 45(1), 35–44. DOI: 10.1111/jasp.12273

Drucker, P., & Maciariello, J. (2014). *Innovation and entrepreneurship*. Routledge. DOI: 10.4324/9781315747453

DuBrin, A. J. (2022). *Leadership: Research findings, practice, and skills*. Cengage Learning.

Duchek, S., Raetze, S., & Scheuch, I. (2019). The role of diversity in organizational resilience: A theoretical framework. *Business Research*, 13(2), 387–423. DOI: 10.1007/s40685-019-0084-8

Duckworth, A. (2016). *Grit: The power of passion and perseverance* (Vol. 234). Scribner.

Dullayaphut, P., & Untachai, S. (2013). Development of the measurement of human resource competency in SMEs in the upper north-eastern region of Thailand. *Procedia: Social and Behavioral Sciences*, 88, 61–72. DOI: 10.1016/j.sbspro.2013.08.481

Dweck, C. S. (2006). *Mindset: The new psychology of success*. Random house.

Dwi Widyani, A. A., Landra, N., Sudja, N., Ximenes, M., & Sarmawa, I. W. G. (2020). The role of ethical behavior and entrepreneurial leadership to improve organizational performance. *Cogent Business & Management*, 7(1), 1747827. DOI: 10.1080/23311975.2020.1747827

E.I. Nikolaou, An evaluation of the prospects of green entrepreneurship development using a SWOT analysis, Department of Logistics, Technological Education Institution of Chalkida, Greece, Vol. 18, No. 1, February 2011.

Edgecliffe-Johnson, A. (2019, January 6). Muhtar Kent: bottling Coca-Cola's secrets for success. Financial Times. https://www.ft.com/content/f8ca0346-0e72-11e9-a3aa-118c761d2745

Eisenbeiss, S. A., Van Knippenberg, D., & Boerner, S. (2008). Transformational leadership and team innovation: Integrating team climate principles. *The Journal of Applied Psychology*, 93(6), 1438–1446. DOI: 10.1037/a0012716 PMID: 19025260

Eisenhardt, K. M. (2013). Top management teams and the performance of entrepreneurial firms. *Small Business Economics*, 40(4), 805–816. https://link.springer.com/article/10.1007/s11187-013-9473-0. DOI: 10.1007/s11187-013-9473-0

Elegbede, T. (2019). Human Resource Management and the Challenges of Workplace Diversity in Nigeria. African Journal of Education. *Science and Technology*, 5(1), 153–162.

Elia, G. *et al.* (2020) Digital entrepreneurship ecosystem: how digital technologies and collective intelligence are reshaping the entrepreneurial process *Technol. Forecast. Soc. Change*

El-Namaki, M. S. S. (1992). Creating a corporate vision. *Long Range Planning*, 25-29(6), 25–29. Advance online publication. DOI: 10.1016/0024-6301(92)90166-Y

Emerson, R. M. (1962). Power-dependence relations. *American Sociological Review*, 27(5), 31–41. DOI: 10.2307/2089716

Enayat, T., Ardebili, M. M., Kivi, R. R., Amjadi, B., & Jamali, Y. (2022). A Computational Approach to Homans Social Exchange Theory. *Physica A*, 597, 127263. DOI: 10.1016/j.physa.2022.127263

Engelbrecht, A. S., Heine, G., & Mahembe, B. (2014). The influence of ethical leadership on trust and work engagement: An exploratory study. *SA Journal of Industrial Psychology*, 40(1), 1–9. DOI: 10.4102/sajip.v40i1.1210

Ercantan, K., Eyupoglu, Ş. Z., & Ercantan, Ö. (2024). The Entrepreneurial Leadership, Innovative Behaviour, and Competitive Advantage Relationship in Manufacturing Companies: A Key to Manufactural Development and Sustainable Business. *Sustainability (Basel)*, 16(6), 2407. DOI: 10.3390/su16062407

Espasandín-Bustelo, F., Ganaza-Vargas, J., & Diaz-Carrion, R. (2021). Employee happiness and corporate social responsibility: The role of organizational culture. *Employee Relations*, 43(3), 609–629. DOI: 10.1108/ER-07-2020-0343

Eyüp, Y. U. R. T., & Polat, S. (2015). The effectiveness of multiple intelligence applications on academic achievement: A meta-analysis. *Journal of Social Studies Education Research*, 6(1).

Farinelli, F., Bottini, M., Akkoyunlu, S., & Aerni, P. (2011). Green entrepreneurship: The missing link towards a greener economy. *Atdf Journal.*, 8(3/4), 42–48.

Feldman, M., & Lowe, N. (2015). Triangulating Regional Economies: Realizing the Promise of Digital Data. *Research Policy*, 44(9), 1785–1793. DOI: 10.1016/j.respol.2015.01.015

Félix, C. B., Aparicio, S., & Urbano, D. (2019). Leadership as a driver of entrepreneurship: An international exploratory study. *Journal of Small Business and Enterprise Development*, 26(3), 397–420. DOI: 10.1108/JSBED-03-2018-0106

Fellnhofer, K., & Mueller, S. (2018). I want to be like you!: The influence of role models on entrepreneurial intention. *Journal of Enterprising Culture*, 26(02), 113–153. DOI: 10.1142/S021849581850005X

Fernald, L. W.Jr, Solomon, G. T., & Tarabishy, A. (2005). A New Paradigm: Entrepreneurial Leadership. *Southern Business Review*, 30(2), 1–10. https://digitalcommons.georgiasouthern.edu/sbr/vol30/iss2/3

Fernald, L. W., Solomon, G. T., & Tarabishy, A. (2005). A new paradigm: Entrepreneurial leadership. *Southern Business Review*, 30(2), 1–10.

Ferraris, A., Giudice, M. D., Grandhi, B., & Cillo, V. (2020a). Refining the relation between cause-related marketing and consumers purchase intentions: A cross-country analysis. *International Marketing Review*, 37(4), 651–669. DOI: 10.1108/IMR-11-2018-0322

Ferraris, A., Santoro, G., & Pellicelli, A. C. (2020b). Openness of public governments in smart cities: Removing the barriers for innovation and entrepreneurship. *The International Entrepreneurship and Management Journal*, 16(4), 1259–1280. DOI: 10.1007/s11365-020-00651-4

Ferrary, M., & Déo, S. (2023). Gender diversity and firm performance: When diversity at middle management and staff levels matter. *International Journal of Human Resource Management*, 34(14), 2797–2831. DOI: 10.1080/09585192.2022.2093121

Fillis, I. (2002). An 'Andalusian dog or a rising star? Creativity and the marketing/entrepreneurship interface. *Journal of Marketing Management*, 18(3-4), 379–395. DOI: 10.1362/0267257022872415

Flor, M. L., Cooper, S. Y., & Oltra, M. J. (2018). External knowledge search, absorptive capacity and radical Innovation in high technology firms. *European Management Journal*, 36(2), 183–194. DOI: 10.1016/j.emj.2017.08.003

Franco, C., & Landini, F. (2022). Organizational drivers of innovation: The role of workforce agility. *Research Policy*, 51(2), 104423. DOI: 10.1016/j.respol.2021.104423

Frazier, M. L., & Bowler, W. M. (2015). Voice climate, supervisor undermining, and work outcomes: A group-level examination. *Journal of Management*, 41(3), 841–863. DOI: 10.1177/0149206311434533

Fredin, S., & Lidén, A. (2020). Entrepreneurial ecosystems: Towards a systemic approach to entrepreneurship? *Geografisk Tidskrift*, 120(2), 87–97. DOI: 10.1080/00167223.2020.1769491

Freeman, A. (2023). The 60-year downward trend of economic growth in the industrialized countries of the world. *The Japanese Political Economy*, 1-23.

Fullan, M. (2020). The nature of leadership is changing. *European Journal of Education*, 55(2), 139–142. DOI: 10.1111/ejed.12388

Gardner, H. (2003). Multiple intelligences after twenty years. *American Educational Research Association, Chicago, Illinois, 21*, 1-15.

Gardner, H. (2010). Multiple intelligences. *New York.-1993.*

Gardner, H. (1995). Reflections on multiple intelligences: Myths and messages. *Phi Delta Kappan*, 77, 200–200.

Gardner, H. E. (2011). *Frames of mind: The theory of multiple intelligences*. Basic books.

Gedam, V. V., Raut, R. D., Agrawal, N., & Zhu, Q. (2023). Critical human and behavioural factors on the adoption of sustainable supply chain management practices in the context of automobile industry. *Business Strategy and the Environment*, 32(1), 120–133. DOI: 10.1002/bse.3121

GEM (2018). *Global Entrepreneurship Monitor*. Institut für Internationales Management, Austria – Europe.

GEM (2021) Entrepreneurial Framework Conditions (EFCs). Available at: https://www.gemconsortium.org/wiki/1154 (accessed June 11, 2021).

George, G., Merrill, R. K., & Schillebeeckx, S. J. D. (2021). Digital sustainability and entrepreneurship: How digital innovations are helping tackle climate change and sustainable development. *Entrepreneurship Theory and Practice*, 45(5), 999–1027. DOI: 10.1177/1042258719899425

Getahun Asfaw, A., & Chang, C. C. (2019). The association between job insecurity and engagement of employees at work. *Journal of Workplace Behavioral Health*, 34(2), 96–110. DOI: 10.1080/15555240.2019.1600409 PMID: 32874154

Getz, I., & Robinson, A. G. (2003). Innovate or die: Is that a fact? *Creativity and Innovation Management*, 12(3), 130–136. DOI: 10.1111/1467-8691.00276

Gezahegn, M., Woldesenbet, K., & Hailu, K. (2022). The Role of Entrepreneurial Leadership on MSMEs' Effectiveness: A Systematic Literature Review. Journal of Entrepreneurship & Management 11 (1 & 2), Pp 01-17. http://publishingindia.com/jem/

Ghosh, S. K., Chaudhuri, R., Chatterjee, S., & Chaudhuri, S. (2021). Adoption of AI-integrated CRM system by Indian industry: From security and privacy perspective. *Information and Computer Security*, 29(1), 1–24. DOI: 10.1108/ICS-02-2019-0029

Ginsburg, D. B., Law, A. V., Mann, H. J., Palombi, L., Thomas Smith, W., Truong, H. A., Volino, L. R., & Ekoma, J. O. (2020). Report of the 2018–2019 strategic engagement standing committee. *American Journal of Pharmaceutical Education*, 84(1), 7597. Advance online publication. DOI: 10.5688/ajpe7597 PMID: 32292198

Goh, J. W. P. (2009). 'Parallel leadership in an "unparallel" world'—Cultural constraints on the transferability of Western educational leadership theories across cultures. *International Journal of Leadership in Education*, 12(4), 319–345.

González-Tejero, C. B., Ulrich, K., & Carrilero, A. (2022). The entrepreneurial motivation, Covid-19, and the new normal. *Entrepreneurial Business and Economics Review*, 10(2), 205–217. DOI: 10.15678/EBER.2022.100212

Goosen, C. J., de Coning, T. J., & Smit, E. M. (2002). Corporate entrepreneurship and financial performance: The role of management. *South African Journal of Business Management*, 33(4), 21–27. DOI: 10.4102/sajbm.v33i4.708

Gottfredson, L. S. (1997). Why g matters: The complexity of everyday life. *Intelligence*, 24(1), 79–132. DOI: 10.1016/S0160-2896(97)90014-3

Grant, A. M., Gino, F., & Hofmann, D. A. (2011). Reversing the extraverted leadership advantage: The role of employee proactivity. *Academy of Management Journal*, 54(3), 528–550. DOI: 10.5465/amj.2011.61968043

Greenwich: JAI Press.Wood, E.H. (2002). 'An analysis of the predictors of business performance in small tourism and hospitality firms', *International Journal of Entrepreneurship and Innovation*, 3(3): 201-210.

Greeven, M. J. (2014). The Alibaba Group and Jack Ma. In *Handbook of East Asian Entrepreneurship* (pp. 380–390). Routledge.

Gregori, P., Holzmann, P., & Schwarz, E. J. (2021). My future entrepreneurial self: Antecedents of entrepreneurial identity aspiration. *Education + Training*, 63(7/8), 1175–1194. DOI: 10.1108/ET-02-2021-0059

Guan, S., & Ploner, J. (2020). The influence of cultural capital and mianzi (face) on mature students' orientation towards higher education in China. *Compare: A Journal of Comparative Education*, 50(1), 1–17.

Guberina, T., Wang, A. M., & Obrenovic, B. (2023). An empirical study of entrepreneurial leadership and fear of COVID-19 impact on psychological wellbeing: A mediating. effect of job insecurity. PLoS ONE, 18(5), e0284766. https://doi.org/. pone.0284766DOI: 10.1371/journal

Güçel, C., Tokmak, İ., & Turgut, H. (2012). The relationship of the ethical leadership among the organizational trust, affective commitment and job satisfaction: Case study of a university. *International Journal of Social Sciences and Humanity Studies*, 4(2), 101–110.

Guerrero, M., Liñán, F., & Cáceres-Carrasco, F. (2020). The influence of ecosystems on the entrepreneurship process: A comparison across developed and developing economies. *Small Business Economics*, ●●●, 2020.

Gullop (2022). State of the Global Workplace 2022 Report T H E V O I C E O F T H E WORLD'S EMPLOYEES, https://www.gallup.com/workplace/349484/state -of-the-global-workplace

Gullop (2024). State of the Global Workplace 2022 Report T H E V O I C E O F T H E WORLD'S EMPLOYEES, https://www.gallup.com/workplace/349484/state -of-the-global-workplace

Gupta, V., MacMillan, I. C., & Surie, G. (2004). Entrepreneurial leadership: Developing and measuring a cross-cultural construct. *Journal of Business Venturing*, 19(2), 241–260. DOI: 10.1016/S0883-9026(03)00040-5

Gu, Q., Tang, T., & Jiang, W. (2015). Does moral leadership enhance employee creativity? Employee identification with leader and leader-member exchange (LMX) in the Chinese context. *Journal of Business Ethics*, 126(3), 513–529. DOI: 10.1007/ s10551-013-1967-9

Haider, M., Shannon, R., Moschis, G. P., & Autio, E. (2023). How has the covid-19 crisis transformed entrepreneurs into sustainable leaders? *Sustainability (Basel)*, 15(6), 5358. DOI: 10.3390/su15065358

Hammoud, K., & Abdallah, J. (2019). Empirical analysis on strategy and hyper - competition with Smes. Proceeding of the international management conference. Academy of Economic Studies, 13(1), 951–960.

Hampden-Turner, C., & Trompenaars, F. (1997). Response to geert hofstede. *International Journal of Intercultural Relations*, 21(1), 149–159. https://www.researchgate .net/publication/348109177. DOI: 10.1016/S0147-1767(96)00042-9

Handfield-Jones, H. (2000). How to grow executives. *The McKinsey Quarterly*, 1, 115–123.

Han, P. C. (2013). Confucian leadership and the rising Chinese economy: Implications for developing global leadership. *Chinese Economy*, 46(2), 107–127.

Hanson, K. T., & Tang, V. T. (2020). Perspectives on disruptive innovations and Africa's services sector. In Arthur, P., Hanson, K., & Puplampu, K. (Eds.), *Disruptive technologies, innovation and development in Africa*. International Political Economy Series. Palgrave Macmillan. DOI: 10.1007/978-3-030-40647-9_12

Harrison, C. (2014). Entrepreneurial Leadership: A Systematic Literature Review. *International Council for Small Business. World Conference Proceedings.*

Harrison, C., Burnard, K., & Paul, S. (2018). Entrepreneurial leadership in a developing economy: A skill-based analysis. *Journal of Small Business and Enterprise Development*, 25(3), 521–548. DOI: 10.1108/JSBED-05-2017-0160

Hasan, A. A., Ahmad, S. Z., & Osman, A. (2023). Transformational leadership and work engagement as mediators on nurses' job performance in healthcare clinics: Work environment as a moderator. *Leadership in Health Services*, 36(4), 537–561. Advance online publication. DOI: 10.1108/LHS-10-2022-0097 PMID: 37093237

Hashim, M. K., Ahmad, S. A., & Zakaria, M. (2012). 'A study on leadership style in SMEs', in International conference on Isla mic leadership-2. The Royale Chulan, Kuala Lumpur, September 26-27.

Hassan, S., Mir, A. A., & Khan, S. J. (2023). Digital entrepreneurship and emancipation: Exploring the nexus in a conflict zone. *International Journal of Emerging Markets*, 18(10), 4170–4190. DOI: 10.1108/IJOEM-07-2021-1076

Hatzisotiriou, C., & Angelidis, P. (2018). *European and Multicultural education: From international to school level.* Diadrasi Publishing. (in Greek)

Hechavarria, D., & Ingram, A. (2019). Entrepreneurial ecosystem conditions and gendered national-level entrepreneurial activity: A 14-year panel study of GEM. *Small Business Economics*, 53(2), 431–458. DOI: 10.1007/s11187-018-9994-7

Helfrich, H. (2024). Description and Classification of Cultures. In *Cross-Cultural Psychology* (pp. 53–66). Springer Berlin Heidelberg., DOI: 10.1007/978-3-662-67558-8_5

Hennessey, B. A. (2015). Creative behavior, motivation, environment and culture: The building of a systems model. *The Journal of Creative Behavior*, 49(3), 194–210. DOI: 10.1002/jocb.97

Herring, C. (2009). Does Diversity Pay: Race, Gender, and the Business Case for Diversity. *American Sociological Review*, 74(2), 208–224. DOI: 10.1177/000312240907400203

Hoang, G., Luu, T. T., Du, T., & Nguyen, T. T. (2023). Can both entrepreneurial and ethical leadership shape employees' service innovative behavior? *Journal of Services Marketing*, 37(4), 446–463. DOI: 10.1108/JSM-07-2021-0276

Hoang, G., Luu, T. T., Nguyen, T. T., Du, T., & Le, L. P. (2022). Examining the effect of entrepreneurial leadership on employees' innovative behavior in SME hotels: A mediated moderation model. *International Journal of Hospitality Management*, 102, 103142. DOI: 10.1016/j.ijhm.2022.103142

Hoang, G., Luu, T. T., Nguyen, T. T., Tang, T. T. T., & Pham, N. T. (2024). Entrepreneurial leadership fostering service innovation in the hospitality firms: The roles of knowledge acquisition, market-sensing capability and competitive intensity. *International Journal of Contemporary Hospitality Management*, 36(4), 1143–1169. DOI: 10.1108/IJCHM-08-2022-0969

Hoang, G., Nguyen, H., Luu, T. T., & Nguyen, T. T. (2023). Linking entrepreneurial leadership and innovation performance in hospitality firms: The roles of innovation strategy and knowledge acquisition. *Journal of Service Theory and Practice*, 33(4), 511–536. DOI: 10.1108/JSTP-09-2022-0203

Hoffman, B. J., & Frost, B. C. (2006). Multiple intelligences of transformational leaders: An empirical examination. *International Journal of Manpower*, 27(1), 37–51. DOI: 10.1108/01437720610652826

Hofstede, G. (2001). *Culture's consequences: Comparing values, behaviors, institutions and organizations across nations*. Sage publications. www.googlescholar.com

Hogan, R& R.B. Kaiser, R.B. (2005). What we know about leadership

Hogan, R., & Kaiser, R. B. (2005). What we know about Leadership. *Review of General Psychology*, 9(2), 169–180. DOI: 10.1037/1089-2680.9.2.169

Homans, G. C. (1958). Social behavior as exchange. *American Journal of Sociology*, 63(6), 597–606. DOI: 10.1086/222355

Homans, G. C. (1961). *Social behavior: Its elementary forms*. Harcourt, Brace.

Horan, J. (2007). Business Driven Action Learning: A Powerful Tool for Building World-Class Entrepreneurial Business Leaders. *Human Resource Management International Digest*, 25(3), 75–80. DOI: 10.1108/hrmid.2008.04416aad.001

House, R. J. (2004). *Culture, leadership, and organizations: The GLOBE study of 62 societies*. Sage. www.googlescholar.com

Howieson, B. (2003). Accounting practice in the new millennium: Is accounting education ready to meet the challenge? *The British Accounting Review*, 35(2), 69–103. DOI: 10.1016/S0890-8389(03)00004-0

Hughes, D. J., Lee, A., Tian, A. W., Newman, A., & Legood, A. (2018). Leadership, creativity, and innovation: A critical review and practical recommendations. *The Leadership Quarterly*, 29(5), 549–569. DOI: 10.1016/j.leaqua.2018.03.001

Hughes-Morgan, M., Kolev, K., & Macnamara, G. (2018a). A meta-analytic review of competitive aggressiveness research. *Journal of Business Research*, 85, 73–82. DOI: 10.1016/j.jbusres.2017.10.053

Hurt, H. T., Joseph, K., & Cook, C. D. (1977). Scales for the measurement of innovativeness. *Human Communication Research*, 4(1), 58–65. DOI: 10.1111/j.1468-2958.1977.tb00597.x

Hussain, M., Rasool, S. F., Xuetong, W., Asghar, M. Z., & Alalshiekh, A. S. A. (2023). Investigating the nexus between critical success factors, supportive leadership, and entrepreneurial success: Evidence from the renewable energy projects. *Environmental Science and Pollution Research International*, 30(17), 49255–49269. DOI: 10.1007/s11356-023-25743-w PMID: 36764994

Hussein, S. A., Amanah, A. A., & Kazem, S. A. (2023). Strategic learning and strategic agility: The mediating role of strategic thinking. International Journal of eBusiness and eGovernment Studies, 15(1),1-25. Retrieved from https://sobiad. org/ menu script/index.php/ijebeg/article/view/1369

Hwang, W. S., Choi, H., & Shin, J. (2020). A mediating role of innovation capability between entrepreneurial competencies and competitive advantage. *Technology Analysis and Strategic Management*, 32(1), 1–14. DOI: 10.1080/09537325.2019.1632430

Im, S., & Workman, J. P. Jr. (2004). Market orientation, creativity, and new product performance in high-technology firms. *Journal of Marketing*, 68(April), 114–132. DOI: 10.1509/jmkg.68.2.114.27788

Indrianti, Y., Abdinagoro, S. B., & Rahim, R. K. (2024). A resilient Startup Leader's personal journey: The role of entrepreneurial mindfulness and ambidextrous leadership through scaling-up performance capacity. *Heliyon*, 10(14), e34285. DOI: 10.1016/j.heliyon.2024.e34285 PMID: 39113945

Iqbal, A., Latif, K. F., & Ahmad, M. S. (2020). Servant leadership and employee innovative behaviour: Exploring psychological pathways. *Leadership and Organization Development Journal*, 41(6), 813–827. DOI: 10.1108/LODJ-11-2019-0474

Ireland, R. D., Hitt, M. A., & Sirmon, D. G. (2003). A model of strategic entrepreneurship: The construct and its dimensions. *Journal of Management*, 29(6), 963–989. DOI: 10.1016/S0149-2063(03)00086-2

Isaacson, W. (2011). *Steve Jobs*. Simon & Schuster.

Isenberg, D. (2011). *The Entrepreneurship Ecosystem Strategy as a New Paradigm for Economic Policy: Principles for Cultivating Entrepreneurships*. Babson. Available online: http://www.wheda.com/uploadedFiles/Website/About_Wheda/BabsonEntrepreneurshipEcosystemProject.pdf (accessed on 5 November 2020).

Islam, T., Khatoon, A., Cheema, A. U., & Ashraf, Y. (2023). How does ethical leadership enhance employee work engagement? The roles of trust in leader and harmonious work passion. *Kybernetes*. ahead-of-print.

Islam, M. N., Furuoka, F., & Idris, A. (2020). The impact of trust in leadership on organizational transformation. *Global Business and Organizational Excellence*, 39(4), 25–34. DOI: 10.1002/joe.22001

Islam, T., & Asad, M. (2024). Enhancing employees' creativity through entrepreneurial leadership: Can knowledge sharing and creative self-efficacy matter? *VINE Journal of Information and Knowledge Management Systems*, 54(1), 59–73. DOI: 10.1108/VJIKMS-07-2021-0121

Jabik, B. B., & Bawakyillenuo, S. (2016). Green entrepreneurship for sustainable development in Ghana: A review. *GHANA SOCIAL SCIENCE*, 13(2), 96.

Jain, T. K. Towards the Theory of Green Entrepreneurship. Available at *SSRN* 3284935. 2018 Nov 15.

Jamak, A. B. S. A., Ali, R. M. M., & Ghazali, Z. (2014). A breakout strategy model of Malay, Malaysian Indigenous, micro-entrepreneurs. *Procedia: Social and Behavioral Sciences*, 109, 572–583. DOI: 10.1016/j.sbspro.2013.12.509

Janssen, O. (2000). Job demands, perceptions of effort-reward fairness and innovative work behaviour. *Journal of Occupational and Organizational Psychology*, 73(3), 287–302. DOI: 10.1348/096317900167038

Jarrar, A. S. (2022). Strategic human resource practices and employee's engagement: Evidence from Jordanian commercial banks. *European Journal of Business & Management Research*, 7(1), 66–72. DOI: 10.24018/ejbmr.2022.7.1.1163

Jayanna, U. R., Kumar, J. P. S., Aluvala, R., & Rao, B. (2024). The role of technology in entrepreneurship: A comprehensive systematic and bibliometric analysis. *Kybernetes*. Advance online publication. DOI: 10.1108/K-09-2023-1873

Jeevan, P. (2014). Green Entrepreneurship-A Conceptual Framework. In *National Conference on Change and Its Contemporary Social Relevance-Department of Social Work, SIMS, 27th September*.

Jensen, A. R. (1999). The g factor: The science of mental ability. *Psycoloquy*, 10(04), 36–2443.

Jha, S., & Bhattacharyya, S. S. (2013). Learning orientation and performance orientation: Scale development and its relationship with performance. *Global Business Review*, 14(1), 43–54. DOI: 10.1177/0972150912466443

Jiang, X., Lin, J., Zhou, L., & Wang, C. (2022). How to select employees to participate in interactive innovation: analysis of the relationship between personality, social networks and innovation behavior. *Kybernetes*, (ahead-of-print).

Johannessen, J., Olsen, B., & Lumpkin, G. T. (2001). Innovation as newness: What is new, how new and to whom? *European Journal of Innovation Management*, 4(1), 20–31. DOI: 10.1108/14601060110365547

John, E. P. (2023). A study on effect of work engagement in business process organisations. TIJER International Research Journal, 10(2). Retrieved from https://www. tijer.org/papers/TIJER2302032.pdf

Johnsen, C. G., Olaison, L., & Sørensen, B. M. (2018). In. *Organization Studies*, 39(2-3), 397–415. DOI: 10.1177/0170840617717551

Johnson, D., Bock, A. J., & George, G. (2019). Entrepreneurial dynamism and the built environment in the evolution of university entrepreneurial ecosystems. *Industrial and Corporate Change*, 28(4), 941–959. DOI: 10.1093/icc/dtz034

Jones, G., & George, J. (2009). Contemporary Management (6th ed.). New York: McGrawHill Companies, Inc.

Jones, C., & English, J. (2004). A contemporary approach to entrepreneurship education. *Education + Training*, 46(8/9), 416–423. DOI: 10.1108/00400910410569533

Jones, G. B., Chace, B. C., & Wright, J. M. (2020). Cultural diversity drives innovation: Empowering teams for success. *International Journal of Innovation Science*, 12(3), 323–343. DOI: 10.1108/IJIS-04-2020-0042

Jooss, S., Burbach, R., & Ruël, H. (2021). Examining talent pools as a core talent management practice in multinational corporations. *International Journal of Human Resource Management*, 32(11), 2321–2352. DOI: 10.1080/09585192.2019.1579748

Juma, N., Olabisi, J., & Griffin-EL, E. (2023). External enablers and entrepreneurial ecosystems: The brokering role of the anchor tenant in capacitating grassroots ecopreneurs. *Strategic Entrepreneurship Journal*, 17(2), 372–407. Advance online publication. DOI: 10.1002/sej.1462

Kaci, M., & Sassi, Y. (2007). *Industrie laitière et des corps gras, fiche sous secto-rielle, rapport ED pme.*

Kahn, W. A. (1990). Psychological conditions of personal engagement and dis-engagement at work. *Academy of Management Journal*, 33(4), 692–724. DOI: 10.2307/256287

Kaim, M. (2020). The development of green entrepreneurship in the modern world economy. *Center for Studies in European Integration Working Papers Series*, (16), 14-25.

Kakabadse, N. K., Tatli, A., Nicolopoulou, K., Tankibayeva, A., & Mouraviev, N. (2018). A gender perspective on entrepreneurial leadership: Female leaders in Ka-zakhstan. *European Management Review*, 15(2), 155–170. DOI: 10.1111/emre.12125

Kalev, A., Dobbin, F., & Kelly, E. (2006). Best practices or best guesses? Assessing the efficacy of corporate affirmative action and diversity policies. *American Socio-logical Review*, 71(4), 589–617. DOI: 10.1177/000312240607100404

Kansheba, M., & Wald, A. (2020). Entrepreneurial ecosystems: A systematic literature review and research agenda. *Journal of Small Business and Enterprise Development*, 27(6), 943–964. DOI: 10.1108/JSBED-11-2019-0364

Karlsson, C., Rickardsson, J., & Wincent, J. (2019b). Diversity, innovation and entrepreneurship: Where are we and where should we go in future studies? *Small Business Economics*, 56(2), 759–772. DOI: 10.1007/s11187-019-00267-1

Kauflin, J. (2021, February 8). Inside The Billion-Dollar Plan To Kill Credit Cards. Forbes. https://www.forbes.com/sites/jeffkauflin/2021/02/08/inside-the-billion -dollar-plan-to-kill-credit-cards/?sh=60e2b98011d9

Kaur, M. (2020). GREEN ENTREPRENEURSHIP INDIA PERSPECTIVE. *New Horizons in Commerce, IT &. Social Sciences*, ●●●, 10.

Kempster, S., Jackson, B., & Conroy, M. (2011). Leadership as purpose: Explor-ing the role of purpose in leadership practice. *Leadership*, 7(3), 317–334. DOI: 10.1177/1742715011407384

Kent, T., Dennis, C., & Tanton, S. (2003). An evaluation of mentoring for SME re-tailers. *International Journal of Retail & Distribution Management*, 31(8), 440–448. DOI: 10.1108/09590550310484115

Khalid, S., & Ali, T. (2017). An integrated perspective of social exchange theory and transaction cost approach on the antecedents of trust in international joint ventures. *International Business Review*, 26(3), 491–501. DOI: 10.1016/j.ibusrev.2016.10.008

Khan, A. J., & Iqbal, J. (2020). Training and employee commitment: The social exchange perspective. *Journal of Management Sciences*, 7(1), 88–100. DOI: 10.20547/jms.2014.2007106

Khan, M. M., Mubarik, M. S., & Islam, T. (2021). Leading the innovation: Role of trust and job crafting as sequential mediators relating servant leadership and innovative work behavior. *European Journal of Innovation Management*, 24(5), 1547–1568. DOI: 10.1108/EJIM-05-2020-0187

Khan, M. S., Breitenecker, R. J., Gustafsson, V., & Schwarz, E. J. (2015). Innovative entrepreneurial teams: The give and take of trust and conflict. *Creativity and Innovation Management*, 24(4), 558–573. DOI: 10.1111/caim.12152

Kickul, J., & Gundry, L. K. (2002). Prospecting for strategic advantage: The proactive entrepreneurial personality and small firm innovation. *Journal of Small Business Management*, 40(2), 85–97. DOI: 10.1111/1540-627X.00042

Kiduff, G. J. (2019). Interfirm relational rivalry: Implications for competitive strategy. *Academy of Management Review*, 44(41), 775–799. DOI: 10.5465/amr.2017.0257

Kim, G., Humble, J., Debois, P., Willis, J., & Forsgren, N. (2021). *The DevOps handbook: How tcreate world-class agility, reliability, & security in technology organizations*. IT Revolution.

Kim, S., & Lee, G. (2023). The effects of organizational diversity perception on affective commitment. *Asia Pacific Journal of Public Administration*, 45(2), 160–178. DOI: 10.1080/23276665.2021.2011341

Kim, T., Cha, M., Kim, H., Lee, J. K., & Kim, J. (2017, July). Learning to discover cross-domain relations with generative adversarial networks. In *International conference on machine learning* (pp. 1857-1865). PMLR

King, A. Y. (2018). *China's great transformation: Selected essays on Confucianism, modernization, and democracy*. The Chinese University of Hong Kong Press.

Kirkpatrick, S. A., & Locke, E. A. (1991). Leadership: Do traits matter? *The Academy of Management Executive*, ●●●, 48–60.

Kirzner, I. M. Competition and Entrepreneurship (1973). University of Illinois at Urbana-Champaign's Academy for Entrepreneurial Leadership Historical Research Reference in Entrepreneurship, Available at SSRN: https://ssrn.com/abstract=1496174

Klingbeil, C., Semrau, T., Ebbers, M., & Wilhelm, H. (2019). Logics, leaders, lab coats: A multi- level study on how institutional logics are linked to entrepreneurial intentions in academia. *Journal of Management Studies*, 56(5), 929–965. DOI: 10.1111/joms.12416

Klotz, A. C., Hmieleski, K. M., Bradley, B. H., & Busenitz, L. W. (2014). New venture teams: A review of the literature and roadmap for future research. *Journal of Management*, 40(1), 226–255. DOI: 10.1177/0149206313493325

Kohler, T. (2016). Corporate accelerators: Building bridges between corporations and startups. *Business Horizons*, 59(3), 347–357. DOI: 10.1016/j.bushor.2016.01.008

Kotter, J. P. (2007). Leading change: Why transformation efforts fail.

Kreitner, R., & Kinicki, A. (2004). *Organizational Behavior* (6th ed.). McGraw-Hill/Irwin.

Krueger, N. F. (2017). Entrepreneurial intentions are dead: Long live entrepreneurial intentions. In Brännback, M., & Carsrud, A. (Eds.), *Revisiting the entrepreneurial mind. International studies in entrepreneurship* (Vol. 35). Springer. DOI: 10.1007/978-3-319-45544-0_2

Kumar, A. (2023). Leadership and decision-making: Top management team age demographic and environmental strategy. *Journal of Management & Organization*, 29(1), 69–85. DOI: 10.1017/jmo.2019.91

Kumar, D., Upadhyay, Y., Yadav, R., & Goyal, A. K. (2022). Psychological capital and innovative work behaviour: The role of mastery orientation and creative self-efficacy. *International Journal of Hospitality Management*, 102, 103157. DOI: 10.1016/j.ijhm.2022.103157

Kuratko, D. F. (2007). Entrepreneurial leadership in the 21st century: Guest editor's perspective. *Journal of Leadership & Organizational Studies*, 13(4), 1–11. DOI: 10.1177/10717919070130040201

Kuratko, D. F., & Hodgetts, R. M. (2007). *Entrepreneurship: Theory, Process, Practice* (7th ed.). Thomson/SouthWestern Publishing.

Kuratko, D. F., & Hornsby, J. S. (1999). Corporate entrepreneurial leadership for the 21st century. *Journal of Leadership Studies, 5*(2), 27-39. leadership perceptions and team performance. *The Leadership Quarterly*, 17, 232–245. DOI: 10.1016/j.leaqua.2006.02.003

La Tonya, Y. G. (2012). An examination of Gardner's multiple intelligences of leadership in organizations.

Laguna, M., Walachowska, K., Gorgievski-Duijvesteijn, M. J., & Moriano, J. A. (2019). Authentic leadership and employees' innovative behaviour: A multilevel investigation in three countries. *International Journal of Environmental Research and Public Health*, 16(21), 4201. DOI: 10.3390/ijerph16214201 PMID: 31671565

Lambe, C. J., Wittmann, C. M., & Spekman, R. E. (2001). Social exchange theory and research on business-to-business relational exchange. *Journal of Business-To-Business Marketing*, 8(3), 1–36. DOI: 10.1300/J033v08n03_01

Lancaster, L. C., & Stillman, D. (2009). *When generations collide: Who they are. Why they clash. How to solve the generational puzzle at work*. Harper Collins.

Lazar, M., Miron-Spektor, E., Agarwal, R., Erez, M., Goldfarb, B., & Chen, G. (2020). Entrepreneurial team formation. *The Academy of Management Annals*, 14(1), 29–59. DOI: 10.5465/annals.2017.0131

Leavy, B. (2016). The next wave of global disruption and the role of China's entrepreneurs. *Strategy and Leadership*, 44(3), 27–37.

Leavy, B. (2018). Value innovation and how to successfully incubate "blue ocean" initiatives. *Strategy and Leadership*, 46(3), 10–20. DOI: 10.1108/SL-02-2018-0020

Lee, L., & Yu, H. (2023). Socioeconomic diversity in the hospitality industry: The relationship between social class background, family expectations and career outcomes. *International Journal of Contemporary Hospitality Management*, 35(11), 3844–3863. Advance online publication. DOI: 10.1108/IJCHM-11-2022-1356

Lee, Y., Shin, H. Y., Park, J., Kim, W., & Cho, D. (2017). An integrative literature review on employee engagement in the field of human resource development: Exploring where we are and where we should go. *Asia Pacific Education Review*, 18(4), 541–557. DOI: 10.1007/s12564-017-9508-3

Lehmann-Ortega, L., & Schoettl, J.-M. (2005). From buzzword to managerial tool: the role of business model in strategic innovation. In CLADEA Retrieved from: http://www.businessmodelcommunity.com/fs/root/8jvaa-businessmodelsantiago.pdf

Lehmann-Ortega, L., Musikas, H., & Schoettl, J.-M. (2017). (Ré)inventez votre Business Model - 2e éd. Dunod.

Lehner, O. M., & Harrer, T. (2019). Crowd funding revisited: A neo-institutional field-perspective. *Venture Capital*, 21(1), 75–96. DOI: 10.1080/13691066.2019.1560884

Leitch, C. M., & Volery, T. (2017). Entrepreneurial leadership: Insights and directions. *International Small Business Journal*, 35(2), 147–156. DOI: 10.1177/0266242616681397

Lekutle, N. T., Ebewo, P. E., & Shambare, R. (2023). The Effects of Entrepreneurship Leadership on Youth Entrepreneurial Intentions Post-COVID-19: The Case of Gauteng. *Businesses*, 3(4), 569–584. DOI: 10.3390/businesses3040035

Le, P. B., & Lei, H. (2018). The effects of innovation speed and quality on differentiation and low-cost competitive advantage: The case of Chinese firms. *Chinese Management Studies*, 12(2), 305–322. DOI: 10.1108/CMS-10-2016-0195

Lepnurm, R., & Bergh, C. (1995). Small business: Entrepreneurship or strategy? *The Center for Entrepreneurship Review*: 4.

Leung, T. K. P., Chan, R. Y. K., Lai, K. H., & Ngai, E. W. (2011). An examination of the influence of guanxi and xinyong (utilization of personal trust) on negotiation outcome in China: An old friend approach. *Industrial Marketing Management*, 40(7), 1193–1205.

Liguori, E. W., Muldoon, J., Ogundana, O. M., Lee, Y., & Wilson, G. A. (2024). Charting the future of entrepreneurship: A roadmap for interdisciplinary research and societal impact. *Cogent Business & Management*, 11(1), 2314218. Advance online publication. DOI: 10.1080/23311975.2024.2314218

Lin, L. H. (2011). Cultural and organizational antecedents of guanxi: The Chinese cases. *Journal of Business Ethics*, 99(3), 441–451. DOI: 10.1007/s10551-010-0662-3

Linton, J. D., & Wei, X. (2020). Research on science and technological entrepreneurship education: What needs to happen next? *The Journal of Technology Transfer*, 46(2), 393–406. DOI: 10.1007/s10961-020-09786-6

Linyiru, B. M., & Ketyenya, R. P. (2017). Influence of competitive aggressiveness on performance of state corporations in Kenya. *International Journal of Entrepreneurship*, 2(1), 1–14.

Liu, T. Q., & Stening, B. W. (2016). The contextualization and de-contextualization of Confucian morality: Making Confucianism relevant to China's contemporary challenges in business ethics. *Asia Pacific Journal of Management*, 33(3), 821–841. DOI: 10.1007/s10490-015-9415-2

Liu, W., Liu, R., Chen, H., & Mboga, J. (2020). Perspectives on disruptive technology and innovation: Exploring conflicts, characteristics in emerging economies. *International Journal of Conflict Management*, 31(3), 313–331. DOI: 10.1108/IJCMA-09-2019-0172

Liu, X., Yu, J., Guo, Q., & Li, J. (2022). Employee engagement, its antecedents, and effects on business performance in hospitality industry: A multilevel analysis. *International Journal of Contemporary Hospitality Management*, 34(12), 4631–4652. DOI: 10.1108/IJCHM-12-2021-1512

Lockwood, N. R. (2007). Leveraging employee engagement for competitive advantage: HR's strategic role. SHRM HRMagazine. *Alexandria (Aldershot)*, 52(3), S1–S11.

Loi, R., Lam, L. W., Ngo, H. Y., & Cheong, S. I. (2015). Exchange mechanisms between ethical leadership and affective commitment. *Journal of Managerial Psychology*, 30(6), 645–658. DOI: 10.1108/JMP-08-2013-0278

Long, S. (2017). *Exploring which leadership styles are effective with millennial employees* (Doctoral dissertation, Walden University).

Longenecker, J. G., McKinney, J. A., & Moore, C. W. (1988). Egoism and independence: Entrepreneurial ethics. *Organizational Dynamics*, 16(3), 64–72. DOI: 10.1016/0090-2616(88)90037-X

Lotfi, M., Yousefi, A., & Jafari, S. (2018). The effect of emerging green market on green entrepreneurship and sustainable development in knowledge-based companies. *Sustainability (Basel)*, 10(7), 2308. DOI: 10.3390/su10072308

Lubis, R. (2017). Assessing entrepreneurial leadership and the law: Why are these important for graduate students in Indonesia? *The International Journal of the Arts in Society*, 10(02), 41–76.

Luca, B. (2008). *Innovating for Sustainability: Green Entrepreneurship in personal mobility* (1st ed.). Routledge.

Lucas, D. S., & Fuller, C. S. (2017). Entrepreneurship: Productive, unproductive, and destructive— relative to what? *Journal of Business Venturing Insight*, 7, 45–49. DOI: 10.1016/j.jbvi.2017.03.001

Lumpkin, G. T., & Dess, G. G. (1996). Clarifying the entrepreneurial orientation construct and linking it to performance. *Academy of Management Review*, 21(1), 135–172. DOI: 10.2307/258632

Lv, M., Jiang, S. M., Chen, H., & Zhang, S. X. (2022). Authentic leadership and innovation behaviour among nurses in China: A mediation model of work engagement. *Journal of Nursing Management*, 30(7), 2670–2680. DOI: 10.1111/jonm.13669 PMID: 35580873

Lyons, S. T., Schweitzer, L., & Ng, E. S. (2015). How have careers changed? An investigation of changing career patterns across four generations. *Journal of Managerial Psychology*, 30(1), 8–21. DOI: 10.1108/JMP-07-2014-0210

Lyons, T. S., Alter, T. R., Audretsch, D., & Augustine, D. (2012). Entrepreneurship and community: The next frontier of entrepreneurship inquiry. *Entrepreneurship Research Journal*, 2(1), 1–26. DOI: 10.2202/2157-5665.1064

MacLeod, I., Steckley, L., & Murray, R. (2012). Time is not enough: Promoting strategic engagement with writing for publication. *Studies in Higher Education*, 37(6), 641–654. DOI: 10.1080/03075079.2010.527934

Madanchian, M., Hussein, N., Noordin, F., & Taherdoost, H. (2016). The relationship between ethical leadership, leadership effectiveness, and organizational performance: A review of literature in SMEs context. *European Business and Management*, 2(2), 17–21. DOI: 10.11648/j.ebm.20160202.11

Madhosingh, S. (2022). 4 Key Leadership Lessons from Patagonia Founder, Yvon Chouinard. CEOWORLD Magazine. https://ceoworld.biz/2022/10/14/4-key-leadership-lessons-from-patagonia-founder-yvon-chouinard/

Makki, A. A., Alidrisi, H., Iqbal, A., & Al-Sasi, B. O. (2020). Barriers tGreen Entrepreneurship: An ISM-Based Investigation. *Journal of Risk and Financial Management*, 13(11), 249. DOI: 10.3390/jrfm13110249

Malecki, E. J. (2011). Connecting local entrepreneurial ecosystems to global innovation networks: Open innovation, double networks and knowledge integration. *International Journal of Entrepreneurship and Innovation Management*, 14(1), 36–59. DOI: 10.1504/IJEIM.2011.040821

Malen, J., & Marcus, A. A. (2017). Promoting clean energy technology entrepreneurship: The role of external context. *Energy Policy*, 102(3), 7–15. DOI: 10.1016/j.enpol.2016.11.045

Malibari, M. A., & Bajaba, S. (2022). Entrepreneurial leadership and employees' innovative behavior: A sequential mediation analysis of innovation climate and employees' intellectual agility. *Journal of Innovation & Knowledge*, 7(4), 100255. DOI: 10.1016/j.jik.2022.100255

Malik, S., Awan, T. M., & Nisar, A. (2020). Entrepreneurial leadership and employee innovative behaviour in software industry. *Journal of Business Economics*, 12(1), 63–76.

Mamun, A. A., Fazal, S. A., & Muniady, R. (2019). Entrepreneurial knowledge, skills, competencies and performance: A study of micro-enterprises in Kelantan, Malaysia. *Asia Pacific Journal of Innovation and Entrepreneurship*, 13(1), 29–48. DOI: 10.1108/APJIE-11-2018-0067

Markides, C. (1997). Strategic innovation. *Sloan Management Review*, 39(3), 9–23.

Marques, J. (2017). Leadership and Ambition. In: Marques, J., Dhiman, S. (eds) *Leadership Today*. Springer Texts in Business and Economics. Springer, Cham. DOI: 10.1007/978-3-319-31036-7_20

Martin, K., Shilton, K., & Smith, J. A. (2019). Business and the ethical implications of technology: Introduction to the symposium. *Journal of Business Ethics*, 160(2), 307–317. DOI: 10.1007/s10551-019-04213-9

Maslach, C., Schaufeli, W. B., & Leiter, M. P. (2001). Job burnout. *Annual Review of Psychology*, 52(1), 397–422. DOI: 10.1146/annurev.psych.52.1.397 PMID: 11148311

Matthews, M. D., Hancock, P. A., & Szalma, J. L. (2008). Positive psychology: Adaptation, leadership, and performance in exceptional circumstances. *Performance under stress*, 163-180.

McCarthy, I. O., Moonesinghe, R., & Dean, H. D. (2020). Association of employee engagement factors and turnover intention among the 2015 US federal government workforce. *SAGE Open*, 10(2), 2158244020931847. DOI: 10.1177/2158244020931847 PMID: 39099646

McClelland, D. C. (1961). The achieving society. *Princeton, NJ*: van Nostrand

Megerian, L. E., & Sosik, J. J. (1996). An affair of the heart: Emotional Intelligence and transformational leadership. *The Journal of Leadership Studies*, 3(3), 31–48. DOI: 10.1177/107179199700300305

Mehra, A., Smith, B., Dixon, A., & Robertson, B. (2006). Distributed leadership in teams: the network of

Melay, I., & Kraus, S. (2012). Green entrepreneurship: Definitions of related concepts. *Int. J. Strateg. Manag.*, 12, 1–2.

Mhlongo, T. (2021). 'A systems' thinking approach to entrepreneurial leadership: An analysis of SMES in the Gauteng Province', doctoral dissertation, Durban University of Technology, Durban.

Miao, Q., Eva, N., Newman, A., & Cooper, B. (2019). CEO entrepreneurial leadership and performance outcomes of top management teams in entrepreneurial ventures: The mediating effects of psychological safety. *Journal of Small Business Management*, 57(3), 1119–1135. DOI: 10.1111/jsbm.12465

Mirjana Radovi´c-Markovi´c 1,2,* and BrankŽivanovi´c (2019), Sustainability, 11, 6826; DOI: 10.3390/su11236826

Mishra, P., & Misra, R. K. (2017). Entrepreneurial leadership and organizational effectiveness: A comparative study of executives and non-executives. *Procedia Computer Science*, 122, 71–78. DOI: 10.1016/j.procs.2017.11.343

Mitonga-Monga, J. (2020). Social exchange influences on ethical leadership and employee commitment in a developing country setting. *Journal of Psychology in Africa*, 30(6), 485–491. DOI: 10.1080/14330237.2020.1842587

Monteleone, H., & Turner, M. (2016). Managing multicultural teams: The multiple intelligences of a project manager. In *Proceedings of the 40th Australasian Universities Building Education Association Conference (AUBEA 2016)* (pp. 229-239). Central Queensland University.

Morris, M. H., Kuratko, D. F., Schindehutte, M., & Spivack, A. J. (2012). Framing the entrepreneurial experience. *Entrepreneurship Theory and Practice*, 36(1), 11–40. DOI: 10.1111/j.1540-6520.2011.00471.x

Morrison, A. (2000). Developing a Global Leadership Model. *Human Resource Management*, 39(2-3), 117–131. DOI: 10.1002/1099-050X(200022/23)39:2/3<117::AID-HRM3>3.0.CO;2-1

Muhibbin, A., Fatoni, A., Hidayat, O. T., & Arifin, Z. (2020, November). Transpormation Leadership Based on Local Wisdom in the Multiple Intelligences and the Efforts to Overcome Digital Gap. In *ICSSED 2020: The Proceedings of the 4th International Conference of Social Science and Education, ICSSED 2020, August 4-5 2020, Yogyakarta, Indonesia* (p. 307). European Alliance for Innovation. DOI: 10.4108/eai.4-8-2020.2302531

Mustafa, S. Z., Chatterjee, S., & Kar, A. K. (2019). Securing IoT devices in Smart Cities of India: From ethical and enterprise information system management perspective. *Journal of Enterprise Information System*, 15(4), 585–615.

Mutonyi, B. R., Slåtten, T., & Lien, G. (2020). Empowering leadership, work group cohesiveness, individual learning orientation and individual innovative behaviour in the public sector: Empirical evidence from Norway. *International Journal of Public Leadership*, 16(2), 175–197. DOI: 10.1108/IJPL-07-2019-0045

Nahapiet, J., & Ghoshal, S. (1998). Social capital, intellectual capital, and the organizational advantage. *Academy of Management Review*, 23(2), 242–266. DOI: 10.2307/259373

Nambisan, S., & Baron, R. A. (2013). Entrepreneurship in innovation ecosystems: Entrepreneurs' self–regulatory processes and their implications for new venture success. *Entrepreneurship Theory and Practice*, 37(5), 1071–1097. DOI: 10.1111/j.1540-6520.2012.00519.x

Newman, A., Herman, H. M., Schwarz, G., & Nielsen, I. (2018). The effects of employees' creative self-efficacy on innovative behavior: The role of entrepreneurial leadership. *Journal of Business Research*, 89, 1–9. DOI: 10.1016/j.jbusres.2018.04.001

Ngibe, M., & Lekhanya, L. M. (2019). Critical factors influencing innovative leadership in attaining business innovation: A case of manufacturing SMEs in KwaZulu-Natal. *International Journal of Entrepreneurship*, 23(2), 1–20.

Nguyen, T. T. (2020). A Cultural Comparison Based on Entrepreneurial Personality: Case Comparison Between Finland and Vietnam. https://urn.fi/URN:NBN:fi:amk-2020091220392

Nguyen, P. V., Huynh, H. T. N., Lam, L. N. H., Le, T. B., & Nguyen, N. H. X. (2021). The impact of entrepreneurial leadership on SMEs' performance: The mediating effects of organizational factors. *Heliyon*, 7(6), e07326. DOI: 10.1016/j.heliyon.2021.e07326 PMID: 34195431

Nicolson, R. I., & Fawcett, A. J. (1999). Developmental dyslexia: The role of the cerebellum 1. *Dyslexia (Chichester, England)*, 5(3), 155–177. DOI: 10.1002/(SICI)1099-0909(199909)5:3<155::AID-DYS143>3.0.CO;2-4

Nie, D., & Lämsä, A. M. (2015). The leader–member exchange theory in the Chinese context and the ethical challenge of guanxi. *Journal of Business Ethics*, 128, 851–861.

Northouse, P. G. (2021). *Leadership: Theory and practice*. Sage publications.

Nsereko, I., Balunywa, W., Munene, J., Orobia, L., & Muhammed, N. (2018). Personal initiative: Its power in social entrepreneurial venture creation. *Cogent Bus. Manag.*, 5(1), 1443686. DOI: 10.1080/23311975.2018.1443686

Nunnally, J. C. (1978). *Psychometric theory*. McGraw-Hill.

O'Shea, G., Farny, S., & Hakala, H. (2021). The buzz before business: A design science study of a sustainable entrepreneurial ecosystem. *Small Business Economics*, 2021(56), 1097–1120. DOI: 10.1007/s11187-019-00256-4

Obuobisa-Darko, T., & Ameyaw-Domfeh, K. (2019). Leader behaviour to achieve employee engagement in Ghana: A qualitative study, International Journal of Public Leadership. *International Journal of Public Leadership*, 15(1), 19–37. DOI: 10.1108/IJPL-04-2018-0018

Odhiambo, O. J. (2020). Strategic management of HRM: Implications for organizational engagement. *Annals of Contemporary Developments in Management & HR*, 2(3), 1–8. Advance online publication. DOI: 10.33166/ACDMHR.2020.03.001

Ojo, A. S., & Tijani, A. A. (2021). Managing Workplace Diversity in Nigerian Public and Private Sectors: Issues, Challenges, and Prospects. *Journal of Public Administration and Governance*, 11(3), 70–86.

Olaniran, B. A., Rodriguez, N., & Williams, I. M. (2012). Social information processing theory (SIPT): A cultural perspective for international online communication environments. In *Computer-mediated communication across cultures: International interactions in online environments* (pp. 45-65). IGI Global.

Oplatka, I., & Arar, K. H. (2016). Leadership for social justice and the characteristics of traditional societies: Ponderings of the application of western-grounded models. *International Journal of Leadership in Education*, 19(3), 352–369. https://doi.org/https://doi.org/10.1080/13603124.2015.102846. DOI: 10.1080/13603124.2015.1028464

Opoku, M. A., Choi, S. B., & Kang, S. W. (2019). Servant leadership and innovative behaviour: An empirical analysis of Ghana's manufacturing sector. *Sustainability (Basel)*, 11(22), 6273. DOI: 10.3390/su11226273

Osborn, R. N., & Marion, R. (2009). Contextual leadership, transformational leadership and the performance of international innovation seeking alliances. *The Leadership Quarterly*, 20(2), 191–206. DOI: 10.1016/j.leaqua.2009.01.010

Ozturk, A., Karatepe, O. M., & Okumus, F. (2021). The effect of servant leadership on hotel employees' behavioral consequences: Work engagement versus job satisfaction. *International Journal of Hospitality Management*, 97, 102994. DOI: 10.1016/j.ijhm.2021.102994

Pacheco, D. F., Dean, T. J., & Payne, D. S. (2010). Escaping the green prison: Entrepreneurship and the creation of opportunities for sustainable development. *Journal of Business Venturing*, 25(5), 464–480. DOI: 10.1016/j.jbusvent.2009.07.006

Page, S. E. (2007). *The difference: How the power of diversity creates better groups, firms, schools, and societies*. Princeton University Press.

Palalić, R., Ramadani, V., Dana, L. P., & Ratten, V. (2017). Gender entrepreneurial leadership in family businesses: a case study from Bosnia and Herzegovina. In *Women entrepreneurship in family business* (pp. 208–226). Routledge. DOI: 10.4324/9781315098531-11

Palla, K. K. (2022). The Impact of Emotional Intelligence and Multiple Intelligences on Team Performance in the Information Technology Sector.

Pathak, M. D., Kar, B., & Panda, M. C. (2022). Chaos and complexity: Entrepreneurial planning during pandemic. *Journal of Global Entrepreneurship Research*, 12(1), 1–11. DOI: 10.1007/s40497-022-00306-4

Patrício, L. D., & Fernandes, C. (2022). Technology entrepreneurship and innovation: A Systematic literature review. In *EAI/Springer Innovations in Communication and Computing* (pp. 253–284). DOI: 10.1007/978-3-031-17960-0_13

Pauceanu, A. M., Rabie, N., Moustafa, A., & Jiroveanu, D. C. (2021). Entrepreneurial leadership and sustainable development– A systematic literature review. *Sustainability (Basel)*, 13(21), 11695. DOI: 10.3390/su132111695

Pauluzzo, R., Shen, B., Pauluzzo, R., & Shen, B. (2018). Culture and Its Dimensions: General Implications for Management. *Impact of Culture on Management of Foreign SMEs in China*, 91-138. https://doi.org/DOI: 10.1007/978-3-319-77881-5_4

Pearce, C. L. (2004). The future of leadership: Combining vertical and shared leadership to transform knowledge work. *The Academy of Management Perspectives*, 18(1), 47–57. DOI: 10.5465/ame.2004.12690298

Pearson, J., Pitfield, D., & Ryley, T. (2015). Intangible resources of competitive advantage: Analysis of 49 Asian airlines across three business models. *Journal of Air Transport Management*, 47(C), 179–189. DOI: 10.1016/j.jairtraman.2015.06.002

Pendell, R. (2022). *The World's $7.8 Trillion Workplace Problem*. Gallup Workplace.

Perryman, R. (1982). Commentary on research in the field of entrepreneurship. In Kent, C. A., Sexton, D. L., & Vesper, K. H. (Eds.), *The encyclopedia of entrepreneurship* (pp. 377–378). Prentice Hall.

Petermann, M. K. H., & Zacher, H. (2020). Agility in the workplace: Conceptual analysis, contributing factors, and practical examples. *Industrial and Organizational Psychology: Perspectives on Science and Practice*, 13(4), 599–609. DOI: 10.1017/iop.2020.106

Piaget, J., & Cook, M. (1952). *No. 5* (Vol. 8). The origins of intelligence in children. International Universities Press.

Piccolo, R., Chatterjee, S., Chaudhuri, R., & Vrontis, D. (2021). Enterprise social network for knowledge sharing in MNCs: Examining the role of knowledge contributors and knowledge seekers for cross-country collaboration. *Journal of International Management*, 27(1), 303–327.

Pinela, N., Guevara, R., & Armijos, M. (2022). Entrepreneurial Leadership, Work Engagement, and Innovative Work Behavior: The Moderating Role of Gender. *International Journal of Economics & Business Administration*, 10(2), 19–40. DOI: 10.35808/ijeba/764

Pita, M., Costa, J., & Moreira, A. C. (2021). Entrepreneurial Ecosystems and Entrepreneurial Initiative: Building a Multi-Country Taxonomy. *Sustainability (Basel)*, 2021(13), 4065. DOI: 10.3390/su13074065

Pizzi, S., Corbo, L., & Caputo, A. (2020). Fintech and SMEs sustainable business models: Reflections and considerations for a circular economy. *Journal of Cleaner Production*. Advance online publication. DOI: 10.1016/j.jclepro.2020.125217

Popkova, E. G., & Sergi, B. S. (2020). Human capital and AI in industry 4.0. Convergence and divergence in social entrepreneurship in Russia. *Journal of Intellectual Capital*, 21(4), 565–581. DOI: 10.1108/JIC-09-2019-0224

Popkova, E. G., Sergi, B. S., Rezaei, M., & Ferraris, A. (2021). Digitalisation in transport and logistics: A roadmap for entrepreneurship in Russia. *International Journal of Technology Management*, 87(1), 7–28. DOI: 10.1504/IJTM.2021.118887

Porter, M. E., & van der Linde, C. (1995). Toward a new conception of the environment competitiveness relationship.

PratimaSarangi, D., & Nayak, B. (2018). Employee engagement and its impact on organizational success–A study in manufacturing company, India. *OSR Journal of Business and Management, 18*(4), 52-57.

Pritchard, K. (2008). Employee engagement in the UK: Meeting the challenge in the public sector. *Development and Learning in Organizations*, 22(6), 15–17. DOI: 10.1108/14777280810910302

Pugh, R., Lamine, W., Jack, S., & Hamilton, E. (2018). The entrepreneurial university of the region: What role for entrepreneurship departments? *European Planning Studies*, 26(9), 1835–1855. DOI: 10.1080/09654313.2018.1447551

Qazi, R. R. K., & Bashir, S. (2022). Strategic engagement as means of conflict prevention: Pakistan's defence diplomacy towards Russia. *Central Asia*, 90(Summer), 1–18. DOI: 10.54418/ca-90.167

Qixun Siebers, L. (2024). Transferring paternalistic entrepreneurial leadership behaviours (PELB): Chinese organisations in sub-Saharan Africa. *International Journal of Cross Cultural Management*, 24(2), 14705958241243171. DOI: 10.1177/14705958241243171

Rabiul, M. K., Karatepe, O. M., Al Karim, R., & Panha, I. M. (2023). An investigation of the interrelationships of leadership styles, psychological safety, thriving at work, and work engagement in the hotel industry: A sequential mediation model. *International Journal of Hospitality Management*, 113, 103508. DOI: 10.1016/j. ijhm.2023.103508

Rajagopal, A. (2020). Transforming entrepreneurial business design: Converging leadership and customer-centric approach. *Journal of Transnational Management*, 25(2), 128–153. DOI: 10.1080/15475778.2020.1734418

Rani, J. (2020, December 10). *How Google Trains World-Class Managers*. OpenGrowth. Retrieved June 30, 2023, from https://www.opengrowth.com/resources/how-google-trains-world-class-managers

Ratten, V. (2021). COVID-19 and entrepreneurship: Future research directions. *Strategic Change*, 30(2), 91–98. DOI: 10.1002/jsc.2392

Ravet-Brown, T. É., Furtner, M., & Kallmuenzer, A. (2023). Transformational and entrepreneurial leadership: A review of distinction and overlap. *Review of Managerial Science*, ●●●, 1–46.

Razak, R. A. (2011). Entrepreneurial orientation as a universal remedy for the receding productivity in Malaysian small and medium enterprises: A theoretical perspective. *International Journal of Business and Social Science*, 2(19), 1–9.

Renko, M. (2017). Entrepreneurial leadership. *Forthcoming in" Nature of Leadership", 3rd edition. Edited by David V. Day and John Antonakis. SAGE Publications.* https://ssrn.com/abstract=2977744

Renko, M., El Tarabishy, A., Carsrud, A. L., & Brännback, M. (2015). Understanding and measuring entrepreneurial leadership style. *Journal of Small Business Management*, 53(1), 54–74. DOI: 10.1111/jsbm.12086

Rezaei, S., Goli, M., & Dana, L.-P. (2014). Beyond legal entrepreneurship: The case of Austria. *International Journal of Entrepreneurship and Small Business*, 21(2), 202–215. DOI: 10.1504/IJESB.2014.059473

Ries, E. (2011). *The lean startup: How today's entrepreneurs use continuous innovation to create radically successful businesses*. Currency.

Ritzer, G. (2011). Exchange, Networks, and Rational Choice Theories. *Sociological theory*, (8th ed), pp. 416-453.

Romero-Rodriguez, L. M., & Montoya, M. S. R. (2019). Entrepreneurship competencies in energy sustainability MOOCs. *Journal of Entrepreneurship in Emerging Economies*, 11(4), 598–616. DOI: 10.1108/JEEE-03-2019-0034

Roomi, M. A., & Harrison, P. (2011). Entrepreneurial leadership: What is it and how should it be taught? http://hdl.handle.net/10547/222995

Roomi, M., & Harrison, P. (2011). Entrepreneurial Leadership: What is it and how should it be taught? *International Review of Entrepreneurship*, 9(3), 1–44. http://hdl.handle.net/10547/222995

Saks, A. M. (2006). Antecedents and consequences of employee engagement. *Journal of Managerial Psychology*, 21(7), 600–619. DOI: 10.1108/02683940610690169

Salanova, M., & Schaufeli, W. B. (2008). A cross-national study of work engagement as a mediator between job resources and proactive behaviour. *International Journal of Human Resource Management*, 19(1), 116–131. DOI: 10.1080/09585190701763982

Salazar, M. R., Lant, T. K., Fiore, S. M., & Salas, E. (2012). Facilitating innovation in diverse science teams through integrative capacity. *Small Group Research*, 43(5), 527–558. DOI: 10.1177/1046496412453622

Sandybayev, A. (2019). Impact of effective entrepreneurial leadership style on organizational performance: Critical review. *International Journal of Economics and Management*, 1(1), 47–55.

Sanhokwe, H., & Chinyamurindi, W. (2023). Work engagement and resilience at work: The moderating role of political skill. *SA Journal of Industrial Psychology*, 49, a2017. DOI: 10.4102/sajip.v49i0.2017

Santos, S. C., Morris, M. H., Caetano, A., Costa, S. F., & Neumeyer, X. (2019). Team entrepreneurial competence: Multilevel effects on individual cognitive strategies. *International Journal of Entrepreneurial Behaviour & Research*, 25(6), 1259–1282. DOI: 10.1108/IJEBR-03-2018-0126

Sarasvathy, S. D. (2001). Causation and Effectuation: Toward a Theoretical Shift from Economic Inevitability to Entrepreneurial Contingency. *Academy of Management Review*, 26(2), 243–263. DOI: 10.2307/259121

Sarma, S. & Sanwar A. S., (2017). Civic entrepreneurial ecosystems: Smart city emergence in Kansas City, *Business Horizons*, Elsevier, vol. 60(6), pages 843-853. Handle: DOI: DOI: 10.1016/j.bushor.2017.07.010

Sarmawa, I. W. G., Widyani, A. A. D., Sugianingrat, I. A. P. W., & Martini, I. A. O. (2020). Ethical entrepreneurial leadership and organizational trust for organizational sustainability. *Cogent Business & Management*, 7(1), 1818368. DOI: 10.1080/23311975.2020.1818368

Schaufeli, W. B., Salanova, M., González-Romá, V., & Bakker, A. B. (2002). The measurement of engagement and burnout: A two sample confirmatory factor analytic approach. *Journal of Happiness Studies*, 3(1), 71–92. DOI: 10.1023/A:1015630930326

Schumpeter, J. (1934). The theory of economic development. Cambridge, MA: Harvard University Press. Shapira, P., Gök, A., Klochikhin, E., & Sensier, M. (2014). Probing green industry enterprises in the UK: a new identification approach. *Journal of Technological Forecasting and Social Change*, 85, 93–104.

Scott, S. G., & Bruce, R. A. (1994). Determinants of innovative behavior: A path model of individual innovation in the workplace. *Academy of Management Journal*, 37(3), 580–607. DOI: 10.2307/256701

Sellars, T. (2006). The relationships among multiple intelligences and leadership styles: A study of administrators in Kentucky child care facilities.

Sengupta, S., Sahay, A., & Croce, F. (2018). Conceptualizing social entrepreneurship in the context of emerging economies: An integrative review of past research from BRIICS. *The International Entrepreneurship and Management Journal*, 14(4), 771–803. DOI: 10.1007/s11365-017-0483-2

Setyawati, I., Purnomo, A., Irawan, D. E., Tamyiz, M., & Sutiksno, D. U. (2018). A visual trend of literature on Ecopreneurship research overviewed within the last twdecades. *Journal of Entrepreneurship Education*, 21(4), 1–7.

Shaban, A. (2016). Managing and Leading a Diverse Workforce: One of the Main Challenges in Management. *Procedia: Social and Behavioral Sciences*, 230, 76–84. Retrieved May 10, 2023, from. DOI: 10.1016/j.sbspro.2016.09.010

Shalley, C. E., & Perry-Smith, J. E. (2008). The emergence of team creative cognition: The role of diverse outside ties, sociocognitive network centrality, and team evolution. *Strategic Entrepreneurship Journal*, 2(1), 23–41. DOI: 10.1002/sej.40

Shalley, C. E., Zhou, J., & Oldham, G. R. (2004). The effects of personal and contextual characteristics on creativity: Where should we go from here? *Journal of Management*, 30(6), 933–958. DOI: 10.1016/j.jm.2004.06.007

Shamroukh, W. (2016, January). Green Entrepreneurship. *Conference on Environment and Alternative Power*.

Shane, S. A. (2008). *The illusions of entrepreneurship: The costly myths that entrepreneurs, investors, and policy makers live by.* Yale University Press.

Sharda, A., Goel, A., Mishra, A., & Chandra, S. (2015). Green entrepreneurship in India: global evaluation, needs analysis, and drivers for growth. In *Entrepreneurial Ecosystem* (pp. 261–282). Springer. DOI: 10.1007/978-81-322-2086-2_11

Sijia, Z., Lingfeng, Y., & Yanling, L. (2021). Entrepreneurial Leadership, Organizational Resilience and New Venture Performance. *Foreign Economics & Management*, 43(03), 42–56.

Simatupang, T. M., Schwab, A., & Lantu, D. C. (2015). Introduction: Building Sustainable Entrepreneurship Ecosystems. [Editorial]. *International Journal of Entrepreneurship and Small Business*, 26(4), 389–398.

Simms, C., McGowan, P., Pickernell, D., Vazquez-Brust, D., & Williams, A. (2022). Uncovering the effectual-causal resilience nexus in the era of Covid-19: A case of a food sector SME's resilience in the face of the global pandemic. *Industrial Marketing Management*, 106, 166–182. DOI: 10.1016/j.indmarman.2022.08.012

Simon, S. S. (2011). The essentials of employee engagement in organizations. *Journal of Contemporary Research in Management*, 6(1), 63–72.

Sinek, S. (2011). *Start with why: How great leaders inspire everyone to take action.* Penguin.

Singh, C., & Wasdani, K. P. (2016). Finance for micro, small, and medium-sized enterprises in India: Sources, and challenges, ADBI Working Paper 581, Asian Development Bank Institute, Tokyo, viewed n.d., from https://www.adb.org/publications/finance-micro-Small and-medium-sized-enterprises-India-sources-and-challenges.

Sipahi Dongul, E., & Artantaş, E. (2022). Exploring the link between social work, entrepreneurial leadership, social embeddedness, social entrepreneurship and firm performance: A case of SMES owned by Chinese ethnic community in Turkey. *Journal of Enterprising Communities: People and Places in the Global Economy*, 17(3), 684–707. DOI: 10.1108/JEC-11-2021-0162

Siscan, Z., & Kaim, M. (2020). Green entrepreneurship in the Republic of Moldova and European circular economy trend.

Siwi, M. K., Haryono, A., & Nuryana, I. (2022, July). Intellectual Agility and Entrepreneurial Leadership as Innovation Sustainability Business Cooperative in The Covid 19 Pandemic. In Eighth Padang International Conference On Economics Education, Economics, Business and Management, Accounting and Entrepreneurship (PICEEBA-8 2021) (pp. 212-216). Atlantis Press.

Siyal, S. (2018). Does Leadership lessen turnover of public servants. The moderated mediation effect of leader member exchange and perspective taking [EBSCO open dissertations].

Siyal, S. (2018). Does Leadership lessen turnover of public servants. The moderated mediation effect of leader member exchange and perspective taking [EBSCopen dissertations].

Siyal, M., Siyal, S., Wu, J., Pal, D., & Memon, M. M. (2021). Consumer perceptions of factors affecting online shopping behavior: An empirical evidence from foreign students in China. [JECO]. *Journal of Electronic Commerce in Organizations*, 19(2), 1–16. DOI: 10.4018/JECO.2021040101

Siyal, S. (2023). Inclusive leadership and work engagement: Exploring the role of psychological safety and trust in leader in multiple organizational context. *Business Ethics, the Environment & Responsibility*, 32(4), 1170–1184. DOI: 10.1111/beer.12556

Siyal, S., Liu, J., Ma, L., Kumari, K., Saeed, M., Xin, C., & Hussain, S. N. (2023). Does inclusive leadership influence task performance of hospitality industry employees? Role of psychological empowerment and trust in leader. *Heliyon*, 9(5), e15507. DOI: 10.1016/j.heliyon.2023.e15507 PMID: 37153410

Siyal, S., & Peng, X. (2018). Does leadership lessen turnover? The moderated mediation effect of leader–member exchange and perspective taking on public servants. *Journal of Public Affairs*, 18(4), e1830. DOI: 10.1002/pa.1830

Siyal, S., Peng, X., & Siyal, A. W. (2018). Socioeconomic analysis: A case of Tharparkar. *Journal of Public Affairs*, 18(4), e1847. DOI: 10.1002/pa.1847

Siyal, S., Saeed, M., Pahi, M. H., Solangi, R., & Xin, C. (2021). They can't treat you well under abusive supervision: Investigating the impact of job satisfaction and extrinsic motivation on healthcare employees. *Rationality and Society*, 33(4), 401–423. DOI: 10.1177/10434631211033660

Siyal, S., & Xin, C. (2020). *Public procurement. Global Encyclopedia of Public Administration, Public Policy, and Governance*. Springer International Publishing.

Siyal, S., Xin, C., Umrani, W. A., Fatima, S., & Pal, D. (2021). How do leaders influence innovation and creativity in employees? The mediating role of intrinsic motivation. *Administration & Society*, 53(9), 1337–1361. DOI: 10.1177/0095399721997427

Smith, P. B., Dugan, S., & Trompenaars, F. (1996). National culture and the values of organizational employees: A dimensional analysis across 43 nations. *Journal of Cross-Cultural Psychology*, 27(2), 231–264. DOI: 10.1177/0022022196272006

Smith, R. J. (2021). *Fortune-tellers and philosophers: Divination in traditional Chinese society*. Routledge.

Soares, M. E., Mosquera, P., & Cid, M. (2021). Antecedents of innovative behaviour: Knowledge sharing, open innovation climate and internal communication. *International Journal of Innovation and Learning*, 30(2), 241–257. DOI: 10.1504/IJIL.2021.117223

Soenarto, S., Rahmawati, R., Suprapti, A. R., Handayani, R., & Sudira, P. (2018). Green Entrepreneurship Development Strategy Based on Local Characteristic tSupport Power Eco-Tourism Continuous at Lombok. *Journal of Tourism & Hospitality (Los Angeles, Calif.)*, 7(06), 2167–0269. DOI: 10.4172/2167-0269.1000394

Song, J., Jiao, H., & Wang, C. (2023). How work-family conflict affects knowledge workers' innovative behavior: a spill over-crossover-spill over model of dual-career couples. *Journal of Knowledge Management*. ahead-of-print

Song, A. K. (2019). The digital entrepreneurial ecosystem—A critique and reconfiguration. *Small Business Economics*, 53(3), 569–590. DOI: 10.1007/s11187-019-00232-y

Soomro, B. A., Mangi, S., & Shah, N. (2021). Strategic factors and significance of organizational innovation and organizational learning in organizational performance. *European Journal of Innovation Management*, 24(2), 481–506. DOI: 10.1108/EJIM-05-2019-0114

Spigel, B. (2022). Examining the cohesiveness and nest-edness entrepreneurial ecosystems: Evidence from British FinTechs. *Small Business Economics*, 59(4), 1381–1399. DOI: 10.1007/s11187-021-00589-z

Spigel, B., Kitagawa, F., & Mason, C. (2020). A manifesto for researching entrepreneurial ecosystems. *Local Economy*, 35(5), 482–495. DOI: 10.1177/0269094220959052

Stadnyk, V., Krasovska, G., Pchelianska, G., & Holovchuk, Y. (2021). Determinants of "green entrepreneurship" competitive strategies implementation in the agro-industrial sector of Ukraine. []. IOP Publishing.]. *IOP Conference Series. Earth and Environmental Science*, 628(1), 012032. DOI: 10.1088/1755-1315/628/1/012032

Stam, E. (2015). Entrepreneurial Ecosystems and Regional Policy: A Sympathetic Critique. *European Planning Studies*, 2015(23), 1759–1769. DOI: 10.1080/09654313.2015.1061484

Steenkamp, J. B. (2017). *Global brand strategy: World-wise marketing in the age of branding*. Springer.

Steidle, S. B., Glass, C., Rice, M., & Henderson, D. A. (2024). Addressing Wicked Problems (SDGs) Through Community Colleges: Leveraging Entrepreneurial Leadership for Economic Development Post-COVID. *Journal of the Knowledge Economy*, ●●●, 1–26. DOI: 10.1007/s13132-024-01890-4

Sternberg, R. J. (2001). Successful Intelligence: A new approach to leadership. *Multiple intelligences and leadership*, 22-41.

Stewart, D. W. (2006). Continuing the investigation into personality traits and work-family conflict. Dallas: Poster presented at the *Twenty-First Annual Meeting of the Society for Industrial and Organizational Psychology*.

Stewart, A. (1989). *Team entrepreneurship*. Sage.

Stogdill, R. M., & Shartle, C. L. (1948). Methods for determining patterns of leadership behavior in relation to organization structure and objectives. *The Journal of Applied Psychology*, 32(3), 286–291. DOI: 10.1037/h0057264 PMID: 18867065

Stone, A. G., Russell, R. F., & Patterson, K. (2004). Transformational versus servant leadership: A difference in leader focus. *Leadership and Organization Development Journal*, 25(4), 349–361. DOI: 10.1108/01437730410538671

Stone, B. (2012). *The rebel sell: Why the culture can't be jammed*. Harper Collins.

Stone, B. (2013). *The everything store: Jeff Bezos and the age of Amazon*. Little, Brown and Company.

Storme, M., Suleyman, O., Gotlib, M., & Lubart, T. (2020). Who is agile? An investigation of the psychological antecedents of workforce agility. *Global Business and Organizational Excellence*, 39(6), 28–38. DOI: 10.1002/joe.22055

Stoudemire, T. (2024). Diversity Done Right: Navigating Cultural Difference to Create Positive Change In the Workplace. John Wiley & Sons. www.booksgoogle.com.na

Strangler, D., & Bell-Masterson, J. (2015). *Measuring an Entrepreneurial Ecosystem*. Kauffman Foundation.

Subramaniam, R., & Shankar, R. K. (2020). Three mindsets of entrepreneurial leaders. *The Journal of Entrepreneurship*, 29(1), 7–37. DOI: 10.1177/0971355719893498

Sullivan, R. (2000). Entrepreneurial learning and mentoring. *International Journal of Entrepreneurial Behaviour & Research*, 6(3), 160–175. DOI: 10.1108/13552550010346587

Sumukadas, N., & Sawhney, R. (2004). Workforce agility through employee involvement. *IIE Transactions*, 36(10), 1011–1021. DOI: 10.1080/07408170490500997

Suudin, H., & Brown, D. A. (2017). Greening the black box: Integrating the environment and management control systems. Journal of Accounting. *Accounting, Auditing & Accountability Journal*, 30(3), 620–642. DOI: 10.1108/AAAJ-03-2014-1649

Svensson, F., & Molén, S. (2024). Unravelling the mystery of municipal employer branding-An exploratory case study of employer branding strategies in a Swedish public organisation. https://hdl.handle.net/2077/79595

Tamvada, J. P. (2015). The spatial distribution of self-employment in India: Evidence from semiparametric geoadditive models. *Regional Studies*, 49(2), 300–322. DOI: 10.1080/00343404.2013.779656

Tan, K. L., Suhaida, S., & Leong, Y. P. (2013, June). Self-Efficacy and green entrepreneurship. []. IOP Publishing.]. *IOP Conference Series. Earth and Environmental Science*, 16(1), 012119. DOI: 10.1088/1755-1315/16/1/012119

Tansley, A. G. (1935). The use and abuse of vegetational concepts and terms. *Ecology*, 16(3), 284–307. DOI: 10.2307/1930070

Tee, M., Abdulahi, R., Din, J., Abdulahi, S., & Wu, L. (2017). Green SD Adoption using knowledge management facilitation – Motivational perspective. *Journal of Theoretical and Applied Information Technology*, 5(17), 4291–4301.

Terzieva, K. (2023, February 28). The Rise Of Ethical Leadership In Modern Business Enterprises. *Forbes*. https://www.forbes.com/sites/forbescoachescouncil/2023/02/28/the-rise-of-ethical-leadership-in-modern-business-enterprises/?sh=245881b337dd

Thomas, D. A. (2004). Diversity as strategy. *Harvard Business Review*, 82(9), 98–108. PMID: 15449859

Tohidi, H., & Jabbari, M. M. (2012). The important of innovation and its crucial role in growth, survival and success of organizations. *Procedia Technology*, 1, 535–538. DOI: 10.1016/j.protcy.2012.02.116

Tomlinson, G. (2010). Building a culture of high employee engagement. *Strategic HR Review*, 9(3), 25–31. DOI: 10.1108/14754391011040046

Tracey, P., Phillips, N., & Jarvis, O. (2011). Bridging institutional entrepreneurship and the creation of new organizational forms: A multilevel model. *Organization Science*, 22(1), 60–80. DOI: 10.1287/orsc.1090.0522

Trompenaars, F., & Hampden-Turner, C. (1997). *Riding the Waves of Culture: Understanding Diversity in Global Business*. McGraw-Hill. www.googlescholar.com

Trompenaars, F. (1996). Resolving international conflict: Culture and business strategy. *Business Strategy Review*, 7(3), 51–68. DOI: 10.1111/j.1467-8616.1996.tb00132.x

Trompenaars, F. (2021). A trans-cultural leadership paradigm. In *Transformative Strategies* (pp. 180–197). Routledge., https://www.taylorfrancis.com/chapters/edit/10.4324/9780429274381-13/trans-cultural-leadership-paradigm-fons-trompenaars DOI: 10.4324/9780429274381-13

Trompenaars, F., & Woolliams, P. (2024). Career Developing/Supporting Cultures. In *New Approaches to Recruitment and Selection* (pp. 79–82). Emerald Publishing Limited. DOI: 10.1108/978-1-83797-759-820241016

Truong, T. D., Hallinger, P., & Sanga, K. (2017). Confucian values and school leadership in Vietnam: Exploring the influence of culture on principal decision making. *Educational Management Administration & Leadership*, 45(1), 77–100.

Tsai, J. C. A., & Kang, T. C. (2019). Reciprocal intention in knowledge seeking: Examining social exchange theory in an online professional community. *International Journal of Information Management*, 48, 161–174. DOI: 10.1016/j.ijinfomgt.2019.02.008

Tse, T., & Tsang, L. T. (2021). Reconceptualising prosumption beyond the 'cultural turn': Passive fashion prosumption in Korea and China. *Journal of Consumer Culture*, 21(4), 703–723.

Tucker, J. (2019, February 7). Creative entrepreneurs: The story behind Innocent Drinks | Headspace. Headspace. https://www.headspacegroup.co.uk/creative-entrepreneurs-the-story-behind-innocent-drinks/

Udin, U. (2024). Leadership styles and innovative work behaviour: The role of work engagement. *International Journal of Economics and Business Research*, 28(1), 65–81. DOI: 10.1504/IJEBR.2024.139287

Ullah, I., Hameed, R. M., & Mahmood, A. (2023). The impact of proactive personality and psychological capital on innovative work behavior: evidence from software houses of Pakistan. *European Journal of Innovation Management*. ahead-of-print

UN report (2021). United Nations report. Report of the Secretary-General on the Work of the Organization (A/76/1, seventy-sixth session). United Nations.

UNESCO. (1994). The Salamanca statement and framework for action. In: Final Report of the World Conference on Special Needs Education: Access and Quality, Spain. Salamanca: UNESCO

United Nations (2015). *Transforming Our World: The 2030 Agenda for Sustainable Development.* Resolution Adopted by the General Assembly on 25 September 2015, 42809, 1-13. https://doi.org/DOI: 10.1007/s13398-014-0173-7.2

Universidad Europea. (2022). What is entrepreneurial leadership? Universidad Europea. https://universidadeuropea.com/en/blog/entrepreneurial-leadership/

Van der Leeuw, S., Wiek, A., Harlow, J., & Buizer, J. (2012). How much time do we have? Urgency and rhetoric in sustainability science. *Sustainability Science*, 7(S1), 115–120. DOI: 10.1007/s11625-011-0153-1

Van Knippenberg, D., Nishii, L. H., & Dwertmann, D. J. (2020). Synergy from diversity: Managing team diversity to enhance performance. *Behavioral Science & Policy*, 6(1), 75–92. DOI: 10.1177/237946152000600108

Van Knippenberg, D., & Schippers, M. C. (2007). Work group diversity. *Annual Review of Psychology*, 58(1), 515–541. DOI: 10.1146/annurev.psych.58.110405.085546 PMID: 16903805

Van Zyl, H. J. C., & Mathur-Helm, B. (2007). Exploring a conceptual model, based on the combined effects of entrepreneurial leadership, market orientation and relationship marketing orientation on South Africa's small tourism business performance. *South African Journal of Business Management*, 38(2), 17–24. DOI: 10.4102/sajbm.v38i2.580

Vance, R. J. (2006). Employee engagement and commitment. *SHRM foundation*, *1*, 1-53.

Vance, A. (2015). *Elon Musk: Tesla, SpaceX, and the quest for a fantastic future.* Ecco.

Vargas, G. M., Campo, C. H. G., & Orejuela, H. A. R. (2010). Corporate social responsibility in the context of institutional and organizational change in the Colombian financial sector. *AD-Minister*, (17), 59–85.

Vecchio, R. P. (2003). Entrepreneurship and leadership: Common Trends and Common Threads. *Human Resource Management Review*, 13(2), 303–327. DOI: 10.1016/S1053-4822(03)00019-6

Vedula, S., Doblinger, C., Pacheco, D., York, J. G., Bacq, S., Russo, M. V., & Dean, T. J. (2022). Entrepreneurship for the public good: A review, critique, and path forward for social and environmental entrepreneurship research. *The Academy of Management Annals*, 16(1), 391–425. DOI: 10.5465/annals.2019.0143

Velez-Calle, A., Robledo-Ardila, C., & Rodriguez-Rios, J. D. (2015). On the influence of interpersonal relations on business practices in Latin America: A comparison with the Chinese guanxi and the Arab Wasta. *Thunderbird International Business Review*, 57(4), 281–293.

Verhees, J. H. M., & Meulenberg, M. T. G. (2004). Market orientation, innovation, and performance in small firms. *Journal of Small Business Management*, 42(2), 134–154. DOI: 10.1111/j.1540-627X.2004.00102.x

Volkmann, C., Fichter, K., Klofsten, M., & Audretsch, D. (2021). Sustainable entrepreneurial ecosystems: An emerging field of research. *Small Business Economics*, 56(3), 1047–1055. DOI: 10.1007/s11187-019-00253-7

Vries, H. D., Bekkers, V., & Tummers, L. (2016). Innovation in the public sector: A systematic review and future research agenda. *Public Administration*, 94(1), 146–166. DOI: 10.1111/padm.12209

Wah, S. S. (2004). Entrepreneurial leaders in family business organisations. *Journal of Enterprising Culture*, 12(1), 1–34. DOI: 10.1142/S0218495804000026

Wallace, W., & Creelman, D. (2015, June 18). *Leading People When They Know More than You Do*. Harvard Business Review. Retrieved June 30, 2023, from https://hbr.org/2015/06/leading-people-when-they-know-more-than-you-do

Wang, C.-J., & Wu, L.-Y. (2012). Team member commitments and start-up competitiveness. *Journal of Business Research*, 65(5), 708–715. DOI: 10.1016/j.jbusres.2011.04.004

Wang, H. (2021). *Contemporary Daoism, organic relationality, and curriculum of integrative creativity*. IAP.

Wang, J. (2021). Research on the Influence of Dynamic Work Environment on Employees' Innovative Performance in the Post-epidemic Era–The Role of Job Crafting and Voice Behaviour. *Frontiers in Psychology*, 12, 5948. DOI: 10.3389/fpsyg.2021.795218

Wang, S. Y., Wong, Y. J., & Yeh, K. H. (2016). Relationship harmony, dialectical coping, and nonattachment: Chinese indigenous well-being and mental health. *The Counseling Psychologist*, 44(1), 78–108.

Wang, T., Yu, Z., Ahmad, R., Riaz, S., Khan, K. U., Siyal, S., Chaudhry, M. A., & Zhang, T. (2022). Transition of bioeconomy as a key concept for the agriculture and agribusiness development: An extensive review on ASEAN countries. *Frontiers in Sustainable Food Systems*, 6, 998594. DOI: 10.3389/fsufs.2022.998594

Wang, Y., Widrow, B., Zadeh, L. A., Howard, N., Wood, S., Bhavsar, V. C., Budin, G., Chan, C., Fiorini, R. A., Gavrilova, M. L., & Shell, D. F. (2016). Cognitive Intelligence: Deep learning, thinking, and reasoning by brain-inspired systems. [IJCINI]. *International Journal of Cognitive Informatics and Natural Intelligence*, 10(4), 1–20. DOI: 10.4018/IJCINI.2016100101

Watson, M., Kuofie, M., & Dool, R. (2018). Relationship between Spiritually Intelligent Leadership and Employee Engagement. *Journal of Marketing Management*, 9(2).

Webb, J. W., Khoury, T. A., & Hitt, M. A. (2019). The influence of formal and informal institutional voids on entrepreneurship. *Entrepreneurship Theory and Practice*, 104225871983031. Advance online publication. DOI: 10.1177/1042258719830310

Wee, J., & Morse, O. (2007). Juggling People—Secrets for Successful Teams. *Cost Engineering (Morgantown, W. Va.)*, 49(8), 38.

Weinstein, B. PhD. (2019, October 14). Seven Bold Leaders Reveal How Ethical Leadership Is A Boon To Business. *Forbes.* https://www.forbes.com/sites/bruceweinstein/2019/10/14/seven-bold-leaders-reveal-how-ethical-leadership-is-a-boon-to-business/?sh=6b12154e454c

West, M. A. (1987). A measure of role innovation at work. *British Journal of Social Psychology*, 26(1), 83–85. DOI: 10.1111/j.2044-8309.1987.tb00764.x

West, M. A., & Sacramento, C. A. (2023). Creativity and innovation: The role of team and organizational climate. In *Handbook of Organizational Creativity* (pp. 317–337). Academic Press., DOI: 10.1016/B978-0-323-91840-4.00024-4

Williams, K. Y., & O'Reilly, C. A. (1998). Demography and diversity in organizations: A review of 40 years of research. In B. Staw & R. Sutton (Eds.), *Research in organizational behavior*, Vol. 20: 77–140.

Wilson, S. D. (2004). The relationship between leadership and domains of multiple intelligences.

Wilson, C. (2012). Strategic engagement and alignment of corporate talent. *Development and Learning in Organizations*, 26(5), 4–8. DOI: 10.1108/14777281211258626

Wilson, S. D. (2007). A study of multiple intelligences and higher education faculty in the United States. [TLC]. *Journal of College Teaching and Learning*, 4(7). Advance online publication. DOI: 10.19030/tlc.v4i7.1560

Wilson, S. D., & Mujtaba, B. G. (2010). The relationship between leadership and multiple intelligences with the 21st century's higher education faculty. *The Journal of Applied Business and Economics*, 11(3), 106.

Winston, B., & Fields, D. (2015). Seeking and measuring the essential behaviors of servant leadership. *Leadership and Organization Development Journal*, 36(4), 413–434.

Wong, Y. T., Wong, S. H., & Wong, Y. W. (2014). A study of subordinate-supervisor guanxi in Chinese joint ventures. In *Confucian HRM in greater China* (pp. 90–103). Routledge.

World Health Organization. (2023). Statement on the fifteenth meeting of the IHR (2005) Emergency Committee on the COVID-19 pandemic. *World Heal Organ*.

Xu, A. J., Loi, R., & Ngo, H. Y. (2016). Ethical leadership behavior and employee justice perceptions: The mediating role of trust in organization. *Journal of Business Ethics*, 134(3), 493–504. DOI: 10.1007/s10551-014-2457-4

Xu, Z., & Dobson, S. (2019). Challenges of building entrepreneurial ecosystems in peripheral places. *Journal of Entrepreneurship and Public Policy*, 8(3), 408–430. DOI: 10.1108/JEPP-03-2019-0023

Xu, Z., Wang, H., & Suntrayuth, S. (2022). Organizational climate, innovation orientation, and innovative work behaviour: The mediating role of psychological safety and intrinsic motivation. *Discrete Dynamics in Nature and Society*, 2022(1), 1–10. DOI: 10.1155/2022/9067136

Yanbin, R., & Chao, S. (2011). Application of the Concept "People-Oriented" to Improve the Working Team Safety Construction. *Procedia Engineering*, 26, 2080–2084. DOI: 10.1016/j.proeng.2011.11.2409

Yang, Y., & Zhang, X. (2024). A Review of the Influence of Different Leadership Styles on Employees' Initiative Behavior. In SHS Web of Conferences (Vol. 181, p. 01035). EDP Sciences

Yang, J., Pu, B., & Guan, Z. (2019). Entrepreneurial leadership and turnover intention of employees: The role of affective commitment and person-job fit. *International Journal of Environmental Research and Public Health*, 16(13), 2380. DOI: 10.3390/ijerph16132380 PMID: 31277473

Yousuf, N. A., Awang, H., & Iranmanesh, M. (2017). Determinants and outcome of environmental practices in Malaysian construction projects. *Journal of Cleaner Production*, 156(17), 345–354. DOI: 10.1016/j.jclepro.2017.04.064

Yu, S., Liu, S., Gong, X., Lu, W., & Liu, C. E. (2023). How does deviance tolerance enhance innovative behaviour? The mediating role of cognitive crafting and the moderating role of regulatory focus. *Chinese Management Studies*. ahead-of-print

Yuan, L., Chia, R., & Gosling, J. (2023). Confucian virtue ethics and ethical leadership in modern China. *Journal of Business Ethics*, 182(1), 119–133.

Yukl, G. (2002). *Leadership in Organizations* (5th ed.). Prentice-Hall.

Yukl, G. (2008, April). The importance of flexible leadership. In *23rd Annual Conference of the Society for Industrial-Organizational Psychology,* San Francisco, CA.

Yukl, G. (2009). Leading organizational learning: Reflections on theory and research. *The Leadership Quarterly*, 20(1), 49–53. DOI: 10.1016/j.leaqua.2008.11.006

Yulivan, I. (2022). The Influence of Entrepreneurial Leadership, Work Culture and Organizational Trust on Employee Engagement of Employees in the Ministry of Religious Affairs Republic of Indonesia. *International Journal of Multicultural and Multireligious Understanding*, 8(12), 633–638.

Yu, S., Gong, X., & Wu, N. (2020). Job insecurity and employee engagement: A moderated dual path model. *Sustainability (Basel)*, 12(23), 10081. DOI: 10.3390/su122310081

Yu, Y., Zhang, X., Huang, S., Chen, Z., & Chen, Z. (2020). Entrepreneurial leadership and innovation performance in new ventures: Examining the roles of strategic flexibility and environmental turbulence. *Entrepreneurship Research Journal*, 12(4), 629–652. DOI: 10.1515/erj-2018-0090

Zaccaro, S. J. (2001). Organizational leadership and social intelligence. *Multiple intelligences and leadership*, 42-68.

Zahra, S. A., Liu, W., & Si, S. (2023). How digital technology promotes entrepreneurship in ecosystems. *Technovation*, 119, 102457. DOI: 10.1016/j.technovation.2022.102457

Zahra, S. A., Sapienza, H. J., & Davidsson, P. (2006). Entrepreneurship and dynamic capabilities: A review, model and research agenda. *Journal of Management Studies*, 43(4), 917–955. DOI: 10.1111/j.1467-6486.2006.00616.x

Zaleznik, (1990). The leadership gap. *Academy of Management Executive*: 7–22.

Zeitlin, W., Lawrence, C. K., Armendariz, S., & Chontow, K. (2023). Predicting retention for a diverse and inclusive child welfare workforce. *Human Service Organizations, Management, Leadership & Governance*, 47(1), 9–27. DOI: 10.1080/23303131.2022.2115432

Zhang, H., & Baker, G. (2008). *Think like Chinese*. Federation Press.

Zhang, Y., Lu, B., & Zheng, H. (2020). Can buzzing bring business? Social interactions, network centrality and sales performance: An empirical study on business-to-business communities. *Journal of Business Research*, 112, 170–189. DOI: 10.1016/j.jbusres.2020.02.034

Zhaojun, Y., Jun, S., Yali, Z., & Ying, W. (2017). Green, Green, It's Green: A Triad Model of Technology, Culture, and Innovation for Corporate Sustainability. *Sustainability*, 9, 1–23.

Zhou, W. (2016). When does shared leadership matter in entrepreneurial teams: The role of personality composition. *The International Entrepreneurship and Management Journal*, 12(1), 153–169. DOI: 10.1007/s11365-014-0334-3

Zhu, J., & Grigoriadis, T. N. (2022). Chinese dialects, culture & economic performance. *China Economic Review*, 73, 101783.

Zhu, W., Zheng, X., He, H., Wang, G., & Zhang, X. (2019). Ethical leadership with both "moral person" and "moral manager" aspects: Scale development and cross-cultural validation. *Journal of Business Ethics*, 158, 547–565.

Zijlstra, P. H. (2014). *When is entrepreneurial leadership most effective* (Master's thesis, University of Twente). https://purl.utwente.nl/essays/66030

Zreik, M. (2021). Europe: An attractive region for Chinese investment. *Journal of the Belarusian State University.International Relations*, 1, 51–61.

Zreik, M. (2022). "Rethinking China's Leadership through an Analysis of the Belt and Road Initiative "Information & Security. *International Journal (Toronto, Ont.)*, 52, 81–100.

Zreik, M. (2023). From Boom to Bust: A Study of China's Economy in the Wake of COVID-19 Outbreak in H1 2020. *BRICS Journal of Economics*, 4(1), 147–171. DOI: 10.3897/brics-econ.4.e101050

Related References

To continue our tradition of advancing information science and technology research, we have compiled a list of recommended IGI Global readings. These references will provide additional information and guidance to further enrich your knowledge and assist you with your own research and future publications.

Abdul Razak, R., & Mansor, N. A. (2021). Instagram Influencers in Social Media-Induced Tourism: Rethinking Tourist Trust Towards Tourism Destination. In M. Dinis, L. Bonixe, S. Lamy, & Z. Breda (Eds.), *Impact of New Media in Tourism* (pp. 135-144). IGI Global. https://doi.org/10.4018/978-1-7998-7095-1.ch009

Abir, T., & Khan, M. Y. (2022). Importance of ICT Advancement and Culture of Adaptation in the Tourism and Hospitality Industry for Developing Countries. In Ramos, C., Quinteiro, S., & Gonçalves, A. (Eds.), *ICT as Innovator Between Tourism and Culture* (pp. 30–41). IGI Global. https://doi.org/10.4018/978-1-7998-8165-0.ch003

Abir, T., & Khan, M. Y. (2022). Importance of ICT Advancement and Culture of Adaptation in the Tourism and Hospitality Industry for Developing Countries. In Ramos, C., Quinteiro, S., & Gonçalves, A. (Eds.), *ICT as Innovator Between Tourism and Culture* (pp. 30–41). IGI Global. https://doi.org/10.4018/978-1-7998-8165-0.ch003

Abtahi, M. S., Behboudi, L., & Hasanabad, H. M. (2017). Factors Affecting Internet Advertising Adoption in Ad Agencies. *International Journal of Innovation in the Digital Economy*, 8(4), 18–29. DOI: 10.4018/IJIDE.2017100102

Afenyo-Agbe, E., & Mensah, I. (2022). Principles, Benefits, and Barriers to Community-Based Tourism: Implications for Management. In Mensah, I., & Afenyo-Agbe, E. (Eds.), *Prospects and Challenges of Community-Based Tourism and Changing Demographics* (pp. 1–29). IGI Global. DOI: 10.4018/978-1-7998-7335-8.ch001

Agbo, V. M. (2022). Distributive Justice Issues in Community-Based Tourism. In Mensah, I., & Afenyo-Agbe, E. (Eds.), *Prospects and Challenges of Community-Based Tourism and Changing Demographics* (pp. 107–129). IGI Global. https://doi.org/10.4018/978-1-7998-7335-8.ch005

Agrawal, S. (2017). The Impact of Emerging Technologies and Social Media on Different Business(es): Marketing and Management. In Rishi, O., & Sharma, A. (Eds.), *Maximizing Business Performance and Efficiency Through Intelligent Systems* (pp. 37–49). Hershey, PA: IGI Global. DOI: 10.4018/978-1-5225-2234-8.ch002

Ahmad, A., & Johari, S. (2022). Georgetown as a Gastronomy Tourism Destination: Visitor Awareness Towards Revisit Intention of Nasi Kandar Restaurant. In Valeri, M. (Ed.), *New Governance and Management in Touristic Destinations* (pp. 71–83). IGI Global. https://doi.org/10.4018/978-1-6684-3889-3.ch005

Alkhatib, G., & Bayouq, S. T. (2021). A TAM-Based Model of Technological Factors Affecting Use of E-Tourism. *International Journal of Tourism and Hospitality Management in the Digital Age*, 5(2), 50–67. https://doi.org/10.4018/IJTHMDA.20210701.oa1

Altinay Ozdemir, M. (2021). Virtual Reality (VR) and Augmented Reality (AR) Technologies for Accessibility and Marketing in the Tourism Industry. In C. Eusébio, L. Teixeira, & M. Carneiro (Eds.), *ICT Tools and Applications for Accessible Tourism* (pp. 277-301). IGI Global. https://doi.org/10.4018/978-1-7998-6428-8.ch013

Anantharaman, R. N., Rajeswari, K. S., Angusamy, A., & Kuppusamy, J. (2017). Role of Self-Efficacy and Collective Efficacy as Moderators of Occupational Stress Among Software Development Professionals. *International Journal of Human Capital and Information Technology Professionals*, 8(2), 45–58. DOI: 10.4018/IJHCITP.2017040103

Aninze, F., El-Gohary, H., & Hussain, J. (2018). The Role of Microfinance to Empower Women: The Case of Developing Countries. *International Journal of Customer Relationship Marketing and Management*, 9(1), 54–78. DOI: 10.4018/IJCRMM.2018010104

Antosova, G., Sabogal-Salamanca, M., & Krizova, E. (2021). Human Capital in Tourism: A Practical Model of Endogenous and Exogenous Territorial Tourism Planning in Bahía Solano, Colombia. In Costa, V., Moura, A., & Mira, M. (Eds.), *Handbook of Research on Human Capital and People Management in the Tourism Industry* (pp. 282–302). IGI Global. https://doi.org/10.4018/978-1-7998-4318-4.ch014

Arsenijević, O. M., Orčić, D., & Kastratović, E. (2017). Development of an Optimization Tool for Intangibles in SMEs: A Case Study from Serbia with a Pilot Research in the Prestige by Milka Company. In Vemić, M. (Ed.), *Optimal Management Strategies in Small and Medium Enterprises* (pp. 320–347). Hershey, PA: IGI Global. DOI: 10.4018/978-1-5225-1949-2.ch015

Aryanto, V. D., Wismantoro, Y., & Widyatmoko, K. (2018). Implementing Eco-Innovation by Utilizing the Internet to Enhance Firm's Marketing Performance: Study of Green Batik Small and Medium Enterprises in Indonesia. *International Journal of E-Business Research*, 14(1), 21–36. DOI: 10.4018/IJEBR.2018010102

Asero, V., & Billi, S. (2022). New Perspective of Networking in the DMO Model. In Valeri, M. (Ed.), *New Governance and Management in Touristic Destinations* (pp. 105–118). IGI Global. https://doi.org/10.4018/978-1-6684-3889-3.ch007

Atiku, S. O., & Fields, Z. (2017). Multicultural Orientations for 21st Century Global Leadership. In Baporikar, N. (Ed.), *Management Education for Global Leadership* (pp. 28–51). Hershey, PA: IGI Global. DOI: 10.4018/978-1-5225-1013-0.ch002

Atiku, S. O., & Fields, Z. (2018). Organisational Learning Dimensions and Talent Retention Strategies for the Service Industries. In Baporikar, N. (Ed.), *Global Practices in Knowledge Management for Societal and Organizational Development* (pp. 358–381). Hershey, PA: IGI Global. DOI: 10.4018/978-1-5225-3009-1.ch017

Atsa'am, D. D., & Kuset Bodur, E. (2021). Pattern Mining on How Organizational Tenure Affects the Psychological Capital of Employees Within the Hospitality and Tourism Industry: Linking Employees' Organizational Tenure With PsyCap. *International Journal of Tourism and Hospitality Management in the Digital Age*, 5(2), 17–28. https://doi.org/10.4018/IJTHMDA.2021070102

Ávila, L., & Teixeira, L. (2018). The Main Concepts Behind the Dematerialization of Business Processes. In M. Khosrow-Pour, D.B.A. (Ed.), *Encyclopedia of Information Science and Technology, Fourth Edition* (pp. 888-898). Hershey, PA: IGI Global. https://doi.org/DOI: 10.4018/978-1-5225-2255-3.ch076

Ayorekire, J., Mugizi, F., Obua, J., & Ampaire, G. (2022). Community-Based Tourism and Local People's Perceptions Towards Conservation: The Case of Queen Elizabeth Conservation Area, Uganda. In Mensah, I., & Afenyo-Agbe, E. (Eds.), *Prospects and Challenges of Community-Based Tourism and Changing Demographics* (pp. 56–82). IGI Global. https://doi.org/10.4018/978-1-7998-7335-8.ch003

Baleiro, R. (2022). Tourist Literature and the Architecture of Travel in Olga To-karczuk and Patti Smith. In R. Baleiro & R. Pereira (Eds.), *Global Perspectives on Literary Tourism and Film-Induced Tourism* (pp. 202-216). IGI Global. https://doi.org/10.4018/978-1-7998-8262-6.ch011

Barat, S. (2021). Looking at the Future of Medical Tourism in Asia. *International Journal of Tourism and Hospitality Management in the Digital Age*, 5(1), 19–33. https://doi.org/10.4018/IJTHMDA.2021010102

Barbosa, C. A., Magalhães, M., & Nunes, M. R. (2021). Travel Instagramability: A Way of Choosing a Destination? In M. Dinis, L. Bonixe, S. Lamy, & Z. Breda (Eds.), *Impact of New Media in Tourism* (pp. 173-190). IGI Global. https://doi.org/10.4018/978-1-7998-7095-1.ch011

Bari, M. W., & Khan, Q. (2021). Pakistan as a Destination of Religious Tourism. In E. Alaverdov & M. Bari (Eds.), *Global Development of Religious Tourism* (pp. 1-10). IGI Global. https://doi.org/10.4018/978-1-7998-5792-1.ch001

Bartens, Y., Chunpir, H. I., Schulte, F., & Voß, S. (2017). Business/IT Alignment in Two-Sided Markets: A COBIT 5 Analysis for Media Streaming Business Models. In De Haes, S., & Van Grembergen, W. (Eds.), *Strategic IT Governance and Alignment in Business Settings* (pp. 82–111). Hershey, PA: IGI Global. DOI: 10.4018/978-1-5225-0861-8.ch004

Bashayreh, A. M. (2018). Organizational Culture and Organizational Performance. In Lee, W., & Sabetzadeh, F. (Eds.), *Contemporary Knowledge and Systems Science* (pp. 50–69). Hershey, PA: IGI Global. DOI: 10.4018/978-1-5225-5655-8.ch003

Bechthold, L., Lude, M., & Prügl, R. (2021). Crisis Favors the Prepared Firm: How Organizational Ambidexterity Relates to Perceptions of Organizational Resilience. In Zehrer, A., Glowka, G., Schwaiger, K., & Ranacher-Lackner, V. (Eds.), *Resiliency Models and Addressing Future Risks for Family Firms in the Tourism Industry* (pp. 178–205). IGI Global. https://doi.org/10.4018/978-1-7998-7352-5.ch008

Bedford, D. A. (2018). Sustainable Knowledge Management Strategies: Aligning Business Capabilities and Knowledge Management Goals. In Baporikar, N. (Ed.), *Global Practices in Knowledge Management for Societal and Organizational Development* (pp. 46–73). Hershey, PA: IGI Global. DOI: 10.4018/978-1-5225-3009-1.ch003

Bekjanov, D., & Matyusupov, B. (2021). Influence of Innovative Processes in the Competitiveness of Tourist Destination. In Soares, J. (Ed.), *Innovation and Entrepreneurial Opportunities in Community Tourism* (pp. 243–263). IGI Global. https://doi.org/10.4018/978-1-7998-4855-4.ch014

Bharwani, S., & Musunuri, D. (2018). Reflection as a Process From Theory to Practice. In M. Khosrow-Pour, D.B.A. (Ed.), *Encyclopedia of Information Science and Technology, Fourth Edition* (pp. 1529-1539). Hershey, PA: IGI Global. DOI: 10.4018/978-1-5225-2255-3.ch132

Bhatt, G. D., Wang, Z., & Rodger, J. A. (2017). Information Systems Capabilities and Their Effects on Competitive Advantages: A Study of Chinese Companies. *Information Resources Management Journal*, 30(3), 41–57. DOI: 10.4018/IRMJ.2017070103

Bhushan, M., & Yadav, A. (2017). Concept of Cloud Computing in ESB. In Bhadoria, R., Chaudhari, N., Tomar, G., & Singh, S. (Eds.), *Exploring Enterprise Service Bus in the Service-Oriented Architecture Paradigm* (pp. 116–127). Hershey, PA: IGI Global. DOI: 10.4018/978-1-5225-2157-0.ch008

Bhushan, S. (2017). System Dynamics Base-Model of Humanitarian Supply Chain (HSCM) in Disaster Prone Eco-Communities of India: A Discussion on Simulation and Scenario Results. *International Journal of System Dynamics Applications*, 6(3), 20–37. DOI: 10.4018/IJSDA.2017070102

Binder, D., & Miller, J. W. (2021). A Generations' Perspective on Employer Branding in Tourism. In Costa, V., Moura, A., & Mira, M. (Eds.), *Handbook of Research on Human Capital and People Management in the Tourism Industry* (pp. 152–174). IGI Global. https://doi.org/10.4018/978-1-7998-4318-4.ch008

Birch Freeman, A. A., Mensah, I., & Antwi, K. B. (2022). Smiling vs. Frowning Faces: Community Participation for Sustainable Tourism in Ghanaian Communities. In Mensah, I., & Afenyo-Agbe, E. (Eds.), *Prospects and Challenges of Community-Based Tourism and Changing Demographics* (pp. 83–106). IGI Global. https://doi.org/10.4018/978-1-7998-7335-8.ch004

Biswas, A., & De, A. K. (2017). On Development of a Fuzzy Stochastic Programming Model with Its Application to Business Management. In Trivedi, S., Dey, S., Kumar, A., & Panda, T. (Eds.), *Handbook of Research on Advanced Data Mining Techniques and Applications for Business Intelligence* (pp. 353–378). Hershey, PA: IGI Global. DOI: 10.4018/978-1-5225-2031-3.ch021

Boragnio, A., & Faracce Macia, C. (2021). "Taking Care of Yourself at Home": Use of E-Commerce About Food and Care During the COVID-19 Pandemic in the City of Buenos Aires. In Korstanje, M. (Ed.), *Socio-Economic Effects and Recovery Efforts for the Rental Industry: Post-COVID-19 Strategies* (pp. 45–71). IGI Global. https://doi.org/10.4018/978-1-7998-7287-0.ch003

Borges, V. D. (2021). Happiness: The Basis for Public Policy in Tourism. In Perinotto, A., Mayer, V., & Soares, J. (Eds.), *Rebuilding and Restructuring the Tourism Industry: Infusion of Happiness and Quality of Life* (pp. 1–25). IGI Global. https://doi.org/10.4018/978-1-7998-7239-9.ch001

Bücker, J., & Ernste, K. (2018). Use of Brand Heroes in Strategic Reputation Management: The Case of Bacardi, Adidas, and Daimler. In Erdemir, A. (Ed.), *Reputation Management Techniques in Public Relations* (pp. 126–150). Hershey, PA: IGI Global. DOI: 10.4018/978-1-5225-3619-2.ch007

Buluk Eşitti, B. (2021). COVID-19 and Alternative Tourism: New Destinations and New Tourism Products. In Demir, M., Dalgıç, A., & Ergen, F. (Eds.), *Handbook of Research on the Impacts and Implications of COVID-19 on the Tourism Industry* (pp. 786–805). IGI Global. https://doi.org/10.4018/978-1-7998-8231-2.ch038

Bureš, V. (2018). Industry 4.0 From the Systems Engineering Perspective: Alternative Holistic Framework Development. In Brunet-Thornton, R., & Martinez, F. (Eds.), *Analyzing the Impacts of Industry 4.0 in Modern Business Environments* (pp. 199–223). Hershey, PA: IGI Global. DOI: 10.4018/978-1-5225-3468-6.ch011

Buzady, Z. (2017). Resolving the Magic Cube of Effective Case Teaching: Benchmarking Case Teaching Practices in Emerging Markets – Insights from the Central European University Business School, Hungary. In Latusek, D. (Ed.), *Case Studies as a Teaching Tool in Management Education* (pp. 79–103). Hershey, PA: IGI Global. DOI: 10.4018/978-1-5225-0770-3.ch005

Camillo, A. (2021). *Legal Matters, Risk Management, and Risk Prevention: From Forming a Business to Legal Representation*. IGI Global. DOI: 10.4018/978-1-7998-4342-9.ch004

Căpusneanu, S., & Topor, D. I. (2018). Business Ethics and Cost Management in SMEs: Theories of Business Ethics and Cost Management Ethos. In Oncioiu, I. (Ed.), *Ethics and Decision-Making for Sustainable Business Practices* (pp. 109–127). Hershey, PA: IGI Global. DOI: 10.4018/978-1-5225-3773-1.ch007

Chan, R. L., Mo, P. L., & Moon, K. K. (2018). Strategic and Tactical Measures in Managing Enterprise Risks: A Study of the Textile and Apparel Industry. In Strang, K., Korstanje, M., & Vajjhala, N. (Eds.), *Research, Practices, and Innovations in Global Risk and Contingency Management* (pp. 1–19). Hershey, PA: IGI Global. DOI: 10.4018/978-1-5225-4754-9.ch001

Charlier, S. D., Burke-Smalley, L. A., & Fisher, S. L. (2018). Undergraduate Programs in the U.S: A Contextual and Content-Based Analysis. In Mendy, J. (Ed.), *Teaching Human Resources and Organizational Behavior at the College Level* (pp. 26–57). Hershey, PA: IGI Global. DOI: 10.4018/978-1-5225-2820-3.ch002

Chumillas, J., Güell, M., & Quer, P. (2022). The Use of ICT in Tourist and Educational Literary Routes: The Role of the Guide. In Ramos, C., Quinteiro, S., & Gonçalves, A. (Eds.), *ICT as Innovator Between Tourism and Culture* (pp. 15–29). IGI Global. https://doi.org/10.4018/978-1-7998-8165-0.ch002

Dahlberg, T., Kivijärvi, H., & Saarinen, T. (2017). IT Investment Consistency and Other Factors Influencing the Success of IT Performance. In De Haes, S., & Van Grembergen, W. (Eds.), *Strategic IT Governance and Alignment in Business Settings* (pp. 176–208). Hershey, PA: IGI Global. DOI: 10.4018/978-1-5225-0861-8.ch007

Damnjanović, A. M. (2017). Knowledge Management Optimization through IT and E-Business Utilization: A Qualitative Study on Serbian SMEs. In Vemić, M. (Ed.), *Optimal Management Strategies in Small and Medium Enterprises* (pp. 249–267). Hershey, PA: IGI Global. DOI: 10.4018/978-1-5225-1949-2.ch012

Daneshpour, H. (2017). Integrating Sustainable Development into Project Portfolio Management through Application of Open Innovation. In Vemić, M. (Ed.), *Optimal Management Strategies in Small and Medium Enterprises* (pp. 370–387). Hershey, PA: IGI Global. DOI: 10.4018/978-1-5225-1949-2.ch017

Daniel, A. D., & Reis de Castro, V. (2018). Entrepreneurship Education: How to Measure the Impact on Nascent Entrepreneurs. In Carrizo Moreira, A., Guilherme Leitão Dantas, J., & Manuel Valente, F. (Eds.), *Nascent Entrepreneurship and Successful New Venture Creation* (pp. 85–110). Hershey, PA: IGI Global. DOI: 10.4018/978-1-5225-2936-1.ch004

David, R., Swami, B. N., & Tangirala, S. (2018). Ethics Impact on Knowledge Management in Organizational Development: A Case Study. In Baporikar, N. (Ed.), *Global Practices in Knowledge Management for Societal and Organizational Development* (pp. 19–45). Hershey, PA: IGI Global. DOI: 10.4018/978-1-5225-3009-1.ch002

De Uña-Álvarez, E., & Villarino-Pérez, M. (2022). Fostering Ecocultural Resources, Identity, and Tourism in Inland Territories (Galicia, NW Spain). In G. Fernandes (Ed.), *Challenges and New Opportunities for Tourism in Inland Territories: Ecocultural Resources and Sustainable Initiatives* (pp. 1-16). IGI Global. https://doi.org/10.4018/978-1-7998-7339-6.ch001

Delias, P., & Lakiotaki, K. (2018). Discovering Process Horizontal Boundaries to Facilitate Process Comprehension. *International Journal of Operations Research and Information Systems*, 9(2), 1–31. DOI: 10.4018/IJORIS.2018040101

Denholm, J., & Lee-Davies, L. (2018). Success Factors for Games in Business and Project Management. In *Enhancing Education and Training Initiatives Through Serious Games* (pp. 34–68). Hershey, PA: IGI Global. DOI: 10.4018/978-1-5225-3689-5.ch002

Deshpande, M. (2017). Best Practices in Management Institutions for Global Leadership: Policy Aspects. In Baporikar, N. (Ed.), *Management Education for Global Leadership* (pp. 1–27). Hershey, PA: IGI Global. DOI: 10.4018/978-1-5225-1013-0.ch001

Deshpande, M. (2018). Policy Perspectives for SMEs Knowledge Management. In Baporikar, N. (Ed.), *Knowledge Integration Strategies for Entrepreneurship and Sustainability* (pp. 23–46). Hershey, PA: IGI Global. DOI: 10.4018/978-1-5225-5115-7.ch002

Dezdar, S. (2017). ERP Implementation Projects in Asian Countries: A Comparative Study on Iran and China. *International Journal of Information Technology Project Management*, 8(3), 52–68. DOI: 10.4018/IJITPM.2017070104

Domingos, D., Respício, A., & Martinho, R. (2017). Reliability of IoT-Aware BPMN Healthcare Processes. In Reis, C., & Maximiano, M. (Eds.), *Internet of Things and Advanced Application in Healthcare* (pp. 214–248). Hershey, PA: IGI Global. DOI: 10.4018/978-1-5225-1820-4.ch008

Dosumu, O., Hussain, J., & El-Gohary, H. (2017). An Exploratory Study of the Impact of Government Policies on the Development of Small and Medium Enterprises in Developing Countries: The Case of Nigeria. *International Journal of Customer Relationship Marketing and Management*, 8(4), 51–62. DOI: 10.4018/IJCRMM.2017100104

Durst, S., Bruns, G., & Edvardsson, I. R. (2017). Retaining Knowledge in Smaller Building and Construction Firms. *International Journal of Knowledge and Systems Science*, 8(3), 1–12. DOI: 10.4018/IJKSS.2017070101

Edvardsson, I. R., & Durst, S. (2017). Outsourcing, Knowledge, and Learning: A Critical Review. *International Journal of Knowledge-Based Organizations*, 7(2), 13–26. DOI: 10.4018/IJKBO.2017040102

Edwards, J. S. (2018). Integrating Knowledge Management and Business Processes. In M. Khosrow-Pour, D.B.A. (Ed.), *Encyclopedia of Information Science and Technology, Fourth Edition* (pp. 5046-5055). Hershey, PA: IGI Global. DOI: 10.4018/978-1-5225-2255-3.ch437

Eichelberger, S., & Peters, M. (2021). Family Firm Management in Turbulent Times: Opportunities for Responsible Tourism. In Zehrer, A., Glowka, G., Schwaiger, K., & Ranacher-Lackner, V. (Eds.), *Resiliency Models and Addressing Future Risks for Family Firms in the Tourism Industry* (pp. 103–124). IGI Global. https://doi.org/10.4018/978-1-7998-7352-5.ch005

Eide, D., Hjalager, A., & Hansen, M. (2022). Innovative Certifications in Adventure Tourism: Attributes and Diffusion. In R. Augusto Costa, F. Brandão, Z. Breda, & C. Costa (Eds.), *Planning and Managing the Experience Economy in Tourism* (pp. 161-175). IGI Global. https://doi.org/10.4018/978-1-7998-8775-1.ch009

Ejiogu, A. O. (2018). Economics of Farm Management. In *Agricultural Finance and Opportunities for Investment and Expansion* (pp. 56–72). Hershey, PA: IGI Global. DOI: 10.4018/978-1-5225-3059-6.ch003

Ekanem, I., & Abiade, G. E. (2018). Factors Influencing the Use of E-Commerce by Small Enterprises in Nigeria. *International Journal of ICT Research in Africa and the Middle East*, 7(1), 37–53. DOI: 10.4018/IJICTRAME.2018010103

Ekanem, I., & Alrossais, L. A. (2017). Succession Challenges Facing Family Businesses in Saudi Arabia. In Zgheib, P. (Ed.), *Entrepreneurship and Business Innovation in the Middle East* (pp. 122–146). Hershey, PA: IGI Global. DOI: 10.4018/978-1-5225-2066-5.ch007

El Faquih, L., & Fredj, M. (2017). Ontology-Based Framework for Quality in Configurable Process Models. *Journal of Electronic Commerce in Organizations*, 15(2), 48–60. DOI: 10.4018/JECO.2017040104

Faisal, M. N., & Talib, F. (2017). Building Ambidextrous Supply Chains in SMEs: How to Tackle the Barriers? *International Journal of Information Systems and Supply Chain Management*, 10(4), 80–100. DOI: 10.4018/IJISSCM.2017100105

Fernandes, T. M., Gomes, J., & Romão, M. (2017). Investments in E-Government: A Benefit Management Case Study. *International Journal of Electronic Government Research*, 13(3), 1–17. DOI: 10.4018/IJEGR.2017070101

Figueira, L. M., Honrado, G. R., & Dionísio, M. S. (2021). Human Capital Management in the Tourism Industry in Portugal. In Costa, V., Moura, A., & Mira, M. (Eds.), *Handbook of Research on Human Capital and People Management in the Tourism Industry* (pp. 1–19). IGI Global. DOI: 10.4018/978-1-7998-4318-4.ch001

Gao, S. S., Oreal, S., & Zhang, J. (2018). Contemporary Financial Risk Management Perceptions and Practices of Small-Sized Chinese Businesses. In I. Management Association (Ed.), *Global Business Expansion: Concepts, Methodologies, Tools, and Applications* (pp. 917-931). Hershey, PA: IGI Global. DOI: 10.4018/978-1-5225-5481-3.ch041

Garg, R., & Berning, S. C. (2017). Indigenous Chinese Management Philosophies: Key Concepts and Relevance for Modern Chinese Firms. In Christiansen, B., & Koc, G. (Eds.), *Transcontinental Strategies for Industrial Development and Economic Growth* (pp. 43–57). Hershey, PA: IGI Global. DOI: 10.4018/978-1-5225-2160-0.ch003

Gencer, Y. G. (2017). Supply Chain Management in Retailing Business. In Akkucuk, U. (Ed.), *Ethics and Sustainability in Global Supply Chain Management* (pp. 197–210). Hershey, PA: IGI Global. DOI: 10.4018/978-1-5225-2036-8.ch011

Gera, R., Arora, S., & Malik, S. (2021). Emotional Labor in the Tourism Industry: Strategies, Antecedents, and Outcomes. In Costa, V., Moura, A., & Mira, M. (Eds.), *Handbook of Research on Human Capital and People Management in the Tourism Industry* (pp. 73–91). IGI Global. https://doi.org/10.4018/978-1-7998-4318-4.ch004

Giacosa, E. (2018). The Increasing of the Regional Development Thanks to the Luxury Business Innovation. In Carvalho, L. (Ed.), *Handbook of Research on Entrepreneurial Ecosystems and Social Dynamics in a Globalized World* (pp. 260–273). Hershey, PA: IGI Global. DOI: 10.4018/978-1-5225-3525-6.ch011

Glowka, G., Tusch, M., & Zehrer, A. (2021). The Risk Perception of Family Business Owner-Manager in the Tourism Industry: A Qualitative Comparison of the Intra-Firm Senior and Junior Generation. In Zehrer, A., Glowka, G., Schwaiger, K., & Ranacher-Lackner, V. (Eds.), *Resiliency Models and Addressing Future Risks for Family Firms in the Tourism Industry* (pp. 126–153). IGI Global. https://doi.org/10.4018/978-1-7998-7352-5.ch006

Glykas, M., & George, J. (2017). Quality and Process Management Systems in the UAE Maritime Industry. *International Journal of Productivity Management and Assessment Technologies*, 5(1), 20–39. DOI: 10.4018/IJPMAT.2017010102

Glykas, M., Valiris, G., Kokkinaki, A., & Koutsoukou, Z. (2018). Banking Business Process Management Implementation. *International Journal of Productivity Management and Assessment Technologies*, 6(1), 50–69. DOI: 10.4018/IJPMAT.2018010104

Gomes, J., & Romão, M. (2017). The Balanced Scorecard: Keeping Updated and Aligned with Today's Business Trends. *International Journal of Productivity Management and Assessment Technologies*, 5(2), 1–15. DOI: 10.4018/IJPMAT.2017070101

Gomes, J., & Romão, M. (2017). Aligning Information Systems and Technology with Benefit Management and Balanced Scorecard. In De Haes, S., & Van Grembergen, W. (Eds.), *Strategic IT Governance and Alignment in Business Settings* (pp. 112–131). Hershey, PA: IGI Global. DOI: 10.4018/978-1-5225-0861-8.ch005

Goyal, A. (2021). Communicating and Building Destination Brands With New Media. In M. Dinis, L. Bonixe, S. Lamy, & Z. Breda (Eds.), *Impact of New Media in Tourism* (pp. 1-20). IGI Global. https://doi.org/10.4018/978-1-7998-7095-1.ch001

Grefen, P., & Turetken, O. (2017). Advanced Business Process Management in Networked E-Business Scenarios. *International Journal of E-Business Research*, 13(4), 70–104. DOI: 10.4018/IJEBR.2017100105

Guasca, M., Van Broeck, A. M., & Vanneste, D. (2021). Tourism and the Social Reintegration of Colombian Ex-Combatants. In J. da Silva, Z. Breda, & F. Carbone (Eds.), *Role and Impact of Tourism in Peacebuilding and Conflict Transformation* (pp. 66-86). IGI Global. https://doi.org/10.4018/978-1-7998-5053-3.ch005

Haider, A., & Saetang, S. (2017). Strategic IT Alignment in Service Sector. In Rozenes, S., & Cohen, Y. (Eds.), *Handbook of Research on Strategic Alliances and Value Co-Creation in the Service Industry* (pp. 231–258). Hershey, PA: IGI Global. DOI: 10.4018/978-1-5225-2084-9.ch012

Hajilari, A. B., Ghadaksaz, M., & Fasghandis, G. S. (2017). Assessing Organizational Readiness for Implementing ERP System Using Fuzzy Expert System Approach. *International Journal of Enterprise Information Systems*, 13(1), 67–85. DOI: 10.4018/IJEIS.2017010105

Haldorai, A., Ramu, A., & Murugan, S. (2018). Social Aware Cognitive Radio Networks: Effectiveness of Social Networks as a Strategic Tool for Organizational Business Management. In Bansal, H., Shrivastava, G., Nguyen, G., & Stanciu, L. (Eds.), *Social Network Analytics for Contemporary Business Organizations* (pp. 188–202). Hershey, PA: IGI Global. DOI: 10.4018/978-1-5225-5097-6.ch010

Hall, O. P.Jr. (2017). Social Media Driven Management Education. *International Journal of Knowledge-Based Organizations*, 7(2), 43–59. DOI: 10.4018/IJKBO.2017040104

Hanifah, H., Halim, H. A., Ahmad, N. H., & Vafaei-Zadeh, A. (2017). Innovation Culture as a Mediator Between Specific Human Capital and Innovation Performance Among Bumiputera SMEs in Malaysia. In Ahmad, N., Ramayah, T., Halim, H., & Rahman, S. (Eds.), *Handbook of Research on Small and Medium Enterprises in Developing Countries* (pp. 261–279). Hershey, PA: IGI Global. DOI: 10.4018/978-1-5225-2165-5.ch012

Hartlieb, S., & Silvius, G. (2017). Handling Uncertainty in Project Management and Business Development: Similarities and Differences. In Raydugin, Y. (Ed.), *Handbook of Research on Leveraging Risk and Uncertainties for Effective Project Management* (pp. 337–362). Hershey, PA: IGI Global. DOI: 10.4018/978-1-5225-1790-0.ch016

Hass, K. B. (2017). Living on the Edge: Managing Project Complexity. In Raydugin, Y. (Ed.), *Handbook of Research on Leveraging Risk and Uncertainties for Effective Project Management* (pp. 177–201). Hershey, PA: IGI Global. DOI: 10.4018/978-1-5225-1790-0.ch009

Hawking, P., & Carmine Sellitto, C. (2017). Developing an Effective Strategy for Organizational Business Intelligence. In Tavana, M. (Ed.), *Enterprise Information Systems and the Digitalization of Business Functions* (pp. 222–237). Hershey, PA: IGI Global. DOI: 10.4018/978-1-5225-2382-6.ch010

Hawking, P., & Sellitto, C. (2017). A Fast-Moving Consumer Goods Company and Business Intelligence Strategy Development. *International Journal of Enterprise Information Systems*, 13(2), 22–33. DOI: 10.4018/IJEIS.2017040102

Hawking, P., & Sellitto, C. (2017). Business Intelligence Strategy: Two Case Studies. *International Journal of Business Intelligence Research*, 8(2), 17–30. DOI: 10.4018/IJBIR.2017070102

Hee, W. J., Jalleh, G., Lai, H., & Lin, C. (2017). E-Commerce and IT Projects: Evaluation and Management Issues in Australian and Taiwanese Hospitals. *International Journal of Public Health Management and Ethics*, 2(1), 69–90. DOI: 10.4018/IJPHME.2017010104

Hernandez, A. A. (2018). Exploring the Factors to Green IT Adoption of SMEs in the Philippines. *Journal of Cases on Information Technology*, 20(2), 49–66. DOI: 10.4018/JCIT.2018040104

Hollman, A., Bickford, S., & Hollman, T. (2017). Cyber InSecurity: A Post-Mortem Attempt to Assess Cyber Problems from IT and Business Management Perspectives. *Journal of Cases on Information Technology*, 19(3), 42–70. DOI: 10.4018/JCIT.2017070104

Ibrahim, F., & Zainin, N. M. (2021). Exploring the Technological Impacts: The Case of Museums in Brunei Darussalam. *International Journal of Tourism and Hospitality Management in the Digital Age*, 5(1), 1–18. https://doi.org/10.4018/IJTHMDA.2021010101

Igbinakhase, I. (2017). Responsible and Sustainable Management Practices in Developing and Developed Business Environments. In Fields, Z. (Ed.), *Collective Creativity for Responsible and Sustainable Business Practice* (pp. 180–207). Hershey, PA: IGI Global. DOI: 10.4018/978-1-5225-1823-5.ch010

Iwata, J. J., & Hoskins, R. G. (2017). Managing Indigenous Knowledge in Tanzania: A Business Perspective. In Jain, P., & Mnjama, N. (Eds.), *Managing Knowledge Resources and Records in Modern Organizations* (pp. 198–214). Hershey, PA: IGI Global. DOI: 10.4018/978-1-5225-1965-2.ch012

Jain, P. (2017). Ethical and Legal Issues in Knowledge Management Life-Cycle in Business. In Jain, P., & Mnjama, N. (Eds.), *Managing Knowledge Resources and Records in Modern Organizations* (pp. 82–101). Hershey, PA: IGI Global. DOI: 10.4018/978-1-5225-1965-2.ch006

James, S., & Hauli, E. (2017). Holistic Management Education at Tanzanian Rural Development Planning Institute. In Baporikar, N. (Ed.), *Management Education for Global Leadership* (pp. 112–136). Hershey, PA: IGI Global. DOI: 10.4018/978-1-5225-1013-0.ch006

Janošková, M., Csikósová, A., & Čulková, K. (2018). Measurement of Company Performance as Part of Its Strategic Management. In Leon, R. (Ed.), *Managerial Strategies for Business Sustainability During Turbulent Times* (pp. 309–335). Hershey, PA: IGI Global. DOI: 10.4018/978-1-5225-2716-9.ch017

Jean-Vasile, A., & Alecu, A. (2017). Theoretical and Practical Approaches in Understanding the Influences of Cost-Productivity-Profit Trinomial in Contemporary Enterprises. In Jean Vasile, A., & Nicolò, D. (Eds.), *Sustainable Entrepreneurship and Investments in the Green Economy* (pp. 28–62). Hershey, PA: IGI Global. DOI: 10.4018/978-1-5225-2075-7.ch002

Joia, L. A., & Correia, J. C. (2018). CIO Competencies From the IT Professional Perspective: Insights From Brazil. *Journal of Global Information Management*, 26(2), 74–103. DOI: 10.4018/JGIM.2018040104

Juma, A., & Mzera, N. (2017). Knowledge Management and Records Management and Competitive Advantage in Business. In Jain, P., & Mnjama, N. (Eds.), *Managing Knowledge Resources and Records in Modern Organizations* (pp. 15–28). Hershey, PA: IGI Global. DOI: 10.4018/978-1-5225-1965-2.ch002

K., I., & A, V. (2018). Monitoring and Auditing in the Cloud. In K. Munir (Ed.), *Cloud Computing Technologies for Green Enterprises* (pp. 318-350). Hershey, PA: IGI Global. https://doi.org/DOI: 10.4018/978-1-5225-3038-1.ch013

Kabra, G., Ghosh, V., & Ramesh, A. (2018). Enterprise Integrated Business Process Management and Business Intelligence Framework for Business Process Sustainability. In Paul, A., Bhattacharyya, D., & Anand, S. (Eds.), *Green Initiatives for Business Sustainability and Value Creation* (pp. 228–238). Hershey, PA: IGI Global. DOI: 10.4018/978-1-5225-2662-9.ch010

Kaoud, M. (2017). Investigation of Customer Knowledge Management: A Case Study Research. *International Journal of Service Science, Management, Engineering, and Technology*, 8(2), 12–22. DOI: 10.4018/IJSSMET.2017040102

Katuu, S. (2018). A Comparative Assessment of Enterprise Content Management Maturity Models. In Gwangwava, N., & Mutingi, M. (Eds.), *E-Manufacturing and E-Service Strategies in Contemporary Organizations* (pp. 93–118). Hershey, PA: IGI Global. DOI: 10.4018/978-1-5225-3628-4.ch005

Khan, M. Y., & Abir, T. (2022). The Role of Social Media Marketing in the Tourism and Hospitality Industry: A Conceptual Study on Bangladesh. In Ramos, C., Quinteiro, S., & Gonçalves, A. (Eds.), *ICT as Innovator Between Tourism and Culture* (pp. 213–229). IGI Global. https://doi.org/10.4018/978-1-7998-8165-0.ch013

Kinnunen, S., Ylä-Kujala, A., Marttonen-Arola, S., Kärri, T., & Baglee, D. (2018). Internet of Things in Asset Management: Insights from Industrial Professionals and Academia. *International Journal of Service Science, Management, Engineering, and Technology*, 9(2), 104–119. DOI: 10.4018/IJSSMET.2018040105

Klein, A. Z., Sabino de Freitas, A., Machado, L., Freitas, J. C.Jr, Graziola, P. G.Jr, & Schlemmer, E. (2017). Virtual Worlds Applications for Management Education. In Tomei, L. (Ed.), *Exploring the New Era of Technology-Infused Education* (pp. 279–299). Hershey, PA: IGI Global. DOI: 10.4018/978-1-5225-1709-2.ch017

Kővári, E., Saleh, M., & Steinbachné Hajmásy, G. (2022). The Impact of Corporate Digital Responsibility (CDR) on Internal Stakeholders' Satisfaction in Hungarian Upscale Hotels. In Valeri, M. (Ed.), *New Governance and Management in Touristic Destinations* (pp. 35–51). IGI Global. https://doi.org/10.4018/978-1-6684-3889-3.ch003

Kożuch, B., & Jabłoński, A. (2017). Adopting the Concept of Business Models in Public Management. In Lewandowski, M., & Kożuch, B. (Eds.), *Public Sector Entrepreneurship and the Integration of Innovative Business Models* (pp. 10–46). Hershey, PA: IGI Global. DOI: 10.4018/978-1-5225-2215-7.ch002

Kumar, J., Adhikary, A., & Jha, A. (2017). Small Active Investors' Perceptions and Preferences Towards Tax Saving Mutual Fund Schemes in Eastern India: An Empirical Note. *International Journal of Asian Business and Information Management*, 8(2), 35–45. DOI: 10.4018/IJABIM.2017040103

Latusi, S., & Fissore, M. (2021). Pilgrimage Routes to Happiness: Comparing the Camino de Santiago and Via Francigena. In Perinotto, A., Mayer, V., & Soares, J. (Eds.), *Rebuilding and Restructuring the Tourism Industry: Infusion of Happiness and Quality of Life* (pp. 157–182). IGI Global. https://doi.org/10.4018/978-1-7998 -7239-9.ch008

Lavassani, K. M., & Movahedi, B. (2017). Applications Driven Information Systems: Beyond Networks toward Business Ecosystems. *International Journal of Innovation in the Digital Economy*, 8(1), 61–75. DOI: 10.4018/IJIDE.2017010104

Lazzareschi, V. H., & Brito, M. S. (2017). Strategic Information Management: Proposal of Business Project Model. In Jamil, G., Soares, A., & Pessoa, C. (Eds.), *Handbook of Research on Information Management for Effective Logistics and Supply Chains* (pp. 59–88). Hershey, PA: IGI Global. DOI: 10.4018/978-1-5225-0973-8.ch004

Lechuga Sancho, M. P., & Martín Navarro, A. (2022). Evolution of the Literature on Social Responsibility in the Tourism Sector: A Systematic Literature Review. In Fernandes, G. (Ed.), *Challenges and New Opportunities for Tourism in Inland Territories: Ecocultural Resources and Sustainable Initiatives* (pp. 169–186). IGI Global. https://doi.org/10.4018/978-1-7998-7339-6.ch010

Lederer, M., Kurz, M., & Lazarov, P. (2017). Usage and Suitability of Methods for Strategic Business Process Initiatives: A Multi Case Study Research. *International Journal of Productivity Management and Assessment Technologies*, 5(1), 40–51. DOI: 10.4018/IJPMAT.2017010103

Lee, I. (2017). A Social Enterprise Business Model and a Case Study of Pacific Community Ventures (PCV). In Potocan, V., Üngan, M., & Nedelko, Z. (Eds.), *Handbook of Research on Managerial Solutions in Non-Profit Organizations* (pp. 182–204). Hershey, PA: IGI Global. DOI: 10.4018/978-1-5225-0731-4.ch009

Leon, L. A., Seal, K. C., Przasnyski, Z. H., & Wiedenman, I. (2017). Skills and Competencies Required for Jobs in Business Analytics: A Content Analysis of Job Advertisements Using Text Mining. *International Journal of Business Intelligence Research*, 8(1), 1–25. DOI: 10.4018/IJBIR.2017010101

Levy, C. L., & Elias, N. I. (2017). SOHO Users' Perceptions of Reliability and Continuity of Cloud-Based Services. In Moore, M. (Ed.), *Cybersecurity Breaches and Issues Surrounding Online Threat Protection* (pp. 248–287). Hershey, PA: IGI Global. DOI: 10.4018/978-1-5225-1941-6.ch011

Levy, M. (2018). Change Management Serving Knowledge Management and Organizational Development: Reflections and Review. In Baporikar, N. (Ed.), *Global Practices in Knowledge Management for Societal and Organizational Development* (pp. 256–270). Hershey, PA: IGI Global. DOI: 10.4018/978-1-5225-3009-1.ch012

Lewandowski, M. (2017). Public Organizations and Business Model Innovation: The Role of Public Service Design. In Lewandowski, M., & Kożuch, B. (Eds.), *Public Sector Entrepreneurship and the Integration of Innovative Business Models* (pp. 47–72). Hershey, PA: IGI Global. DOI: 10.4018/978-1-5225-2215-7.ch003

Lhannaoui, H., Kabbaj, M. I., & Bakkoury, Z. (2017). A Survey of Risk-Aware Business Process Modelling. *International Journal of Risk and Contingency Management*, 6(3), 14–26. DOI: 10.4018/IJRCM.2017070102

Li, J., Sun, W., Jiang, W., Yang, H., & Zhang, L. (2017). How the Nature of Exogenous Shocks and Crises Impact Company Performance?: The Effects of Industry Characteristics. *International Journal of Risk and Contingency Management*, 6(4), 40–55. DOI: 10.4018/IJRCM.2017100103

Lopez-Fernandez, M., Perez-Perez, M., Serrano-Bedia, A., & Cobo-Gonzalez, A. (2021). Small and Medium Tourism Enterprise Survival in Times of Crisis: "El Capricho de Gaudí. In Toubes, D., & Araújo-Vila, N. (Eds.), *Risk, Crisis, and Disaster Management in Small and Medium-Sized Tourism Enterprises* (pp. 103–129). IGI Global. DOI: 10.4018/978-1-7998-6996-2.ch005

Mahajan, A., Maidullah, S., & Hossain, M. R. (2022). Experience Toward Smart Tour Guide Apps in Travelling: An Analysis of Users' Reviews on Audio Odigos and Trip My Way. In R. Augusto Costa, F. Brandão, Z. Breda, & C. Costa (Eds.), *Planning and Managing the Experience Economy in Tourism* (pp. 255-273). IGI Global. https://doi.org/10.4018/978-1-7998-8775-1.ch014

Malega, P. (2017). Small and Medium Enterprises in the Slovak Republic: Status and Competitiveness of SMEs in the Global Markets and Possibilities of Optimization. In Vemić, M. (Ed.), *Optimal Management Strategies in Small and Medium Enterprises* (pp. 102–124). Hershey, PA: IGI Global. DOI: 10.4018/978-1-5225-1949-2.ch006

Malewska, K. M. (2017). Intuition in Decision-Making on the Example of a Non-Profit Organization. In Potocan, V., Üngan, M., & Nedelko, Z. (Eds.), *Handbook of Research on Managerial Solutions in Non-Profit Organizations* (pp. 378–399). Hershey, PA: IGI Global. DOI: 10.4018/978-1-5225-0731-4.ch018

Maroofi, F. (2017). Entrepreneurial Orientation and Organizational Learning Ability Analysis for Innovation and Firm Performance. In Baporikar, N. (Ed.), *Innovation and Shifting Perspectives in Management Education* (pp. 144–165). Hershey, PA: IGI Global. DOI: 10.4018/978-1-5225-1019-2.ch007

Marques, M., Moleiro, D., Brito, T. M., & Marques, T. (2021). Customer Relationship Management as an Important Relationship Marketing Tool: The Case of the Hospitality Industry in Estoril Coast. In M. Dinis, L. Bonixe, S. Lamy, & Z. Breda (Eds.), *Impact of New Media in Tourism* (pp. 39-56). IGI Global. https://doi.org/DOI: 10.4018/978-1-7998-7095-1.ch003

Martins, P. V., & Zacarias, M. (2017). A Web-based Tool for Business Process Improvement. *International Journal of Web Portals*, 9(2), 68–84. DOI: 10.4018/IJWP.2017070104

Matthies, B., & Coners, A. (2017). Exploring the Conceptual Nature of e-Business Projects. *Journal of Electronic Commerce in Organizations*, 15(3), 33–63. DOI: 10.4018/JECO.2017070103

Mayer, V. F., Fraga, C. C., & Silva, L. C. (2021). Contributions of Neurosciences to Studies of Well-Being in Tourism. In Perinotto, A., Mayer, V., & Soares, J. (Eds.), *Rebuilding and Restructuring the Tourism Industry: Infusion of Happiness and Quality of Life* (pp. 108–128). IGI Global. https://doi.org/10.4018/978-1-7998-7239-9.ch006

McKee, J. (2018). Architecture as a Tool to Solve Business Planning Problems. In M. Khosrow-Pour, D.B.A. (Ed.), *Encyclopedia of Information Science and Technology, Fourth Edition* (pp. 573-586). Hershey, PA: IGI Global. DOI: 10.4018/978-1-5225-2255-3.ch050

McMurray, A. J., Cross, J., & Caponecchia, C. (2018). The Risk Management Profession in Australia: Business Continuity Plan Practices. In Bajgoric, N. (Ed.), *Always-On Enterprise Information Systems for Modern Organizations* (pp. 112–129). Hershey, PA: IGI Global. DOI: 10.4018/978-1-5225-3704-5.ch006

Meddah, I. H., & Belkadi, K. (2018). Mining Patterns Using Business Process Management. In Hamou, R. (Ed.), *Handbook of Research on Biomimicry in Information Retrieval and Knowledge Management* (pp. 78–89). Hershey, PA: IGI Global. DOI: 10.4018/978-1-5225-3004-6.ch005

Melian, A. G., & Camprubí, R. (2021). The Accessibility of Museum Websites: The Case of Barcelona. In Eusébio, C., Teixeira, L., & Carneiro, M. (Eds.), *ICT Tools and Applications for Accessible Tourism* (pp. 234–255). IGI Global. https://doi.org/10.4018/978-1-7998-6428-8.ch011

Mendes, L. (2017). TQM and Knowledge Management: An Integrated Approach Towards Tacit Knowledge Management. In Jaziri-Bouagina, D., & Jamil, G. (Eds.), *Handbook of Research on Tacit Knowledge Management for Organizational Success* (pp. 236–263). Hershey, PA: IGI Global. DOI: 10.4018/978-1-5225-2394-9.ch009

Menezes, V. D., & Cavagnaro, E. (2021). Communicating Sustainable Initiatives in the Hotel Industry: The Case of the Hotel Jakarta Amsterdam. In F. Brandão, Z. Breda, R. Costa, & C. Costa (Eds.), *Handbook of Research on the Role of Tourism in Achieving Sustainable Development Goals* (pp. 224-234). IGI Global. https://doi.org/10.4018/978-1-7998-5691-7.ch013

Menezes, V. D., & Cavagnaro, E. (2021). Communicating Sustainable Initiatives in the Hotel Industry: The Case of the Hotel Jakarta Amsterdam. In F. Brandão, Z. Breda, R. Costa, & C. Costa (Eds.), *Handbook of Research on the Role of Tourism in Achieving Sustainable Development Goals* (pp. 224-234). IGI Global. https://doi.org/10.4018/978-1-7998-5691-7.ch013

Mitas, O., Bastiaansen, M., & Boode, W. (2022). If You're Happy, I'm Happy: Emotion Contagion at a Tourist Information Center. In R. Augusto Costa, F. Brandão, Z. Breda, & C. Costa (Eds.), *Planning and Managing the Experience Economy in Tourism* (pp. 122-140). IGI Global. https://doi.org/10.4018/978-1-7998-8775-1.ch007

Mnjama, N. M. (2017). Preservation of Recorded Information in Public and Private Sector Organizations. In Jain, P., & Mnjama, N. (Eds.), *Managing Knowledge Resources and Records in Modern Organizations* (pp. 149–167). Hershey, PA: IGI Global. DOI: 10.4018/978-1-5225-1965-2.ch009

Mokoqama, M., & Fields, Z. (2017). Principles of Responsible Management Education (PRME): Call for Responsible Management Education. In Fields, Z. (Ed.), *Collective Creativity for Responsible and Sustainable Business Practice* (pp. 229–241). Hershey, PA: IGI Global. DOI: 10.4018/978-1-5225-1823-5.ch012

Monteiro, A., Lopes, S., & Carbone, F. (2021). Academic Mobility: Bridging Tourism and Peace Education. In J. da Silva, Z. Breda, & F. Carbone (Eds.), *Role and Impact of Tourism in Peacebuilding and Conflict Transformation* (pp. 275-301). IGI Global. https://doi.org/10.4018/978-1-7998-5053-3.ch016

Muniapan, B. (2017). Philosophy and Management: The Relevance of Vedanta in Management. In Ordóñez de Pablos, P. (Ed.), *Managerial Strategies and Solutions for Business Success in Asia* (pp. 124–139). Hershey, PA: IGI Global. DOI: 10.4018/978-1-5225-1886-0.ch007

Murad, S. E., & Dowaji, S. (2017). Using Value-Based Approach for Managing Cloud-Based Services. In Turuk, A., Sahoo, B., & Addya, S. (Eds.), *Resource Management and Efficiency in Cloud Computing Environments* (pp. 33–60). Hershey, PA: IGI Global. DOI: 10.4018/978-1-5225-1721-4.ch002

Mutahar, A. M., Daud, N. M., Thurasamy, R., Isaac, O., & Abdulsalam, R. (2018). The Mediating of Perceived Usefulness and Perceived Ease of Use: The Case of Mobile Banking in Yemen. *International Journal of Technology Diffusion*, 9(2), 21–40. DOI: 10.4018/IJTD.2018040102

Naidoo, V. (2017). E-Learning and Management Education at African Universities. In Baporikar, N. (Ed.), *Management Education for Global Leadership* (pp. 181–201). Hershey, PA: IGI Global. DOI: 10.4018/978-1-5225-1013-0.ch009

Naidoo, V., & Igbinakhase, I. (2018). Opportunities and Challenges of Knowledge Retention in SMEs. In Baporikar, N. (Ed.), *Knowledge Integration Strategies for Entrepreneurship and Sustainability* (pp. 70–94). Hershey, PA: IGI Global. DOI: 10.4018/978-1-5225-5115-7.ch004

Naumov, N., & Costandachi, G. (2021). Creativity and Entrepreneurship: Gastronomic Tourism in Mexico. In Soares, J. (Ed.), *Innovation and Entrepreneurial Opportunities in Community Tourism* (pp. 90–108). IGI Global. https://doi.org/10.4018/978-1-7998-4855-4.ch006

Nayak, S., & Prabhu, N. (2017). Paradigm Shift in Management Education: Need for a Cross Functional Perspective. In Baporikar, N. (Ed.), *Management Education for Global Leadership* (pp. 241–255). Hershey, PA: IGI Global. DOI: 10.4018/978-1-5225-1013-0.ch012

Nedelko, Z., & Potocan, V. (2017). Management Solutions in Non-Profit Organizations: Case of Slovenia. In Potocan, V., Üngan, M., & Nedelko, Z. (Eds.), *Handbook of Research on Managerial Solutions in Non-Profit Organizations* (pp. 1–22). Hershey, PA: IGI Global. DOI: 10.4018/978-1-5225-0731-4.ch001

Nedelko, Z., & Potocan, V. (2017). Priority of Management Tools Utilization among Managers: International Comparison. In Wang, V. (Ed.), *Encyclopedia of Strategic Leadership and Management* (pp. 1083–1094). Hershey, PA: IGI Global. DOI: 10.4018/978-1-5225-1049-9.ch075

Nedelko, Z., Raudeliūnienė, J., & Črešnar, R. (2018). Knowledge Dynamics in Supply Chain Management. In Baporikar, N. (Ed.), *Knowledge Integration Strategies for Entrepreneurship and Sustainability* (pp. 150–166). Hershey, PA: IGI Global. DOI: 10.4018/978-1-5225-5115-7.ch008

Nguyen, H. T., & Hipsher, S. A. (2018). Innovation and Creativity Used by Private Sector Firms in a Resources-Constrained Environment. In Hipsher, S. (Ed.), *Examining the Private Sector's Role in Wealth Creation and Poverty Reduction* (pp. 219–238). Hershey, PA: IGI Global. DOI: 10.4018/978-1-5225-3117-3.ch010

Obicci, P. A. (2017). Risk Sharing in a Partnership. In *Risk Management Strategies in Public-Private Partnerships* (pp. 115–152). Hershey, PA: IGI Global. DOI: 10.4018/978-1-5225-2503-5.ch004

Obidallah, W. J., & Raahemi, B. (2017). Managing Changes in Service Oriented Virtual Organizations: A Structural and Procedural Framework to Facilitate the Process of Change. *Journal of Electronic Commerce in Organizations*, 15(1), 59–83. DOI: 10.4018/JECO.2017010104

Ojo, O. (2017). Impact of Innovation on the Entrepreneurial Success in Selected Business Enterprises in South-West Nigeria. *International Journal of Innovation in the Digital Economy*, 8(2), 29–38. DOI: 10.4018/IJIDE.2017040103

Okdinawati, L., Simatupang, T. M., & Sunitiyoso, Y. (2017). Multi-Agent Reinforcement Learning for Value Co-Creation of Collaborative Transportation Management (CTM). *International Journal of Information Systems and Supply Chain Management*, 10(3), 84–95. DOI: 10.4018/IJISSCM.2017070105

Olivera, V. A., & Carrillo, I. M. (2021). Organizational Culture: A Key Element for the Development of Mexican Micro and Small Tourist Companies. In Soares, J. (Ed.), *Innovation and Entrepreneurial Opportunities in Community Tourism* (pp. 227–242). IGI Global. DOI: 10.4018/978-1-7998-4855-4.ch013

Ossorio, M. (2022). Corporate Museum Experiences in Enogastronomic Tourism. In R. Augusto Costa, F. Brandão, Z. Breda, & C. Costa (Eds.), *Planning and Managing the Experience Economy in Tourism* (pp. 107-121). IGI Global. https://doi.org/DOI: 10.4018/978-1-7998-8775-1.ch006

Ossorio, M. (2022). Enogastronomic Tourism in Times of Pandemic. In Fernandes, G. (Ed.), *Challenges and New Opportunities for Tourism in Inland Territories: Eco-cultural Resources and Sustainable Initiatives* (pp. 241–255). IGI Global. https://doi.org/10.4018/978-1-7998-7339-6.ch014

Özekici, Y. K. (2022). ICT as an Acculturative Agent and Its Role in the Tourism Context: Introduction, Acculturation Theory, Progress of the Acculturation Theory in Extant Literature. In Ramos, C., Quinteiro, S., & Gonçalves, A. (Eds.), *ICT as Innovator Between Tourism and Culture* (pp. 42–66). IGI Global. https://doi.org/10.4018/978-1-7998-8165-0.ch004

Pal, K. (2018). Building High Quality Big Data-Based Applications in Supply Chains. In Kumar, A., & Saurav, S. (Eds.), *Supply Chain Management Strategies and Risk Assessment in Retail Environments* (pp. 1–24). Hershey, PA: IGI Global. DOI: 10.4018/978-1-5225-3056-5.ch001

Palos-Sanchez, P. R., & Correia, M. B. (2018). Perspectives of the Adoption of Cloud Computing in the Tourism Sector. In Rodrigues, J., Ramos, C., Cardoso, P., & Henriques, C. (Eds.), *Handbook of Research on Technological Developments for Cultural Heritage and eTourism Applications* (pp. 377–400). Hershey, PA: IGI Global. DOI: 10.4018/978-1-5225-2927-9.ch018

Papadopoulou, G. (2021). Promoting Gender Equality and Women Empowerment in the Tourism Sector. In F. Brandão, Z. Breda, R. Costa, & C. Costa (Eds.), *Handbook of Research on the Role of Tourism in Achieving Sustainable Development Goals* (pp. 152-174). IGI Global. https://doi.org/DOI: 10.4018/978-1-7998-5691-7.ch009

Papp-Váry, Á. F., & Tóth, T. Z. (2022). Analysis of Budapest as a Film Tourism Destination. In R. Baleiro & R. Pereira (Eds.), *Global Perspectives on Literary Tourism and Film-Induced Tourism* (pp. 257-279). IGI Global. https://doi.org/10.4018/978-1-7998-8262-6.ch014

Patiño, B. E. (2017). New Generation Management by Convergence and Individual Identity: A Systemic and Human-Oriented Approach. In Baporikar, N. (Ed.), *Innovation and Shifting Perspectives in Management Education* (pp. 119–143). Hershey, PA: IGI Global. DOI: 10.4018/978-1-5225-1019-2.ch006

Patro, C. S. (2021). Digital Tourism: Influence of E-Marketing Technology. In M. Dinis, L. Bonixe, S. Lamy, & Z. Breda (Eds.), *Impact of New Media in Tourism* (pp. 234-254). IGI Global. https://doi.org/10.4018/978-1-7998-7095-1.ch014

Pawliczek, A., & Rössler, M. (2017). Knowledge of Management Tools and Systems in SMEs: Knowledge Transfer in Management. In Bencsik, A. (Ed.), *Knowledge Management Initiatives and Strategies in Small and Medium Enterprises* (pp. 180–203). Hershey, PA: IGI Global. DOI: 10.4018/978-1-5225-1642-2.ch009

Pejic-Bach, M., Omazic, M. A., Aleksic, A., & Zoroja, J. (2018). Knowledge-Based Decision Making: A Multi-Case Analysis. In Leon, R. (Ed.), *Managerial Strategies for Business Sustainability During Turbulent Times* (pp. 160–184). Hershey, PA: IGI Global. DOI: 10.4018/978-1-5225-2716-9.ch009

Perano, M., Hysa, X., & Calabrese, M. (2018). Strategic Planning, Cultural Context, and Business Continuity Management: Business Cases in the City of Shkoder. In Presenza, A., & Sheehan, L. (Eds.), *Geopolitics and Strategic Management in the Global Economy* (pp. 57–77). Hershey, PA: IGI Global. DOI: 10.4018/978-1-5225-2673-5.ch004

Pereira, R., Mira da Silva, M., & Lapão, L. V. (2017). IT Governance Maturity Patterns in Portuguese Healthcare. In De Haes, S., & Van Grembergen, W. (Eds.), *Strategic IT Governance and Alignment in Business Settings* (pp. 24–52). Hershey, PA: IGI Global. DOI: 10.4018/978-1-5225-0861-8.ch002

Pérez-Uribe, R. I., Torres, D. A., Jurado, S. P., & Prada, D. M. (2018). Cloud Tools for the Development of Project Management in SMEs. In Perez-Uribe, R., Salcedo-Perez, C., & Ocampo-Guzman, D. (Eds.), *Handbook of Research on Intrapreneurship and Organizational Sustainability in SMEs* (pp. 95–120). Hershey, PA: IGI Global. DOI: 10.4018/978-1-5225-3543-0.ch005

Petrisor, I., & Cozmiuc, D. (2017). Global Supply Chain Management Organization at Siemens in the Advent of Industry 4.0. In Saglietto, L., & Cezanne, C. (Eds.), *Global Intermediation and Logistics Service Providers* (pp. 123–142). Hershey, PA: IGI Global. DOI: 10.4018/978-1-5225-2133-4.ch007

Pierce, J. M., Velliaris, D. M., & Edwards, J. (2017). A Living Case Study: A Journey Not a Destination. In Silton, N. (Ed.), *Exploring the Benefits of Creativity in Education, Media, and the Arts* (pp. 158–178). Hershey, PA: IGI Global. DOI: 10.4018/978-1-5225-0504-4.ch008

Pipia, S., & Pipia, S. (2021). Challenges of Religious Tourism in the Conflict Region: An Example of Jerusalem. In E. Alaverdov & M. Bari (Eds.), *Global Development of Religious Tourism* (pp. 135-148). IGI Global. https://doi.org/10.4018/978-1-7998-5792-1.ch009

Poulaki, P., Kritikos, A., Vasilakis, N., & Valeri, M. (2022). The Contribution of Female Creativity to the Development of Gastronomic Tourism in Greece: The Case of the Island of Naxos in the South Aegean Region. In Valeri, M. (Ed.), *New Governance and Management in Touristic Destinations* (pp. 246–258). IGI Global. https://doi.org/10.4018/978-1-6684-3889-3.ch015

Radosavljevic, M., & Andjelkovic, A. (2017). Multi-Criteria Decision Making Approach for Choosing Business Process for the Improvement: Upgrading of the Six Sigma Methodology. In Stanković, J., Delias, P., Marinković, S., & Rochhia, S. (Eds.), *Tools and Techniques for Economic Decision Analysis* (pp. 225–247). Hershey, PA: IGI Global. DOI: 10.4018/978-1-5225-0959-2.ch011

Radovic, V. M. (2017). Corporate Sustainability and Responsibility and Disaster Risk Reduction: A Serbian Overview. In Camilleri, M. (Ed.), *CSR 2.0 and the New Era of Corporate Citizenship* (pp. 147–164). Hershey, PA: IGI Global. DOI: 10.4018/978-1-5225-1842-6.ch008

Raghunath, K. M., Devi, S. L., & Patro, C. S. (2018). Impact of Risk Assessment Models on Risk Factors: A Holistic Outlook. In Strang, K., Korstanje, M., & Vajjhala, N. (Eds.), *Research, Practices, and Innovations in Global Risk and Contingency Management* (pp. 134–153). Hershey, PA: IGI Global. DOI: 10.4018/978-1-5225-4754-9.ch008

Raman, A., & Goyal, D. P. (2017). Extending IMPLEMENT Framework for Enterprise Information Systems Implementation to Information System Innovation. In Tavana, M. (Ed.), *Enterprise Information Systems and the Digitalization of Business Functions* (pp. 137–177). Hershey, PA: IGI Global. DOI: 10.4018/978-1-5225-2382-6.ch007

Rao, Y., & Zhang, Y. (2017). The Construction and Development of Academic Library Digital Special Subject Databases. In Ruan, L., Zhu, Q., & Ye, Y. (Eds.), *Academic Library Development and Administration in China* (pp. 163–183). Hershey, PA: IGI Global. DOI: 10.4018/978-1-5225-0550-1.ch010

Ravasan, A. Z., Mohammadi, M. M., & Hamidi, H. (2018). An Investigation Into the Critical Success Factors of Implementing Information Technology Service Management Frameworks. In Jakobs, K. (Ed.), *Corporate and Global Standardization Initiatives in Contemporary Society* (pp. 200–218). Hershey, PA: IGI Global. DOI: 10.4018/978-1-5225-5320-5.ch009

Rezaie, S., Mirabedini, S. J., & Abtahi, A. (2018). Designing a Model for Implementation of Business Intelligence in the Banking Industry. *International Journal of Enterprise Information Systems*, 14(1), 77–103. DOI: 10.4018/IJEIS.2018010105

Richards, V., Matthews, N., Williams, O. J., & Khan, Z. (2021). The Challenges of Accessible Tourism Information Systems for Tourists With Vision Impairment: Sensory Communications Beyond the Screen. In Eusébio, C., Teixeira, L., & Carneiro, M. (Eds.), *ICT Tools and Applications for Accessible Tourism* (pp. 26–54). IGI Global. https://doi.org/10.4018/978-1-7998-6428-8.ch002

Rodrigues de Souza Neto, V., & Marques, O. (2021). Rural Tourism Fostering Welfare Through Sustainable Development: A Conceptual Approach. In Perinotto, A., Mayer, V., & Soares, J. (Eds.), *Rebuilding and Restructuring the Tourism Industry: Infusion of Happiness and Quality of Life* (pp. 38–57). IGI Global. https://doi.org/10.4018/978-1-7998-7239-9.ch003

Romano, L., Grimaldi, R., & Colasuonno, F. S. (2017). Demand Management as a Success Factor in Project Portfolio Management. In Romano, L. (Ed.), *Project Portfolio Management Strategies for Effective Organizational Operations* (pp. 202–219). Hershey, PA: IGI Global. DOI: 10.4018/978-1-5225-2151-8.ch008

Rubio-Escuderos, L., & García-Andreu, H. (2021). Competitiveness Factors of Accessible Tourism E-Travel Agencies. In Eusébio, C., Teixeira, L., & Carneiro, M. (Eds.), *ICT Tools and Applications for Accessible Tourism* (pp. 196–217). IGI Global. https://doi.org/10.4018/978-1-7998-6428-8.ch009

Rucci, A. C., Porto, N., Darcy, S., & Becka, L. (2021). Smart and Accessible Cities?: Not Always – The Case for Accessible Tourism Initiatives in Buenos Aries and Sydney. In Eusébio, C., Teixeira, L., & Carneiro, M. (Eds.), *ICT Tools and Applications for Accessible Tourism* (pp. 115–145). IGI Global. https://doi.org/10.4018/978-1-7998-6428-8.ch006

Ruhi, U. (2018). Towards an Interdisciplinary Socio-Technical Definition of Virtual Communities. In M. Khosrow-Pour, D.B.A. (Ed.), *Encyclopedia of Information Science and Technology, Fourth Edition* (pp. 4278-4295). Hershey, PA: IGI Global. DOI: 10.4018/978-1-5225-2255-3.ch371

Ryan, L., Catena, M., Ros, P., & Stephens, S. (2021). Designing Entrepreneurial Ecosystems to Support Resource Management in the Tourism Industry. In Costa, V., Moura, A., & Mira, M. (Eds.), *Handbook of Research on Human Capital and People Management in the Tourism Industry* (pp. 265–281). IGI Global. https://doi.org/10.4018/978-1-7998-4318-4.ch013

Sabuncu, I. (2021). Understanding Tourist Perceptions and Expectations During Pandemic Through Social Media Big Data. In Demir, M., Dalgıç, A., & Ergen, F. (Eds.), *Handbook of Research on the Impacts and Implications of COVID-19 on the Tourism Industry* (pp. 330–350). IGI Global. https://doi.org/10.4018/978-1 -7998-8231-2.ch016

Safari, M. R., & Jiang, Q. (2018). The Theory and Practice of IT Governance Maturity and Strategies Alignment: Evidence From Banking Industry. *Journal of Global Information Management*, 26(2), 127–146. DOI: 10.4018/JGIM.2018040106

Sahoo, J., Pati, B., & Mohanty, B. (2017). Knowledge Management as an Academic Discipline: An Assessment. In Gunjal, B. (Ed.), *Managing Knowledge and Scholarly Assets in Academic Libraries* (pp. 99–126). Hershey, PA: IGI Global. DOI: 10.4018/978-1-5225-1741-2.ch005

Saini, D. (2017). Relevance of Teaching Values and Ethics in Management Education. In Baporikar, N. (Ed.), *Management Education for Global Leadership* (pp. 90–111). Hershey, PA: IGI Global. DOI: 10.4018/978-1-5225-1013-0.ch005

Sambhanthan, A. (2017). Assessing and Benchmarking Sustainability in Organisations: An Integrated Conceptual Model. *International Journal of Systems and Service-Oriented Engineering*, 7(4), 22–43. DOI: 10.4018/IJSSOE.2017100102

Sambhanthan, A., & Potdar, V. (2017). A Study of the Parameters Impacting Sustainability in Information Technology Organizations. *International Journal of Knowledge-Based Organizations*, 7(3), 27–39. DOI: 10.4018/IJKBO.2017070103

Sánchez-Fernández, M. D., & Manríquez, M. R. (2018). The Entrepreneurial Spirit Based on Social Values: The Digital Generation. In Isaias, P., & Carvalho, L. (Eds.), *User Innovation and the Entrepreneurship Phenomenon in the Digital Economy* (pp. 173–193). Hershey, PA: IGI Global. DOI: 10.4018/978-1-5225-2826-5.ch009

Sanchez-Ruiz, L., & Blanco, B. (2017). Process Management for SMEs: Barriers, Enablers, and Benefits. In Vemić, M. (Ed.), *Optimal Management Strategies in Small and Medium Enterprises* (pp. 293–319). Hershey, PA: IGI Global. DOI: 10.4018/978-1-5225-1949-2.ch014

Sanz, L. F., Gómez-Pérez, J., & Castillo-Martinez, A. (2018). Analysis of the European ICT Competence Frameworks. In Ahuja, V., & Rathore, S. (Eds.), *Multidisciplinary Perspectives on Human Capital and Information Technology Professionals* (pp. 225–245). Hershey, PA: IGI Global. DOI: 10.4018/978-1-5225-5297-0.ch012

Sarvepalli, A., & Godin, J. (2017). Business Process Management in the Classroom. *Journal of Cases on Information Technology*, 19(2), 17–28. DOI: 10.4018/JCIT.2017040102

Saxena, G. G., & Saxena, A. (2021). Host Community Role in Medical Tourism Development. In Singh, M., & Kumaran, S. (Eds.), *Growth of the Medical Tourism Industry and Its Impact on Society: Emerging Research and Opportunities* (pp. 105–127). IGI Global. https://doi.org/10.4018/978-1-7998-3427-4.ch006

Saygili, E. E., Ozturkoglu, Y., & Kocakulah, M. C. (2017). End Users' Perceptions of Critical Success Factors in ERP Applications. *International Journal of Enterprise Information Systems*, 13(4), 58–75. DOI: 10.4018/IJEIS.2017100104

Saygili, E. E., & Saygili, A. T. (2017). Contemporary Issues in Enterprise Information Systems: A Critical Review of CSFs in ERP Implementations. In Tavana, M. (Ed.), *Enterprise Information Systems and the Digitalization of Business Functions* (pp. 120–136). Hershey, PA: IGI Global. DOI: 10.4018/978-1-5225-2382-6.ch006

Schwaiger, K. M., & Zehrer, A. (2021). The COVID-19 Pandemic and Organizational Resilience in Hospitality Family Firms: A Qualitative Approach. In Zehrer, A., Glowka, G., Schwaiger, K., & Ranacher-Lackner, V. (Eds.), *Resiliency Models and Addressing Future Risks for Family Firms in the Tourism Industry* (pp. 32–49). IGI Global. https://doi.org/10.4018/978-1-7998-7352-5.ch002

Scott, N., & Campos, A. C. (2022). Cognitive Science of Tourism Experiences. In R. Augusto Costa, F. Brandão, Z. Breda, & C. Costa (Eds.), *Planning and Managing the Experience Economy in Tourism* (pp. 1-21). IGI Global. https://doi.org/DOI: 10.4018/978-1-7998-8775-1.ch001

Seidenstricker, S., & Antonino, A. (2018). Business Model Innovation-Oriented Technology Management for Emergent Technologies. In M. Khosrow-Pour, D.B.A. (Ed.), *Encyclopedia of Information Science and Technology, Fourth Edition* (pp. 4560-4569). Hershey, PA: IGI Global. DOI: 10.4018/978-1-5225-2255-3.ch396

Selvi, M. S. (2021). Changes in Tourism Sales and Marketing Post COVID-19. In Demir, M., Dalgıç, A., & Ergen, F. (Eds.), *Handbook of Research on the Impacts and Implications of COVID-19 on the Tourism Industry* (pp. 437–460). IGI Global. DOI: 10.4018/978-1-7998-8231-2.ch021

Senaratne, S., & Gunarathne, A. D. (2017). Excellence Perspective for Management Education from a Global Accountants' Hub in Asia. In Baporikar, N. (Ed.), *Management Education for Global Leadership* (pp. 158–180). Hershey, PA: IGI Global. DOI: 10.4018/978-1-5225-1013-0.ch008

Sensuse, D. I., & Cahyaningsih, E. (2018). Knowledge Management Models: A Summative Review. *International Journal of Information Systems in the Service Sector*, 10(1), 71–100. DOI: 10.4018/IJISSS.2018010105

Seth, M., Goyal, D., & Kiran, R. (2017). Diminution of Impediments in Implementation of Supply Chain Management Information System for Enhancing its Effectiveness in Indian Automobile Industry. *Journal of Global Information Management*, 25(3), 1–20. DOI: 10.4018/JGIM.2017070101

Seyal, A. H., & Rahman, M. N. (2017). Investigating Impact of Inter-Organizational Factors in Measuring ERP Systems Success: Bruneian Perspectives. In Tavana, M. (Ed.), *Enterprise Information Systems and the Digitalization of Business Functions* (pp. 178–204). Hershey, PA: IGI Global. DOI: 10.4018/978-1-5225-2382-6.ch008

Shaqrah, A. A. (2018). Analyzing Business Intelligence Systems Based on 7s Model of McKinsey. *International Journal of Business Intelligence Research*, 9(1), 53–63. DOI: 10.4018/IJBIR.2018010104

Sharma, A. J. (2017). Enhancing Sustainability through Experiential Learning in Management Education. In Baporikar, N. (Ed.), *Management Education for Global Leadership* (pp. 256–274). Hershey, PA: IGI Global. DOI: 10.4018/978-1-5225-1013-0.ch013

Shetty, K. P. (2017). Responsible Global Leadership: Ethical Challenges in Management Education. In Baporikar, N. (Ed.), *Innovation and Shifting Perspectives in Management Education* (pp. 194–223). Hershey, PA: IGI Global. DOI: 10.4018/978-1-5225-1019-2.ch009

Sinthupundaja, J., & Kohda, Y. (2017). Effects of Corporate Social Responsibility and Creating Shared Value on Sustainability. *International Journal of Sustainable Entrepreneurship and Corporate Social Responsibility*, 2(1), 27–38. DOI: 10.4018/IJSECSR.2017010103

Škarica, I., & Hrgović, A. V. (2018). Implementation of Total Quality Management Principles in Public Health Institutes in the Republic of Croatia. *International Journal of Productivity Management and Assessment Technologies*, 6(1), 1–16. DOI: 10.4018/IJPMAT.2018010101

Skokic, V. (2021). How Small Hotel Owners Practice Resilience: Longitudinal Study Among Small Family Hotels in Croatia. In Zehrer, A., Glowka, G., Schwaiger, K., & Ranacher-Lackner, V. (Eds.), *Resiliency Models and Addressing Future Risks for Family Firms in the Tourism Industry* (pp. 50–73). IGI Global. DOI: 10.4018/978-1-7998-7352-5.ch003

Smuts, H., Kotzé, P., Van der Merwe, A., & Loock, M. (2017). Framework for Managing Shared Knowledge in an Information Systems Outsourcing Context. *International Journal of Knowledge Management*, 13(4), 1–30. DOI: 10.4018/IJKM.2017100101

Sousa, M. J., Cruz, R., Dias, I., & Caracol, C. (2017). Information Management Systems in the Supply Chain. In Jamil, G., Soares, A., & Pessoa, C. (Eds.), *Handbook of Research on Information Management for Effective Logistics and Supply Chains* (pp. 469–485). Hershey, PA: IGI Global. DOI: 10.4018/978-1-5225-0973-8.ch025

Spremic, M., Turulja, L., & Bajgoric, N. (2018). Two Approaches in Assessing Business Continuity Management Attitudes in the Organizational Context. In Bajgoric, N. (Ed.), *Always-On Enterprise Information Systems for Modern Organizations* (pp. 159–183). Hershey, PA: IGI Global. DOI: 10.4018/978-1-5225-3704-5.ch008

Steenkamp, A. L. (2018). Some Insights in Computer Science and Information Technology. In *Examining the Changing Role of Supervision in Doctoral Research Projects: Emerging Research and Opportunities* (pp. 113–133). Hershey, PA: IGI Global. DOI: 10.4018/978-1-5225-2610-0.ch005

Stipanović, C., Rudan, E., & Zubović, V. (2022). Reaching the New Tourist Through Creativity: Sustainable Development Challenges in Croatian Coastal Towns. In Valeri, M. (Ed.), *New Governance and Management in Touristic Destinations* (pp. 231–245). IGI Global. https://doi.org/10.4018/978-1-6684-3889-3.ch014

Tabach, A., & Croteau, A. (2017). Configurations of Information Technology Governance Practices and Business Unit Performance. *International Journal of IT/Business Alignment and Governance*, 8(2), 1–27. DOI: 10.4018/IJITBAG.2017070101

Talaue, G. M., & Iqbal, T. (2017). Assessment of e-Business Mode of Selected Private Universities in the Philippines and Pakistan. *International Journal of Online Marketing*, 7(4), 63–77. DOI: 10.4018/IJOM.2017100105

Tam, G. C. (2017). Project Manager Sustainability Competence. In *Managerial Strategies and Green Solutions for Project Sustainability* (pp. 178–207). Hershey, PA: IGI Global. DOI: 10.4018/978-1-5225-2371-0.ch008

Tambo, T. (2018). Fashion Retail Innovation: About Context, Antecedents, and Outcome in Technological Change Projects. In I. Management Association (Ed.), *Fashion and Textiles: Breakthroughs in Research and Practice* (pp. 233-260). Hershey, PA: IGI Global. https://doi.org/DOI: 10.4018/978-1-5225-3432-7.ch010

Tantau, A. D., & Frățilă, L. C. (2018). Information and Management System for Renewable Energy Business. In *Entrepreneurship and Business Development in the Renewable Energy Sector* (pp. 200–244). Hershey, PA: IGI Global. DOI: 10.4018/978-1-5225-3625-3.ch006

Teixeira, N., Pardal, P. N., & Rafael, B. G. (2018). Internationalization, Financial Performance, and Organizational Challenges: A Success Case in Portugal. In Carvalho, L. (Ed.), *Handbook of Research on Entrepreneurial Ecosystems and Social Dynamics in a Globalized World* (pp. 379–423). Hershey, PA: IGI Global. DOI: 10.4018/978-1-5225-3525-6.ch017

Teixeira, P., Teixeira, L., Eusébio, C., Silva, S., & Teixeira, A. (2021). The Impact of ICTs on Accessible Tourism: Evidence Based on a Systematic Literature Review. In Eusébio, C., Teixeira, L., & Carneiro, M. (Eds.), *ICT Tools and Applications for Accessible Tourism* (pp. 1–25). IGI Global. DOI: 10.4018/978-1-7998-6428-8.ch001

Trad, A., & Kalpić, D. (2018). The Business Transformation Framework, Agile Project and Change Management. In M. Khosrow-Pour, D.B.A. (Ed.), *Encyclopedia of Information Science and Technology, Fourth Edition* (pp. 620-635). Hershey, PA: IGI Global. https://doi.org/DOI: 10.4018/978-1-5225-2255-3.ch054

Trad, A., & Kalpić, D. (2018). The Business Transformation and Enterprise Architecture Framework: The Financial Engineering E-Risk Management and E-Law Integration. In Sergi, B., Fidanoski, F., Ziolo, M., & Naumovski, V. (Eds.), *Regaining Global Stability After the Financial Crisis* (pp. 46–65). Hershey, PA: IGI Global. DOI: 10.4018/978-1-5225-4026-7.ch003

Trengereid, V. (2022). Conditions of Network Engagement: The Quest for a Common Good. In R. Augusto Costa, F. Brandão, Z. Breda, & C. Costa (Eds.), *Planning and Managing the Experience Economy in Tourism* (pp. 69-84). IGI Global. https://doi.org/10.4018/978-1-7998-8775-1.ch004

Turulja, L., & Bajgoric, N. (2018). Business Continuity and Information Systems: A Systematic Literature Review. In Bajgoric, N. (Ed.), *Always-On Enterprise Information Systems for Modern Organizations* (pp. 60–87). Hershey, PA: IGI Global. DOI: 10.4018/978-1-5225-3704-5.ch004

Vargas-Hernández, J. G. (2017). Professional Integrity in Business Management Education. In Baporikar, N. (Ed.), *Management Education for Global Leadership* (pp. 70–89). Hershey, PA: IGI Global. DOI: 10.4018/978-1-5225-1013-0.ch004

Varnacı Uzun, F. (2021). The Destination Preferences of Foreign Tourists During the COVID-19 Pandemic and Attitudes Towards: Marmaris, Turkey. In Demir, M., Dalgıç, A., & Ergen, F. (Eds.), *Handbook of Research on the Impacts and Implications of COVID-19 on the Tourism Industry* (pp. 285–306). IGI Global. https://doi.org/10.4018/978-1-7998-8231-2.ch014

Vasista, T. G., & AlAbdullatif, A. M. (2017). Role of Electronic Customer Relationship Management in Demand Chain Management: A Predictive Analytic Approach. *International Journal of Information Systems and Supply Chain Management*, 10(1), 53–67. DOI: 10.4018/IJISSCM.2017010104

Vieru, D., & Bourdeau, S. (2017). Survival in the Digital Era: A Digital Competence-Based Multi-Case Study in the Canadian SME Clothing Industry. *International Journal of Social and Organizational Dynamics in IT*, 6(1), 17–34. DOI: 10.4018/IJSODIT.2017010102

Vijayan, G., & Kamarulzaman, N. H. (2017). An Introduction to Sustainable Supply Chain Management and Business Implications. In Khan, M., Hussain, M., & Ajmal, M. (Eds.), *Green Supply Chain Management for Sustainable Business Practice* (pp. 27–50). Hershey, PA: IGI Global. DOI: 10.4018/978-1-5225-0635-5.ch002

Vlachvei, A., & Notta, O. (2017). Firm Competitiveness: Theories, Evidence, and Measurement. In Vlachvei, A., Notta, O., Karantininis, K., & Tsounis, N. (Eds.), *Factors Affecting Firm Competitiveness and Performance in the Modern Business World* (pp. 1–42). Hershey, PA: IGI Global. DOI: 10.4018/978-1-5225-0843-4.ch001

Wang, C., Schofield, M., Li, X., & Ou, X. (2017). Do Chinese Students in Public and Private Higher Education Institutes Perform at Different Level in One of the Leadership Skills: Critical Thinking?: An Exploratory Comparison. In Wang, V. (Ed.), *Encyclopedia of Strategic Leadership and Management* (pp. 160–181). Hershey, PA: IGI Global. DOI: 10.4018/978-1-5225-1049-9.ch013

Wang, J. (2017). Multi-Agent based Production Management Decision System Modelling for the Textile Enterprise. *Journal of Global Information Management*, 25(4), 1–15. DOI: 10.4018/JGIM.2017100101

Wiedemann, A., & Gewald, H. (2017). Examining Cross-Domain Alignment: The Correlation of Business Strategy, IT Management, and IT Business Value. *International Journal of IT/Business Alignment and Governance*, 8(1), 17–31. DOI: 10.4018/IJITBAG.2017010102

Wolf, R., & Thiel, M. (2018). Advancing Global Business Ethics in China: Reducing Poverty Through Human and Social Welfare. In Hipsher, S. (Ed.), *Examining the Private Sector's Role in Wealth Creation and Poverty Reduction* (pp. 67–84). Hershey, PA: IGI Global. DOI: 10.4018/978-1-5225-3117-3.ch004

Yablonsky, S. (2018). Innovation Platforms: Data and Analytics Platforms. In *Multi-Sided Platforms (MSPs) and Sharing Strategies in the Digital Economy: Emerging Research and Opportunities* (pp. 72–95). Hershey, PA: IGI Global. DOI: 10.4018/978-1-5225-5457-8.ch003

Yaşar, B. (2021). The Impact of COVID-19 on Volatility of Tourism Stocks: Evidence From BIST Tourism Index. In Demir, M., Dalgıç, A., & Ergen, F. (Eds.), *Handbook of Research on the Impacts and Implications of COVID-19 on the Tourism Industry* (pp. 23–44). IGI Global. https://doi.org/10.4018/978-1-7998-8231-2.ch002

Yusoff, A., Ahmad, N. H., & Halim, H. A. (2017). Agropreneurship among Gen Y in Malaysia: The Role of Academic Institutions. In Ahmad, N., Ramayah, T., Halim, H., & Rahman, S. (Eds.), *Handbook of Research on Small and Medium Enterprises in Developing Countries* (pp. 23–47). Hershey, PA: IGI Global. DOI: 10.4018/978-1-5225-2165-5.ch002

Zacher, D., & Pechlaner, H. (2021). Resilience as an Opportunity Approach: Challenges and Perspectives for Private Sector Participation on a Community Level. In Zehrer, A., Glowka, G., Schwaiger, K., & Ranacher-Lackner, V. (Eds.), *Resiliency Models and Addressing Future Risks for Family Firms in the Tourism Industry* (pp. 75–102). IGI Global. https://doi.org/10.4018/978-1-7998-7352-5.ch004

Zanin, F., Comuzzi, E., & Costantini, A. (2018). The Effect of Business Strategy and Stock Market Listing on the Use of Risk Assessment Tools. In *Management Control Systems in Complex Settings: Emerging Research and Opportunities* (pp. 145–168). Hershey, PA: IGI Global. DOI: 10.4018/978-1-5225-3987-2.ch007

Zgheib, P. W. (2017). Corporate Innovation and Intrapreneurship in the Middle East. In Zgheib, P. (Ed.), *Entrepreneurship and Business Innovation in the Middle East* (pp. 37–56). Hershey, PA: IGI Global. DOI: 10.4018/978-1-5225-2066-5.ch003

About the Contributors

Saeed Siyal is associated with Zhejiang University; Business School, NingboTech University, Ningbo. He has more than 10 years of teaching and research experience in different universities in Pakistan and China. He has published in well-reputed peer-reviewed and impact factor research journals. Recently his research has been accepted in the European Academy of Management Annual Conference (EURAM), British Academy of Management Annual Conference (BAM) and 3rd international conference on environmental research and public health (an MDPI conference). He is a member of "Association for Psychological Science (APS)" and "The Society of Digital Information and Wireless Communications (SDIWC)". His current research interests include HRM, Management, organizational behavior, and leadership,.

***

Biju M, presently working as an Asst. Professor at Kristu Jayanti College Autonomous, Bengaluru, India.

Anjali Daisy is an assistant professor at Loyola Institute of Business Administration,Chennai,TamilNadu, India. She holds a Ph.D. degree in the field of Emotional Intelligence. She assessed and developed an Emotional Competence Inventory for IT employees in Tamil Nadu as the outcome of her research work. She has done her MBA in PSG Institute of Management, Coimbatore. She secured University second position in B.Sc(Computer Science).She holds a Post Graduate Diploma in Labour Law and Administrative Law(PGDLL). She conducted EI training programs for diversified working professionals. She has published research papers in SCOPUS and SSCI indexed journals and wrote book chapters as well. She has presented papers at International conferences. She is also a reviewer in IGI Global. She has completed certification courses in the areas of Mind control, Competency

Mapping, Strategic Performance Management, Psychology and Teaching in higher education offered by international premier institutes viz the University of Michigan, the University of Toronto, Yale University, and the University of Washington. She is able to incorporate global teaching-learning pedagogies in the courses she handles.

Kiran Thakur CPHR, SHRP-SCP is currently an Assistant Professor at University Canada West. She has over 12 years of teaching experience in higher education in the field of Human Resource Management and Organization Behavior. Born and raised in India, Kiran received her Bachelor's in Science and Bachelor of Education from Himachal Pradesh University, Master's of Business Administration from Sikkim Manipal University and Ph.D. from I.K.G. Punjab Technical University, India. Dr. Kiran is an active researcher, with publications in reputed academic journals. She has also participated in and presented her work at various international conferences. Her research interest areas are Work-Life Balance, Spirituality at the Workplace, employee engagement, leadership, Digital HR and Sustainability. In addition to her scholarly activities, Kiran is also regarded as a passionate and engaging teacher who encourages students to think critically and creatively. Kiran believes in creating a conducive learning environment, where students feel free to share their experiences and thoughts to reflect upon the topic of discussion and can learn through active participation and peer learning. When not teaching or researching, Kiran enjoys exploring courses on Coursera, cooking, and spending time with family.

Omar Guirette-Barbosa, Business Management Ph D.Experience in quality systems based on ISO standards such as 9001, 17025, etc. Consultant on accreditation and certification issues, as well as on the application of continuous improvement tools and industrial engineering.

Ancia Katjiteo is an entrepreneurship lecturer at the University of Namibia, within the School of Education, Department of Applied Education Sciences. She has authored several textbooks and study guides on entrepreneurship, which are currently being used in secondary schools. In addition, she has written numerous articles and book chapters. Ancia is passionate about entrepreneurship and is dedicated to instilling this passion in her students. She is currently pursuing a Doctorate in Education with a focus on Organizational Change and Leadership at UNICAF University in Zambia and has been accepted for a PhD in Sustainable Development: Entrepreneurship and Innovation. Ancia holds a master's degree in education, specializing in Educational Leadership and Administration, from the University of Nicosia, Cyprus, and a Postgraduate Diploma in Education with majors in Accounting and Business Studies from the Institute for Open Learning,

Namibia. She also holds a bachelor's degree in business administration from the Namibia University of Science and Technology. With extensive experience as an entrepreneurship teacher at the secondary school level, she is committed to shaping future entrepreneurs.

Sateesh Kumar T K, presently working as an Asst. Professor at Kristu Jayanti College Autonomous, Bengaluru, India.

Daniel Kwalipo Mbangula is currently employed as a lecturer in the Faculty of Applied Educational Sciences at the University of Namibia, Namibia. He currently holds a PhD in Education from the University of Namibia. A Masters' degree from Midland State University, Zimbabwe. With over 15 years' experience in the education sector, he has been able to contribute and improve the learning environment in Namibia through series of school based projects. His research interests are on social science related field with key focus on the Education sector. Daniel Kwalipo Mbangula has published in different peer reviewed journals and book chapters in different areas.

Manoj Kumar Mishra is currently working as an Assistant Professor in Faculty of Management studies, Marwadi University, Rajkot, Gujarat, India. He is pursuing his Ph.D from Jagannath University Jaipur, India on "Green Entrepreneurship". He did his MBA from VTU with a specialization in marketing and graduated from AKTU. He has presented several research papers in many national and international conferences including presentations at IITs and IIMs. His papers are published in various journals of National Repute which include Scopus-indexed and UGC –Care Listed Journals. Mr Mishra has conducted two workshops and six FDPs on research methodology across different institutes in India.

Surjit Singha is an academician with a broad spectrum of interests, including UN Sustainable Development Goals, Organizational Climate, Workforce Diversity, Organizational Culture, HRM, Marketing, Finance, IB, Global Business, Business, AI, K12 & Higher Education, Gender and Cultural Studies. Currently a faculty member at Kristu Jayanti College, Dr. Surjit also serves as an Editor, reviewer, and author for prominent global publications and journals, including being on the Editorial review board of Information Resources Management Journal and contributor to various publications. With over 13 years of experience in Administration, Teaching, and Research, Dr. Surjit is dedicated to imparting knowledge and guiding students in their research pursuits. As a research mentor, Dr. Surjit has nurtured young minds and fostered academic growth. Dr. Surjit has an impressive track record of over 75 publications, including articles, book chapters, and textbooks, holds two US

Copyrights, and has successfully completed and published two fully funded minor research projects from Kristu Jayanti College.

Kiran Thakur CPHR, SHRP-SCP is currently an Assistant Professor at University Canada West. She has over 12 years of teaching experience in higher education in the field of Human Resource Management and Organization Behavior. Born and raised in India, Kiran received her Bachelor's in Science and Bachelor of Education from Himachal Pradesh University, Master's of Business Administration from Sikkim Manipal University and Ph.D. from I.K.G. Punjab Technical University, India. Dr. Kiran is an active researcher, with publications in reputed academic journals. She has also participated in and presented her work at various international conferences. Her research interest areas are Work-Life Balance, Spirituality at the Workplace, employee engagement, leadership, Digital HR and Sustainability. In addition to her scholarly activities, Kiran is also regarded as a passionate and engaging teacher who encourages students to think critically and creatively. Kiran believes in creating a conducive learning environment, where students feel free to share their experiences and thoughts to reflect upon the topic of discussion and can learn through active participation and peer learning. When not teaching or researching, Kiran enjoys exploring courses on Coursera, cooking, and spending time with family.

Akanksha Upadhyaya is an Associate Professor at JIMS rohini sector 5, Delhi. With over 13 years of experience in academia, she holds a Ph.D. in data authentication and fraud detection from Amity University, Noida. Dr. Upadhyaya has presented papers at national and international conferences, receiving best paper awards and recognition for her outstanding thesis. She has authored over 25 research papers published in journals and conferences indexed by Scopus. She has chaired sessions at prestigious conferences, served as a guest editor for international book publications, and reviewed articles for reputable publishers. Dr. Upadhyaya holds two patents and is currently a guest editor for books by CRC Press, Apple Academic Press, and Nova Science Publisher. She is a respected speaker and Resource Person, providing expertise in Research Methodology and Data Authentication through workshops and faculty development programs.

Omar Vargas-González, Professor, research assistant and former Head of Computer Systems Department at Tecnologico Nacional de Mexico Campus Ciudad Guzman, professor at Telematic Engineering at Centro Universitario del Sur Universidad de Guadalajara with a master degree in Computer Systems. Has been trained in Innovation and Multidisciplinary Entrepreneurship at Arizona State University (2018) and a Generation of Ecosystems of Innovation, Entrepreneurship and Sustainability for Jalisco course by Harvard University T.H. Chan School of Health. At present conduct research on diverse fields such as Entrepreneurship, Economy, Statistics, Mathematics and Information and Computer Sciences. Has colaborated in the publication of many scientific articles and conducted diverse Innovation and Technological Development projects.

Mohamad Zreik, a Postdoctoral Fellow at Sun Yat-sen University, is a recognized scholar in International Relations, specializing in China's Arab-region foreign policy. His recent work in soft power diplomacy compares China's methods in the Middle East and East Asia. His extensive knowledge spans Middle Eastern Studies, China-Arab relations, East Asian and Asian Affairs, Eurasian geopolitics, and Political Economy, providing him a unique viewpoint in his field. Dr. Zreik is a proud recipient of a PhD from Central China Normal University (Wuhan). He's written numerous acclaimed papers, many focusing on China's Belt and Road Initiative and its Arab-region impact. His groundbreaking research has established him as a leading expert in his field. Presently, he furthers his research on China's soft power diplomacy tactics at Sun Yat-sen University. His significant contributions make him a crucial figure in understanding contemporary international relations.

Index

30, 37, 44

G

General Intelligence 77, 80, 87
Globalization 31, 36, 50, 59, 185, 201
Green 36, 203, 204, 205, 206, 208, 209,
210, 211, 212, 213, 214, 215, 216
Guanxi 181, 190, 192, 196, 197, 217, 218,
219, 221, 222, 223, 224, 225, 226, 227,
228, 230, 231, 232, 233

I

Inclusion 1, 2, 3, 10, 12, 13, 14, 15, 33,
54, 56, 63, 64, 65, 68, 81, 102, 110,
188, 195, 196
Innovative Culture 28
institutional environmental 153, 154,
156, 165

L

Leadership 1, 2, 3, 4, 5, 6, 7, 8, 9, 10, 11,
12, 13, 14, 15, 16, 17, 18, 19, 20, 21,
23, 24, 25, 26, 27, 28, 29, 30, 31, 32,
33, 34, 35, 36, 37, 38, 39, 40, 41, 42,
43, 44, 45, 46, 50, 51, 56, 61, 66, 69,
70, 71, 72, 73, 74, 75, 76, 77, 79, 80,
81, 82, 83, 84, 85, 86, 87, 88, 89, 90,
91, 93, 94, 95, 96, 99, 100, 101, 102,
103, 105, 106, 107, 109, 110, 111,
112, 113, 114, 115, 116, 117, 118,
119, 120, 121, 122, 123, 124, 125,
126, 128, 130, 140, 145, 146, 147,
149, 150, 151, 173, 177, 178, 179,
180, 181, 182, 183, 184, 185, 186,
187, 188, 189, 190, 191, 192, 193,
194, 195, 196, 197, 198, 199, 200,
201, 205, 215, 217, 218, 219, 220,
221, 222, 223, 224, 225, 226, 227,
228, 229, 230, 231, 232, 233
Leadership behaviours 6, 15, 118, 185,
186, 187, 188, 189, 190, 201

M

Mianzi 217, 218, 219, 221, 222, 223, 224,
225, 226, 227, 228, 229, 233
Multiple Intelligence 73, 74, 75, 76, 80,
81, 83, 85, 86, 87

O

Overcoming Challenges 63, 72

P

Paternalistic Leadership 223, 224, 225,
229, 233

R

R-software 203, 206, 207

S

Sensorimotor Intelligence 77
Shared Leadership 34, 37, 39, 43, 46
Skills Development 60, 72, 164
Social 3, 7, 9, 10, 12, 19, 21, 25, 26, 29, 35,
36, 40, 41, 43, 45, 49, 53, 55, 56, 66,
68, 69, 70, 74, 79, 81, 82, 84, 85, 87,
89, 91, 93, 95, 96, 97, 98, 102, 103,
105, 107, 109, 110, 111, 112, 113,
114, 115, 117, 119, 120, 121, 122,
127, 133, 134, 149, 155, 156, 157,
159, 160, 161, 162, 163, 164, 165,
166, 168, 169, 172, 173, 181, 188,
189, 190, 194, 208, 209, 210, 211,
212, 213, 214, 215, 216, 219, 220,
221, 222, 224, 228, 232, 233
sustainable 3, 8, 9, 10, 11, 14, 16, 19, 30,
43, 45, 48, 49, 56, 66, 67, 112, 127,
138, 140, 145, 148, 154, 155, 160,
161, 162, 163, 164, 165, 166, 168,
169, 170, 172, 173, 174, 190, 193,
204, 205, 206, 208, 209, 210, 211,
212, 213, 214, 215

Printed in the United States
by Baker & Taylor Publisher Services